D1473951

THE LOGIC OF SENSE

EUROPEAN PERSPECTIVES
A Series of the Columbia University Press

THE LOGIC OF SENSE

Gilles Deleuze

TRANSLATED BY Mark Lester
WITH Charles Stivale

EDITED BY
Constantin V. Boundas

COLUMBIA UNIVERSITY PRESS
New York

Columbia University Press wishes to express its appreciation for assistance given by the government of France through Le Ministère de la Culture in the preparation of this translation.

COLUMBIA UNIVERSITY PRESS
New York

Copyright © 1990 Columbia University Press
All rights reserved
© 1969 Les Editions de Minuit

LIBRARY OF CONGRESS CATALOGING-IN-PUBLICATION DATA
Deleuze, Gilles.
 [Logique du sens. English]
 The logic of sense / Gilles Deleuze : translated by Mark Lester
with Charles Stivale : edited by Constantin V. Boundas.
  p. cm.
 Translation of: Logique du sens.
 Includes index.
 ISBN 0-231-05982-5
 1. Semantics (Philosophy) 2. Carroll, Lewis, 1832–1898. Alice's
adventures in Wonderland. I. Title.
B840.D3813 1989
149'.94—dc20   89-33677
          CIP

Casebound editions of Columbia University Press books are Smyth-
sewn and printed on permanent and durable acid-free paper

∞

Printed in the United States of America
c 10 9 8 7 6 5 4 3 2 1

Book design by Ken Venezio

Contents

tion of the event into predicate—From the individual to the person—Persons, properties, and classes

Transition of the dimensions of the proposition—Sense and proposition—Neutrality of sense—Surface and lining

Philosophy and height—Philosophy and depth—A new type of philosopher: the Stoic—Hercules and the surfaces

From signification to designation—Stoicism and Zen—Classical discourse and the individual, romantic discourse and the person: irony—Groundless discourse—The discourse of singularities: humour or the "fourth person singular"

The two poles of morality: physical divination of things and logical use of representation—Representation, usage and expression—To understand, to will, and to represent the event

The eternal truth of the event—Actualization and counter-actualization: the actor—The two aspects of death as event—The meaning of "to will the event"

The "crack up" (Fitzgerald)—The two processes and the problem of their distinction—Alcoholism and depressive mania—Homage to psychedelia

Third step of genesis: from the physical surface to the metaphysical surface (the double screen)

TRANSLATOR'S NOTE

There are many to whom I owe a debt of gratitude for the encouragement and friendship they provided during the time I was engaged in translating *Logique du sens*. But I would especially like to acknowledge Linda Cognato. Her valuable suggestions and criticisms, as well as her unwavering support, make her as deserving of credit as anyone for the appearance of this piece in English. I would like to dedicate the translation to her.

———M.L.

Preface: From Lewis Carroll
to the Stoics

The work of Lewis Carroll has everything required to please the modern reader: children's books or, rather, books for little girls; splendidly bizarre and esoteric words; grids; codes and decodings; drawings and photographs; a profound psychoanalytic content; and an exemplary logical and linguistic formalism. Over and above the immediate pleasure, though, there is something else, a play of sense and nonsense, a chaos-cosmos. But since the marriage of language and the unconscious has already been consummated and celebrated in so many ways, it is necessary to examine the precise nature of this union in Carroll's work: what else is this marriage connected with, and what is it that, thanks to him, this marriage celebrates?

We present here a series of paradoxes which form the theory of sense. It is easy to explain why this theory is inseparable from paradoxes: sense is a nonexisting entity, and, in fact, maintains very special relations with nonsense. The privileged place assigned to Lewis Carroll is due to his having provided the first great account, the first great *mise en scène* of the paradoxes of sense—sometimes collecting, sometimes renewing, sometimes inventing, and sometimes preparing them. The privileged place assigned to the Stoics is due to their having been the initiators of a new image of the philosopher which broke away from the pre-Socratics, Socratic philosophy, and Platonism. This new image is already closely linked to the paradoxical constitution of the theory of sense. Thus to each series there correspond figures which are not only historical but topological and logical as well. As on a pure surface, certain points of one figure in a series refer to the points of another figure: an entire galaxy of problems with their corresponding dice-throws, stories, and places, a complex place; a "convoluted story." This book is an attempt to develop a logical and psychological novel.

In the appendixes we present five articles which have already been published. While reprinted here in modified form, their theme remains unchanged and develops certain points which are but briefly touched on in the preceding series (each connection being indicated by means of a note). The articles are: 1) "Reversing Platonism," *Revue de Métaphysique et de Morale*, 1967; 2) "Lucretius and Naturalism," *Études Philosophiques*, 1961; 3) "Klossowski and Bodies-Language," *Critique*, 1965; 4) "A Theory of the Other" (Michel Tournier), *Critique*, 1967; 5) "Introduction to Zola's *La Bête humaine*," Cercle Précieux du Livre, 1967. We wish to thank the editors for having authorized their reproduction.

THE LOGIC OF SENSE

First Series of Paradoxes
of Pure Becoming

Alice and *Through the Looking-Glass* involve a category of very special things: events, pure events. When I say "Alice becomes larger," I mean that she becomes larger than she was. By the same token, however, she becomes smaller than she is now. Certainly, she is not bigger and smaller at the same time. She is larger now; she was smaller before. But it is at the same moment that one becomes larger than one was and smaller than one becomes. This is the simultaneity of a becoming whose characteristic is to elude the present. Insofar as it eludes the present, becoming does not tolerate the separation or the distinction of before and after, or of past and future. It pertains to the essence of becoming to move and to pull in both directions at once: Alice does not grow without shrinking, and vice versa. Good sense affirms that in all things there is a determinable sense or direction *(sens);* but paradox is the affirmation of both senses or directions at the same time.

Plato invites us to distinguish between two dimensions: (1) that of limited and measured things, of fixed qualities, permanent or temporary which always presuppose pauses and rests, the fixing of presents, and the assignation of subjects (for example, a particular subject having a particular largeness or a particular smallness at a particular moment); and (2) a pure becoming without measure, a veritable becoming-mad, which never rests. It moves in both directions at once. It always eludes the present, causing future and past, more and less, too much and not enough to coincide in the simultaneity of a rebellious matter. " '[H]otter' never stops where it is but is always going a point further, and the same applies to 'colder,' whereas definite quality is something that has stopped going on and is fixed;" ". . . the younger becoming older than the older, the older becoming younger than the younger—but they can never finally become so; if they did they would no longer be becoming, but would be so." [1]

We recognize this Platonic dualism. It is not at all the dualism of the intelligible and the sensible, of Idea and matter, or of Ideas and bodies. It is a more profound and secret dualism hidden in sensible and material bodies themselves. It is a subterranean dualism between that which receives the action of the Idea and that which eludes this action. It is not the distinction between the Model and the copy, but rather between copies and simulacra. Pure becoming, the unlimited, is the matter of the simulacrum insofar as it eludes the action of the Idea and insofar as it contests *both* model *and* copy at once. Limited things lie beneath the Ideas; but even beneath things, is there not still this mad element which subsists and occurs on the other side of the order that Ideas impose and things receive? Sometimes Plato wonders whether this pure becoming might not have a very peculiar relation to language. This seems to be one of the principal meanings of the *Cratylus.* Could this relation be, perhaps, essential to language, as in the case of a "flow" of speech, or a wild discourse which would incessantly slide over its referent, without ever stopping? Or might there not be two languages and two sorts of "names," one designating the pauses and rests which receive the action of the Idea, the other expressing the movements or rebel becomings?[2] Or further still, is it not possible that there are two distinct dimensions internal to language in general—one always concealed by the other, yet continuously coming to the aid of, or subsisting under, the other?

The paradox of this pure becoming, with its capacity to elude the present, is the paradox of infinite identity (the infinite identity of both directions or senses at the same time—of future and past, of the day before and the day after, of more and less, of two much and not enough, of active and passive, and of cause and effect). It is language which fixes the limits (the moment, for example, at which the excess begins), but it is language as well which transcends the limits and restores them to the infinite equivalence of an unlimited becoming ("A red-hot poker will burn you if you hold it too long; and . . . if you cut your finger *very* deeply with a knife, it usually bleeds"). Hence the reversals which constitute Alice's adventures: the reversal of becoming larger and becoming smaller—"which way, which way?" asks Alice, sensing that it is always in both directions at the same time, so that for once she stays the same, through an optical illusion; the reversal of the day before and the day after, the present always being eluded—"jam tomorrow and jam yesterday—but never jam *to-day*"; the reversal of more and less: five nights are five times hotter than a single one, "but they must be five times as cold for the same reason"; the reversal of active and passive: "do cats eat bats?" is as good as "do bats eat cats?"; the reversal of cause and effect: to be punished before having committed a fault, to cry before having pricked oneself, to serve before having divided up the servings.

All these reversals as they appear in infinite identity have one consequence: the contesting of Alice's personal identity and the loss of her proper name. The loss of the proper name is the adventure which is repeated throughout all Alice's adventures. For the proper or singular name is guaranteed by the permanence of *savoir*. The latter is embodied in general names designating pauses and rests, in substantives and adjectives, with which the proper name maintains a constant connection. Thus the personal self requires God and the world in general. But when substantives and adjectives begin to dissolve, when the names of pause and rest are carried away by the verbs of pure becoming and slide into the language of events, all identity disappears from the self, the world, and God. This is the test of *savoir* and recitation which strips Alice of her identity. In it words may go awry, being obliquely swept away by the verbs. It is as if events enjoyed an irreality which is communicated through language to the *savoir* and to persons. For personal uncertainty is not a doubt foreign to what is happening, but rather an objective structure of the event itself, insofar as it moves in two directions at once, and insofar as it fragments the subject following this double direction. Paradox is initially that which destroys good sense as the only direction, but it is also that which destroys common sense as the assignation of fixed identities.

Second Series of Paradoxes
of Surface Effects

The Stoics also distinguish between two kinds of things. First, there are bodies with their tensions, physical qualities, actions and passions, and the corresponding "states of affairs." These states of affairs, actions and passions, are determined by the mixtures of bodies. At the limit, there is a unity of all bodies in virtue of a primordial Fire into which they become absorbed and from which they develop according to their respective tensions. The only time of bodies and states of affairs is the present. For the living present is the temporal extension which accompanies the act, expresses and measures the action of the agent and the passion of the patient. But to the degree that there is a unity of bodies among themselves, to the degree that there is a unity of active and passive principles, a cosmic present embraces the entire universe: only bodies exist in space, and only the present exists in time. There are no causes *and* effects among bodies. Rather, all bodies are causes—causes in relation to each other and for each other. In the scope of the cosmic present, the unity is called Destiny.

Second, all bodies are causes in relation to each other, and causes for each other—but causes of what? They are causes of certain things of an entirely different nature. These *effects* are not bodies, but, properly speaking, "incorporeal" entities. They are not physical qualities and properties, but rather logical or dialectical attributes. They are not things or facts, but events. We can not say that they exist, but rather that they subsist or inhere (having this minimum of being which is appropriate to that which is not a thing, a nonexisting entity). They are not substantives or adjectives but verbs. They are neither agents nor patients, but results of actions and passions. They are "impassive" entities—impassive results. They are not living presents, but infinitives: the unlimited Aion, the becoming which divides itself infinitely in past and future and always eludes the present. Thus time must be grasped twice, in two complementary though mutually exclusive fashions. First, it must be grasped entirely as the living present in bodies which act and are acted upon. Second, it must be grasped entirely as an entity infinitely divisible into past and future, and into the incorporeal effects which result from bodies, their actions and their passions. Only the present exists in time and gathers together or absorbs the past and future. But only the past and future inhere in time and divide each present infinitely. These are not three successive dimensions, but two simultaneous readings of time.

In his fine reconstruction of Stoic thought, Émile Bréhier says:

> when the scalpel cuts through the flesh, the first body produces upon the second not a new property but a new attribute, that of being cut. The *attribute* does not designate any real *quality . . . ,* it is, to the contrary, always expressed by the verb, which means that it is not a being, but a way of being. . . . This way of being finds itself somehow at the limit, at the surface of being, the nature of which it is not able to change: it is, in fact, neither active nor passive, for passivity would presuppose a corporeal nature which undergoes an action. It is purely and simply a result, or an effect which is not to be classified among beings. . . . [The Stoics distinguished] radically two planes of being, something that no one had done before them: on the one hand, real and profound being, force; on the other, the plane of facts, which frolic on the surface of being, and constitute an endless multiplicity of incorporeal beings.[1]

Yet, what is more intimate or essential to bodies than events such as growing, becoming smaller, or being cut? What do the Stoics mean when they contrast the thickness of bodies with these incorporeal events which would play only on the surface, like a mist over the prairie (even less than a mist, since a mist is after all a body)? Mixtures are in bodies, and in the depth of bodies: a body penetrates another and coexists with it in all of its parts, like a drop of wine in the ocean, or fire in iron. One body withdraws from another, like liquid from a vase. Mixtures in general determine the quantitative and qualitative states of affairs: the dimensions of an ensemble—the red of iron, the green of a tree. But what we mean by "to grow," "to diminish," "to become red," "to become green," "to cut," and "to be cut," etc., is something entirely different. These are no longer states of affairs—mixtures deep inside bodies—but incorporeal events at the surface which are the results of these mixtures. The tree "greens." . . .[2] The genius of a philosophy must first be measured by the new distribution which it imposes on beings and concepts. The Stoics are in the process of tracing out and of forming a frontier where there had not been one before. In this sense they displace all reflection.

They are in the process of bringing about, first, an entirely new cleavage of the causal relation. They dismember this relation, even at the risk of recreating a unity on each side. They refer causes to causes and place a bond of causes between them (destiny). They refer effects to effects and pose certain bonds of effects between them. But these two operations are not accomplished in the same manner. Incorporeal effects are never themselves causes in relation to each other; rather, they are only "quasi-causes" following laws which perhaps express in each case the relative unity or mixture of bodies on which they depend for their real causes. Thus freedom is preserved in two complementary manners: once in the interiority of destiny as a connection between causes, and once more in the exteriority of events as a bond of effects. For this reason the Stoics can oppose destiny and necessity.[3] The Epicureans formulated another cleavage of causality, which also grounds freedom. They conserve the homogeneity of cause and effect, but cut up causality according to atomic series whose respective independence is guaranteed by the *clinamen*—no longer destiny without necessity, but causality without destiny.[4] In either case, one begins by splitting the causal relation, instead of distinguishing types of causality as Aristotle had done and Kant would do. And this split always refers us back to language, either to the existence of a *declension* of causes or, as we shall see, to the existence of a *conjugation* of effects.

This new dualism of bodies or states of affairs and effects or incorporeal events entails an upheaval in philosophy. In Aristotle, for example, all categories are said of Being; and difference is present in Being, between substance as the primary sense and the other categories which are related to it as accidents. For the Stoics, on the other hand, states of affairs, quantities, and qualities are no less beings (or bodies) than substance is; they are a part of substance, and in this sense they are contrasted with an *extra-Being* which constitutes the incorporeal as a nonexisting entity. The highest term therefore is not Being, but *Something (aliquid)*, insofar as it subsumes being and non-being, existence and inherence.[5] Moreover, the Stoics are the first to reverse Platonism and to bring about a radical inversion. For if bodies with their states, qualities, and quantities, assume all the characteristics of substance and cause, conversely, the characteristics of the Idea are relegated to the other side, that is to this impassive extra-Being which is sterile, ineffi-cacious, and on the surface of things: *the ideational or the incorporeal can no longer be anything other than an "effect."*

These consequences are extremely important. In Plato, an obscure debate was raging in the depth of things, in the depth of the earth, between that which undergoes the action of the Idea and that which eludes this action (copies and simulacra). An echo of this debate resonates when Socrates asks: is there an Idea of everything, even of hair, dirt, and mud—or rather is there something which always and obstinately escapes the Idea? In Plato, however, this something is never sufficiently hidden, driven back, pushed deeply into the depth of the body, or drowned in the ocean. *Everything now returns to the surface.* This is the result of the Stoic operation: the unlimited returns. Becoming-mad, becoming unlimited is no longer a ground which rumbles. It climbs to the surface of things and becomes impassive. It is no longer a question of simulacra which elude the ground and insinuate themselves everywhere, but rather a question of effects which manifest themselves and act in their place. These are effects in the causal sense, but also sonorous, optical, or linguistic "effects"—and even less, or much more, since they are no longer corporeal entities, but rather form the entire Idea. What was eluding the Idea climbed up to the surface, that is, the incorporeal limit, and represents now all possible *ideality*, the latter being stripped of its causal and spiritual efficacy. The Stoics discovered surface effects. Simulacra cease to be subterranean rebels and make the most of their effects (that is, what might be called "phantasms," independently of the Stoic terminology). The most concealed becomes the most manifest. All the old paradoxes of becoming must again take shape in a new youthfulness—transmutation.

Becoming unlimited comes to be the ideational and incorporeal event, with all of its characteristic reversals between future and past, active and passive, cause and effect, more and less, too much and not enough, already and not yet. The infinitely divisible event is always *both at once*. It is eternally that which has just happened and that which is about to happen, but never that which is happening (to cut too deeply and not enough). The event, being itself impassive, allows the active and the passive to be interchanged more easily, since it is *neither the one nor the other,* but rather their common result (to cut—to be cut). Concerning the cause and the effect, events, *being always only effects,* are better able to form among themselves functions of quasi-causes or relations o. quasi-causality which are always reversible (the wound and the scar).

The Stoics are amateurs and inventors of paradoxes. It is necessary to reread the astonishing portrait of Chrysippus given in several pages written by Diogenes Laertius. Perhaps the Stoics used the paradox in a completely new manner—both as an instrument for the analysis of language and as a means of synthesizing events. *Dialectics* is precisely this science of incorporeal events as they are expressed in propositions, and of the connections between events as they are expressed in relations between propositions. Dialectics is, indeed, the art of *conjugation* (see the *confatalia* or series of events which depend on one another). But it is the task of language both to establish limits and to go beyond them. Therefore language includes terms which do not cease to displace their extension and which make possible a reversal of the connection in a given series (thus too much and not enough, few and many). The event is coextensive with becoming, and becoming is itself coextensive with language; the paradox is thus essentially a "sorites," that is a series of interrogative propositions which, following becoming, proceed through successive additions and retrenchments. Everything happens at the boundary between things and propositions. Chrysippus taught: "If you say something, it passes through your lips; so, if you say "chariot," a chariot passes through your lips." Here is a use of paradox the only equivalents of which are to be found in Zen Buddhism on one hand and in English or American *nonsense* on the other. In one case, that which is most profound is the immediate, in the other, the immediate is found in language. Paradox appears as a dismissal of depth, a display of events at the surface, and a deployment of language along this limit. Humor is the art of the surface, which is opposed to the old irony, the art of depths and heights. The Sophists and Cynics had already made humor a philosophical weapon against Socratic irony; but with the Stoics, humor found its dialectics, its dialectical principle or its natural place and its pure philosophical concept.

Lewis Carroll carries out this operation, inaugurated by the Stoics, or rather, he takes it up again. In all his works, Carroll examines the difference between events, things, and states of affairs. But the entire first half of *Alice* still seeks the secret of events and of the becoming unlimited which they imply, in the depths of the earth, in dug out shafts and holes which plunge beneath, and in the mixture of bodies which interpenetrate and coexist. As one advances in the story, however, the digging and hiding gives way to a lateral sliding from right to left and left to right. The animals below ground become secondary, giving way to *card figures* which have no thickness. One could say that the old depth having been spread out became width. The becoming unlimited is maintained entirely within this inverted width. "Depth" is no longer a complement. Only animals are deep, and they are not the noblest for that; the noblest are the flat animals. Events are like crystals, they become and grow only out of the edges, or on the edge. This is, indeed, the first secret of the stammerer or of the left-handed person: no longer to sink, but to slide the whole length in such a way that the old depth no longer exists at all, having been reduced to the opposite side of the surface. By sliding, one passes to the other side, since the other side is nothing but the opposite direction. If there is nothing to see behind the curtain, it is because everything is visible, or rather all possible science is along the length of the curtain. It suffices to follow it far enough, precisely enough, and superficially enough, in order to reverse sides and to make the right side become the left or vice versa. It is not therefore a question of *the adventures* of Alice, but of Alice's *adventure:* her climb to the surface, her disavowal of false depth and her discovery that everything happens at the border. This is why Carroll abandons the original title of the book: *Alice's Adventures Underground.*

This is the case—even more so—in *Through the Looking-Glass.* Here events, differing radically from things, are no longer sought in the depths, but at the surface, in the faint incorporeal mist which escapes from bodies, a film without volume which envelops them, a mirror which reflects them, a chessboard on which they are organized according to plan. Alice is no longer able to make her way through to the depths. Instead, she releases her incorporeal double. *It is by following the border, by skirting the surface, that one passes from bodies to the incorporeal.* Paul Valéry had a profound idea: what is most deep is the skin. This is a Stoic discovery, which presupposes a great deal of wisdom and entails an entire ethic. It is the discovery of the little girl, who grows and diminishes only from the edges—a surface which reddens and becomes green. She knows that the more the events traverse the entire, depthless extension, the more they affect bodies which they cut and bruise. Later, the adults are snapped up by the ground, fall again, and, being too deep, they no longer understand. Why do the same Stoic examples continue to inspire Lewis Carroll?—the tree greens, the scalpel cuts, the battle will or will not take place. . . . It is in front of the trees that Alice loses her name. It is a tree which Humpty Dumpty addresses without looking at Alice. Recitations announce battles, and everywhere there are injuries and cuts. But are these examples? Or rather, is it the case that every event is of this type—forest, battle and wound—all the more profound since *it* occurs at the surface? The more it skirts bodies, the more incorporeal it is. History teaches us that sound roads have no foundation, and geography that only a thin layer of the earth is fertile.

This rediscovery of the Stoic sage is not reserved to the little girl. Indeed, it is true that Lewis Carroll detests boys in general. They have too much depth, and false depth at that, false wisdom, and animality. The male baby in *Alice* is transformed into a pig. As a general rule, only little girls understand Stoicism; they have the sense of the event and release an incorporeal double. But it happens sometimes that a little boy is a stutterer and left-handed, and thus conquers sense as the double sense or direction of the surface. Carroll's hatred of boys is not attributable to a deep ambivalence, but rather to a superficial inversion, a properly Carrollian concept. In *Sylvie and Bruno,* it is the little boy who has the inventive role, learning his lessons in all manners, inside-out, outside-in, above and below, but never "in depth." This important novel pushes to the extreme the evolution which had begun in *Alice,* and which continued in *Through the Looking-Glass.* The admirable conclusion of the first part is to the glory of the East, from which comes all that is good, "the substance of things hoped for, and the existence of things not seen." Here even the barometer neither rises nor falls, but goes lengthwise, sideways, and gives a horizontal weather. A stretching machine even lengthens songs. And Fortunatus' purse, presented as a Möbius strip, is made of handkerchiefs sewn *in the wrong way,* in such a manner that its outer surface is continuous with its inner surface: it envelops the entire world, and makes that which is inside be on the outside and vice versa.[6] In *Sylvie and Bruno,* the technique of passing from reality to dream, and from bodies to the incorporeal, is multiplied, completely renewed, and carried out to perfection. It is, however, still by skirting the surface, or the border, that one passes to the other side, by virtue of the strip. The continuity between reverse and right side replaces all the levels of depth; and the surface effects in one and the same Event, which would hold for all events, bring to language becoming and its paradoxes.[7] As Carroll says in an article entitled *The Dynamics of a Parti-cle:* "Plain Superficiality is the character of a speech. . . ."

Third Series of the Proposition

Between these events-effects and language, or even the possibility of language, there is an essential relation. It is the characteristic of events to be expressed or expressible, uttered or utterable, in propositions which are at least possible. There are many relations inside a proposition. Which is the best suited to surface effects or events?

Many authors agree in recognizing three distinct relations within the proposition. The first is called denotation or indication: it is the relation of the proposition to an external state of affairs (*datum*). The state of affairs is *individuated;* it includes particular bodies, mixtures of bodies, qualities, quantities, and relations. Denotation functions through the association of the words themselves with *particular* images *which ought to* "represent" the state of affairs. From all the images associated with a word—with a particular word in the proposition—we must choose or select those which correspond to the given whole. The denoting intuition is then expressed by the form: "it is that," or "it is not that." The question of knowing whether the association of words and images is primitive or derived, necessary or arbitrary, can not yet be formulated. What matters for the moment is that certain words in the proposition, or certain linguistic particles, function in all cases as empty forms for the selection of images, and hence for the denotation of each state of affairs. It would be wrong to treat them as universal concepts, for they are formal particulars *(singuliers)* which function as pure "designators" or, as Benveniste says, indexicals *(indicateurs)*. These formal indexicals are: this, that, it, here, there, yesterday, now, etc. Proper names are also indexicals or designators, but they have special importance since they alone form properly material singularities. Logically, denotation has as its elements and its criterion the true and the false. "True" signifies that a denotation is effectively filled by the state of affairs or that the indexicals are "realized" or that the correct image has been selected. "True in all cases" signifies that the infinity of particular images associable to words is filled, without any selection being necessary. "False" signifies that the denotation is not filled, either as a result of a defect in the selected images or as a result of the radical impossibility of producing an image which can be associated with words.

A second relation of the proposition is often called "manifestation." It concerns the relation of the proposition to the person who speaks and expresses himself. Manifestation therefore is presented as a statement of desires and beliefs which correspond to the proposition. Desires and beliefs are causal inferences, not associations. Desire is the internal causality of an image with respect to the existence of the object or the corresponding state of affairs. Correlatively, belief is the anticipation of this object or state of affairs insofar as its existence must be produced by an external causality. We should not conclude from this that manifestation is secondary in relation to denotation. Rather, it makes denotation possible, and inferences form a systematic unity from which the associations derive. Hume had seen this clearly: in the association of cause and effect, it is "inference according to the relation" which precedes the relation itself. The primacy of manifestation is confirmed by linguistic analysis, which reveals that there are in the proposition "manifesters" like the special particles I, you, tomorrow, always, elsewhere, everywhere, etc. In the same way that the proper name is a privileged indicator, "I" is the basic manifester. But it is not only the other manifesters which depend on the "I": all indicators are related to it as well.[1] Indication, or denotation, subsumes the individual states of affairs, the particular images and the singular designators; but manifesters, beginning with the "I," constitute the domain of the *personal,* which functions as the principle of all possible denotation. Finally, from denotation to manifestation, a displacement of logical values occurs which is represented by the Cogito: no longer the true and the false, but veracity and illusion. In his celebrated analysis of the piece of wax, for example, Descartes is not at all looking for that which was dwelling in the wax—this problem is not even formulated in this text; rather, he shows how the I, manifest in the Cogito, grounds the judgment of denotation by which the wax is identified.

We ought to reserve the term "signification" for a third dimension of the proposition. Here it is a question of the relation of the word to *universal or general* concepts, and of syntactic connections to the implications of the concept. From the standpoint of signification, we always consider the elements of the proposition as "signifying" conceptual implications capable of referring to other propositions, which serve as premises of the first. Signification is defined by this order of conceptual implication where the proposition under consideration intervenes only as an element of a "demonstration," in the most general sense of the word, that is, either as premise or as conclusion. Thus, "implies" and "therefore" are essentially linguistic signifiers. *"Implication"* is the sign which defines the relation between premises and conclusion; "therefore" is the sign of *assertion,* which defines the possibility of affirming the conclusion itself as the outcome of implications. When we speak of demonstration in the most general sense, we mean that the signification of the proposition is always found in the indirect process which corresponds to it, that is, in its relation to other propositions from which it is inferred, or conversely, whose conclusion it renders possible. Denotation, on the other hand, refers to a direct process. Demonstration must not be understood in a restricted, syllogistic or mathematical sense, but also in the physical sense of probabilities or in the moral sense of promises and commitments. In this last case, the assertion of the conclusion is represented by the moment the promise is effectively kept.[2] The logical value of signification or demonstration thus understood is no longer the truth, as is shown by the hypothetical mode of implications, but rather the *condition of truth,* the aggregate of conditions under which the proposition "would be" true. The conditioned or concluded proposition may be false, insofar as it actually denotes a nonexisting state of affairs or is not directly verified. Signification does not establish the truth without also establishing the possibility of error. For this reason, the condition of truth is not opposed to the false, but

to the absurd: that which is without signification or that which may be neither true nor false.

The question of whether signification is in turn primary in relation to manifestation and denotation requires a complex response. For if manifestation itself is primary in relation to denotation, if it is the foundation, it is so only from a very specific point of view. To borrow a classic distinction, we say that it is from the standpoint of speech (parole), be it a speech that is silent. In the order of speech, it is the I which begins, and begins absolutely. In this order, therefore, the I is primary, not only in relation to all possible denotations which are founded upon it, but also in relation to the significations which it envelops. But precisely from this standpoint, conceptual significations are neither valid nor deployed for themselves: they are only implied (though not expressed) by the I, presenting itself as having signification which is immediately understood and identical to its own manifestation. This is why Descartes could contrast the definition of man as a rational animal with his determination as Cogito: for the former demands an explicit development of the signified concepts (what is animal? what is rational?), whereas the latter is supposed to be understood as soon as it is said.[3]

This primacy of manifestation, not only in relation to denotation but also in relation to signification, must be understood within the domain of "speech" in which significations remain naturally implicit. It is only here that the I is primary in relation to concepts—in relation to the world and to God. But if another domain exists in which significations are valid and developed for themselves, significations would be primary in it and would provide the basis of manifestation. This domain is precisely that of language (langue). In it, a proposition is able to appear only as a premise or a conclusion, signifying concepts before manifesting a subject, or even before denoting a state of affairs. It is from this point of view that signified concepts, such as God or the world, are always primary in relation to the self as manifested person and to things as designated objects. More generally, Benveniste has shown that the relation between the word (or rather its own acoustic image) and the concept was alone necessary, and not arbitrary. Only the relation between the word and the concept enjoys a necessity which the other relations do not have. The latter remain arbitrary insofar as we consider them directly and escape the arbitrary only insofar as we connect them to this primary relation. Thus, the possibility of causing particular images associated with the word to vary, of substituting one image for another in the form "this is not that, it's that," can be explained only by the constancy of the signified concept. Similarly, desires would not form an order of demands or even of duties, distinct from a simple urgency of needs, and beliefs would not form an order of inferences distinct from simple opinions, if the words in which they were mani-fested did not refer first to concepts and conceptual implications ren-dering these desires and beliefs significative.

The presupposed primacy of signification over denotation, however, still raises a delicate problem. When we say "therefore," when we consider a proposition as concluded, we make it the object of an assertion. We set aside the premises and affirm it for itself, indepen-dently. We relate it to the state of affairs which it denotes, indepen-dently of the implications which constitute its signification. To do so, however, two conditions have to be filled. It is first necessary that the premises be posited as effectively true, which already forces us to depart from the pure order of implication in order to relate the premises to a denoted state of affairs which we presuppose. But then, even if we suppose that the premises A and B are true, we can only conclude from this the proposition in question (let us call it Z)—we can only detach it from its premises and affirm it for itself independently of the impli-cation—by admitting that Z is, in turn, true if A and B are true. This amounts to a proposition, C, which remains within the order of impli-cation, and is unable to escape it, since it refers to a proposition, D, which states that "Z is true if A, B, and C are true . . . ," and so on to infinity. This paradox, which lies at the heart of logic, and which had decisive importance for the entire theory of symbolic implication and signification, is Lewis Carroll's paradox in the celebrated text, "What the Tortoise Said to Achilles."[4] In short, the conclusion can be detached from the premises, but only on the condition that one always adds other premises from which alone the conclusion is not detachable. This amounts to saying that signification is never homogeneous; or that the two signs "implies" and "therefore" are completely heterogeneous; or that implication never succeeds in grounding denotation except by giving itself a ready-made denotation, once in the premises and again in the conclusion.

From denotation to manifestation, then to signification, but also from signification to manifestation and to denotation, we are carried along a circle, which is the circle of the proposition. Whether we ought to be content with these three dimensions of the proposition, or whether we should add *a fourth—which would be sense*—is an economic or strategic question. It is not that we must construct an a posteriori model corresponding to previous dimensions, but rather the model itself must have the aptitude to function a priori from within, were it forced to introduce a supplementary dimension which, because of its evanescence, could not have been recognized in experience from outside. It is thus a question *de jure,* and not simply a question of fact. Nevertheless, there is also a question of fact, and it is necessary to begin by asking whether sense is capable of being localized in one of these three dimensions— denotation, manifestation, or signification. We could answer first that such a localization seems impossible within denotation. Fulfilled deno- tation makes the proposition true; unfulfilled denotation makes the proposition false. Sense, evidently, can not consist of that which renders the proposition true or false, nor of the dimension in which these values are realized. Moreover, denotation would be able to support the weight of the proposition only to the extent that one would be able to show a correspondence between words and denoted things or states of affairs. Brice Parain has discussed the paradoxes that such a hypothesis causes to arise in Greek philosophy.[5] How are we to avoid paradoxes, like a chariot passing through one's lips? More directly still, Carroll asks: how could names have a "respondent"? What does it mean for something to respond to its name? And if things do not respond to their name, what is it that prevents them from losing it? What is it then that would remain, save arbitrariness of denotations to which nothing responds, and the emptiness of indexicals or formal designators of the "that" type —both being stripped of sense? It is undeniable that all denotation presupposes sense, and that we position ourselves *straight away* within sense whenever we denote.

To identify sense with manifestation has a better chance of success, since the designators themselves have sense only in virtue of an I which manifests itself in the proposition. This I is indeed primary, since it allows speech to begin; as Alice says, "if you only spoke when you were spoken to, and the other person always waited for *you* to begin, you see nobody would ever say anything. . . ." It shall be concluded from this that sense resides in the beliefs (or desires) of the person who expresses herself.[6] " 'When *I* use a word,' said Humpty Dumpty, 'it means just what I choose it to mean—neither more nor less. . . . The question is . . . which is to be master—that's all.' " We have, however, seen that the order of beliefs and desires was founded on the order of the conceptual implications of signification, and that even the identity of the self which speaks, or says "I," was guaranteed only by the permanence of certain signifieds (the concepts of God, the world . . .). The I is primary and sufficient in the order of speech only insofar as it envelops significations which must be developed for themselves in the order of language *(langue)*. If these significations collapse, or are not established in themselves, personal identity is lost, as Alice painfully experiences, in conditions where God, the world, and the self become the blurred characters of the dream of someone who is poorly determined. This is why the last recourse seems to be identifying sense with signification.

We are then sent back to the circle and led back to Carroll's paradox, in which signification can never exercise its role of last foundation, since it presupposes an irreducible denotation. But perhaps there is a very general reason why signification fails and why there is a circularity between ground and grounded. When we define signification as the condition of truth, we give it a characteristic which it shares with sense, and which is already a characteristic of sense. But how does signification assume this characteristic? How does it make use of it? In discussing the conditions of truth, we raise ourselves above the true and the false, since a false proposition also has a sense or signification. But at the same time, we define this superior condition solely as the possibility for the proposition to be true.[7] This possibility is nothing other than the *form of possibility* of the proposition itself. There are many forms of possibility for propositions: logical, geometrical, algebraic, physical, syntactic . . . ; Aristotle defined the form of logical possibility by means of the relation between the terms of the proposition and the *loci* of the accident, *proprium,* genus, or definition; Kant even invented two new forms of possibility, the transcendental and the moral. But by whatever manner one defines form, it is an odd procedure since it involves rising from the conditioned to the condition, in order to think of the condition as the simple possibility of the conditioned. Here one rises to a foundation, but that which is founded remains what it was, independently of the operation which founded it and unaffected by it. Thus denotation remains external to the order which conditions it, and the true and the false remain indifferent to the principle which determines the possibility of the one, by allowing it only to subsist in its former relation to the other. One is perpetually referred from the conditioned to the condition, and also from the condition to the conditioned. For the condition of truth to avoid this defect, it ought to have an element of its own, distinct from the form of the conditioned. It ought to have *something unconditioned* capable of assuring a real genesis of denotation and of the other dimensions of the proposition. Thus the condition of truth would be defined no longer as the form of conceptual possibility, but rather as ideational material or "stratum," that is to say, no longer as signification, but rather as sense.

Sense is the fourth dimension of the proposition. The Stoics discovered it along with the event: sense, *the expressed of the proposition,* is an incorporeal, complex, and irreducible entity, at the surface of things, a pure event which inheres or subsists in the proposition. The discovery was made a second time in the fourteenth century, in Ockham's school, by Gregory of Rimini and Nicholas d'Autrecourt. It was made a third time at the end of the nineteenth century, by the great philosopher and logician Meinong.[8] Undoubtedly there are reasons for these moments: we have seen that the Stoic discovery presupposed a reversal of Platonism; similarly Ockham's logic reacted against the problem of Universals, and Meinong against Hegelian logic and its lineage. The question is as follows: is there something, *aliquid,* which merges neither with the proposition or with the terms of the proposition, nor with the object or with the state of affairs which the proposition denotes, neither with the "lived," or representation or the mental activity of the person who expresses herself in the proposition, nor with concepts or even signified essences? If there is, sense, or that which is expressed by the proposition, would be irreducible to individual states of affairs, particular images, personal beliefs, and universal or general concepts. The Stoics said it all: neither word nor body, neither sensible representation nor *rational representation.*[9] Better yet, perhaps sense would be "neutral," altogether indifferent to both particular and general, singular and universal, personal and impersonal. It would be of an entirely different nature. But is it necessary to recognize such a supplementary instance? Or must we indeed manage to get along with what we already have: denotation, manifestation, and signification? In each period the controversy is taken up anew (André de Neufchateau and Pierre d'Ailly against Rimini, Brentano and Russell against Meinong). In truth, the attempt to make this fourth dimension evident is a little like Carroll's Snark hunt. Perhaps the dimension is the hunt itself, and sense is the Snark. It is difficult to respond to those who wish to be satisfied with words, things, images, and ideas. For we may not even say that sense exists either in things or in the mind; it has neither physical nor mental existence. Shall we at least say that it is useful, and that it is necessary to admit it for its utility? Not even this, since it is endowed with an inefficacious, impassive, and sterile splendor. This is why we said that *in fact* we can only infer it indirectly, on the basis of the circle where the ordinary dimensions of the proposition lead us. It is only by breaking open the circle, as in the case of the Möbius strip, by unfolding and untwisting it, that the dimension of sense appears for itself, in its irreducibility, and also in its genetic power as it animates an a priori internal model of the proposition.[10] The logic of sense is inspired in its entirety by empiricism. Only empiricism knows how to transcend the experiential dimensions of the visible without falling into Ideas, and how to track down, invoke, and perhaps produce a phantom at the limit of a lengthened or unfolded experience.

Husserl calls *"expression"* this ultimate dimension, and he distinguishes it from denotation, manifestation, and demonstration.[11] Sense is that which is expressed. Husserl, no less than Meinong, rediscovered the living sources of the Stoic inspiration. For example, when Husserl reflects on the "perceptual noema," or the "sense of perception," he at once distinguishes it from the physical object, from the psychological or "lived," from mental representations and from logical concepts. He presents it as an impassive and incorporeal entity, without physical or mental existence, neither acting nor being acted upon—a pure result or pure "appearance." The real tree (the *denotatum*) can burn, be the subject and object of actions, and enter into mixtures. This is not the case, however, for the noema "tree." There are many noemata or senses for the same *denotatum*: evening star and morning star are two noemata, that is, two ways in which the same *denotatum* may be presented in expressions. When therefore Husserl says that the noema is the perceived such as it appears in a presentation, "the perceived as such" or the appearance, we ought not understand that the noema involves a sensible given or quality; it rather involves an ideational objective unity as the intentional correlate of the act of perception. The noema is not given in a perception (nor in a recollection or an image). It has an entirely different status which consists in *not* existing outside the proposition which expresses it—whether the proposition is perceptual, or whether it is imaginative, recollective, or representative. We distinguish between green as a sensible color or quality and "to green" as a noematic color or attribute. *"The tree greens"*—is this not finally the sense of the color of the tree; and is not *"the tree greens"* its global meaning? Is the noema anything more than a pure event—the tree occurrence (although Husserl does not speak of it in this manner for terminological reasons)? And is that which he calls "appearance" anything more than a surface effect? Between the noemata of the same object, or even of different objects, complex ties are developed, analogous to those which the Stoic dialectic established between events. Could phenomenology be this rigorous science of surface effects?

Let us consider the complex status of sense or of that which is expressed. On one hand, it does not exist outside the proposition which expresses it; what is expressed does not exist outside its expression. This is why we cannot say that sense exists, but rather that it inheres or subsists. On the other hand, it does not merge at all with the proposition, for it has an objective *(objectité)* which is quite distinct. What is expressed has no resemblance whatsoever to the expression. Sense is indeed attributed, but it is not at all the attribute of the proposition— it is rather the attribute of the thing or state of affairs. The attribute of the proposition is the predicate—a qualitative predicate like green, for example. It is attributed to the subject of the proposition. But the attribute of the thing is the verb: to green, for example, or rather the event expressed by this verb. It is attributed to the thing denoted by the subject, or to the state of affairs denoted by the entire proposition. Conversely, this logical attribute does not merge at all with the physical state of affairs, nor with a quality or relation of this state. The attribute is not a being and does not qualify a being; it is an extra-being. "Green" designates a quality, a mixture of things, a mixture of tree and air where chlorophyll coexists with all the parts of the leaf. "To green," on the contrary, is not a quality in the thing, but an attribute which is said of the thing. This attribute does not exist outside of the proposition which expresses it in denoting the thing. Here we return to our point of departure: sense does not exist outside of the proposition . . . , etc.

But this is not a circle. It is rather the coexistence of two sides without thickness, such that we pass from one to the other by following their length. *Sense is both the expressible or the expressed of the proposition, and the attribute of the state of affairs.* It turns one side toward things and one side toward propositions. But it does not merge with the proposition which expresses it any more than with the state of affairs or the quality which the proposition denotes. It is exactly the boundary between propositions and things. It is this *aliquid* at once extra-Being and inherence, that is, this minimum of being which befits inherences.[12] It is in this sense that it is an "event": *on the condition that the event is not confused with its spatio-temporal realization in a state of affairs.* We will not ask therefore what is the sense of the event: the event is sense itself. The event belongs essentially to language; it has an essential relationship to language. But language is what is said of things. Jean Gattegno has indeed noted the difference between Carroll's stories and classical fairy tales: in Carroll's work, everything that takes place occurs in and by means of language; "it is not a story which he tells us, it is a discourse which he addresses to us, a discourse in several pieces. . . ."[13] It is indeed into this flat world of the sense-event, or of the expressible-attribute, that Carroll situates his entire work. Hence the connection between the fantastic work signed "Carroll" and the mathematico-logical work signed "Dodgson." It seems difficult to say, as has been done, that the fantastic work presents simply the traps and difficulties into which we fall when we do not observe the rules and laws formulated by the logical work. Not only because many of the traps subsist in the logical work itself, but also because the distribution seems to be of an entirely different sort. It is surprising to find that Carroll's entire logical work is directly about *signification,* implications, and conclusions, and only indirectly about sense—precisely, through the paradoxes which signification does not resolve, or indeed which it creates. On the contrary, the fantastic work is immediately concerned with *sense* and attaches the power of paradox directly to it. This corresponds well to the two states of sense, de facto and de jure, a posteriori and a priori, one by which the circle of the proposition is indirectly inferred, the other by which it is made to appear for itself, by unfolding the circle along the length of the border between propositions and things.

Fourth Series of
Dualities

The first important duality was that of causes and effects, of corporeal things and incorporeal events. But insofar as events-effects do not exist outside the propositions which express them, this duality is prolonged in the duality of things and propositions, of bodies and language. This is the source of the alternative which runs through all the works of Carroll: to eat or to speak. In *Sylvie and Bruno,* the alternative is between "bits of things" and "bits of Shakespeare." At Alice's coronation dinner, you either eat what is presented to you, *or* you are presented to what you eat. To eat and to be eaten—this is the operational model of bodies, the type of their mixture in depth, their action and passion, and the way in which they coexist within one another. To speak, though, is the movement of the surface, and of ideational attributes or incorporeal events. What is more serious: to speak of food or to eat words? In her alimentary obsessions, Alice is overwhelmed by nightmares of absorbing and being absorbed. She finds that the poems she hears recited are about edible fish. If we then speak of food, how can we avoid speaking in front of the one who is to be served as food? Consider, for example, Alice's blunders in front of the Mouse. How can we avoid eating the pudding to which we have been *presented?* Further still, spoken words may go awry, as if they were attracted by the depth of bodies; they may

23

be accompanied by verbal hallucinations, as in the case of maladies where language disorders are accompanied by unrestricted oral behavior (everything brought to the mouth, eating any object at all, gritting one's teeth). "I'm sure those are not the right words," says Alice, summarizing the fate of the person who speaks of food. To eat words, however, is exactly the opposite: in this case, we raise the operation of bodies up to the surface of language. We bring bodies to the surface, as we deprive them of their former depth, even if we place the entire language through this challenge in a situation of risk. This time the disorders are of the surface; they are lateral and spread out from right to left. *Stuttering* has replaced the *gaffe;* the phantasms of the surface have replaced the hallucination of depth; dreams of accelerated gliding replace the painful nightmare of burial and absorption. The ideal little girl, incorporeal and anorexic, and the ideal little boy, stuttering and left-handed, must disengage themselves from their real, voracious, gluttonous, or blundering images.

But this second duality — body/language, to eat/to speak — is not sufficient. We have seen that although sense does not exist outside of the proposition which expresses it, it is nevertheless the attribute of states of affairs and not the attribute of the proposition. The event subsists in language, but it happens to things. Things and propositions are less in a situation of radical duality and more on the two sides of a frontier represented by sense. This frontier does not mingle or reunite them (for there is no more monism here than dualism); it is rather something along the line of an articulation of their difference: body/language. Comparing the event to a mist rising over the prairie, we could say that this mist rises precisely at the frontier, at the juncture of things and propositions. As a result, the duality is reflected from both sides and in each of the two terms. On the side of the thing, there are physical qualities and real relations which constitute the state of affairs; there are also ideational logical attributes which indicate incorporeal events. And on the side of the proposition, there are names and adjectives which *denote* the state of affairs; and also there are verbs which *express* events or logical attributes. On one hand, there are singular proper names, substantives, and general adjectives which indicate limits, pauses, rests, and presences; on the other, there are verbs carrying off with them becoming and its train of reversible events and infinitely dividing their present into past and future. Humpty Dumpty forcefully distinguished between two sorts of words: "They've a temper, some of them—particularly verbs: they're the proudest—adjectives you can do anything with, but not verbs—however, *I* can manage the whole lot of them! Impenetrability! That's what *I* say." And when Humpty Dumpty explains the use of the odd word "impenetrability," he provides a much too modest explanation ("I meant . . . that we've had enough of that subject"). In fact, impenetrability does mean something else. Humpty Dumpty opposes the impassibility of events to the actions and passions of bodies, the non-consumable nature of sense to the edible nature of things, the impenetrability of incorporeal entities without thickness to the mixtures and reciprocal penetrations of substances, and the resistance of the surface to the softness of depths—in short, the "pride" of verbs to the complacency of substantives and adjectives. Impenetrability also means the frontier between the two—and that the person situated on the frontier, precisely as Humpty Dumpty is seated on his narrow wall, has both at his disposal, being the impenetrable master of the articulation of their difference (". . . however, *I* can manage the whole lot of them").

But this is not yet sufficient. Duality's last word is not to be found in this return to the hypothesis of *Cratylus*. The duality in the proposition is not between two sorts of names, names of stasis and names of becoming, names of substances or qualities and names of events; rather, it is between two dimensions of the proposition, that is, between denotation and expression, or between the denotation of things and the expression of sense. It is like the two sides of a mirror, only what is on one side has no resemblance to what is on the other (". . . all the rest was as different as possible"). To pass to the other side of the mirror is to pass from the relation of denotation to the relation of expression—without pausing at the intermediaries, namely, at manifestation and signification. It is to reach a region where language no longer has any relation to that which it denotes, but only to that which it expresses, that is, to sense. This is the final displacement of the duality: it has now moved inside the proposition.

The Mouse recounts that when the lords proposed to offer the crown to William the Conqueror,

"the archbishop of Canterbury found *it* advisable—,"—"Found *what?*" asked the Duck.—"Found *it,*" the Mouse replied rather crossly: "of course you know what 'it' means."—"I know what 'it' means well enough, when *I* find a thing," said the Duck: "it's generally a frog, or a worm. The question is, what did the archbishop find?"

It is clear that the Duck employs and understands "it" as a denoting term for all things, state of affairs and possible qualities (an indicator). It specifies even that the denoted thing is essentially something which is (or may be) eaten. Everything denoted or capable of denotation is, in principle, consumable and penetrable; Alice remarks elsewhere that she is only able to "imagine" food. But the Mouse made use of "it" in an entirely different manner: as the sense of an earlier proposition, as the event expressed by the proposition (to go and offer the crown to William). The equivocation of "it" is therefore distributed in accordance with the duality of denotation and expression. The two dimensions of the proposition are organized in two series which converge asymptotically, in a term as ambiguous as "it," since they meet one another only at the frontier which they continuously stretch. One series resumes "eating" in its own way, while the other extracts the essence of "speaking." For this reason, in many of Carroll's poems, one witnesses the autonomous development of two simultaneous dimensions, one referring to denoted objects which are always consumable or recipients of consumption, the other referring to always expressible meanings or at least to objects which are the bearers of language and sense. These two dimensions converge only in an esoteric word, in a non-identifiable *aliquid.* Take, for example, the refrain of the Snark: "They sought it with thimbles, they sought it with care; / They pursued it with forks and hope"—where the "thimble" and "fork" refer to designated instruments, but "hope" and "care" to considerations of sense and events (sense, in Carroll's works, is often presented as that which one must "take care of," the object of a fundamental "care"). The strange word "Snark" is the frontier which is stretched as it is drawn by both series. Even more typical is the wonderful Gardener's song in *Sylvie and Bruno.* Every stanza puts into play two terms of very different kinds, which offer two distinct readings: "He thought he saw . . . He looked again and saw it was . . ." Thus, the ensemble of stanzas develops two heterogeneous series. One is composed of animals, of beings or objects which either consume or are consumed; they are described by physical qualities, either sensible or sonorous; the other is composed of objects or of eminently symbolic characters, defined by logical attributes, or sometimes by parental names, and bearers of events, news, messages, or sense. In the conclusion of each verse, the Gardener draws a melancholic path, bordered on both sides by both series; for this song, we learn, is its own story.

> He thought he saw an Elephant,
>   That practiced on a fife:
> He looked again, and found it was
>   A letter from his wife.
> "At length I realize," he said,
>   "The bitterness of life."
>
> He thought he saw an Albatross
>   That fluttered round the lamp:
> He looked again, and found it was
>   A Penny-Postage-Stamp.
> "You'd best be getting home," he said:
>   "The nights are very damp!"
>
> He thought he saw an Argument
>   That proved he was the Pope:
> He looked again, and found it was
>   A Bar of Mottled Soap.
> "A fact so dread," he faintly said,
>   "Extinguishes all hope!"[1]

Fifth Series of
Sense

Sense is never only one of the two terms of the duality which contrasts things and propositions, substantives and verbs, denotations and expressions; it is also the frontier, the cutting edge, or the articulation of the difference between the two terms, since it has at its disposal an impenetrability which is its own and within which it is reflected. For these reasons, sense must be developed for its own sake in a new series of paradoxes, which are now internal.

The paradox of regress, or of indefinite proliferation. When I designate something, I always suppose that the sense is understood, that it is already there. As Bergson said, one does not proceed from sounds to images and from images to sense; rather, one is established "from the outset" within sense. Sense is like the sphere in which I am already established in order to enact possible denotations, and even to think their conditions. Sense is always presupposed as soon as *I* begin to speak; I would not be able to begin without this presupposition. In other words, I never state the sense of what I am saying. But on the other hand, I can always take the sense of what I say as the object of another proposition whose sense, in turn, I cannot state. I thus enter into the infinite regress of that which is presupposed. This regress testifies both to the great impotence of the speaker and to the highest power of language: my impotence to state the sense of what I say, to say at the same time something and its meaning; but also the infinite power of language to speak about words. In short, given a proposition which denotes a state of affairs, one may always take its sense as that which another proposition denotes. If we agree to think of a proposition as a name, it would then appear that every name which denotes an object may itself become the object of a new name which denotes its sense: n_1 refers to n_2, which denotes the sense of n_1; n_2 refers to n_3; etc. For each one of its names, language must contain a name for the sense of this name. This infinite proliferation of verbal entities is known as Frege's paradox.[1] But it is also Carroll's paradox. It appears in rigorous form on the other side of the looking-glass, in the meeting of Alice and the Knight. The Knight announces the title of the song he is going to sing:

"The name of the song is called *'Haddock's Eyes'* "—"Oh, that's the name of the song, is it?" Alice said, trying to feel interested.—"No, you don't understand," the Knight said, looking a little vexed. "That's what the name of the song is *called.* The name really is *'The Aged Aged Man.'* "—"Then I ought to have said 'That's what the *song* is called'?" Alice corrected herself.—"No, you oughtn't: that's quite another thing! The song is called *'Ways and Means':* but that's only what it's *called,* you know!"—"Well, what *is* the song then?" said Alice, who was by this time completely bewildered.—"I was coming to that," the Knight said. "The song really *is 'A-sitting on a Gate'!* . . ."

This passage[2] distinguishes a series of nominal entities. It does not generate an infinite regress but, precisely in order to limit itself, proceeds according to a conventionally finite progression. We must therefore start at the end in order to restore the natural regress. 1) Carroll says: the song *really* is "A-sitting on a Gate." The song itself is a proposition, a name (n_1). "A-sitting on a Gate" is this name, the name which is the song and which appears as far back as the first stanza. 2) But it is not the name *of* the song. Being itself a name, the song is designated by another name. The second name (n_2) is "Ways and Means," which forms the theme of the second, third, fourth, and fifth stanzas. "Ways and Means" is thus the name which designates the song, or *what the song is called.* 3) But the *real* name, Carroll adds, is "The Aged Aged Man," who in fact appears in the entire song. The denoting name itself has a meaning which forms a new name (n_3). 4) This third name in its turn, however, must be designated by a fourth. That is to say, the meaning of n_2, namely n_3, must be designated by n_4. The fourth name is *what the name of the song is called,* namely, "Haddock's Eyes," which appears in the sixth stanza.

There are indeed in Carroll's classification four names: there is the name of what the song really is; the name denoting this reality, which thus denotes the song or represents what the song is called; the sense of this name, which forms a new name or a new reality; and the name which denotes this reality, which thus denotes the sense of the name of the song, or represents what the name of the song is called. At this point, several remarks are necessary. First, Carroll has voluntarily limited himself, since he does not take into account each particular stanza, and since his progressive presentation of the series permits him to give himself an arbitrary point of departure: "Haddock's Eyes." But it goes without saying that the series, taken in its regressive sense, may be extended to infinity in the alternation of a real name and a name which designates this reality. It will be noted, however, that Carroll's series is much more complex than what we have just indicated. Hitherto, in fact, the question was only about a name which, in denoting something, sends us over to another name which denotes the previous name's sense, and on to infinity. In Carroll's classification, this precise situation is represented only by n_2 and n_4: n_4 is the name which denotes the sense of n_2. But Carroll added two other names: a first name, because it treats the originally denoted thing as being itself a name (the song); and a third name, because it treats the sense of the denoting name itself as a name, independently of the name which is going to denote it in turn. Carroll forms therefore the regress with four nominal entities which are displaced ad infinitum. That is to say, he decomposes each couplet and freezes it, in order to draw from it a supplementary couplet. We shall see why. But we can be satisfied with a regress of two alternating terms: the name which denotes something and the name which denotes the sense of this name. This two-term regress is the minimal condition of indefinite proliferation.

This simpler expression appears in a passage from *Alice* in which the Duchess is always discovering the moral or the morality which must be drawn from everything—at least from everything on the condition that it be a proposition. For when Alice does not speak, the Duchess is disarmed: "You're thinking about something, my dear, and that makes you forget to talk. I can't tell you just what the moral of that is, but I shall remember in a bit." But as soon as Alice does speak, the Duchess is busy finding morals:

"The game's going on rather better now," she (Alice) said, by way of keeping up the conversation a little.——" 'Tis so," said the Duchess: "and the moral of that is, 'Oh, 'tis love, 'tis love that makes the world go round!' "——"Somebody said," Alice whispered, "that it's done by everybody minding their own business!"——"Ah well! It means much the same thing," said the Duchess, . . . "and the moral of *that* is, 'Take care of the sense, and the sounds will take care of themselves.' "

In this passage, it is not a question of association of ideas, from one sentence to another; rather, the moral of each proposition consists of another proposition which denotes the sense of the first. Making sense the object of the new proposition amounts to "taking care of the sense," in such conditions that propositions proliferate and "the sounds take care of themselves." Thus, the possibility of a profound link between the logic of sense and ethics, morals or morality, is confirmed.

The paradox of sterile division, or of dry reiteration. There is indeed a way of avoiding this infinite regress. It is to fix the proposition, to immobilize it, just long enough to extract from it its sense—the thin film at the limit of things and words. (Hence the doubling up which we just observed in Carroll's work at each stage of the regress.) But is it the destiny of sense that this dimension be indispensable, or that we do not know what to do with it as soon as we attain it? What have we done, indeed, aside from disengaging a neutralized double of the proposition, a phantom, and a phantasm without thickness? Is it because the sense is expressed by a verb in the proposition that the verb is expressed in its infinitive, participial, or interrogative form: God-to be; or the being-blue of the sky, or is the sky blue? Sense brings about the suspension of both affirmation and negation. Is this the meaning of the propositions "God is," "the sky is blue"? As an attribute of states of affairs, sense is extra-being. It is not of being; it is an *aliquid* which is appropriate to non-being. As that which is expressed by the proposition, sense does not exist, but inheres or subsists in the proposition. One of the most remarkable points of Stoic logic is the sterility of sense-event: only bodies act and suffer, not the incorporeal entities, which are the mere results of actions and passions. This paradox may be called the Stoics' paradox. All the way down to Husserl, there resounds the declaration of a splendid sterility of the expressed, coming to confirm the status of the noema: "The stratum of expression—and this constitutes its peculiarity—apart from the fact that it lends expression to all other intentionalities, is not productive. Or if one prefers: its productivity, its noematic service, exhausts itself in *expressing*." [3]

Extracted from the proposition, sense is independent of it, since it suspends its affirmation and negation, and is nevertheless only its evanescent double: Carroll's smile without the cat or flame without a candle. The two paradoxes, that of infinite regress and that of sterile division, form the two terms of an alternative: one *or* the other. If the first forces us to combine the greatest power with the greatest impotence, the second imposes upon us a similar task, which we must later on fulfill: the task is to combine the sterility of sense in relation to the proposition from which it was extracted with its power of genesis in relation to the dimensions of the proposition. In any case, it seems that Carroll had been acutely aware of the fact that the two paradoxes form an alternative. In *Alice,* the characters have only two possible means of drying themselves after falling into the pool of tears: either to listen to the Mouse's story, the "dryest" story one could be acquainted with, since it isolates the sense of a proposition in a ghostly "it"; or to be launched into a Caucus Race, running around from one proposition to another, stopping when one wishes, without winners or losers, in the circuit of infinite proliferation. At any rate, dryness is what shall later on be named impenetrability. And the two paradoxes represent the essential forms of stuttering, the choreic or clonic form of a convulsive circular proliferation, and the tetanic or tonic form of a fitful immobilization. As is said in *"Poeta Fit, non Nascitur,"* spasm or whiz—these are the two rules of the poem.

The paradox of neutrality, or of essence's third estate. The second paradox necessarily catapults us into a third. For if sense as the double of the proposition is indifferent to affirmation and negation, if it is no more passive than active, then no mode of the proposition is able to affect it. Sense is strictly the same for propositions which are opposed from the point of view of quality, quantity, relation, or modality. For all of these points of view affect denotation and the diverse aspects of its actualiza-

32   FIFTH SERIES OF SENSE

tion or fulfillment in a state of affairs. But they do not affect either sense or expression. Let us take first quality, affirmation and negation: "God is" and "God is not" must have the same sense, by virtue of the autonomy of sense in relation to the existence of the *denotatum.* This was, in fact, in the fourteenth century, the fantastic paradox of Nicolas d'Autrecourt, the object of reprobation: *contradictoria ad invicem idem significant.*[4]

Let us take quantity: all men are white, no man is white, some men are not white . . . ; or relation: sense must be the same in the case of inverse relations, since the relation with regard to sense is always established in both directions at once, insofar as it causes all the paradoxes of becoming-mad to appear yet again. Sense is always a double sense and excludes the possibility that there may be a "good sense" in the relation. Events are never causes of one another, but rather enter the relations of quasi-causality, an unreal and ghostly causality, endlessly reappearing in the two senses. It is neither at the same time, nor in relation to the same thing, that I am younger and older, but it is at the same time and by the same relation that I become so. Hence the innumerable examples dotting Carroll's work, where one finds that "cats eat bats" and "bats eat cats," "I say what I mean" and "I mean what I say," "I like what I get" and "I get what I like," and "I breathe when I sleep" and "I sleep when I breathe," have one and the same sense. This includes the final example of *Sylvie and Bruno,* in which the red jewel carrying the proposition "All will love Sylvie" and the blue jewel carrying the proposition "Sylvie will love all" are two sides of one and the same jewel, so that one can never be preferred except *to itself,* following the law of becoming (to choose a thing from itself).

Let us finally examine modality: how would the possibility, the reality, or the necessity of the denoted object affect sense? The event, for its part, must have one and the same modality, in both future and past, in line with which it divides its presence ad infinitum. If the event is possible in the future and real in the past, it is necessary that it be both at once, since it is divided in them at the same time. Is this to say that it is necessary? One is here reminded of the paradox of contingent futures and its importance in Stoic thought. The hypothesis of necessity, however, rests on the application of the principle of contradiction to the proposition which announces a future. In this perspective, the Stoics went to astonishing lengths in order to escape necessity and to affirm the "fated" without affirming the necessary.[5] We must rather leave this perspective, even if it means rediscovering the Stoic thesis from another point of view. For the principle of contradiction concerns the impossibility of the realization of denotation and, also, the minimal condition of signification. But perhaps it does not concern sense: neither possible, nor real, nor necessary, yet fated. . . . The event subsists in the proposition which expresses it and also happens to things at the surface and outside of being; this is, as we shall see, the "fated." It behooves therefore the event to be cited by the proposition as future, but it behooves the proposition no less to cite the event as past. One of Carroll's general techniques consists of presenting the event *twice*, precisely because everything occurs by way of, and within, language. It is presented once in the proposition in which it subsists, and again in the state of affairs where it crops up at the surface. It is presented once in the verse of a song which relates it to the proposition, and again in the surface effect which relates it to beings, to things, and states of affairs. (Thus the battle between Tweedledum and Tweedledee, or that between the lion and the unicorn. The same occurs in *Sylvie and Bruno*, where Carroll asks the reader to guess whether he composed the verses of the gardener's song in accordance with the events, or the events in accordance with the verses.) But is it necessary to relate the event *twice*, since both are always *at the same time*, since they are two simultaneous faces of one and the same surface, whose inside and outside, their "insistence" and "extra-being," past and future, are in an always reversible continuity?

How could we summarize these paradoxes of neutrality, all of which display sense as unaffected by the modes of the proposition? The philosopher Avicenna distinguished three states of essence: universal in relation to the intellect which thinks it in general; and singular in relation to the particular things in which it is embodied. But neither of these two states is essence itself. An animal is nothing other than an animal *("animal non est nisi animal tantum")* being indifferent to the universal and to the singular, to the particular and to the general.[6] The first state of essence is essence as signified by the proposition, in the order of the concept and of conceptual implications. The second state of essence is essence as designated by the proposition in the particular things in which it is involved. But the third state of essence is essence as sense, essence as expressed—always in this dryness *(animal tantum)* and this splendid sterility or neutrality. It is indifferent to the universal and to the singular, to the general and to the particular, to the personal and to the collective; it is also indifferent to affirmation and negation, etc. In short, it is indifferent to all opposites. This is so because all of these opposites are but modes of the proposition considered in its relations of denotation and signification, and not the traits of the sense which it expresses. Is it, then, the status of the pure event, or of the *fatum* which accompanies it, to surmount all the oppositions in this way? Neither private nor public, neither collective nor individual . . . , it is more terrible and powerful in this neutrality, to the extent that it is all of these things at once?

The paradox of the absurd, or of the impossible objects. From this paradox is derived yet another: the propositions which designate contradictory objects themselves have a sense. Their denotation, however, cannot at all be fulfilled; nor do they have a signification, which would define the type of possibility for such a fulfillment. They are without signification, that is, they are absurd. Nevertheless, they have a sense, and the two notions of absurdity and nonsense must not be confused. Impossible objects—square circles, matter without extension, *perpetuum mobile,* mountain without valley, etc.—are objects "without a home," outside of being, but they have a precise and distinct position within this outside: they are of "extra being"—pure, ideational events, unable to be realized in a state of affairs. We are obliged to call this paradox "Meinong's paradox," for Meinong knew how to draw from it the most beautiful and brilliant effects. If we distinguish two sorts of beings, the being of the real as the matter of denotations and the being of the possible as the form of significations, we must yet add this extra-being which defines a minimum common to the real, the possible *and the impossible.* For the principle of contradiction is applied to the possible and to the real, but *not* to the impossible: impossible entities are "extra-existents," reduced to this minimum, and insisting as such in the proposition.

Sixth Series on
Serialization

The paradox of indefinite regress is the one from which all the other paradoxes are derived. Now, regress has, necessarily, a serial form: each denoting name has a sense which must be denoted by another name: $n_1 \rightarrow n_2 \rightarrow n_3 \rightarrow n_4 \ldots$ If we consider only the succession of names, the series brings about a synthesis of the homogeneous, whereby each name is distinguished from the one preceding it only by its rank, degree, or type. In fact, in compliance with the theory of "types," each name denoting the sense of the one preceding it is superior in degree to that name and to that which it denotes. But if, instead of considering the simple succession of names, we consider that which alternates in this succession, we see that each name is taken first in the denotation which it brings about, and then in the sense which it expresses, because it is this sense which serves as the *denotation* of the other name. The advantage of Carroll's procedure lies precisely in making apparent this difference in nature. This time we are confronted with a synthesis of the heterogeneous; *the serial form is necessarily realized in the simultaneity of at least two series.* Every unique series, whose homogeneous terms are distinguished only according to type or degree, necessarily subsumes under it two heterogeneous series, each one of which is constituted by terms of the same type or degree, although these terms differ in nature from those of the other series (they can of course differ also in degree). The serial form is thus essentially multi-serial. This is indeed the case in mathematics, where a series constructed in the vicinity of a point is significant only in relation to another series, constructed around another point, and converging with, or diverging from, the first. *Alice* is the story of an oral *regress,* but "regress" must be understood first in a logical sense, as the synthesis of names. The homogeneous form of this synthesis subsumes under it two heterogeneous series of orality: to eat/to speak, consumable things/expressible senses. The serial form itself therefore refers us to the already described paradoxes of duality and forces us to address them again from this new point of view.

These two heterogeneous series can, in fact, be determined in various ways. We can consider a series of events and a series of things in which these events are or are not realized; or we can consider a series of denoting propositions and a series of denoted things; or a series of verbs and a series of adjectives and substantives; or a series of expressions and senses and a series of denotations and *denotata.* These variations are unimportant, since they represent solely degrees of freedom in the organization of heterogeneous series. The same duality, we have seen, occurs *outside,* between events and states of affairs; *at the surface,* between propositions and denoted objects; and *inside* the proposition between expressions and denotations. What is more important is that we can construct the two series under an apparently homogeneous form: in this case, we can consider two series of things or states of affairs, two series of events, two series of propositions or denotations, and two series of senses or expressions. Is this to say that the constitution of series is surrendered to the arbitrary?

The law governing two simultaneous series is that they are never equal. One represents the *signifier,* the other the *signified.* But thanks to our terminology, these two terms acquire a particular meaning. We call "signifier" any sign which presents in itself an aspect of sense; we call "signified," on the contrary, that which serves as the correlative to this aspect of sense, that is, that which is defined in a duality relative to this aspect. What is signified therefore is never sense itself. In a restrained sense, signified is the concept; in an extended sense, signified is any thing which may be defined on the basis of the distinction that a certain aspect of sense establishes with this thing. Thus, the signifier is primarily the event as the ideal logical attribute of a state of affairs, and the signified is the state of affairs together with its qualities and real relations. The signifier is also the entire proposition, insofar as it includes dimensions of denotation, manifestation, and signification in the strict sense. And the signified is the independent term which corresponds to these dimensions, that is, the concept, and also the denoted thing or manifested subject. Finally, the signifier is the sole dimension of expression, which in fact has the privilege of not being relative to an independent term, since sense as expressed does not exist outside of the expression; and the signified, in this case, is the denotation, the manifestation, or even the signification in the strict sense. In other words, the signified is the proposition insofar as sense, or that which is expressed, is distinguished from it. However, when we extend the serial method — in order to consider two series of events, two series of things, two series of propositions, or two series of expressions — homogeneity is only apparent: it is always the case that one series has the role of the signifier, and the other the role of the signified, even if these roles are interchanged as we change points of view.

Jacques Lacan has brought to light the existence of two series in one of Edgar Allan Poe's stories. First series: the king who does not see the compromising letter received by his wife; the queen who is relieved to have hidden it so cleverly by leaving it out in the open; the minister who sees everything and takes possession of the letter. Second series: the police who find nothing at the minister's hotel; the minister who thought of leaving the letter in the open in order better to hide it; Dupin who sees everything and takes back possession of the letter.[1] It is obvious that differences between series may be more or less great — very great with certain authors, or very small with those others who introduce only infinitesimal, and yet equally efficacious, variations. It is also obvious that series relations — that which relates the signifying series to the signified and the signified to the signifying — may be assured in the simplest fashion by the continuation of a story, the resemblance of situations, or the identity of the characters. But nothing in all this is essential. On the contrary, the essential appears when small *or* great differences predominate over resemblances and become primary; in other words, when two quite distinct stories are developed simultaneously, or when the characters have a vacillating and ill-determined identity.

It is easy to cite various authors, who have known how to create serial techniques of an exemplary formalism. Joyce, for example, secured the relation between the signifying series "Bloom" and the signified series "Ulysses," thanks to multiple forms which included an archeology of narrative modes, a system of correspondence between numbers, a prodigious employment of esoteric words, a method of question and answer and the establishment of currents of thought or multiple trains of thought (Carroll's double thinking?). Raymond Roussel based the communication of series on a phonematic relation (*"les bandes du vieux pillard," "les bandes du vieux billard"* = b/p), and filled up the difference with a marvelous story in which the signifying series *p* links up with the signified series *b:* the enigmatic nature of the story is emphasized in this general procedure, to the extent that the signified series may remain hidden.[2] Robbe-Grillet established his series of descriptions of states of affairs and rigorous designations with small differences. He did it by having them revolve around themes which, although fixed, are nevertheless suited to almost imperceptible modification and displacement in each series. Pierre Klossowski relies on the *proper name* "Roberte," certainly not in order to designate a character and manifest its identity, but on the contrary, in order to express a "primary intensity," to distribute difference and to obtain the doubling up of two series: the first, signifying, which refers to "the husband being unable to imagine his wife otherwise than as surprising herself as she would allow herself to be surprised"; the second, signified, which refers to the wife "rushing into initiatives which ought to convince her of her freedom, when these initiatives confirm only the vision of her spouse."[3] Witold Gombrowicz established a signifying series of hanged animals (what do they signify?), and a signified series of feminine mouths (what is signifying them?); each series develops a system of signs, sometimes by excess, sometimes by default, and communicates with another by means of strange interfering objects and by means of the esoteric words pronounced by Léon.[4]

Three characteristics, therefore, permit the specification of the relation and distribution of series in general. First, the terms of each series are in perpetual relative displacement in relation to those of the other (thus, for example, the position occupied by the minister in Poe's two series). There is an essential lack of correspondence. This shift or displacement is not a disguise covering up or hiding the resemblances of series through the introduction of secondary variations in them. This relative displacement is, on the contrary, the primary variation without which neither series would open up onto the other. Without it, the series would not constitute themselves through this doubling up, nor would they refer to one another through this variation alone. There is thus a double sliding of one series over or under the other, which constitutes both, in a perpetual disequilibrium vis-à-vis each other. Second, this disequilibrium must itself be oriented: one of the two series —the one determined as signifying, to be precise, presents an excess over the other. For there is always a blurred excess of signifier. Finally, we reach the most important point, a very special and paradoxical case, which ensures the relative displacement of the two series, the excess of the one over the other, without being reducible to any of the terms of the series or to any relation between these terms. The *letter* in Lacan's commentary on Edgar Allan Poe's story, for example, is one such case. Another example is given by Lacan in his commentary on the Freudian case study of the Wolf Man in which the existence of series in the unconscious is made evident. Here Lacan describes the signified paternal series and the signifying filial series, and shows in both the particular role of a special element: the *debt.*[5] In *Finnegans Wake,* once again a letter causes an entire world of series to communicate in a chaos-cosmos. In Robbe-Grillet's writing, the series of designations, the more rigorous or rigorously descriptive they become, the more they converge on the expression of indetermined or overdetermined objects such as the eraser, the fine cord, or the insect bite. According to Klossowski, the name "Roberte" expresses an "intensity," that is, a difference of intensity, before designating or manifesting any person.

What are the characteristics of this paradoxical entity? It circulates without end in both series and, for this reason, assures their communication. It is a two-sided entity, equally present in the signifying and the signified series. It is the mirror. Thus, it is at once word and thing, name and object, sense and *denotatum,* expression and designation, etc. It guarantees, therefore, the convergence of the two series which it traverses, but precisely on the condition that it makes them endlessly diverge. It has the property of being always displaced in relation to itself. If the terms of each series are relatively displaced, *in relation to one another,* it is primarily because they have in themselves an *absolute* place; but this absolute place is always determined by the terms' distance from this element which is always displaced, in the two series, *in relation to itself.* We must say that the paradoxical entity is never where we look for it, and conversely that we never find it where it is. As Lacan says, *it fails to observe its place (elle manque à sa place).*[6] It also fails to observe its own identity, resemblance, equilibrium, and origin. We will not say, therefore, of the two series it animates, that the one is originary and the other derived, though they certainly may be originary or derived in relation to one another. They can also be successive in relation to one another. But they are strictly simultaneous in relation to the entity by means of which they communicate. They are simultaneous without ever being equal, since the entity has two sides, one of which is always absent from the other. It behooves it, therefore, to be in excess in the one series which it constitutes as signifying, and lacking in the other which it constitutes as signified: split apart, incomplete by nature or in relation to itself. Its excess always refers to its own lack, and conversely, its lack always refers to its excess. But even these determinations are still relative. For that which is in excess in one case is nothing but an extremely mobile *empty place;* and that which is lacking in another case is a rapidly moving object, an *occupant without a place,* always supernumerary and displaced.

In fact, there is no stranger element than this double-headed thing with two unequal or uneven "halves." As in a game, we participate in the combination of the empty place and the perpetual displacement of a piece. Or rather, it is as in the Sheep's shop, where Alice discovers the complementarity of "the empty shelf" and of the "bright thing always in the shelf next above," that is, of the place without an occupant and of the occupant without a place. "The most provoking of all" (oddest: the most incomplete, the most disjoined) was that "whenever Alice looked hard at any shelf, to make out exactly what it had on it, *that particular shelf was always quite empty,* though the others round it were crowded as full as they could hold." How things disappear here, says she finally in a plaintive tone, after having spent about a minute in a vain pursuit of a "large bright thing that looked sometimes like a doll and sometimes like a work-box, and *was always in the shelf next above the one she was looking at* . . . I'll follow it up to the very top shelf of all. It'll puzzle it to go through the ceiling, I expect!" But even this plan failed: "the *thing* went through the ceiling as quietly as possible, as if it were quite used to it."

Seventh Series of
Esoteric Words

Lewis Carroll explored and established a serial method in literature. We find in his work several methods for developing series. *We find first two series of events with slight internal differences being regulated by a strange object.* In *Sylvie and Bruno,* for example, the accident of a young cyclist is displaced from one series to the other (chapter 23). Undoubtedly, these two series are successive in relation to each other, yet simultaneous in relation to the strange object—in this case, an eight-handed watch with reversing pin which never follows time. On the contrary, time follows it. It makes events return in two ways, either in a becoming-mad which reverses their sequential order, or with slight variations according to the Stoic fatum. The young cyclist, who falls over a box in the first series of events, now proceeds uninjured. But when the hands of the watch return to their original position, the cyclist lies once again wounded on the wagon which takes him to the hospital. It is as if the watch knew how to conjure up the accident, that is, the temporal occurrence of the event, but not the Event itself, the result, the wound as an eternal truth. . . . The same thing again happens in the second part of *Sylvie and Bruno* (chapter 2). We find in it a scene which reproduces, albeit with slight differences, a scene of the first part (the variable position of the old man which is determined by the "purse."

The latter is a strange object, displaced in relation to itself, since the heroine is forced to run with a fairy's swiftness in order to return it to him).

Second, we find also in Carroll's work *two series of events with great internal and accelerated differences being regulated by propositions, or at least by sounds and onomatopoeias.* This is the law of the mirror as Carroll describes it: ". . . what could be seen from the old room was quite uninteresting, but . . . all the rest was as different as possible." The dream-reality series of *Sylvie and Bruno* are constructed in accordance with this law of divergence, with the splitting of characters from one series to another and their further splitting in each one of them. In the preface to the second part, Carroll presents a detailed table of *states,* both human and fairy, which guarantees the correspondence of the two series in each passage of the book. The transitions from one series to another, and the communication between series, are generally secured through a proposition which begins in one series and ends in another, or through onomatopoeia, that is, a sound which partakes of both. (We do not understand why the best of Carroll's commentators, above all the French, have so many reservations and trifling criticisms with respect to *Sylvie and Bruno,* a masterpiece which, in comparison with *Alice* and *Through the Looking-Glass,* displays a set of entirely new techniques.)

Third, we find two series of propositions (or rather, one series of propositions and one series of "consumptions," or one series of pure expressions and one series of denotations). These series are characterized by *great disparity, and are regulated by means of an esoteric word.* We must first, however, acknowledge that Carroll's esoteric words belong to very different types. One type is formed by contracting the syllabic elements of one proposition, or of many propositions which follow one another. For example, in *Sylvie and Bruno* (chapter 1), *"y'reince"* takes the place of *"Your royal Highness."* This contraction aims at the extraction of the global sense of the entire proposition in order to name it with a single syllable—or an "Unpronounceable Monosyllable," as Carroll says. We know of different procedures in Rabelais and Swift: for example, the syllabic elongation with an overload of consonants; or the simple devocalization, where only consonants are preserved (as if they were suited to express the sense and as if vowels were merely elements of denotation).[1] In any case, esoteric words of this first type form a connection, a synthesis of succession which bears upon a single series.

The esoteric words which are characteristic of Carroll, however, belong to another type. They belong to a synthesis of coexistence intended to guarantee the conjunction of two series of heterogeneous propositions, or of dimensions of propositions. (This of course amounts to the same thing, since it is always possible to construct the propositions of one series by making them embody a particular dimension.) We have seen that the best example of this was the word "Snark": it circulates throughout the two series of alimentary and semiological orality, or throughout the two dimensions of the proposition—the denotative and the expressive. *Sylvie and Bruno* offers other examples as well: the Phlizz, a fruit without taste, or the Azzigoom Pudding. This variety of names can easily be explained: not one of them is the word which circulates; rather, they are names which denote this word ("what the word is called"). The circulating word is of a different nature: in principle, it is the empty square, the empty shelf, the blank word (Lewis Carroll occasionally advised timid people to leave certain words blank in their letters). This word therefore is "called" by names which indicate evanescences and displacements: the Snark is invisible, and the Phlizz is almost an onomatopoeia for something vanishing. Or again, the word is called by names which are quite indeterminate: *aliquid,* it, that, thing, gadget, or "whachamacallit." (See, for example, the *it* in the Mouse's story or the *thing* in the Sheep's shop.) Finally, the word has no name at all; it is rather named by the entire refrain of a song, which circulates throughout the stanzas and causes them to communicate. Or, as it is the case with the Gardener's song, the word is named by the conclusion of each stanza which brings about the communication between premises of two different genres.

Fourth, we find greatly ramified series being regulated by portmanteau words and constituted if necessary through esoteric words of the previous kind. In fact, these portmanteau words are themselves esoteric words of a new kind. They are defined by their function of contracting several words and of enveloping several senses ("frumious" = fuming + furious). The problem, however, is to know when portmanteau words become necessary; for one can always find portmanteau words, and, given good will or arbitrariness, almost all esoteric words may be thus interpreted. But, in fact, the portmanteau word is grounded or formed only if it coincides with a particular function of an esoteric word which it supposedly denotes. For example, an esoteric word with the simple function of contraction within a single series *(y'reince)* is not a portmanteau word. A further example may be found in the famous "Jabberwocky," where a great number of words sketch out a fantastic zoology but do not necessarily form portmanteau words: thus, for example, "toves" (badgers-lizards-corkscrews), "borogoves" (birds-buoys), "raths" (green pigs) and the verb "outgribe" (bellowing-whistling-sneezing).[2] In one final example, we must point out that an esoteric word subsuming two heterogeneous series is not necessarily a portmanteau word. We have just seen that this dual function of subsumption was adequately fulfilled by words like "Phlizz," "thing," and "it."

Nevertheless, portmanteau words *may* appear even on these levels. "Snark" is a portmanteau word which designates a fantastic or composite animal, shark + snake. But it is a secondary or accessory portmanteau word, since its content *(teneur)* does not coincide as such with its function as an esoteric word. By its content, it refers to a composite animal, whereas, by its function, it connotes two heterogeneous series, only one of which is about an animal, albeit composite; the other is about an incorporeal sense. It is not therefore in its "portmanteau" aspect that the word fulfills its function. On the other hand, Jabberwock is undoubtedly a fantastic animal; but it is also a portmanteau word, whose content, this time, coincides with its function. In fact, Carroll suggests that it is formed from "wocer" or "wocor," which means offspring or fruit, and "jabber," which expresses a voluble, animated, or chattering discussion. It is thus as a portmanteau word that "Jabberwock" connotes two series analogous to those of "Snark." It connotes a series of the animal or vegetable provenance of edible and denotable objects and a series of verbal proliferation of expressible senses. It is of course the case that these two series may be connoted otherwise, and that the portmanteau word does not find in them the foundation of its necessity. The definition of the portmanteau word, as contracting several words and encompassing several senses, is therefore a nominal definition only.

Commenting on the first stanza of "Jabberwocky," Humpty Dumpty offers as portmanteau words the words "slithy" (= lithe-slimy-active) "mimsy" (= flimsy-miserable), etc. Here our discomfort increases. We see clearly in each case that there are several contracted words and senses; but these elements are easily organized into a single series in order to compose a global sense. We do not therefore see how the portmanteau word can be distinguished from a simple contraction or from a synthesis of connective succession. We can, of course, introduce a second series; Carroll himself explains that the interpretive possibilities are infinite. For example, we may bring "Jabberwocky" back into the schema of the Gardener's song, with the two series of denotable objects (edible animals), and of objects bearing sense (symbolic or functional beings of the "bank employee," "stamp," or "diligence" types, or even the "action of the railway" type, as in the *Snark*). Thus, on one hand, it is possible to interpret the end of the first stanza in the manner of Humpty Dumpty: green pigs *(raths),* far from home *(mome* = from home), bellowing-whistling-sneezing *(outgribing);* but it is also possible to interpret as follows: taxes, preferential rates *(rath = rate + rather),* far from their point of departure, were prohibitive *(outgrabe).* But, along this route, any serial interpretation may be accepted, and it is not therefore clear how the portmanteau word is distinguished from a conjunctive synthesis of coexistence, or from any esoteric word whatsoever assuring the coordination of two or more heterogeneous series.

The solution to this problem is given by Carroll in the preface to *The Hunting of the Snark:*

Supposing that, when Pistol uttered the well-known words—"Under which king, Bezonian? Speak or die!" Justice Shallow had felt certain that it was either William or Richard, but had not been able to settle which, so that he could not possibly say either name before the other, can it be doubted that, rather than die, he would have gasped out "Rilchiam!"

It seems then that the portmanteau word is grounded upon a strict disjunctive synthesis. Far from being confronted with a particular case, we discover the law of the portmanteau word in general, provided that we disengage each time the disjunction which may have been hidden. Thus, for "frumious" (fuming + furious): "If your thoughts incline ever so little towards 'fuming,' you will say 'fuming-furious'; if they turn, even by a hair's breadth, towards 'furious,' you will say 'furious-fuming'; but if you have that rarest of gifts, a perfectly balanced mind, you will say 'frumious.' " Thus, the necessary disjunction is not between fuming and furious, for one may indeed be both at once; rather, it is between fuming-and-furious on one hand and furious-and-fuming on the other. In this sense, the function of the portmanteau word always consists in the ramification of the series into which it is inserted. This is the reason why it never exists alone. It beckons to other portmanteau words which precede or follow it, and which show that every series is already ramified in principle and still further ramifiable. Michel Butor said it very well: "each of these words can act as a switch, and we can move from one to another by means of many passages; hence the idea of a book which does not simply narrate one story, but a whole ocean of stories."[3] Thus we may now answer the question posed at the outset. When the esoteric word functions not only to connote or coordinate two heterogeneous series but to introduce disjunctions in the series, then the portmanteau word is necessary or necessarily founded. In this case, the esoteric word itself is "named" or denoted by a portmanteau word. The esoteric word in general refers at once to the *empty square* and to the occupant without place. But, in Carroll's work, we must distinguish three sorts of esoteric words: *contracting words,* which perform a synthesis of succession over a single series and bear upon the syllabic elements of a proposition or a succession of propositions in order to extract from them their composite sense ("connection"); *circulating words,* which perform a synthesis of coexistence and coordination between two heterogeneous series and which directly and at once bear upon the respective senses of these series ("conjunction"); and *disjunctive* or portmanteau words, which perform an infinite ramification of coexisting series and bear at once upon words and senses, or syllabic and semiological elements ("disjunction"). The ramifying function or the disjunctive synthesis offers the real definition of the portmanteau word.

Eighth Series of
Structure

Lévi-Strauss has indicated a paradox in the form of an antinomy, which is similar to Lacan's paradox: two series being given, one signifying and the other signified, the first presents an excess and the latter a lack. By means of this excess and this lack, the series refer to each other in eternal disequilibrium and in perpetual displacement. As the hero of *Cosmos* says, there are always too many signifying signs. The primordial signifier is of the order of language. In whatever manner language is acquired, the elements of language must have been given all together, all at once, since they do not exist independently of their possible differential relations. But the signified in general is of the order of the known, though the known is subject to the law of a progressive movement which proceeds from one part to another—*partes extra partes*. And whatever totalizations knowledge may perform, they remain asymptotic to the virtual totality of langue or language. The signifying series organizes a preliminary totality, whereas the signified series arranges the produced totalities. "The Universe signified long before we began to know what it was signifying . . . Man, since his origin, has had at his disposal a completeness of signifier which he is obstructed from allocating to a signifed, given as such without being any better known. There is always an inadequacy between the two."[1]

This paradox might be named Robinson's paradox. It is obvious that Robinson, on his desert island, could reconstruct an analogue of society only by giving himself, all at once, all the rules and laws which are reciprocally implicated, even when they still have no objects. The conquest of nature is, on the contrary, progressive, partial, and advances step by step. Any society whatsoever has all of its rules at once— juridical, religious, political, economic; laws governing love and labor, kinship and marriage, servitude and freedom, life and death. But the conquest of nature, without which it would no longer be a society, is achieved progressively, from one source of energy to another, from one object to another. This is why *law* weighs with all its might, even before its object is known, and without ever its object becoming exactly known. It is this disequilibrium that makes revolutions possible. It is not at all the case that revolutions are determined by technical progress. Rather, they are made possible by this gap between the two series, which solicits realignments of the economic and political totality in relation to the parts of the technical progress. There are therefore two errors which in truth are one and the same: the error of reformism or technocracy, which aspires to promote or impose partial arrangements of social relations according to the rhythm of technical achievements; and the error of totalitarianism, which aspires to constitute a totalization of the signifiable and the known, according to the rhythm of the social totality existing at a given moment. The technocrat is the natural friend of the dictator—computers and dictatorship; but the revolutionary lives in the gap which separates technical progress from social totality, and inscribes there his dream of permanent revolution. This dream, therefore, is itself action, reality, and an effective menace to all established order; it renders possible what it dreams about.

Let us return to Lévi-Strauss' paradox: two series being given, signifying and signified, there is a natural excess of the signifying series and a natural lack of the signified series. There is, necessarily, a *"floating signifier,* which is the servitude of all finite thought, but also the promise of all art, all poetry, all mythic and aesthetic invention." We would like to add that it is the promise of all revolutions. And then there is on the other side a kind of *floated signified,* given by the signifier "without being thereby known," without being thereby assigned or realized. Lévi-Strauss proposes to interpret in this way the words "gadget" or "what-not," "something," *"aliquid,"* but also the famous *"mana"* (or, yet again, *"it"* [ça]). This is a value "in itself void of sense and thus susceptible of taking on any sense, whose unique function would be to fill the gap between signifier and signified." "It is a symbolic value zero, that is, a sign marking the necessity of a symbolic content supplementary to that which already charges the signified, but able to take any value whatsoever, on the condition that it belong to the available reserve . . ." It is necessary to understand that the two series are marked, one by excess, the other by lack, and that the two determinations are interchanged without ever reaching equilibrium. What is in excess in the signifying series is literally an empty square and an always displaced place without an occupant. What is lacking in the signified series is a supernumerary and non-situated given—an unknown, an occupant without a place, or something always displaced. These are two sides of the same thing— two uneven sides—by means of which the series communicate without losing their difference. It is the adventure in the Sheep's shop or the story that the esoteric word narrates.

We may, perhaps, determine certain minimal conditions for a *structure* in general: 1) There must be at least two heterogeneous series, one of which shall be determined as "signifying" and the other as "signified" (a single series never suffices to form a structure). 2) Each of these series is constituted by terms which exist only through the relations they maintain with one another. To these relations, or rather to the values of these relations, there correspond very particular events, that is, *singularities* which are assignable within the structure. The situation is very similar to that of differential calculus, where the distributions of singular points correspond to the values of differential relations.[2] For example, the differential relations among phonemes assign singularities within language, in the "vicinity" of which the sonorities and significations characteristic of the language are constituted. Moreover, it seems that the singularities attached to a series determine in a complex manner the terms of the other series. In any case, a structure includes two distributions of singular points corresponding to the base series. And for this reason, it is imprecise to oppose structure and event: the structure includes a register of ideal *events,* that is, an entire *history* internal to it (for example, if the series include "characters," it is a history which connects all the singular points corresponding to the positions of the characters relative to one another in the two series). 3) The two heterogeneous series converge toward a paradoxical element, which is their "differentiator." This is the principle of the emission of singularities. This element belongs to no series; or rather, it belongs to both series at once and never ceases to circulate throughout them. It has therefore the property of always being displaced in relation to itself, of "being absent from its own place," its own identity, its own resemblance, and its own equilibrium. It appears in one of the series as an excess, but only on the condition that it would appear at the same time in the other as a lack. But if it is in excess in the one, it is so only as an empty square; and if it is lacking in the other, it is so only as a supernumerary pawn or an occupant without a compartment. It is both word and object at once: esoteric word and exoteric object.

It has the function of articulating the two series to one another, of reflecting them in one another, of making them communicate, coexist, and be ramified. Again, it has the function of joining the singularities which correspond to the two series in a "tangled tale," of assuring the passage from one distribution of singularities to the next. In short, it has the function of bringing about the distribution of singular points; of determining as signifying the series in which it appears in excess, and, as signified, the series in which it appears correlatively as lacking and, above all, of assuring the bestowal of sense in both signifying and signified series. For sense is not to be confused with signification; it is rather what is attributed in such a way that it determines both the signifier and the signified as such. We can conclude from this that there is no structure without series, without relations between the terms of each series, or without singular points corresponding to these relations. But above all, we can conclude that there is no structure without the empty square, which makes everything function.

Ninth Series of the
Problematic

What is an ideal event? It is a singularity—or rather a set of singularities or of singular points characterizing a mathematical curve, a physical state of affairs, a psychological and moral person. Singularities are turning points and points of inflection; bottlenecks, knots, foyers, and centers; points of fusion, condensation, and boiling; points of tears and joy, sickness and health, hope and anxiety, "sensitive" points. Such singularities, however, should not be confused either with the personality of the one expressing herself in discourse, or with the individuality of a state of affairs designated by a proposition, or even with the generality or universality of a concept signified by a figure or a curve. The singularity belongs to another dimension than that of denotation, manifestation, or signification. It is essentially pre-individual, non-personal, and a-conceptual. It is quite indifferent to the individual and the collective, the personal and the impersonal, the particular and the general—and to their oppositions. Singularity is *neutral*. On the other hand, it is not "ordinary": the singular point is opposed to the ordinary.[1]

We said that a set of singularities corresponds to each one of the series of a structure. Conversely, each singularity is the source of a series extending in a determined direction right up to the vicinity of another singularity. In this sense, not only are there several divergent series in a structure, but each series is itself constituted by several convergent sub-series. If we examine the singularities corresponding to the two important basic series, we see that they are distinguished, in both cases, by their distribution. From one to the other, certain singular points disappear or are divided, or undergo a change of nature and function. The moment that the two series resonate and communicate, we pass from one distribution to another. The moment that the series are traversed by the paradoxical agent, singularities are displaced, redistributed, transformed into one another, and change sets. If the singularities are veritable events, they communicate in one and the same Event which endlessly redistributes them, while their transformations form a *history*. Péguy clearly saw that history and event were inseparable from those singular points: "Events have critical points just as temperature has critical points—points of fusion, congelation, boiling, condensation, coagulation, and crystallization. And even within the event there are states of surfeit which are precipitated, crystallized, and determined only by the introduction of a fragment of the future event."[2] Péguy was able, as well, to invent an entire language, among the most pathological and aesthetic that one might dream of, in order to explain how a singularity is prolonged in a line of ordinary points, but also how it begins again in another singularity, how it redistributes itself in another set (two repetitions, a bad one and a good one, one that enchains and the other that saves).

Events are ideal. Novalis sometimes says that there are two courses of events, one of them ideal, the other real and imperfect—for example, ideal Protestanism and real Lutheranism.[3] The distinction however is not between two sorts of events; rather, it is between the event, which is ideal by nature, and its spatio-temporal realization in a state of affairs. The distinction is between *event* and *accident*. Events are ideational singularities which communicate in one and the same Event. They have therefore an eternal truth, and their time is never the present which realizes them and makes them exist. Rather, it is the unlimited Aion, the Infinitive in which they subsist and insist. Events are the only idealities. To reverse Platonism is first and foremost to remove essences and to substitute events in their place, as jets of singularities. A double battle has the objective to thwart all dogmatic confusion between event and essence, and also every empiricist confusion between event and accident.

The mode of the event is the problematic. One must not say that there are problematic events, but that events bear exclusively upon problems and define their conditions. In the beautiful pages in which he opposes the theorematic conception of geometry to the problematic, the Neoplatonic philosopher Proclus defines the problem by means of the vents which come to affect a logical subject matter (sections, ablations, adjunctions, etc.), whereas the theorem deals with the properties which are deduced from an essence.[4] The event by itself is problematic and problematizing. A problem is determined only by the singular points which express its conditions. We do not say that the problem is thereby resolved; on the contrary, it is determined as a problem. For example, in the theory of differential equations, the existence and distribution of singularities are relative to a problematic field defined by the equation as such. As for the solution, it appears only with the integral curves and the form they take in the vicinity of singularities inside the field of vectors. It seems, therefore, that a problem always finds the solution it merits, according to the conditions which determine it as a problem. In fact, the singularities preside over the genesis of the solutions of the equation. Nonetheless, it is still the case, as Lautman said, that the instance-problem and the instance-solution differ in nature[5]—as they represent respectively the ideal event and its spatio-temporal realization. We must then break with the long habit of thought which forces us to consider the problematic as a subjective category of our knowledge or as an empirical moment which would indicate only the imperfection of our method and the unhappy necessity for us not to know ahead of time—a necessity which would disappear as we acquire knowledge. Even if the problem is concealed by its solution, it subsists nonetheless in the Idea which relates it to its conditions and organizes the genesis of the solutions. Without this Idea, the solutions would have no *sense*. The problematic is both an objective category of knowledge and a perfectly objective kind of being. "Problematic" qualifies precisely the ideal objectivities. Kant was without doubt the first to accept the problematic not as a fleeting uncertainty but as the very object of the Idea, and thereby as an indispensable horizon of all that occurs or appears.

The relation between mathematics and man may thus be conceived in a new way: the question is not that of quantifying or measuring human properties, but rather, on the one hand, that of problematizing human events, and, on the other, that of developing as various human events the conditions of a problem. The recreational mathematics of which Carroll dreamt offers this double aspect. The first appears precisely in a text entitled "A Tangled Tale." This story is composed of *knots* which, in each case, surround the singularities corresponding to a problem; characters incarnate these singularities and are displaced or rearranged from one problem to another, until they find each other again in the tenth knot, caught in the network of their kinship relations. The Mouse's *it,* which used to refer either to consumable objects or to expressible senses, is now replaced by *data,* which refer sometimes to alimentary gifts, and sometimes to givens or problem conditions. The second, and more profound, attempt appears in *The Dynamics of a Parti-cle:*

... two lines might have been observed wending their way across a plane superficies. The elder of the two had by long practice acquired the art, so painful to young and impulsive loci, of lying evenly between his extreme points; but the younger, in her girlish impetuosity, was ever longing to diverge and become a hyperbola or some such romantic and boundless curve. ... Fate and the intervening superficies had hitherto kept them asunder, but this was no longer to be: a line had intersected them, making the two interior angles together less than two right angles.

We should not see in this passage a simple allegory or a manner of anthropomorphizing mathematics. Nor should we see these tendencies in the celebrated passage from *Sylvie and Bruno.* "Once a coincidence was taking a walk with a little accident, and they met an explanation. ..." When Carroll speaks of a parallelogram which longs for exterior angles and complains at not being able to be inscribed in a circle, or of a curve which suffers from "sections and ablations" that it has been forced to undergo, one must remember rather that psychological and moral characters are also made of pre-personal singularities, and that their feelings or their pathos are constituted in the vicinity of these singularities: sensitive crisis points, turning points, boiling points, knots, and foyers (what Carroll calls *plain anger* or *right anger,* for example). Carroll's two lines evoke two resonating series; and their longings evoke distributions of singularity, merging and being redistributed in the current of a tangled tale. As Carroll said, "(p)lain superficiality is the character of a speech, in which any two points being taken, the speaker is found to lie wholly with regard to those two points."[6] In *The Dynamics of a Parti-cle* Carroll outlines a theory of series and of degrees or powers of particles arranged in these series (*"LSD, a function of great value . . ."*).

We can speak of events only in the context of the problem whose conditions they determine. We can speak of events only as singularities deployed in a problematic field, in the vicinity of which the solutions are organized. This is why an entire method of problems and solutions traverses Carroll's work, constituting the scientific language of events and their realizations. Now, if the distributions of singularities corresponding to each series form fields of problems, how are we to characterize the paradoxical element which runs through the series, makes them resonate, communicate, and branch out, and which exercises command over all the repetitions, transformations, and redistributions? This element must itself be defined as the locus of a question. The *problem* is determined by *singular points* corresponding to the series, but the *question* is determined by an *aleatory point* corresponding to the empty square or mobile element. The metamorphoses or redistributions of singularities form a history; each combination and each distribution is an event. But the paradoxical instance is the Event in which all events communicate and are distributed. It is the Unique event, and all other events are its bits and pieces. Later on, James Joyce will be able to give sense to a method of questions and answers which doubles that of problems—the Inquisitory which grounds the Problematic. The question is developed in problems, and the problems are enveloped in a fundamental question. And just as solutions do not suppress problems, but on the contrary discover in them the subsisting conditions without which they would have no sense, answers do not at all suppress, nor do they saturate, the question, which persists in all of the answers. There is therefore an aspect in which problems remain without a solution, and the question without an answer. It is in this sense that problem and question designate ideational objectivities and have their own being, *a minimum of being* (see the "answerless riddles" of *Alice*). We have already seen how esoteric words were essentially tied to them. On one hand, the portmanteau words are inseparable from a problem which is deployed in the ramified series. This problem does not at all express a subjective uncertainty, but, on the contrary, it expresses the objective equilibrium of a mind situated in front of the horizon of what happens or appears: Is it Richard or William? Is it fuming-furious or furious-fuming? In each case, there is a distribution of singularities. On the other hand, blank words, or, rather, words denoting the blank word are inseparable from a question which is enveloped and displaced throughout the series. It belongs to this element which is always absent from its proper place, proper resemblance, and proper identity to be the object of a fundamental question which is displaced along with it: what is the Snark? what is the Phlizz? what is It *(Ça)?* Being the refrain of a song, whose verses form the many series through which the element circulates, being the magic word, in whose case all the names by which it is "called" do not fill in the "blank," the paradoxical instance has precisely this singular being, this "objective," which corresponds to the question as such, and corresponds without ever answering it.

Tenth Series of the
Ideal Game

Not only does Lewis Carroll invent games, or transform the rules of known games (tennis, croquet), but he invokes a sort of ideal game whose meaning and function are at first glance difficult to assess: for example, the caucus-race in *Alice,* in which one begins when one wishes and stops at will; and the croquet match in which the balls are hedgehogs, the mallets pink flamingos, and the loops soldiers who endlessly displace themselves from one end of the game to the other. These games have the following in common: they have a great deal of movement, they seem to have no precise rules, and they permit neither winner nor loser. We are not "acquainted" with such games which seem to contradict themselves.

The games with which we are acquainted respond to a certain number of principles, which may make the object of a theory. This theory applies equally to games of skill and to games of chance; only the nature of the rules differs. 1) It is necessary that in every case a set of rules preexists the playing of the game, and, when one plays, this set takes on a categorical value; 2) these rules determine hypotheses which divide and apportion chance, that is, hypotheses of loss or gain (what happens if . . .); 3) these hypotheses organize the playing of the game according to a plurality of throws, which are really and numerically distinct. Each one of them brings about a fixed distribution corresponding to one case or another. (Even when the game is based on a single throw, this throw is good only because of the fixed distribution which it brings about and because of its numerical particularity); 4) the consequences of the throws range over the alternative "victory or defeat." The characteristics of normal games are therefore the preexisting categorical rules, the distributing hypotheses, the fixed and numerically distinct distributions, and the ensuing results. These games are partial in two ways: first, they characterize only one part of human activity, and second, even if they are pushed to the absolute, they *retain chance only at certain points,* leaving the remainder to the mechanical development of consequences or to skill, understood as the art of causality. It is inevitable therefore that, being themselves mixed, they refer to another type of activity, labor, or morality, whose caricature or counterpart they are, and whose elements they integrate in a new order. Whether it be Pascal's gambling man or Leibniz's chess-playing God, the game is explicitly taken as a model only because it has implicit models which are not games: the moral model of the Good or the Best, the economic model of causes and effects, or of means and ends.

It is not enough to oppose a "major" game to the minor game of man, nor a divine game to the human game; it is necessary to imagine other principles, even those which appear inapplicable, by means of which the game would become pure. 1) There are no preexisting rules, each move invents its own rules; it bears upon its own rule. 2) Far from dividing and apportioning chance in a really distinct number of throws, all throws affirm chance and endlessly ramify it with each throw. 3) The throws therefore are not really or numerically distinct. They are qualitatively distinct, but are the qualitative forms of a single cast which is ontologically one. Each throw is itself a series, but *in a time much smaller than the minimum* of continuous, thinkable time; and, to this serial minimum, a distribution of singularities corresponds.[1] Each throw emits singular points—the points on the dice, for example. But the set of throws is included in the aleatory point, a unique cast which is endlessly displaced throughout all series, *in a time greater than the maximum* of continuous, thinkable time. These throws are successive in relation to one another, yet simultaneous in relation to this point which always changes the rule, or coordinates and ramifies the corresponding series as it insinuates chance over the entire length of each series. The unique cast is a chaos, each throw of which is a fragment. Each throw operates a distribution of singularities, a constellation. But instead of dividing a closed space between fixed results which correspond to hypotheses, the mobile results are distributed in the open space of the unique and undivided cast. This is a *nomadic* and non-sedentary *distribution,* wherein each system of singularities communicates and resonates with the others, being at once implicated by the others and implicating them in the most important cast. It is the game of problems and of the question, no longer the game of the categorical and the hypothetical.

4) Such a game—without rules, with neither winner nor loser, without responsibility, a game of innocence, a caucus-race, in which skill and chance are no longer distinguishable—seems to have no reality. Besides, it would amuse no one. Certainly, it is not the game played by Pascal's gambler, nor by Leibniz's God. What cheating is there in Pascal's moralizing wager! What a bad move is there in Leibniz's economic combination! This is not at all the world as a work of art. The ideal game of which we speak cannot be played by either man or God. It can only be thought as nonsense. But precisely for this reason, it is the reality of thought itself and the unconscious of pure thought. Each thought forms a series in a time which is smaller than the minimum of consciously thinkable continuous time. Each thought emits a distribution of singularities. All of these thoughts communicate in one long thought, causing all the forms or figures of the nomadic distribution to correspond to its own displacement, everywhere insinuating chance and ramifying each thought, linking the "once and for all" to "each time" for the sake of "all time." For only thought finds it possible *to affirm all chance and to make chance into an object of affirmation.* If one tries to play this game other than in thought, nothing happens; and if one tries to produce a result other than the work of art, nothing is produced. This game is reserved then for thought and art. In it there is nothing but victories for those who know how to play, that is, how to affirm and ramify chance, instead of dividing it *in order to* dominate it, *in order to* wager, *in order to* win. This game, which can only exist in thought and which has no other result than the work of art, is also that by which thought and art are real and disturbing reality, morality, and the economy of the world.

In games with which we are familiar, chance is fixed at certain points. These are the points at which independent causal series encounter one another (for example, the rotation of the roulette and the rolling ball). Once the encounter is made, the mixed series follow a single track, protected from any new interference. If a player suddenly bent over and blew with all his might in order to speed up or to thwart the rolling ball, he would be stopped, thrown out, and the move would be annulled. What would have been accomplished, however, other than breathe a little more chance into the game? This is how J. L. Borges describes the Babylonian lottery:

if the lottery is an intensification of chance, a periodic infusion of chaos into the cosmos, would it not be desirable for chance to intervene at all stages of the lottery and not merely in the drawing? Is it not ridiculous for chance to dictate the death of someone while the circumstances of his death—its silent reserve or publicity, the time limit of one hour or one century—should remain immune to hazard? . . . In reality, *the number of drawings is infinite. No decision is final, all diverge into others. The ignorant suppose that an infinite number of drawings requires an infinite amount of time; in reality, it suffices that time be infinitely subdivisible,* as is the case in the famous parable of the Tortoise and Hare.[2]

The fundamental question with which this text leaves us is this: what is this time which need not be infinite but only "infinitely subdivisible"? It is the Aion. We have seen that past, present, and future were not at all three parts of a single temporality, but that they rather formed two readings of time, each one of which is complete and excludes the other: on one hand, the always limited present, which measures the action of bodies as causes and the state of their mixtures in depth (Chronos); on the other, the essentially unlimited past and future, which gather incorporeal events, at the surface, as effects (Aion).

The greatness of Stoic thought is to show at once the necessity of these two readings and their reciprocal exclusion. *Sometimes* it will be said that only the present exists; that it absorbs or contracts in itself the past and the future, and that, from contraction to contraction, with ever greater depth, it reaches the limits of the entire Universe and becomes a living cosmic present. It suffices in this case to proceed according to the order of the decontractions, in order that the Universe begin again and that all its presents be restored. Thus the time of the present is always a limited but infinite time; infinite because cyclical, animating a physical eternal return as the return of the Same, and a moral eternal wisdom as the wisdom of the Cause. *Sometimes, on the other hand,* it will be said that only the past and future subsist, that they subdivide each present, ad infinitum, however small it may be, stretching it out over their empty line. The complementarity of past and future appears then clearly: each present is divided into past and future, ad infinitum. Or rather, such time is not infinite, since it never comes back upon itself; it is unlimited, a pure straight line the two extremities of which endlessly distance themselves from each other and become deferred into the past and the future. Is there not in the Aion a labyrinth very different from that of Chronos—a labyrinth more terrible still, which commands *another* eternal return and another ethic (an ethic of Effects)? Let us think again of Borge's words: "I know of a Greek labyrinth which is a single straight line. . . . The next time I kill you . . . I promise you the labyrinth made of the single straight line which is invisible and everlasting." [3]

In the one case, the present is everything; the past and future indicate only the relative difference between two presents. One of these has a smaller extension, while the other has a contraction bearing upon a greater extension. In the other case, the present is nothing; it is a pure mathematical instant, a being of reason which expresses the past and the future into which it is divided. Briefly, *there are two times, one of which is composed only of interlocking presents; the other is constantly decomposed into elongated pasts and futures.* There are two times, one of which is always definite, active or passive; the other is eternally Infinitive and eternally neutral. One is cyclical, measures the movement of bodies and depends on the matter which limits and fills it out; the other is a pure straight line at the surface, incorporeal, unlimited, an empty form of time, independent of all matter. One of the esoteric words found in "Jabberwocky" contaminates both times: "wabe." For, according to one sense, "wabe" must be understood as having been derived from "swab" or "soak." In this case, it would designate the rain-drenched lawn surrounding a sundial; it is the physical and cyclical Chronos of the variable living present. But in another sense, it is the lane extending far ahead and far behind, "way-be," "a long way before, a long way behind." It is the incorporeal Aion which has been unfolded. It has become autonomous in the act of disinvesting itself from its matter and flees in both directions at once, toward the future and toward the past. In it, even rain falls horizontally following the hypothesis of *Sylvie and Bruno*. This Aion, being straight line and empty form, is the time of events-effects.

Just as the present measures the temporal realization of the event—that is, its incarnation in the depth of acting bodies and its incorporation in a state of affairs—the event in turn, in its impassibility and impenetrability, has no present. It rather retreats and advances in two directions at once, being the perpetual object of a double question: What is going to happen? What has just happened? The agonizing aspect of the pure event is that it is always and at the same time something which has just happened and something about to happen; never something which is happening. The x, with respect to which one feels that *it* just happened, is the object of the "novella"; and the x which is always about to happen, is the object of the "tale" *("conte")*. The pure event is both tale and novella, never an actuality. It is in this sense that events are *signs*.

Sometimes the Stoics say that signs are always present, that they are signs of present things. One cannot *say* of someone mortally wounded that he has been wounded and that he will die, but that he *is* having been wounded *(il est ayant blessé),* and that he *is* due to die *(il est devant mourir).* This present does not contradict the Aion; on the contrary, it is the present as being of reason which is subdivided ad infinitum into something that has just happened and something that is going to happen, always flying in both directions at once. The other present, the living present, happens and brings about the event. But the event nonetheless retains an eternal truth upon the line of the Aion, which divides it eternally into a proximate past and an imminent future. The Aion endlessly subdivides the event and pushes away past as well as future, without ever rendering them less urgent. The event is that no one ever dies, but has always just died or is always going to die, in the empty present of the Aion, that is, in eternity. As he was describing a murder such that it had to be mimed—pure ideality—Mallarmé said: "Here advancing, there remembering, to the future, to the past, under the false appearance of the present—in such a manner the Mime proceeds, whose game is limited to a perpetual allusion, without breaking the mirror."[4] Each event is the smallest time, smaller than the minimum of continuous thinkable time, because it is divided into proximate past and imminent future. But it is also the longest time, longer than the maximum of continuous thinkable time, because it is endlessly subdivided by the Aion which renders it equal to its own unlimited line. Let us understand that each event in the Aion is smaller than the smallest subdivision of Chronos; but it is also greater than the greatest divisor of Chronos, namely, the entire cycle. Through its unlimited subdivision in both directions at once, each event runs along the entire Aion and becomes coextensive to its straight line in both directions. Do we then sense the approach of an eternal return no longer having anything to do with the cycle, or indeed of the entrance to a labyrinth, all the more terrible since it is the labyrinth of the unique line, straight and without thickness? The Aion is the straight line traced by the aleatory point. The singular points of each event are distributed over this line, always in relation to the aleatory point which subdivides them ad infinitum, and it causes them to communicate with each other, as it extends and stretches them out over the entire line. Each event is adequate to the entire Aion; each event communicates with all others, and they all form one and the same Event, an event of the Aion where they have an eternal truth. This is the secret of the event: it exists on the line of the Aion, and yet it does not fill it. How could an incorporeal fill up the incorporeal or the impenetrable fill up the impenetrable? Only bodies penetrate each other, only Chronos is filled up with states of affairs and the movements of the objects that it measures. But being an empty and unfolded form of time, the Aion subdivides ad infinitum that which haunts it without ever inhabiting it —the Event for all events. This is why the unity of events or effects among themselves is very different from the unity of corporeal causes among themselves.

The Aion is the ideal player of the game; it is an infused and ramified chance. It is the unique cast from which all throws are qualitatively distinguished. It plays or is played on at least two tables, or at the border of two tables. There, it traces its straight and bisecting line. It gathers together and distributes over its entire length the singularities corresponding to both. The two tables or series are like the sky and the earth, propositions and things, expressions and consumptions. Carroll would say that they are the multiplication table and the dinner table. The Aion is precisely the border of the two, the straight line which separates them; but it is also the plain surface which connects them, an impenetrable window or glass. It circulates *therefore* throughout the series and never ceases to reflect and to ramify them. It makes one and the same event the expressed of propositions and the attribute of things. It is Mallarmé's game, that is, "the book." This book has its two tables (the first and last pages on a single folded sheet); its multiple internal series endowed with singularities (mobile, interchangeable pages, constellations-problems); its two-sided straight line which reflects and ramifies the series ("central purity," "an equation under god Janus"), and over this line the aleatory point endlessly displaced, appearing as an empty square on one side and as a supernumerary object on the other (hymn and drama, or "a bit priest, a bit dancer"; or again, a lacquered piece of furniture made of pigeonholes and the hat without a shelf, as the architectonic elements of the book). Now, inside the four, a little too elaborate, fragments of the Book of Mallarmé, something in his thought resonates which vaguely conforms to Carroll's series. One fragment develops the double series: things or propositions, to eat or to speak, to feed or to be presented, to eat the inviting lady or to answer the invitation. A second fragment releases the "firm and benevolent neutrality" of the word, a neutrality of sense in relation to the proposition and also of the order expressed in relation to the person who hears it. Another fragment displays in two intertwined female figures the unique line of the Event which, being always in disequilibrium, presents one of its sides as the sense of propositions and the other as the attribute of states of affairs. And finally, another fragment shows the aleatory point which is displaced over the line, the point of *Igitur,* or of the *dice-throw,* doubly indicated by an old man who has died of hunger and by an infant born of speech—"for dying of hunger gives him the right to begin anew. . . ." [5]

Eleventh Series of
Nonsense

Let us summarize the characteristics of this paradoxical element or *perpetuum mobile*. Its function is to traverse the heterogeneous series, to coordinate them, to make them resonate and converge, but also to ramify them and to introduce into each one of them multiple disjunctions. It is both word = x and thing = x. Since it belongs simultaneously to both series, it has two sides. But the sides are never balanced, joined together, or paired off, because the paradoxical element is always in disequilibrium in relation to itself. To account for this correlation and this dissymmetry we made use of a number of dualities: it is at once excess and lack, empty square and supernumerary object, a place without an occupant and an occupant without a place, "floating signifier" and floated signified, esoteric word and exoteric thing, white word and black object. This is why it is constantly denoted in two ways: "For the Snark was a Boojum, you see." We should not imagine that the Boojum is a particularly frightening species of Snark; the relation of genus and species is here inappropriate. Rather, we are faced with the two dissymmetrical halves of an ultimate instance. Likewise, from Sextus Empiricus we learn that the Stoics had at their disposal a word stripped of meaning, *"Blituri,"* and that they employed it in a doublet with the correlate *"Skindapsos."* [1] "For Blituri was a Skindapsos, you see." Word = x in a series, but at the same time, thing = x in another series; perhaps (we shall see this later) it is necessary to add to the Aion yet a third aspect, action = x, insofar as the series resonate and communicate and form a "tangled tale." "Snark" is an unheard-of name, but it is also an invisible monster. It refers to a formidable action, the hunt, at the end of which the hunter is dissipated and loses his identity. "Jabberwock" is an unheard-of name, a fantastic beast, but also the object of a formidable action or of a great murder.

The blank word is designated by esoteric words in general (it, thing, Snark, etc.). The function of the blank word, or of the esoteric words of the first order, is to coordinate the two heterogeneous series. Esoteric words, in turn, may also be designated by portmanteau words, words of the second order, whose function is to ramify the series. Two different figures correspond to these two powers. *First figure:* the paradoxical element is at once word and thing. In other words, both the blank word denoting it and the esoteric word denoting the blank word have the function to express the thing. It is a word that denotes exactly what it expresses and expresses what it denotes. It expresses its *denotatum* and designates its own sense. It says something, but at the same time it says the sense of what it says: it says its own sense. It is therefore completely abnormal. We know that the normal law governing all names endowed with sense is precisely that their sense may be denoted only by another name ($n_1 \rightarrow n_2 \rightarrow n_3 \ldots$). The name saying its own sense can only be *nonsense* (N_n). Nonsense is of a piece with the word "nonsense," and the word "nonsense" is of a piece with words which have no sense, that is, with the conventional words that we use to denote it. *Second figure:* the portmanteau word is itself the principle of an alternative the two terms of which it forms (frumious = fuming-and-furious or furious-and-fuming). Each virtual part of such a word denotes the sense of the other or expresses the other part which in turn denotes it. Under the same form, the entire word says its own sense and is, for this reason, nonsense. Indeed, the second normal law governing names endowed with sense is that their sense can not determine an alternative into which they themselves enter. Nonsense thus has two sides, one corresponding to the regressive synthesis, the other to the disjunctive synthesis.

One could object that all of this means nothing. It is a bad play on words to suppose that nonsense expresses its own sense since, by definition, it has none. But this objection is unfounded. The play on words would be to say that nonsense has a sense, the sense being precisely that it hasn't any. This is not our hypothesis at all. When we assume that nonsense says its own sense, we wish to indicate, on the contrary, that sense and nonsense have a specific relation which can not copy that of the true and false, that is, which can not be conceived simply on the basis of a relation of exclusion. This is indeed the most general problem of the logic of sense: what would be the purpose of rising from the domain of truth to the domain of sense, if it were only to find between sense and nonsense a relation analogous to that of the true and the false? We have already seen that it is futile to go from the conditioned to the condition in order to think of the condition in the image of the conditioned as the simple form of possibility. The condition cannot have with its negative the same kind of relation that the conditioned has with its negative. The logic of sense is necessarily determined to posit between sense and nonsense an original type of intrinsic relation, a mode of co-presence. For the time being, we may only hint at this mode by dealing with nonsense as a word which says its own sense.

The paradoxical element, under the two preceding figures, is nonsense. But the normal laws are not exactly opposed to the two figures. These figures, on the contrary, subsume normal words endowed with sense under these laws which do not apply to them. Any normal name has a sense which must be denoted by another name and which must determine the disjunctions filled by other names. Insofar as these names, which are endowed with sense, are subject to these laws, they receive *determinations of signification*. The determination of signification and the law are not the same thing; the former derives from the latter and relates names, that is, words and propositions, to concepts, properties, or classes. Thus, when the regressive law states that the sense of a name must be denoted by another name, these names of different degrees refer, from the point of view of signification, to classes or properties of different "types." Every property must belong to a type higher than the properties or individuals over which it presides, and every class must belong to a type higher than the objects which it contains. It follows that a class cannot be a member of itself, nor may it contain members of different types. Likewise, according to the disjunctive law, a determination of signification states that the property or the term in relation to which a classification is made cannot belong to any of the groups of the same type which are classified in relation to it. An element cannot be part of the sub-sets which it determines, nor a part of the set whose existence it presupposes. Thus, two forms of the absurd correspond to the two figures of nonsense, and these forms are defined as "stripped of signification" and as constituting *paradoxes:* a set which is included in itself as a member; the member dividing the set which it presupposes — the set of all sets, and the "barber of the regiment." The absurd then is sometimes a confusion of formal levels in the regressive synthesis, sometimes a vicious circle in the disjunctive synthesis.[2] The interest of the determinations of signification lies in the fact that they engender the principles of non-contradiction and the excluded middle, instead of these principles being given ready-made. The paradoxes themselves enact the genesis of contradiction and inclusion in the propositions stripped of signification. Perhaps we should envisage from this point of view certain Stoic conceptions concerning the connection of propositions. For when the Stoics display so much interest in hypothetical propositions of the sort "if it is day, it is light," or "if this woman has milk, she has given birth," commentators are certainly right to recall that the question here is not about a relation of physical consequence or of causality in the modern sense of the word. But they are perhaps wrong to see in them a simple logical consequence in the form of identity. The Stoics used to number the members of the hypothetical proposition: we can consider "being day" or "having given birth" as signifying properties of a higher type than those over which they preside ("being light," "having milk"). The link between propositions cannot be reduced either to an analytic identity or to an empirical synthesis; rather it belongs to the domain of signification—so that contradiction may be engendered, not in the relation of a term to its opposite, but in the relation of a term to the *other* term. Given the transformation of the hypothetical to the conjunctive, "if it is day, it is light" implies that it is not possible that it be day and not light. Perhaps this is the case, because "being day" would have to be an element of a set which it would presuppose and would have to belong to one of the groups classified in relation to it.

No less than the determination of signification, nonsense enacts a *donation of sense.* But it does so in an entirely different manner. From the point of view of sense, the regressive law no longer relates the names of different degrees to classes or properties, but rather distributes them in a heterogeneous series of events. These series are undoubtedly determined, one as signifying, the other as signified. But the distribution of sense in each one of them is entirely independent of the precise relation of signification. This is why, as we have seen, a term devoid of signification has nonetheless a sense, and the sense or the event is independent of all the modalities affecting classes and properties, being neutral in relation to all of these characteristics. The event differs in nature from properties and classes. That which has a sense has also a signification, but for reasons which are different from its having a sense. Sense is thus inseparable from a new kind of paradoxes which mark the presence of nonsense within sense, just as the preceding paradoxes marked the presence of nonsense within signification. This time, we are confronted with paradoxes of subdivision ad infinitum and also with paradoxes of the distribution of singularities. Inside the series, each term has sense only by virtue of its position relative to every other term. But this relative position itself depends on the absolute position of each term relative to the instance $= x$. The latter is determined as nonsense and circulates endlessly throughout the series. Sense is actually *produced* by this circulation as sense which affects both the signifier and the signified. In short, sense is always an *effect*. It is not an effect merely in the causal sense; it is also an effect in the sense of an "optical effect" or a "sound effect," or, even better, a surface effect, a position effect, and a language effect. Such an effect is not at all an appearance or an illusion. It is a product which spreads out over, or extends itself the length of, the surface; it is strictly co-present to, and coextensive with, its own cause, and determines this cause as an imminent cause, inseparable from its effects, pure *nihil* or *x*, outside of the effects themselves. Such effects, or such a product, have usually been designated by a proper or a singular name. A proper name can be considered fully as a sign only to the extent that it refers to an effect of this kind. Thus, physics speaks of the "Kelvin effect," of the "Seebeck effect," of the "Zeeman effect," etc. Medicine designates diseases by the names of the doctors who were able to elaborate the lists of their symptoms. Following this path, the discovery of sense as an incorporeal effect, being always produced by the circulation of the element $= x$ in the series of terms which it traverses, must be named the "Chryssipus effect" or the "Carroll effect."

Authors referred to as "structuralists" by recent practice may have no essential point in common other than this: sense, regarded not at all as appearance but as surface effect and position effect, and produced by the circulation of the empty square in the structural series (the place of the dummy, the place of the king, the blind spot, the floating signifier, the value degree zero, the off-stage or absent cause, etc.). Structuralism, whether consciously or not, celebrates new findings of a Stoic and Carrollian inspiration. Structure is in fact a machine for the production of incorporeal sense *(skindapsos)*. But when structuralism shows in this manner that sense is produced by nonsense and its perpetual displacement, and that it is born of the respective position of elements which are not by themselves "signifying," we should not at all compare it with what was called the philosophy of the absurd: Carroll, yes; Camus, no. This is so because, for the philosophy of the absurd, nonsense is what is opposed to sense in a simple relation with it, so that the absurd is always defined by a deficiency of sense and a lack (there is not enough of it . . .). From the point of view of structure, on the contrary, there is always too much sense: an excess produced and over-produced by nonsense as a lack of itself. Jakobson defines a phoneme zero, having no phonetically determined value, by its opposition to the *absence of the phoneme* rather than to the phoneme itself. Likewise, nonsense does not have any particular sense, but is opposed to the absence of sense rather than to the sense that it produces in excess—without ever maintaining with its product the simple relation of exclusion to which some people would like to reduce them.[3] Nonsense is that which has no sense, and that which, as such and as it enacts the donation of sense, is opposed to the absence of sense. This is what we must understand by *"nonsense."*

In the final analysis, the importance of structuralism in philosophy, and for all thought, is that it displaces frontiers. When the emphasis shifted from failing Essences to the notion of sense, the philosophical dividing line seemed to be established between those who linked sense to a new transcendence, a new avatar of God and a transformed heaven, and those who found sense in man and his abyss, a newly excavated depth and underground. New theologians of a misty sky (the sky of Koenigsberg), and new humanists of the caverns, sprang upon the stage in the name of the God-man or the Man-god as the secret of sense. Sometimes it was difficult to distinguish between them. But what today renders the distinction impossible is, first and foremost, our current fatigue with this interminable discourse, in which one wonders whether it is the ass which loads man or man who loads the ass and himself. Moreover, we have the impression of a pure counter-sense imposed on sense; for, in any case, heavenly or subterranean, sense is presented as Principle, Reservoir, Reserve, Origin. As heavenly Principle, it is said to be fundamentally forgotten and veiled or, as subterranean principle, it is said to be deeply erased, diverted, and alienated. But beneath the erasure and the veil, we are summoned to rediscover and to restore meaning, in either a God which was not well enough understood, or in a man not fully fathomed. It is thus pleasing that there resounds today the news that sense is never a principle or an origin, but that it is produced. It is not something to discover, to restore, and to re-employ; it is something to produce by a new machinery. It belongs to no height or depth, but rather to a surface effect, being inseparable from the surface which is its proper dimension. It is not that sense lacks depth or height, but rather that height and depth lack surface, that they lack sense, or have it only by virtue of an "effect" which presupposes sense. We no longer ask ourselves whether the "originary meaning" of religion is to be found in a God betrayed by men, or in a man alienated in the image of God. We do not, for example, seek in Nietzsche a prophet of reversal or transcendence. If there is an author for whom the death of God or the free fall of the ascetic ideal has no importance so long as it is compensated by the false depth of the human, by bad faith and *ressentiment,* it is indeed Nietzsche. He pursues his discoveries elsewhere, in the aphorism and the poem (where neither God nor man speak), in machines for the production of sense and for the survey of the surface. Nietzsche establishes the effective ideal game. We do not seek in Freud an explorer of human depth and originary sense, but rather the prodigious discoverer of the machinery of the unconscious by means of which sense is produced always as a function of nonsense.[4] And how could we not feel that our freedom and strength reside, not in the divine universal nor in the human personality, but in these singularities which are more us than we ourselves are, more divine than the gods, as they animate concretely poem and aphorism, permanent revolution and partial action? What is bureaucratic in these fantastic machines which are peoples and poems? It suffices that we dissipate ourselves a little, that we be able to be at the surface, that we stretch our skin like a drum, in order that the "great politics" begin. An empty square for neither man nor God; singularities which are neither general nor individual, neither personal nor universal. All of this is traversed by circulations, echoes, and events which produce more sense, more freedom, and more strength than man has ever dreamed of, or God ever conceived. Today's task is to make the empty square circulate and to make pre-individual and nonpersonal singularities speak—in short, to produce sense.

Twelfth Series of
the Paradox

We cannot get rid of paradoxes by saying that they are more worthy of Carroll's work than they are of the *Principia Mathematica.* What is good for Carroll is good for logic. We cannot get rid of paradoxes by saying that the barber of the regiment does not exist, any more than the abnormal set exists. For paradoxes, on the contrary, inhere in language, and the whole problem is to know whether language would be able to function without bringing about the insistence of such entities. Nor could we say that paradoxes give a false image of thought, improbable and uselessly complicated. One would have to be too "simple" to believe that thought is a simple act, clear unto itself, and not putting into play all the powers of the unconscious, or all the powers of nonsense in the unconscious. Paradoxes are recreational only when they are considered as initiatives of thought. They are not recreational when they are considered as "the Passion of thought," or as discovering what can only be thought, what can only be spoken, despite the fact that it is both ineffable and unthinkable—a mental Void, the Aion. Finally, we cannot invoke the contradictory character of the insinuated entities, nor can we say that the barber cannot belong to the regiment. The force of paradoxes is that they are not contradictory; they rather allow us to be present at the genesis of the contradiction. The principle of contradic-

74

tion is applicable to the real and the possible, but not to the impossible from which it derives, that is, to paradoxes or rather to what paradoxes represent. The paradoxes of signification are essentially that of the *abnormal set* (which is included as a member or which includes members of different types) and that of the *rebel element* (which forms part of a set whose existence it presupposes and belongs to two sub-sets which it determines). The paradoxes of sense are essentially that of the *subdivision ad infinitum* (always past-future and never present), and that of the *nomadic distribution* (distributing in an open space instead of distributing a closed space). They always have the characteristic of going in both directions at once, and of rendering identification impossible, as they emphasize sometimes the first, sometimes the second, of these effects. This is the case with Alice's double adventure—the becoming-mad and the lost name.

Paradox is opposed to *doxa,* in both aspects of *doxa,* namely, good sense and common sense. Now, good sense is said of one direction only: it is the unique sense and expresses the demand of an order according to which it is necessary to choose one direction and to hold onto it. This direction is easily determined as that which goes from the most differentiated to the least differentiated, from things to the primordial fire. The arrow of time gets its orientation from this direction, since the most differentiated necessarily appears as past, insofar as it defines the origin of an individual system, whereas the least differentiated appears as future and end. This order of time, from the past to the future, is thus established in relation to the present, that is, in relation to a determined phase of time chosen within the particular system under consideration. Good sense therefore is given the condition under which it fulfills its function, which is essentially to foresee. It is clear that foresight would be impossible in the other direction, that is, if one went from the least differentiated to the most differentiated—for example, if temperatures which were at first indiscernible were to go on differentiating themselves. This is why good sense rediscovered itself in the context of thermodynamics. At its point of origin, though, good sense claims kinship with the highest models. Good sense is essentially distributive; "on one hand and on the other hand" is its formula.

But the distribution which it puts into motion is accomplished in conditions which place difference at the beginning and involve it in a controlled movement which is supposed to saturate, equalize, annul, and compensate it. This is indeed the meaning of such phrases as "from things to the primordial fire," or "from worlds (individual systems) to God." Such a distribution, implied by good sense, is defined precisely as a fixed or sedentary distribution. The essense of good sense is to give itself a singularity, *in order to* stretch it out over the whole line of ordinary and regular points which depend on it, but which also avert and dilute it. Good sense is altogether combustive and digestive. It is agricultural, inseparable from the agrarian problem, the establishment of enclosures, and the dealings of middle classes the parts of which are supposed to balance and to regulate one another. The steam engine and the livestock, but also properties and classes, are the living sources of good sense, not only as facts which spring up in a particular period, but as eternal archetypes. This is not a mere metaphor; it ties together all the senses of the terms "properties" and "classes." The systematic characteristics of good sense are thus the following: it affirms a single direction; it determines this direction to go from the most to the least differentiated, from the singular to the regular, and from the remarkable to the ordinary; it orients the arrow of time from past to future, according to this determination; it assigns to the present a directing role in this orientation; it renders possible thereby the function of prevision; and it selects the sedentary type of distribution in which all of the preceding characteristics are brought together.

Good sense plays a capital role in the determination of signification, but plays no role in the donation of sense. This is because good sense always comes second, and because the sedentary distribution which it enacts presupposes another distribution, just as the problem of enclosures presupposes first a free, opened, and unlimited space—the side of a hill or knoll. Is it then enough to say that the paradox follows a direction other than that of good sense, and that it goes from the least to the most differentiated, through a whim that might only be a mental diversion? To repeat some famous examples, it is certain that if temperature goes on differentiating itself, or if viscosity goes on accelerating itself, one could no longer "foresee." But why not? It is not because things would be happening in the other sense or direction. The other direction would still encompass a unique sense. Good sense is not content with determining the particular direction of the unique sense. It first determines the principle of a unique sense or direction in general, ready to show that this principle, once given, forces us to choose one direction over the other. The power of the paradox therefore is not all in following the other direction, but rather in showing that sense always takes on both senses at once, or follows two directions at the same time. The opposite of good sense is not the other direction *(sens),* for this direction is only a recreation for the mind, its amusing initiative. But the paradox as passion reveals that one cannot separate two directions, that a unique sense cannot be established—neither a unique sense for serious thought and work, nor an inverse sense for recreations and minor games. If viscosity went on accelerating itself, it would eliminate the reasons behind rest in an unpredictable sense. "Which way, which way?" asks Alice. The question has no answer, since it is the characteristic of sense not to have any direction or "good sense." Rather, sense always goes to both directions at once, in the infinitely subdivided and elongated past-future. The physicist Boltzmann explained that the arrow of time, moving from past to future, functions only in individual worlds or systems, and in relation to a present determined within such systems: "For the entire universe, the two directions of time are thus impossible to distinguish, and the same holds for space; there is neither above nor below" (that is, there is neither height nor depth).[1] Here we rediscover the opposition between Aion and Chronos. Chronos is the present which alone exists. It makes of the past and future its two oriented dimensions, so that one goes always from the past to the future—but only to the degree that presents follow one another inside partial worlds or partial systems. Aion is the past-future, which in an infinite subdivision of the abstract moment endlessly decomposes itself in both directions at once and forever sidesteps the present. For no present can be fixed in a Universe which is taken to be the system of all systems, or the abnormal set. To the oriented line of the present, which "regularizes" in an individual system each singular point which it takes in, the line of Aion is opposed. This line leaps from one pre-individual singularity to another and recovers them all, each one of them within the others. It recovers all the systems as it follows the figures of the nomadic distribution wherein each event is already past and yet in the future, at once more and less, always the day before and the day after, inside the subdivision which makes them communicate with one another.

In common sense, "sense" is no longer said of a direction, but of an organ. It is called "common," because it is an organ, a function, a faculty of identification that brings diversity in general to bear upon the form of the Same. Common sense identifies and recognizes, no less than good sense foresees. Subjectively, common sense subsumes under itself the various faculties of the soul, or the differentiated organs of the body, and brings them to bear upon a unity which is capable of saying "I." One and the same self perceives, imagines, remembers, knows, etc.; one and the same self breathes, sleeps, walks, and eats. . . . Language does not seem possible without this subject which expresses and mani-fests itself in it, and which says what it does. Objectively, common sense subsumes under itself the given diversity and relates it to the unity of a particular form of object or an individualized form of a world. It is the same object which I see, smell, taste, or touch; it is the same object which I perceive, imagine, and remember. . . ; and, it is the same world that I breathe, walk, am awake or asleep in, as I move from one object to another following the laws of a determined system. Here again, language does not seem possible outside of these identities which it designates. The complementarity of the two forces of good sense and common sense are clearly seen. Good sense could not fix any beginning, end, or direction, it could not distribute any diversity, if it did not transcend itself toward an instance capable of relating the diverse to the form of a subject's identity, or to the form of an object's or a world's permanence, which one assumes to be present from beginning to end. Conversely, this form of identity within common sense would remain empty if it did not transcend itself toward an instance capable of determining it by means of a particular diversity, which would begin here, end there, and which one would suppose to last as long as it is necessary to assure the equalization of its parts. It is necessary that quality be at once stopped and measured, attributed and identified. In this complementarity of good sense and common sense, the alliance between the self, the world, and God is sealed—God being the final outcome of directions and the supreme principle of identities. The paradox therefore is the simultaneous reversal of good sense and com-mon sense: on one hand, it appears in the guise of the two simultaneous senses or directions of the becoming-mad and the unforeseeable; on the other hand, it appears as the nonsense of the lost identity and the unrecognizable. Alice is the one who always goes in two directions at once: Wonderland exists in an always subdivided double direction. Alice is also the one who loses the identity, whether her own or the identity of things and the world. In *Sylvie and Bruno,* Fairyland is opposed to the Common-Place. Alice submits to (and fails at) all the tests of common sense: the test of self-consciousness as an organ—"Who are *you?*" said the caterpillar; the test of the perception of an object as a test of recognition—the woods which is stripped off all identification; the test of memory as recitation—"It is wrong from beginning to end"; the test of the dream as unity of the world—wherein each individual system comes undone to the benefit of a universe in which one is always an element in someone else's dream—". . . you're only one of the things in his dream. You know very well you're not real." How could Alice have any common sense left, since she no longer had good sense? Language, in any case, seems impossible, having no subject which expresses or manifests itself in it, no object to denote, no classes and no properties to signify according to a fixed order.

It is here, however, that the gift of meaning occurs, in this region which precedes all good sense and all common sense. For here, with the passion of the paradox, language attains its highest power. Beyond good sense, Carroll's doubles represent the two senses or two directions of the becoming-mad. Let us look first at the doublet of the Hatter and the March Hare in *Alice:* each one of them lives in one direction, but the two directions are inseparable; each direction subdivides itself into the other, to the point that both are found in either. Two are necessary for being mad; one is always mad *in tandem.* The Hatter and the Hare went mad together the day they "murdered time," that is, the day they destroyed the measure, suppressed the pauses and the rests which relate quality to something fixed. The Hatter and the Hare killed the present which no longer survives between them except in the sleepy image of the Dormouse, their tortured companion. But also this present no longer subsists except in the abstract moment, at tea time, being indefinitely subdivisible into past and future. The result is that they now change places endlessly, they are always late and early, in both directions at once, but never on time. On the other side of the looking-glass, the Hare and the Hatter are taken up again in the two messengers, one going and the other coming, one searching and the other bringing back, on the basis of the two simultaneous directions of the Aion. Tweedledee and Tweedledum testify to the indiscernibility of the two directions, and to the infinite subdivision of the two senses in each direction, over the bifurcating route pointing to their house. But, just as the doubles render impossible any limit of becoming, any fixing of quality, and thus any exercise of good sense, Humpty Dumpty is royal simplicity, the Master of words, the Giver of sense. He destroys the exercise of common sense, as he distributes differences in such a manner that no fixed quality and no measured time are brought to bear upon an identifiable or recognizable object. Humpty Dumpty (whose waist and neck, tie and belt, are indiscernible) lacks common sense as much as he lacks differentiated organs; he is uniquely made of shifting and "disconcerting" singularities. Humpty Dumpty will not recognize Alice, for each of Alice's singularities seems to him assimilated in the ordinary arrangement of an organ (eye, nose, mouth) and to belong to the Commonplace of an all too regular face, arranged just like everyone else's. In the singularity of paradoxes, nothing begins or ends, everything proceeds at once in the direction of both past and future. As Humpty Dumpty says, it is always possible to prevent that we grow *in tandem*. One does not grow without the other shrinking. There is nothing astonishing in the fact that the paradox is the force of the unconscious: it occurs always in the space between *(l'entre-deux)* consciousnesses, contrary to good sense or, behind the back of consciousness, contrary to common sense. To the question as to when one becomes bald, or when there is a pile, Chrysippus' answer used to be that we would be better off to stop counting, that we could even go to sleep, we could think later on. Carneades does not seem to understand this response very well and he objects that, at Chrysippus' reawakening, everything will begin anew and the same question will be raised. Chrysippus answers more explicitly: one can always manage *in tandem,* slowing the horses when the slope becomes steeper, or decreasing with one hand while increasing with the other.[2] For if it is a question of knowing "why at this moment rather than at another," "why water changes its state of quality at $0°$ centigrade," the question is poorly stated insofar as $0°$ is considered as an ordinary point on the thermometer. But if it is considered, on the contrary, as a singular point, it is inseparable from the event occurring at that point, always being zero in relation to its realization on the line of ordinary points, always forthcoming and already passed.

We may therefore propose a table of the development of language at the surface and of the donation of sense at the frontier, between propositions and things. Such a table represents an organization which is said to be secondary and proper to language. It is animated by the paradoxical element or aleatory point to which we have given various double names. To introduce this element as running through the two series at the surface, or as tracing between the two series the straight line of the Aion, amounts to the same thing. It is nonsense, and it defines the two verbal figures of nonsense. But, precisely because nonsense has an internal and original relation to sense, this paradoxical element bestows sense upon the terms of each series. The relative positions of these terms in relation to one another depend on their "absolute" position in relation to it. Sense is always an effect produced in the series by the instance which traverses them. This is why sense, such as it is gathered over the line of the Aion, has two sides which correspond to the dissymmetrical sides of the paradoxical element: one tending toward the series determined as signifying, the other tending toward the series determined as signified. Sense insists in one of the series (propositions): it is that which can be expressed by propositions, but does not merge with the propositions which express it. Sense crops up suddenly in the other series (states of affairs): it is the attribute of states of affairs, but does not merge with the state of affairs to which it is attributed, or with the things and qualities which realize it. What permits therefore the determination of one of those series as signifying and of the other as signified are precisely these two aspects of sense (insistence and extra-being) and the two aspects of nonsense or of the paradoxical element from which they derive (empty square and super-numerary object; place without occupant in one series and occupant without place in the other). This is why sense is the object of fundamental paradoxes which repeat the figures of nonsense. But the gift of sense occurs only when the conditions of signification are also being determined. The terms of the series, once provided with sense, will subsequently be submitted to these conditions, in a tertiary organization which will relate them to the laws of possible indications and manifestations (good sense, common sense). This presentation of a total deployment at the surface is necessarily affected, at each of these points, by an extreme and persistent fragility.

Thirteenth Series of the Schizophrenic and the Little Girl

Nothing is more fragile than the surface. Is not this secondary organization threatened by a monster even more awesome than the Jabberwocky—by a formless, fathomless nonsense, very different from what we previously encountered in the two figures still inherent in sense? At first, the threat is imperceptible, but a few steps suffice to make us aware of an enlarged crevice; the whole organization of the surface has already disappeared, overturned in a terrible primordial order. Nonsense no longer gives sense, for it has consumed everything. We might have thought at first that we were inside the same element, or in a neighboring element. But we see now that we have changed elements, that we have entered a storm. We might have thought to be still among little girls and children, but we are already in an irreversible madness. We might have believed to be at the latest edge of literary research, at the point of the highest invention of languages and words; we are already faced by the agitations of a convulsive life, in the night of a pathological creation affecting bodies. It is for this reason that the observer must be attentive: it is hardly acceptable, under the pretext of portmanteau words, for example, to run together a child's nursery rhymes, poetic experimentations, and experiences of madness. A great poet may write in a direct relation to the child that she was and the children she loves;

a madman may carry along with him an immense poetical work, in a direct relation to the poet that he was and which he does not cease to be. But this does not at all justify the grotesque trinity of child, poet, and madman. With all the force of admiration and veneration, we must be attentive to the sliding which reveals a profound difference underlying these crude similarities. We must be attentive to the very different functions and abysses of nonsense, and to the heterogeneity of portmanteau words, which do not authorize the grouping together of those who invent or even those who use them. A little girl may sing *"Pimpanicaille"*; an artist may write "frumious"; and a schizophrenic may utter "perspendicace."[1] But we have no reason to believe that the problem is the same in all of these cases and the results roughly analogous. One could not seriously confuse Babar's song with Artaud's howls-breaths *(cris-souffles),* "Ratara ratara ratara Atara tatara rana Otara otara katara. . . ." We may add that the mistake made by logicians, when they speak of nonsense, is that they offer laboriously constructed, emaciated examples fitting the needs of their demonstration, as if they had never heard a little girl sing, a great poet recite, or a schizophrenic speak. There is a poverty of so-called logical examples (except in Russell, who was always inspired by Lewis Carroll). But here still the weakness of the logician does not authorize us to reconstruct a trinity against him. On the contrary, the problem is a clinical problem, that is, a problem of sliding from one organization to another, or a problem of the formation of a progressive and creative disorganization. It is also a problem of criticism, that is, of the determination of differential levels at which nonsense changes shape, the portmanteau word undergoes a change of nature, and the entire language changes dimension.

Crude similarities set their trap. We would like to consider two texts in which these traps of similarity can be found. Occasionally Antonin Artaud confronts Lewis Carroll: first in a transcription of the Humpty Dumpty episode; and again in a letter, written from the asylum at Rodez, in which he passes judgment on Carroll. As we read the first stanza of "Jabberwocky," such as Artaud renders it, we have the impression that the two opening verses still correspond to Carroll's criteria and conform to the rules of translation generally held by Carroll's other French translators, Parisot and Brunius. But beginning with the last word of the second line, from the third line onward, a sliding is produced, and even a creative, central collapse, causing us to be in another world and in an entirely different language.[2] With horror, we recognize it easily: it is the language of schizophrenia. Even the portmanteau words seem to function differently, being caught up in syncopes and being overloaded with gutturals. We measure at the same moment the distance separating Carroll's language and Artaud's language—the former emitted at the surface, the latter carved into the depth of bodies. We measure the difference between their respective problems. We are thus able to acknowledge the full impact of the declarations made by Artaud in his letter from Rodez:

I have not produced a translation of "Jabberwocky." I tried to translate a fragment of it, but it bored me. I never liked this poem, which always struck me as an affected infantilism. . . . *I do not like poems or languages of the surface* which smell of happy leisures and of intellectual success—as if the intellect relied on the anus, but without any heart or soul in it. The anus is always terror, and I will not admit that one loses an excrement without being torn from, thereby losing one's soul as well, and there is no soul in "Jabberwocky." . . . One may invent one's language, and make pure language speak with an extra-grammatical or a-grammatical meaning, but this meaning must have value in itself, that is, it must issue from torment. . . . "Jabberwocky" is the work of a profiteer who, satiated after a fine meal, seeks to indulge himself in the pain of others. . . . When one digs through the shit of being and its language, the poem necessarily smells badly, and "Jabberwocky" is a poem whose author took steps to keep himself from the uterine being of suffering into which every great poet has plunged, and having been born from it, smells badly. There are in "Jabberwocky" passages of fecality, but it is the fecality of an English snob, who curls the obscene within himself like ringlets of hair around a curling iron. . . . It is the work of a man who ate well—and this makes itself felt in his writing. . . .[3]

Summing this up, we could say that Artaud considers Lewis Carroll a pervert, a little pervert, who holds onto the establishment of a surface language, and who has not felt the real problem of a language in depth —namely, the schizophrenic problem of suffering, of death, and of life. To Artaud, Carroll's games seem puerile, his food too worldly, and even his fecality hypocritical and too well-bred.

Leaving Artaud's genius behind, let us consider another text whose beauty and density remain clinical.[4] In Louis Wolfson's book, the person who refers to himself as the patient or the schizophrenic "student of languages" experiences the existence and disjunction of two series of orality: the duality of things/words, consumptions/expressions, or consumable objects/expressible propositions. This duality between *to eat* and *to speak* may be even more violently expressed in the duality between *to pay/to eat* and to *shit/to speak*. But in particular, this duality is transported to, and is recovered in, a duality of two sorts of words, propositions, or two kinds of language: namely, the mother tongue, English, which is essentially alimentary and excremental; and foreign languages, which are essentially expressive, and which the patient strives to acquire. The mother threatens him in two equivalent ways and keeps him from making progress in these languages. Sometimes she brandishes before him tempting but indigestible food, sealed in cans; sometimes she pounces on him in order to speak abruptly in English before he has had time to cover his ears. He wards off this threat with a number of ever more refined procedures. First, he eats like a glutton, crams himself full of food, and stomps on the cannisters while repeating endlessly some foreign words. At a deeper level, he ensures a resonance between the two series and a conversion from one to the other, as he translates English words into foreign words according to their phonetic elements (consonants being the most important). "Tree," for example, is converted as a result of the R which recurs in the French word *"arbre,"* and again as a result of the T which recurs in the Hebrew term; and since the Russians say *"derevo"* for tree, one can equally well transform "tree" into "tere," with T becoming D. This already complex procedure is replaced by a more generalized one, as soon as the patient has the idea of evoking a number of associations: "early," whose consonants R and L pose particularly delicate problems, is transformed into various associated French locutions: *"surR-Le-champ,"* *"de bonne heuRe,"* *"matinaLement,"* *"à la paRole,"* *"dévoRer L'espace,"* or even into an esoteric and fictional word of German consonance, *"urlich."* (One recalls that Raymond Roussel, in the techniques he invented in order to constitute and to convert series within the French language, distinguishes a primary, restricted procedure and a secondary, generalized procedure based on associations.) It is often the case that some rebellious words resist all of these procedures, giving rise to insufferable paradoxes. Thus, "ladies," for example, which applies to only half of the human population, can be transcribed only by the German *"leutte"* or the Russian *"loudi,"* which, on the contrary, designate the totality of humankind.

Here again, one's first impression is that there is a certain resemblance between all of this and the Carrollian series. In Carroll's works as well, the basic oral duality (to eat/to speak) is sometimes displaced and passes between two kinds or two dimensions of propositions. Some other times it hardens and becomes "to pay/to speak," or "excrement/ language" (Alice has to buy an egg in the Sheep's shop, and Humpty Dumpty pays his words; as for fecality, as Artaud says, it underlies Carroll's work everywhere). Likewise, when Artaud develops his own antinomic series—"to be and to obey, to live and to exist, to act and to think, matter and soul, body and mind"—he himself has the impression of an extraordinary resemblance with Carroll. He translates this impression by saying that Carroll had reached out across time to pillage and plagiarize him, Antonin Artaud, both with respect to Humpty Dumpty's poem about the little fishes and with respect to "Jabber-wocky." And yet, why did Artaud add that his writing has nothing to do with Carroll's? Why is this extraordinary familiarity also a radical and definite strangeness? It suffices to ask once more how and where Carroll's series are organized. The two series are articulated at the surface. On this surface, a line is like the frontier between two series, propositions and things, or between dimensions of the same proposi-tion. Along this line, sense is elaborated, both as what is expressed by the proposition and as the attribute of things—the "expressible" of expressions and the "attributable" of denotations. The two series are therefore articulated by their difference, and sense traverses the entire surface, although it remains on its own line. Undoubtedly, this imma-terial sense is the result of corporeal things, of their mixtures, and of their actions and passions. But the result has a very different nature than the corporeal cause. It is for this reason that sense, as an effect, being always at the surface, refers to a quasi-cause which is itself incorporeal. This is the always mobile nonsense, which is expressed in esoteric and in portmanteau words, and which distributes sense on both sides simultaneously. All of this forms the surface organization upon which Carroll's work plays a mirror-like effect.

Artaud said that this is only surface. The revelation which enlivened Artaud's genius is known to any schizophrenic, who lives it as well in his or her own manner. For him, *there is not, there is no longer, any surface.* How could Carroll not strike him as an affected little girl, protected from all deep problems? The first schizophrenic evidence is that the surface has split open. Things and propositions have no longer any frontier between them, precisely because bodies have no surface. The primary aspect of the schizophrenic body is that it is a sort of body-sieve. Freud emphasized this aptitude of the schizophrenic to grasp the surface and the skin as if they were punctured by an infinite number of little holes.[5] The consequence of this is that the entire body is no longer anything but depth—it carries along and snaps up everything into this gaping depth which represents a fundamental involution. Everything is body and corporeal. Everything is a mixture of bodies, and inside the body, interlocking and penetration. Artaud said that everything is physical: "We have in our back full vertebrae, transfixed by the nail of pain, which through walking, the effort of lifting weights, and the resistance to letting go, become cannisters by being nested in one another."[6] A tree, a column, a flower, or a cane grow inside the body; other bodies always penetrate our body and coexist with its parts. Everything is really a can—canned food and excrement. As there is no surface, the inside and the outside, the container and the contained, no longer have a precise limit; they plunge into a universal depth or turn in the circle of a present which gets to be more contracted as it is filled. Hence the schizophrenic manner of living the contradiction: either in the deep fissure which traverses the body, or in the fragmented parts which encase one another and spin about. Body-sieve, fragmented body, and dissociated body—these are the three primary dimensions of the schizophrenic body.

In this collapse of the surface, the entire world loses its meaning. It maintains perhaps a certain power of denotation, but this is experienced as empty. It maintains a certain power of manifestation, but this is experienced as indifferent. And it maintains a certain signification, experienced as "false." Nevertheless, the word loses its sense, that is, its power to draw together or to express an incorporeal effect distinct from the actions and passions of the body, and an ideational event distinct from its present realization. Every event is realized, be it in a hallucinatory form. Every word is physical, and immediately affects the body. The procedure is this: a word, often of an alimentary nature, appears in capital letters, printed as in a collage which freezes it and strips it of its sense. But the moment that the pinned-down word loses its sense, it bursts into pieces; it is decomposed into syllables, letters, and above all into consonants which act directly on the body, penetrating and bruising it. We have already seen that this was the case for the schizophrenic student of languages. The moment that the maternal language is stripped of its sense, its *phonetic elements* become singularly wounding. The word no longer expresses an attribute of the state of affairs; its fragments merge with unbearable sonorous qualities, invade the body where they form a mixture and a new state of affairs, as if they themselves were a noisy, poisonous food and canned excrement. The parts of the body, its organs, are determined in virtue of decomposed elements which affect and assail them.[7] In this passion, a pure language-affect is substituted for the effect of language: "All writing is PIG SHIT" (that is to say, every fixed or written word is decomposed into noisy, alimentary, and excremental bits).

For the schizophrenic, then, it is less a question of recovering meaning than of destroying the word, of conjuring up the affect, and of transforming the painful passion of the body into a triumphant action, obedience into command, always in this depth beneath the fissured surface. The student of languages provides the example of the means by which the painful explosions of the word in the maternal language are converted into actions relative to the foreign languages. We saw a little while ago that wounding was accomplished by means of *phonetic elements* affecting the articulated or disarticulated parts of the body. Triumph may now be reached only through the creation of breath-words *(mots-souffles)* and howl-words *(mots-cris),* in which all literal, syllabic, and phonetic values have been replaced by *values which are exclusively tonic* and not written. To these values a glorious body corresponds, being a new dimension of the schizophrenic body, an organism without parts which operates entirely by insufflation, respiration, evaporation, and fluid transmission (the superior body or body without organs of Antonin Artaud).[8] Undoubtedly, this characterization of the active procedure, in opposition to the procedure of passion, appears initially insufficient: fluids, in fact, do not seem less harmful than fragments. But this is so because of the action-passion ambivalence. It is here that the contradiction lived in schizophrenia finds its real point of application: passion and action are the inseparable poles of an ambivalence, because the two languages which they form belong inseparably to the body and to the depth of bodies. One is thus never sure that the ideal fluids of an organism without parts does not carry parasitic worms, fragments of organs, solid food, and excremental residue. In fact, it is certain that the maleficent forces make effective use of fluids and insufflations in order to introduce bits of passion into the body. The fluid is necessarily corrupted, but not by itself. It is corrupted only by the other pole from which it cannot be separated. The fact, though, is that it represents the active pole and the state of perfect mixture. The latter is opposed to the encasings and bruisings of the imperfect mixtures which represent the passive pole. In schizophrenia, there is a way of living the Stoic distinction between two corporeal mixtures: the partial mixture which alters the body, and the total and liquid mixture which leaves the body intact. In the fluid element, or in the insufflated liquid, there is the unwritten secret of an active mixture which is like the "principle of the Sea," in opposition to the passive mixtures of the encased parts. It is in this sense that Artaud transforms Humpty Dumpty's poem about the sea and the fish into a poem about the problem of obedience and command.

What defines this second language and this method of action, practically, is its consonantal, guttural, and aspirated overloads, its apostrophes and internal accents, its breaths and its scansions, and its modulation which replaces all syllabic or even literal values. It is a question of transforming the word into an action by rendering it incapable of being decomposed and incapable of disintegrating: *language without articulation.* The cement here is a palatalized, an-organic principle, a sea-block or a sea-mass. With respect to the Russian word *"derevo"* ("tree") the student of language is overjoyed at the existence of a plural form *derev'ya*—whose internal apostrophe seems to assure the fusion of consonants (the linguist's soft sign). Rather than separating the consonants and rendering them pronounceable, one could say that the vowel, once reduced to the soft sign, renders the consonants indissociable from one another, by palatalizing them. It leaves them illegible and even unpronounceable, as it transforms them into so many active howls in one continuous breath.[9] These howls are welded together in breath, like the consonants in the sign which liquifies them, like fish in the ocean-mass, or like the bones in the blood of the body without organs. A sign of fire, a wave "which hesitates between gas and water," said Artaud. The howls are gurglings in breath.

When Artaud says in his "Jabberwocky" "Until rourghe is to rouarghe has rangmbde and rangmbde has rouarghambde," he means to activate, insufflate, palatalize, and set the word aflame so that the word becomes the action of a body without parts, instead of being the passion of a fragmented organism. The task is that of transforming the word into a fusion of consonants—fusion through the use of soft signs and of consonants which cannot be decomposed. Within this language, one can always find words which would be equivalent to portmanteau words. For *"rourghe"* and *"rouarghe,"* Artaud himself indicates *"ruée," "roue," "route," "régle,"* or *"route à régler."* To this list, we could add "Rouergue," that section of Rodez in which Artaud was at the time. Likewise, when he says *"Uk'hatis,"* with an internal apostrophe, he indicates *"ukhase," "hâte,"* and *"abruti,"* and adds "a nocturnal jolt beneath Hecate which means the pigs of the moon thrown off the straight path." As soon as the word appears, however, as a portmanteau word, its structure and the commentary attached to it persuade us of the presence of something very different. Artaud's *"Ghoré Uk'hatis"* are not equivalent to the lost pigs, to Carroll's "mome raths," or to Parisot's *"verchons fourgus."* They do not compete with them on the same plane. They do not secure the ramification of series on the basis of sense. On the contrary, they enact a chain of associations between tonic and consonantal elements, in a region of infra-sense, according to a fluid and burning principle which absorbs and reabsorbs effectively the sense as soon as it is produced: *Uk'hatis* (or the lost pigs of the moon) is K'H (*cahot* = jolt), 'KT (nocturnal), and H'KT (Hecate).

The duality of the schizophrenic word has not been adequately noted: it comprises the passion-word, which explodes into wounding *phonetic* values, and the action-word, which welds inarticulate *tonic* values. These two words are developed in relation to the duality of the body, fragmented body and body without organs. They refer to two theaters, the theater of terror or passion and the theater of cruelty, which is by its essence active. They refer to two types of nonsense, passive and active: the nonsense of the word devoid of sense, which is decomposed into phonetic elements; and the nonsense of tonic elements, which form a word incapable of being decomposed and no less devoid of sense. Here everything happens, acts and is acted upon, beneath sense and far from the surface. Sub-sense, a-sense, *Untersinn*— this must be distinguished from the nonsense of the surface. According to Hölderlin, language in its two aspects is "a sign empty of meaning." Although a sign, it is a sign which merges with an action or a passion of the body.[10] This is why it seems entirely insufficient to say that schizophrenic language is defined by an endless and panic-stricken sliding of the signifying series toward the signified series. In fact, *there are no longer any series at all;* the two series have disappeared. Nonsense has ceased to give sense to the surface; it absorbs and engulfs all sense, both on the side of the signifier and on the side of the signified. Artaud says that Being, which is nonsense, has teeth. In the surface organization which we called secondary, physical bodies and sonorous words are separated and articulated at once by an incorporeal frontier. This frontier is sense, representing, on one side, the pure "expressed" of words, and on the other, the logical attribute of bodies. Although sense results from the actions and the passions of the body, it is a result which differs in nature, since it is neither action nor passion. It is a result which shelters sonorous language from any confusion with the physical body. On the contrary, in this primary order of schizophrenia, the only duality left is that between the actions and the passions of the body. Language is both at once, being entirely reabsorbed into the gaping depth. There is no longer anything to prevent propositions from falling back onto bodies and from mingling their sonorous elements with the body's olfactory, gustatory, or digestive affects. Not only is there no longer any sense, but there is no longer any grammar or syntax either—nor, at the limit, are there any articulated syllabic, literal, or phonetic elements. Antonin Artaud could have entitled his essay "An Antigrammatical Effort Against Lewis Carroll." Carroll needs a very strict grammar, required to conserve the inflection and articulation of words, and to distinguish them from the inflection and articulation of bodies, were it only through the mirror which reflects them and sends a meaning back to them.[11] It is for this reason that we can oppose Artaud and Carroll point for point—primary order and secondary organization. The *surface series* of the "to eat/to speak" type have really nothing in common with the *poles of depth* which are only apparently similar. The two *figures of nonsense* at the surface, which distribute sense between the series, have nothing to do with the two *dives into nonsense* which drag along, engulf, and reabsorb sense *(Untersinn)*. The two forms of stuttering, the clonic and the tonic, are only roughly analogous to the two schizophrenic languages. The break *(coupure)* of the surface has nothing in common with the deep *Spaltung*. The contradiction which was grasped in an infinite subdivision of the past-future over the incorporeal line of the Aion has nothing to do with the opposition of poles in the physical present of bodies. Even portmanteau words have functions which are completely heterogeneous.

One may find a schizoid "position" in the child, before the child has risen to the surface or conquered it. Even at the surface, we can always find schizoid fragments, since its function is precisely to organize and to display elements which have risen from the depth. This does not make it any less abominable or annoying to mix everything together—the child's conquest of the surface, the collapse of the surface in the schizophrenic, or the mastery of surfaces in the person called, for example, "pervert." We can always make of Carroll's work a sort of schizophrenic tale. Some imprudent English psychoanalysts have in fact done so: they note Alice's telescope-body, its foldings and its unfoldings, her manifest alimentary, and latent excremental, obsessions; the bits which designate morsels of food as well as "choice morsels," the collages and labels of alimentary words which are quick to decompose; her loss of identity, the fish and the sea. . . . One can still wonder what kind of madness is clinically represented by the Hatter, the March Hare, and the Dormouse. And one can always recognize in the opposition between Alice and Humpty Dumpty the two ambivalent poles: "fragmented organs—body without organs," body-sieve and glorious body. Artaud had no other reason for confronting the text of Humpty Dumpty. But, at this precise moment, we could listen to Artaud's warning: "I have not produced a translation. . . . I have never liked this poem. . . . I do not like the surface poems or the languages of the surface." Bad psychoanalysis has two ways of deceiving itself: by believing to have discovered identical materials, that one can inevitably find everywhere, or by believing to have discovered analogous forms which create false differences. Thus, the clinical psychiatric aspect and the literary critical aspect are botched simultaneously. Structuralism is right to raise the point that form and matter have a scope only in the original and irreducible structures in which they are organized. Psychoanalysis must have geometrical dimensions, before being concerned with historical anecdotes. For life, and even sexuality, lies within the organization and orientation of these dimensions, before being found in generative matter or engendered form. Psychoanalysis cannot content itself with the designation of cases, the manifestation of histories, or the signification of complexes. Psychoanalysis is the psychoanalysis of sense. It is geographical before it is historical. It distinguishes different countries. Artaud is neither Carroll nor Alice, Carroll is not Artaud, Carroll is not even Alice. Artaud thrusts *the child* into an extremely violent alternative, an alternative of corporeal action and passion, which conforms to the two languages in depth. Either the child is not born, that is, does not leave the foldings of his or her future spinal cord, over which her parents fornicate (a reverse suicide), or she creates a fluid, glorious, and flamboyant body without organs and without parents (like those Artaud called his "daughters" yet to be born). Carroll, on the contrary, awaits *the child,* in a manner conforming to his language of incorporeal sense: he waits at the point and at the moment in which the child has left the depths of the maternal body and has yet to discover the depth of her own body. This is the brief surface moment in which the little girl skirts the surface of the water, like Alice in the pool of her own tears. These are different regions, different and unrelated dimensions. We may believe that the surface has its monsters, the Snark and the Jabberwock, its terrors and its cruelties, which, although not of the depths, have claws just the same and can snap one up laterally, or even make us fall back into the abyss which we believed we had dispelled. For all that, Carroll and Artaud do not encounter one another; only the commentator may change dimensions, and that is his great weakness, the sign that he inhabits no dimension at all. We would not give a page of Artaud for all of Carroll. Artaud is alone in having been an absolute depth in literature, and in having discovered a vital body and the prodigious language of this body. As he says, he discovered them through suffering. He explored the infra-sense, which is still unknown today. But Carroll remains the master and the surveyor of surfaces— surfaces which were taken to be so well-known that nobody was exploring them anymore. On these surfaces, nonetheless, the entire logic of sense is located.

Fourteenth Series of
Double Causality

The fragility of sense can easily be explained. The attribute has an entirely different nature than corporeal qualities. The event has a different nature than the actions and passions of the body. But it *results* from them, since sense is the effect of corporeal causes and their mixtures. It is always therefore in danger of being snapped up by its cause. It escapes and affirms its irreducibility only to the extent that the causal relation comprises the heterogeneity of cause and effect—the connection of causes between themselves *and* the link of effects between themselves. This is to say that incorporeal sense, as the result of the actions and the passions of the body, may preserve its difference from the corporeal cause only to the degree that it is linked, at the surface, to a quasi-cause which is itself incorporeal. The Stoics saw clearly that the event is subject to a double causality, referring on one hand to mixtures of bodies which are its cause and, on the other, to other events which are its quasi-cause.[1] On the contrary, the Epicureans did not succeed in developing their theory of envelopes and surfaces and they did not reach the idea of incorporeal effects, perhaps because the "simulacra" remain subjected to the single causality of bodies in depth. But the requirement of a double causality is manifest, even from the point of view of a pure physics of surfaces. The events of a liquid surface refer to the inter-molecular modifications on which they depend as their real cause, but also to the variations of a surface tension on which they depend as their (ideational or "fictive") quasi-cause. We have tried to ground this second causality in a way which would conform to the incorporeal character of the surface and the event. It seemed to us that the event, that is, sense, referred *to a paradoxical element, intervening as nonsense or as an aleatory point, and operating as a quasi-cause assuring the full autonomy of the effect.* (This autonomy does not falsify the previously mentioned fragility, since the two figures of nonsense at the surface may in turn be transformed into the two "deep" nonsenses of passion and action, and the incorporeal effect can thus be reabsorbed into the depth of bodies. Conversely, fragility does not falsify autonomy as long as sense has its own dimension.)

The autonomy of the effect is thus defined initially by its difference in nature from the cause; in the second place, it is defined by its relation to the quasi-cause. These two aspects, however, give sense very different and even apparently opposed characteristics. For, insofar as it affirms its difference in nature from corporeal causes, states of affairs, qualities, and physical mixtures, sense as an effect or event is characterized by a striking impassibility (impenetrability, sterility, or inefficacy, which is neither active nor passive). This impassibility marks not only the difference between sense and the denoted states of affairs, but also the difference from the propositions which express it. Viewed from this angle, it appears as a neutrality (a mere double extracted from the proposition, or a suspension of the modalities of the proposition). On the contrary, as soon as sense is grasped, in its relation to the quasi-cause which produces and distributes it at the surface, it inherits, participates in, and even envelops and possesses the force of this ideational cause. We have seen that this cause is nothing outside of its effect, that it haunts this effect, and that it maintains with the effect an immanent relation which turns the product, the moment that it is produced, into something productive. There is no reason to repeat that sense is essentially *produced.* It is never originary but is always caused and derived. However, this derivation is two-fold, and, in relation to the immanence of the quasi-cause, it creates the paths which it traces and causes to bifurcate. Under these conditions, we must understand this genetic power in relation to the proposition itself, insofar as the expressed sense must engender the other dimensions of the proposition (signification, manifestation, and denotation.) But we must also under-stand it in relation to the way in which these dimensions are fulfilled, and even in relation to that which fulfills these dimensions, to one degree or another and in one manner or another. In other words, we must understand it in relation to the denoted states of affairs, to the manifested states of the subject, and to the signified concepts, proper-ties, and classes.

How are we to reconcile these two contradictory aspects? On one hand, we have impassibility in relation to states of affairs and neutrality in relation to propositions; on the other hand, we have the power of genesis in relation to propositions and in relation to states of affairs themselves. How are we to reconcile the logical principle, according to which a false proposition has a sense (so that sense as a condition of truth remains indifferent to both the true and the false), and the no less certain transcendental principle according to which a proposition always has the truth, the part and the kind of truth which it merits, and which belongs to it according to its sense? It would not suffice to say that these two aspects are explained by the double figure of autonomy, where in one case we consider the effect only as it differs in nature from its real cause, whereas in the other case we consider it as bound to its ideational quasi-cause. The fact is that these two figures of autonomy hurl us into contradiction, without ever resolving it.

This opposition between simple formal logic and transcendental logic cuts through the entire theory of sense. Let us consider, for example, Husserl's *Ideas*. We recall that Husserl had uncovered sense as the noema of an act or as that which a proposition expresses. Along this path, following the Stoics, and thanks to the reductive methods of phenomenology, he had recovered the impassibility of sense in the expression. The noema, from the beginning, implies a neutralized dou-ble of the thesis or the modality of the expressive proposition (the perceived, the remembered, the imagined). Moreover, the noema pos-sessed a nucleus quite independent of the modalities of consciousness and the thetic characteristics of the proposition, and also quite distinct from the physical qualities of the object posited as real (for example, pure predicates, like noematic color, in which neither the reality of the object, nor the way in which we are conscious of it, intervenes). In this nucleus of noematic sense, there appears something even more intimate, a "supremely" or transcendentally intimate "center" which is nothing other than the relation between sense itself and the object in its reality. *Relation and reality* must now be engendered or constituted in a transcendental manner. Paul Ricœur, following Fink, has in fact noted this shift in the fourth section of the *Ideas:* "not only is consciousness transcended in an intended meaning, but this intended meaning is transcended in an object. The intended meaning was yet only a content, an intentional, of course, and not a real content. . . . (But now) the relation of the noema to the object must itself be constituted through transcendental consciousness as the ultimate structure of the noema." [2] At the heart of the logic of sense, one always returns to this problem, this immaculate conception, being the passage from sterility to genesis.

But the Husserlian genesis seems to be a slight-of-hand. For the nucleus has indeed been determined as *attribute;* but the attribute is understood as *predicate* and not as verb, that is, as concept and not as *event.* (This is why the expression according to Husserl produces a form of the conceptual, and sense is inseparable from a type of generality, although this generality is not confused with that of a species.) Henceforth, the relation between sense and object is the natural result of the relation between noematic predicates—a something $=$ x which is capable of functioning as their support or principle of unification. This thing $=$ x is not at all therefore like a nonsense internal and co-present to sense, or a point zero presupposing nothing of what it necessarily engenders. It is rather the Kantian object $=$ x, where "x" means "in general." It has in relation to sense an extrinsic, rational relation of transcendence, and gives itself, ready-made, the form of denotation, just as sense, as a predicable generality, was giving itself, ready-made, the form of signification. It seems that Husserl does not think about genesis on the basis of a necessarily "paradoxical" instance, which, properly speaking, would be "non-identifiable" (lacking its own identity and its own origin). He thinks of it, on the contrary, on the basis of an originary faculty of *common sense,* responsible for accounting for the identity of an object in general, and even on the basis of a faculty of *good sense,* responsible for accounting for the process of identification of every object in general ad infinitum. [3] We can clearly see this in the Husserlian theory of *doxa,* wherein the different kinds of belief are engendered with reference to an *Urdoxa,* which acts as a faculty of common sense in relation to the specified faculties. The powerlessness of this philosophy to break with the form of common sense, which was clearly present in

Kant, is also present in Husserl. What is then the fate of a philosophy which knows well that it would not be philosophy if it did not, at least provisionally, break with the particular contents and modalities of the *doxa?* What is the fate of a philosophy which nevertheless conserves the essential (that is, the form), and is satisfied with raising to the transcendental a mere empirical exercise in an image of thought presented as originary? It is not only the dimension of signification that is given ready-made, whenever sense is conceived as a general predicate; and it is not only the dimension of denotation that is given in the alleged relation between sense and any determinable or individualizable object whatsoever. It is the entire dimension of manifestation, in the position of a transcendental subject, which retains the form of the person, of personal consciousness, and of subjective identity, and which is satisfied with creating the transcendental out of the characteristics of the empirical. What is evident in Kant, when he directly deduces the three transcendental syntheses from corresponding psychological syntheses, is no less evident in Husserl when he deduces an originary and transcendental "Seeing" from preceptual "vision."

Thus, not only is everything which must be engendered *by* the notion of sense given *in* the notion of sense, but what is even more important, the whole notion is muddied when we confuse the expression with these other dimensions from which we tried to distinguish it. We confuse it "transcendentally" with the dimensions from which we wanted to distinguish it formally. Nucleus-metaphors are disquieting; they envelop the very thing which is in question. The Husserlian bestowal of sense assumes indeed the adequate appearance of a homogeneous and regressive series degree by degree; it then assumes the appearance of an organization of heterogeneous series, that of noesis and that of noema, traversed by a two-sided instance (*Urdoxa* and object in general).[4] But this is only the rational or rationalized caricature of the true genesis, of the bestowal of sense which must determine this genesis by realizing itself within the series, and of the double nonsense which must preside over this bestowal of sense, acting as its quasi-cause. In fact, this bestowal of sense, on the basis of the immanent quasi-cause and the static genesis which ensues for the other dimensions of the proposition, may occur only within a transcendental field which would correspond to the conditions posed by Sartre in his decisive article of 1937: an impersonal transcendental field, not having the form of a synthetic personal consciousness or a subjective identity—with the subject, on the contrary, being always constituted.[5] The foundation can never resemble what it founds. It does not suffice to say of the foundation that it is another matter—it is also another geography, without being another world. And no less than the form of the personal, the transcendental field of sense must exclude the form of the general and the form of the individual. For the first characterizes only a subject which *manifests* itself; but the second characterizes only objective classes and properties which are *signified;* and the third characterizes only denotable systems which are *individuated* in an objective manner, referring to subjective points of view which are themselves *individuating* and *designating.* It does not seem to us therefore that the problem is really advanced, insofar as Husserl inscribes in the transcendental field centers of individuation and individual systems, monads, and points of view, and *Selves* in the manner of Leibniz, rather than a form of the I in the Kantian manner.[6] One finds there, nevertheless, as we shall see, a very important change. But the transcendental field is no more individual than personal, and no more general than universal. Is this to say that it is a bottomless entity, with neither shape nor difference, a schizophrenic abyss? Everything contradicts such a conclusion, beginning with the surface organization of this field. The idea of singularities, and thus of anti-generalities, which are however impersonal and pre-individual, must now serve as our hypothesis for the determination of this domain and its genetic power.

Fifteenth Series of
Singularities

The two moments of sense, impassiblity and genesis, neutrality and productivity, are not such that one may pass for the appearance of the other. Neutrality, the impassibility of the event, its indifference to the determinations of the inside and the outside, to the individual and the collective, the particular and the general—all these form a constant without which the event would not have eternal truth and could not be distinguished from its temporal actualizations. If the battle is not an example of an event among others, but rather the Event in its essence, it is no doubt because it is actualized in diverse manners at once, and because each participant may grasp it at a different level of actualization within its variable present. And the same is true for the now classic comparisons between Stendahl, Hugo, and Tolstoy when they "see" the battle and make their heroes "see" it. But it is above all because the battle *hovers over* its own field, being neutral in relation to all of its temporal actualizations, neutral and impassive in relation to the victor and the vanquished, the coward and brave; because of this, it is all the more terrible. Never present but always yet to come and already passed, the battle is graspable only by the will of anonymity which it itself inspires. This will, which we must call will "of indifference," is present in the mortally wounded soldier who is no longer brave or cowardly, no longer victor or vanquished, but rather so much beyond, at the place where the Event is present, participating therefore in its terrible impassibility. "Where" is the battle? This is why the soldier flees when he flees and surges when he surges, determined to consider each temporal actualization from the height of the eternal truth of the event which incarnates itself in it and, alas, incarnates itself in his own flesh. Still, the soldier needs a long struggle in order to arrive at this *beyond* of courage and cowardice, to this pure grasping of the event by means of a "volitional intuition," that is, by means of the will that the event creates in him. This intuition is distinct from all the empirical intuitions which still correspond to types of actualization.[1] Hence, the most important book about the event, more important even than those of Stendhal, Hugo, and Tolstoy, is Stephen Crane's *The Red Badge of Courage,* in which the hero designates himself anonymously as "the young man" or "the young soldier." It is a little similar to Carroll's battles, in which a great fuss, an immense black and neutral cloud, or a noisy crow, hovers over the combatants and separates or disperses them only in order to render them even more indistinct. There is indeed a god of war, but of all gods, he is the most impassive, the least permeable to prayers — "Impenetrability," empty sky, Aion.

In relation to propositional modes in general, the neutrality of sense appears from several different perspectives. From the point of view of quantity, sense is neither particular nor general, neither universal nor personal. From the point of view of quality, it is entirely independent of both affirmaiton and negation. From the point of view of modality, it is neither assertoric nor apodeictic, nor even interrogative (the mode of subjective uncertainty or objective possibility). From the point of view of relation, it is not confused within the proposition which expresses it, either with denotation, or with manifestation, or with signification. Finally, from the point of view of the type, it is not confused with any of the intuitions, or any of the "positions" of consciousness that we could empirically determine thanks to the play of the preceding propositional traits: intuitions or positions of empirical perception, imagination, memory, understanding, volition, etc. In conformity with the requirements of the phenomenological methods of reduction, Husserl clearly indicated the independence of sense from a certain number of these modes or points of view. But what prevents him from conceiving sense as a full (impenetrable) neutrality is his concern with retaining in sense the rational mode of a good sense and a common sense, as he presents incorrectly the latter as a matrix or a "non-modalized root-form" *(Urdoxa)*. It is this same concern which makes him conserve the form of consciousness within the transcendental. It follows then that the full neutrality of sense may be attained only as one of the sides of a disjunction within consciousness itself: either the root position of the real cogito under the jurisdiction of reason; or else neutralization as a "counterpart," an "improper cogito," an inactive and impassive "shadow or reflection" withdrawn from the jurisdiction of reason.[2] What is then presented as a radical cleavage of consciousness clearly corresponds to the two aspects of sense, neutrality and genetic power with respect to modes. But the solution which consists of distributing the two aspects in a disjunctive alternative is no more satisfactory than the solution which treated one of these aspects as an appearance. Not only is the genesis, in this case, a false genesis, but the neutrality is a pseudo-neutrality. On the contrary, we have seen that, in relation to the modifications of being and to the modalities of the proposition, the same thing had to be grasped as neutral surface effect and as fruitful principle of production. It had to be grasped, not according to a disjunction of consciousness, but rather according to the division and the conjunction of two causalities.

We seek to determine an impersonal and pre-invididual transcendental field, which does not resemble the corresponding empirical fields, and which nevertheless is not confused with an undifferentiated depth. This field can not be determined as that of a consciousness. Despite Sartre's attempt, we cannot retain consciousness as a milieu while at the same time we object to the form of the person and the point of view of individuation. A consciousness is nothing without a synthesis of unification, but there is no synthesis of unification of consciousness without the form of the I, or the point of view of the Self. What is neither individual nor personal are, on the contrary, emissions of singularities insofar as they occur on an unconscious surface and possess a mobile, immanent principle of auto-unification through a *nomadic distribution,* radically distinct from fixed and sedentary distributions as conditions of the syntheses of consciousness. Singularities are the true transcendental events, and Ferlinghetti calls them "the fourth person singular." Far from being individual or personal, singularities preside over the genesis of individuals and persons; they are distributed in a "potential" which admits neither Self nor I, but which produces them by actualizing or realizing itself, although the figures of this actualization do not at all resemble the realized potential. Only a theory of singular points is capable of transcending the synthesis of the person and the analysis of the individual as these are (or are made) in consciousness. We can not accept the alternative which thoroughly compromises psychology, cosmology, and theology: either singularities already comprised in individuals and persons, or the undifferentiated abyss. Only when the world, teaming with anonymous and nomadic, impersonal and pre-individual singularities, opens up, do we tread at last on the field of the transcendental. Throughout the preceding series, five principal characteristics of such a world have been outlined.

In the first place, singularities-events correspond to heterogeneous series which are organized into a system which is neither stable nor unstable, but rather "metastable," endowed with a potential energy wherein the differences between series are distributed. (Potential energy is the energy of the pure event, whereas forms of actualization correspond to the realization of the event.) In the second place, singularities possess a process of auto-unification, always mobile and displaced to the extent that a paradoxical element traverses the series and makes them resonate, enveloping the corresponding singular points in a single aleatory point and all the emissions, all dice throws, in a single cast. In the third place, singularities or potentials haunt the surface. Everything happens at the surface in a crystal which develops only on the edges. Undoubtedly, an organism is not developed in the same manner. An organism does not cease to contract in an interior space and to expand in an exterior space—to assimilate and to externalize. But membranes are no less important, for they carry potentials and regenerate polarities. They place internal and external spaces into contact, without regard to distance. The internal and the external, depth and height, have biological value only through this topological surface of contact. Thus, even biologically, it is necessary to understand that "the deepest is the skin." The skin has at its disposal a vital and properly superficial potential energy. And just as events do not occupy the surface but rather frequent it, superficial energy is not *localized* at the surface, but is rather bound to its formation and reformation. Gilbert Simondon has expressed this very well:

The living lives at the limit of itself, on its limit. . . . The characteristic polarity of life is at the level of the membrane; it is here that life exists in an essential manner, as an aspect of a dynamic topology which itself maintains the metastability by which it exists. . . . The entire content of internal space is topologically in contact with the content of external space at the limits of the living; there is, in fact, no distance in topology; the entire mass of living matter contained in the internal space is actively present to the external world at the limit of the living. . . . *To belong to interiority does not mean only to "be inside," but to be on the "in-side" of the limit.* . . . At the level of the polarized membrane, internal past and external future face one another . . .[3]

As a fourth determination, we will say therefore that the surface is the locus of *sense:* signs remain deprived of sense as long as they do not enter into the surface organization which assures the resonance of two series (two images-signs, two photographs, two tracks, etc.). But this world of sense does not yet imply unity of direction or community of organs. The latter requires a receptive apparatus capable of bringing about a successive superimposition of surface planes in accordance with another dimension. Furthermore, this world of sense, with its events-singularities, offers a neutrality which is essential to it. And this is the case, not only because it hovers over the dimensions according to which it will be arranged in order to acquire signification, manifestation, and denotation, but also because it hovers over the actualizations of its energy as potential energy, that is, the realization of its events, which may be internal as well as external, collective as well as individual, according to the contact surface or the neutral surface-limit which transcends distances and assures the continuity on both its sides. And this is why (determination number five) this world of sense has a *problematic* status: singularities are distributed in a properly problematic field and crop up in this field as topological events to which no direction is attached. As with chemical elements, with respect to which we know where they are before we know what they are, likewise here we know of the existence and distribution of singular points before we know their nature (bottlenecks, knots, foyers, centers . . .). This allows us, as we have seen, to give an entirely objective definition to the term "problematic" and to the indetermination which it carries along, since the nature of directed singularities and their existence and directionless distribution depend on objectively distinct instances.[4]

Hence, the conditions of the true genesis become apparent. It is true that sense is the characteristic discovery of transcendental philosophy, and that it replaces the old metaphysical Essenses. (Or rather, sense was first discovered in the form of an impassive neutrality by an empirical logic of propositions, which had broken away from Aristotelianism; and then, for a second time, sense was discovered in the form of a genetic productivity by transcendental philosophy which had broken away from metaphysics.) But the question of knowing how the transcendental field is to be determined is very complex. It seems impossible to endow it, in the Kantian manner, with the personal form of an I, or the synthetic unity of apperception, even if this unity were to be given universal extension. On this point, Sartre's objections are decisive. But it is no more possible to preserve for it the form of consciousness, even if we define this impersonal consciousness by means of pure intentionalities and retentions, which still presuppose centers of individuation. The error of all efforts to determine the transcendental as consciousness is that they think of the transcendental in the image of, and in the resemblance to, that which it is supposed to ground. In this case, either we give ourselves ready-made, in the "originary" sense presumed to belong to the constitutive consciousness, whatever we were trying to generate through a transcendental method, or, in agreement with Kant, we give up genesis and constitution and we limit ourselves to a simple transcendental conditioning. But we do not, for all this, escape the vicious circle which makes the condition refer to the conditioned as it reproduces its image. It is said that the definition of the transcendental as originary consciousness is justified, since the conditions of the real object of knowledge must be *the same as* the conditions of knowledge; without this provision, transcendental philosophy would lose all meaning and would be forced to establish autonomous conditions for objects, resurrecting thereby the Essences and the divine Being of the old metaphysics. The double series of the conditioned, that is, of the empirical consciousness and its objects, must therefore be founded on an originary instance which retains the pure form of objectivity (object = x) and the pure form of consciousness, and which constitutes the former on the basis of the latter.

But this requirement does not seem to be at all legitimate. What is common to metaphysics and transcendental philosophy is, above all, this alternative which they both impose on us: *either* an undifferentiated ground, a groundlessness, formless nonbeing, or an abyss without differences and without properties, *or* a supremely individuated Being and an intensely personalized Form. Without this Being or this Form, you will have only chaos. ... In other words, metaphysics and transcendental philosophy reach an agreement to think about *those determinable singularities only which are already imprisoned inside a supreme Self or a superior I*. It seems therefore entirely natural for metaphysics to determine this supreme Self as that which characterizes a Being infinitely and completely determined by its concept and which thereby possesses the entire originary reality. In fact, this Being is necessarily individuated, since it relegates to nonbeing or to the bottomless abyss every predicate or property which expresses nothing real, and delegates to its creatures, that is, to finite individualities, the task of receiving derived predicates which express only limited realities.[5] At the other pole, transcendental philosophy chooses the finite synthetic form of the Person rather than the infinite analytic being of the individual; and it thinks natural to determine this superior I with reference to man and to enact the grand permutation Man-God which has satisfied philosophy for so long. The I is coextensive with representation, as the individual used to be coextensive with Being. But, in both cases, we are faced with the alternative between undifferentiated groundlessness and imprisoned singularities. It is necessary therefore that nonsense and sense enter into a simple opposition, and sense itself appears both as originary and as mistaken for the primary predicates—either predicates considered in the infinite determination of the individuality of the supreme Being, or predicates considered in the finite formal constitution of the superior subject. Human or divine, as Stirner said, the predicates are the same whether they belong analytically to the divine being, or whether they are synthetically bound to the human form. As long as sense is posited as originary and predicable, it makes no difference whether the question is about a divine sense forgotten by man or whether it is about a human sense alienated in God.

Always extraordinary are the moments in which philosophy makes the Abyss *(Sans-fond)* speak and finds the mystical language of its wrath, its formlessness, and its blindness: Boehme, Schelling, Schopenhauer. Nietzsche was in the beginning one of them, a disciple of Schopenhauer, when in *The Birth of Tragedy* he allowed the *groundless* Dionysus to speak, contrasting him to the divine individuation of Apollo, and to the human character of Socrates as well. This is the fundamental problem of "who speaks in philosophy?" or "what is the subject of philosophical discourse?" But even if the formless ground or the undifferentiated abyss is made to speak, with its full voice of intoxication and anger, the alternative imposed by transcendental philosophy and by metaphysics is not left behind: beyond the person and the individual, you *will discern* nothing. . . . Nietzsche's discovery lies elsewhere when, having liberated himself from Schopenhauer and Wagner, he explored a world of impersonal and pre-individual singularities, a world he then called Dionysian or of the will to power, a free and unbound energy. These are nomadic singularities which are no longer imprisoned within the fixed individuality of the infinite Being (the notorious immutability of God), nor inside the sedentary boundaries of the finite subject (the notorious limits of knowledge). This is something neither individual nor personal, but rather singular. Being not an undifferentiated abyss, it leaps from one singularity to another, casting always the dice belonging to the same cast, always fragmented and formed again in each throw. It is a Dionysian sense-producing machine, in which nonsense and sense are no longer found in simple opposition, but are rather co-present to one another within a new discourse. The new discourse is no longer that of the form, but neither is it that of the formless: it is rather that of the pure unformed. To the charge "You shall be a monster, a shapeless mass," Nietzsche responds: "We have realized this prophecy."[6] As for the subject of this new discourse (except that there is no longer any subject), it is not man or God, and even less man in the place of God. The subject is this free, anonymous, and nomadic singularity which traverses men as well as plants and animals independently of the matter of their individuation and the forms of their personality. "Overman" means nothing other than this—the superior type of *everything that is.* This is a strange discourse, which ought to have renewed philosophy, and which finally deals with sense not as a predicate or a property but as an event.

In his own discovery, Nietzsche glimpsed, as if in a dream, at the means of treading over the earth, of touching it lightly, of dancing and leading back to the surface those monsters of the deep and forms of the sky which were left. But it is true that he was overtaken by a more profound task, one which was more grandiose and also more dangerous: in his discovery, he saw a new way of exploring the depth, of bringing a distinct eye to bear upon it, of discerning in it a thousand voices, of making all of these voices speak—being prepared to be snapped up by this depth which he interpreted and populated as it had never been before. He could not stand to stay on the fragile surface, which he had nevertheless plotted through men and gods. Returning to a bottomless abyss that he renewed and dug out afresh, that is where Nietzsche perished in his own manner. It would be preferable to say that he "quasi-perished"; for sickness and death are the event itself, subject as such to a double causality: that of bodies, states of affairs, and mixtures, but also that of the quasi-cause which represents the state of organization or disorganization of the incorporeal surface. Nietzsche, it seems, became insane and died of general paralysis, a corporeal syphilitic mixture. But the pathway which this event followed, this time in relation to the quasi-cause inspiring his entire work and co-inspiring his life, has nothing to do with his general paralysis, the ocular migraines and the vomiting from which he suffered, with the exception of giving them a new causality, that is, an eternal truth independent of their corporeal realization—thus a style in an *œuvre* instead of a mixture in the body. We see no other way of raising the question of the relations between an *œuvre* and illness except by means of this double causality.

Sixteenth Series of the
Static Ontological Genesis

This surface topology, these impersonal and preindividual nomadic singularities constitute the real transcendental field. The way in which the individual is derived out of this field represents the first stage of the genesis. The individual is inseparable from a world; but what is it that we call "world"? In general, as we have seen, a singularity may be grasped in two ways: in its existence and distribution, but also in its nature, in conformity with which it extends and spreads itself out in a determined direction over a line of ordinary points. This second aspect already represents a certain stabilization and a beginning of the actualization of the singularities. A singular point is extended analytically over a series of ordinary points up to the vicinity of another singularity, etc. A world therefore is constituted on the condition that series converge. ("Another" world would begin in the vicinity of those points at which the resulting series would diverge).

A world already envelops an infinite system of singularities selected through convergence. Within this world, however, individuals are constituted which select and envelop a finite number of the singularities of the system. They combine them with the singularities that their own body incarnates. They spread them out over their own ordinary lines, and are even capable of forming them again on the membranes which bring the inside and the outside in contact with each other. Leibniz then was right to say that the individual monad expresses a world according to the relation of other bodies with its own, as much as it expresses this relation according to the relation of the parts of its own body. An individual is therefore always in a world as a circle of convergence, and a world may be formed and thought only in the vicinity of the individuals which occupy or fill it. The question whether the world itself has a surface capable of forming again a potential of singularities is generally resolved in the negative. A world may be infinite in an order of convergence and nevertheless may have a finite energy, in which case this order would be limited. We recognize here the problem of entropy, for it is in the same way that a singularity is extended over a line of ordinary points and that a potential energy is actualized and falls to its lowest level. The power of renewal is conceded only to individuals in the world, and only for a time—the time of their living present, relative to which the past and future of the surrounding world acquire, to the contrary, a permanent and irreversible direction.

From the point of view of the static genesis, the structure individual-world-interindividuality defines the first level of actualization. At this first level, singularities are actualized both in a world and in the individuals which are parts of the world. To be actualized or to actualize oneself means to extend over a series of ordinary points; to be selected according to a rule of convergence; to be incarnated in a body; to become the state of a body; and to be renewed locally for the sake of limited new actualizations and extensions. Not one of these characteristics belongs to singularities as such; they rather belong to the individuated world and to the worldly individuals which envelop them. This is why actualization is always both collective and individual, internal and external, etc.

To be actualized is also to be *expressed*. Leibniz held the famous thesis that each individual monad expresses the world. But this thesis is poorly understood as long as we interpret it to mean the inherence of predicates in the expressive monad. It is indeed true that the expressed world does not exist outside of the monads which express it, and thus that it does exist within the monads as the series of predicates which inhere in them. It is no less true, however, that God created the world rather than monads, and that what is expressed is not confused with its expression, but rather insists and subsists.[1] The expressed world is made of differential relations and of contiguous singularities. It is formed as a world precisely to the extent that the series which depend on each singularity converge with the series which depend on others. *This convergence defines "compossibility" as the rule of a world synthesis.* Where the series diverge, another world begins, incompossible with the first. The extraordinary notion of compossibility is thus defined as a *continuum* of singularities, whereby continuity has the convergence of series as its ideational criterion. It follows that the notion of incompossibility is not reducible to the notion of contradiction. Rather, in a certain way, contradiction is derived from incompossibility. The contradiction between Adam-the-sinner and Adam-non-sinner results from the incompossibility of worlds in which Adam sins or does not sin. In each world, the individual monads express all the singularities of this world—an infinity—as though in a murmur or a swoon; but each monad envelops or expresses "clearly" a certain number of singularities only, that is, *those in the vicinity of which it is constituted and which link up with its own body.* We see that the *continuum* of singularities is entirely distinct from the individuals which envelop it in variable and complementary degrees of clarity: singularities are pre-individual. If it is true that the expressed world exists only in individuals, and that it exists there only as a predicate, it subsists in an entirely different manner, as an event or a verb, in the singularities which preside over the constitution of individuals. It is no longer Adam-the-sinner but rather the world in which Adam has sinned. . . . It would be arbitrary to give a privileged status to the inherence of predicates in Leibniz's philosophy. The inherence of predicates in the expressive monad presupposes the compossibility of the expressed world, which, in turn, presupposes the distribution of pure singularities according to the rules of convergence and divergence. These rules belong to a logic of sense and the event, and not to a logic of predication and truth. Leibniz went very far in this first stage of the genesis. He thought of the constitution of the individual as the center of an envelopment, as enveloping singularities inside a world and on its own body.

The first level of actualization produces correlatively individuated worlds and individual selves which populate each of these worlds. Individuals are constituted in the vicinity of singularities which they envelop; they express worlds as circles of converging series which depend upon these singularities. To the extent that what is expressed does not exist outside of its expressions, that is, outside of the individuals which express it, the world is really the "appurtenance" of the subject and the event has really become the analytic predicate of a subject. "*To green*" indicates a singularity-event in the vicinity of which the tree is constituted. *"To sin"* indicates a singularity-event in the vicinity of which Adam is constituted. But *"to be green"* or *"to be a sinner"* are now the analytic predicates of constituted subjects—namely, the tree and Adam. Since all the individual monads express the totality of their world—although they express clearly only a select part—their bodies form mixtures and aggregates, variable associations with zones of clarity and obscurity. This is why even here relations are analytic predicates of mixtures (Adam ate of the fruit of the tree). Moreover, contrary to certain aspects of the Leibnizian theory, it is necessary to assert that the analytic order of predicates is an order of coexistence or succession, with neither logical hierarchy nor the character of generality. When a predicate is attributed to an individual subject, it does not enjoy any degree of generality; having a color is no more general than being green, being an animal is no more general than being reasonable. The increasing or decreasing generalities appear only when a predicate is determined in a proposition to function as the subject of another predicate. As long as predicates are brought to bear upon individuals, we must recognize in them equal immediacy which blends with their analytic character. To have a color is no more general than to be green, since it is only this color that is green, and this green that has this shade, that are related to the individual subject. This rose is not red without having the red color of this rose. This red is not a color without having the color of this red. We may leave the predicate undetermined, without its acquiring any character of generality. In other words, there is not yet an order of concepts and mediations, but rather an order of mixtures only according to coexistence and succession. Animal and reasonable, green and color are two equally immediate predicates which translate a mixture in the body of the individual subject, without one predicate being attributed to it any less immediately than the other. Reason, as the Stoics say, is a body which enters, and spreads itself over, an animal body. Color is a luminous body which absorbs or reflects another body. Analytic predicates do not yet imply logical considerations of genus and species or of properties and classes; they imply only the actual physical structure and diversity which make them possible inside the mixture of the body. This is why we identify, in the last analysis, the domain of intuitions as immediate representations, the analytic predicates of existence, and the *descriptions* of mixtures or aggregates.

Now, on the terrain of the first actualization, a second level is established and developed. We face again the Husserlian problem of the Fifth Cartesian Meditation: what is it in the Ego that transcends the monad, its appurtenances and predicates? Or more precisely, what is it that gives the monad the "sense-bestowal pertaining to transcendency proper, to constitutionally secondary *Objective transcendency*," as distinct from the "immanent transcendence" of the fist level?[2] The solution here cannot be the phenomenological one, since the Ego is no less constituted than the individual monad. This monad, this living individual, was defined within a world as a *continuum* or circle of convergences; but the Ego as a knowing subject appears when something is *identified* inside worlds which are nevertheless incompossible, and across series which are nevertheless divergent. In this case, the subject is vis-à-vis the world, in a new sense of the word "world" *(Welt)*, whereas the living individual was in the world and the world within him or her *(Umwelt)*. We cannot therefore follow Husserl when he puts into play the highest synthesis of identification inside a *continuum*, all the lines of which converge or concord.[3] This is not the way to transcend the first level. Only when something is identified between divergent series or between incompossible worlds, an object = x appears transcending individuated worlds, and the Ego which thinks it transcends worldly individuals, giving thereby to the world a new value in view of the new value of the subject which is being established.

To understand this operation, we must always return to the theater of Leibniz—and not to the cumbersome machinery of Husserl. On the one hand, we know that a singularity is inseparable from a zone of perfectly objective indetermination which is the open space of its nomadic distribution. In fact, it behooves the *problem* to refer to conditions which constitute this superior and positive indetermination; it behooves the *event* to be subdivided endlessly, and also to be reassembled in one and the same Event; it behooves the *singular points* to be distributed according to mobile and communicating figures which make of every dice throw one and the same cast (an aleatory point), and of this cast a multiplicity of throws. Although Leibniz did not attain the free character of this play, since he neither wanted nor knew how to breathe enough chance into it, or to make of divergence an object of affirmation as such, he nevertheless assembled all consequences at the level of the actualization which preoccupies us at this point. A problem, he said, has conditions which necessarily include "ambiguous signs," or aleatory points, that is, diverse distributions of singularities to which instances of different solutions correspond. Thus, for example, the equation of conic sections expresses one and the same Event that its ambiguous sign subdivides into diverse events—circle, ellipse, hyperbola, parabola, straight line. These diverse events form so many instances corresponding to the problem and determining the genesis of the solutions. We must therefore understand that incompossible worlds, despite their incompossibility, have something in common—something objectively in common—which represents the ambiguous sign of the genetic element in relation to which several worlds appear as instances of solution for one and the same problem (every throw, the result of a single cast). Within these worlds, there is, for example, an objectively indeterminate Adam, that is, an Adam positively defined *solely* through a few singularities which can be combined and can complement each other in a very different fashion in different worlds (to be the first man, to live in a garden, to give birth to a woman from himself, etc.).[4] The incompossible worlds become the variants of the same story: Sextus, for example, hears the oracle. . . ; or, indeed, as Borges says, "Fang, let us say, has a secret. A stranger knocks at his door. Fang makes up his mind to kill him. Naturally there are various possible outcomes. Fang can kill the intruder, the intruder can kill Fang, both can be saved, both can die and so on and so on. In Ts'ui Pen's work, all possible solutions occur, each one being the point of departure for other bifurcations."[5]

We are no longer faced with an individuated world constituted by means of already fixed singularities, organized into convergent series, nor are we faced with determined individuals which express this world. We are now faced with the aleatory point of singular points, with the ambiguous sign of singularities, or rather with that which represents this sign, and which holds good for many of these worlds, or, in the last analysis, for all worlds, despite their divergences and the individuals which inhabit them. There is thus a "vague Adam," that is, a vagabond, a nomad, an Adam = x common to several worlds, just as there is a Sextus = x or a Fang = x. In the end, there is something = x common to all worlds. All objects $= x$ are "persons" and are defined by predicates. But these predicates are no longer the analytic predicates of individuals determined within a world which carry out the *description* of these individuals. On the contrary, they are predicates which *define* persons synthetically, and open different worlds and individualities to them as so many variables or possibilities: "to be the first man and to live in a garden" in the case of Adam; "to hold a secret and to be disturbed by an intruder," in the case of Fang. As far as the absolutely common object in general is concerned, with respect to which all worlds are variables, its predicates are the primary possibilities or the categories. Instead of each world being the analytic predicate of individuals described in series, it is rather the incompossible worlds which are the synthetic predicates of persons defined in relation to disjunctive syntheses. As for the variables which realize the possibilities of a person, we must treat them as concepts which necessarily signify classes and properties, and therefore as essentially affected by an increasing or decreasing generality in a continuous specification against a categorial background. Indeed, the garden may contain a red rose, but there are in other worlds or in other gardens roses which are not red and flowers which are not roses. The variables being properties and classes are quite distinct from the individual aggregates of the first level. Properties and classes are grounded in the order of the person. This is because persons themselves are primarily *classes having one single member,* and their predicates are *properties having one constant.* Each person is the sole member of his or her class, a class which is, nevertheless, constituted by the worlds, possibilities, and individuals which pertain to it. Classes as multiples, and properties as variables, derive from these classes with one single member and these properties with one constant. We believe therefore that the entire deduction is as follows: 1) persons; 2) classes with one single member that they constitute and properties with one constant which belong to them; 3) extensive classes and variable properties— that is, the general concepts which derive from them. It is in this sense that we interpret the fundamental link between the concept and the Ego. The universal Ego is, precisely, the person corresponding to something $= x$ common to all worlds, just as the other egos are the persons corresponding to a particular thing $= x$ common to several worlds.

We cannot follow this entire deduction in detail. What matters is only that we establish the two stages of the passive genesis. First, beginning with the singularities-events which constitute it, sense engenders a first field *(complexe)* wherein it is actualized: the *Umwelt* which organizes the singularities in circles of convergence; individuals which express these worlds; states of bodies; mixtures or aggregates of these individuals; analytic predicates which describe these states. Then, a second, very different field *(complexe)* appears, built upon the first: the *Welt* common to several or to all worlds; the persons who define this "something in common"; synthetic predicates which define these persons; and the classes and properties which derive from them. Just as the first stage of the genesis is the work of sense, the second is the work of nonsense, which is always co-present to sense (aleatory point or ambiguous sign): it is for this reason that the two stages, and their distinction, are necessarily founded. In accordance with the first we find the principle of a "good sense" taking shape, the principle of an already fixed and sedentary organization of differences. In accordance with the second, we find the formation of the principle of a "common sense" as the function of identification. But it would be an error to conceive of these produced principles as if they were transcendentals. That is, it would be an error to conceive, *in their image,* the sense and nonsense from which they are derived. This, however, explains why Leibniz, no matter how far he may have progressed in a theory of singular points and the play, did not truly pose the distributive rules of the ideal game and did at best conceive of the pre-individual very much on the basis of constituted individuals, in regions already formed by good sense (see Leibniz's shameful declaration: he assigns to philosophy the creation of new concepts, provided that they do not overthrow the "established sentiments"). This also explains how Husserl, in his theory of constitution, provides himself with a ready-made form of common sense, conceives of the transcendental as the Person or Ego, and fails to distinguish between *x* as the form of produced identification and the quite different *x,* that is, the productive nonsense which animates the ideal game and the impersonal transcendental field.[6] In truth, the person is Ulysses, no one *(elle n'est personne)* properly speaking, but a produced form, derived from this impersonal transcendental field. And the individual is always an individual in general, born, like Eve, from Adam's side, from a singularity which extends itself over a line of ordinary points and starts from the pre-individual transcendental field. The individual and the person, good sense and common sense, are produced by the passive genesis, on the basis of sense and nonsense which do not resemble them, and whose pre-individual and impersonal transcendental play we have seen. Good sense and common sense are therefore undermined by the prinicple of their production, and are overthrown from within by paradox. In Lewis Carroll's work, Alice would be rather like the individual, or the monad which discovers sense and has already a foreboding of nonsense, while climbing back up to the surface from a world into which she fell, but which is also enveloped in her and imposes on her the difficult law of mixtures. Sylvie and Bruno would be rather like "vague" persons, who discover nonsense and its presence to sense in "something" common to several worlds: a world of men and a world of fairies.

Seventeenth Series of the
Static Logical Genesis

Individuals are infinite analytic propositions. But while they are infinite with respect to what they express, they are finite with respect to their clear expression, with respect to their corporeal zone of expression. Persons are finite synthetic propositions: finite with respect to their definition, indefinite with respect to their application. Individuals and persons are, in themselves, ontological propositions—persons being grounded on individuals (and conversely, individuals being grounded by the person). The third element of the ontological genesis, however, namely the multiple classes and variable properties which in turn depend on persons, is not embodied in a third proposition which would again be ontological. Rather, this element sends us over to another order of the proposition, and constitutes the condition or the form of possibility of the logical proposition in general. In relation to this condition and simultaneously with it, individuals and persons no longer play the role of ontological propositions. They act now as material instances which realize the possibility and determine within the logical proposition the relations necessary to the existence of the conditioned (conditionné): the relation of denotation as the relation to the individual (the world, the state of affairs, the aggregate, individuated bodies); the relation of manifestation as the relation to the personal; and the relation of signification defined by the form of possibility. We are thus better able to understand the complexity of the question: what is primary in the order of the logical proposition? For, if signification is primary as the condition or form of possibility, it nevertheless refers to manifestation, to the extent that the multiple classes and variable properties defining signification are grounded, in the ontological order, upon the person; as for the manifestation, it refers to denotation to the extent that the person is grounded upon the individual.

Furthermore, between the logical genesis and the ontological genesis there is no parallelism. There is rather a relay which permits every sort of shifting and jamming. It is therefore too simple to argue for the correspondence between the individual and denotation, the person and manifestation, multiple classes or variable properties and signification. It is true that the relation of denotation may only be established in a world which is subject to the various aspects of individuation, but this is not sufficient. Besides continuity, denotation requires that an identity be posited and made dependent upon the manifest order of the person. This is what we previously indicated when we said that denotation presupposes manifestation. Conversely, when the person is manifested or expressed in the proposition, this does not occur independently of individuals, states of affairs, or states of bodies, which, not content with being denoted, form so many cases and possibilities in relation to the person's desires, beliefs, or constitutive projects. Finally, signification presupposes the formation of a good sense which comes about with individuation, just as the formation of a common sense finds its source in the person. It implicates an entire play of denotation and manifestation both in the power to affirm premises and in the power to state the conclusion. There is therefore, as we have seen, a very complex structure in view of which each of the three relations of the logical proposition in general is, in turn, primary. This structure as a whole forms the tertiary arrangement of language. Precisely because it is produced by the ontological and logical genesis, it is contingent upon sense, that is, upon that which constitutes by itself a secondary organization which is very different and also distributed in an entirely different manner. (Notice, for example, the distinction between the two x's: the x of the unformed paradoxical element which, in the case of pure sense, misses its own identity; and the x of the object in general which characterizes only the form of identity produced in common sense). If we consider therefore this complex structure of the tertiary arrangement, where every relation of the proposition must be based upon the others in a circular way, we see that the whole or each one of its parts can collapse if it loses this complementarity. This is the case, not only because the circuit of the logical proposition can always be undone, the way that a ring might be snapped, and reveal the otherwise organized sense, but also and above all because with sense, being fragile to the point of a possible toppling over into nonsense, the relations of the logical proposition run the risk of losing all measure. Similarly, signification, manifestation, and denotation run the risk of sinking into the undifferentiated abyss of a groundlessness which only permits the pulsation of a monstrous body. This is why, beyond the tertiary order of the proposition and even the secondary organization of sense, we anticipate a terrible primary order wherein the entire language becomes enfolded.

It appears that sense, in its organization of aleatory and singular points, problems and questions, series and displacement, is doubly generative: not only does it engender the logical proposition with its determinate dimensions (denotation, manifestation, and signification); it engenders also the objective correlates of this proposition which were themselves first produced as ontological propositions (the denoted, the manifested, and the signified). The lack of synchronicity and the blurring between the two aspects of the genesis explains a phenomenon like *error,* since something denoted, for example, may be given in an ontological proposition which does not correspond with the logical proposition under consideration. Error however is a very artificial notion, an abstract philosophical concept, because it affects only the truth of propositions which are assumed to be ready-made and isolated. The genetic element is discovered only when the notions of true and false are transferred from propositions to the problem these propositions are supposed to resolve, and they therefore alter completely their meaning in this transfer. Or rather, it is the category of sense which replaces the category of truth, when "true" and "false" qualify the problem instead of the propositions which correspond to it. From this point of view, we know that the problem, far from indicating a subjective and provisional state of empirical knowledge, refers on the contrary to an ideational objectivity or to a structure constitutive of sense which grounds both knowledge and the known, the proposition and its correlates. The relation between the problem and its conditions defines sense as the truth of the problem as such. It may happen that the conditions remain insufficiently determined or, on the other hand, that they are overdetermined, in such a manner that the problem may turn out to be a false problem. As for the determination of conditions, it implies, on the one hand, a space of nomad distribution in which singularities are distributed *(Topos);* on the other hand, it implies a time of decomposition whereby this space is subdivided into sub-spaces. Each one of these sub-spaces is successively defined by the adjunction of new points ensuring the progressive and complete determination of the domain under consideration (Aion). There is always a space which condenses and precipitates singularities, just as there is always a time which progressively completes the event through fragments of future and past events. Thus, there is a spatio-temporal self-determination of the problem, in the sequence of which the problem advances, making up for the deficiencies and thwarting the excess of its own conditions. It is at this point that truth becomes sense and productivity. Solutions are engendered at precisely the same time that the problem determines *itself.* This is why people quite often believe that the solution does not allow the problem to subsist, and that it assigns to it retrospectively the status of a subjective moment which is necessarily transcended as soon as a solution is found. The opposite though is the case. By means of an appropriate process, the problem is determined in space and time and, as it is determined, it determines the solutions in which it persists. The synthesis of the problem with its conditions engenders propositions, their dimensions, and their correlates.

Sense is thus expressed as the problem to which propositions correspond insofar as they indicate particular responses, signify instances of a general solution, and manifest subjective acts of resolution. This is why, rather than expressing sense in an infinitive or participial form — to be-snow white, the being-white of snow — it seems desirable to express it in the interrogative form. It is true that the interrogative form is conceived on the basis of a given (or capable of being given) solution and that it is only the neutralized double of a response supposedly held by someone (what is the color of the snow? what time is it?). It does have, at least, the advantage of setting us on the track of what we are looking for, namely, the true problem. The latter bears no resemblance to the propositions it subsumes under it; it rather engenders them as it determines its own conditions and assigns the individual order of permutation of the engendered propositions within the framework of general significations and personal manifestations. Interrogation is the shadow only of the problem projected, or rather reconstructed on the basis of empirical propositions. But the problem in itself is the reality of the genetic element, the complex *theme* which does not allow itself to be reduced to any propositional *thesis*.[1] It is one and the same illusion which, from an empirical point of view, formulates the problem from the propositions which function as its "answers," and which, from a philosophical or scientific point of view, defines the problem through the form of the possibility of the "corresponding" propositions. This form of possibility may be logical, or it may be geometrical, algebraic, physical, transcendental, moral, etc. It does not matter. As long as we define the problem by its "resolvability," we confuse sense with signification, and we conceive of the condition only in the image of the conditioned. In fact, the domains of resolvability are relative to the process of the self-determination of the problem. The synthesis of the problem with *its* own conditions constitutes something ideational or unconditioned, determining at once the condition and the conditioned, that is, the domain of resolvability and the solutions present in this domain, the form of the propositions and their determination in this form, signification as the condition of truth and proposition as the conditional truth. The problem bears resemblance neither to the propositions which it subsumes under it, nor to the relations which it engenders in the proposition: it *is not* propositional, although it does not exist outside of the propositions which express it. We cannot therefore follow Husserl when he claims that the expression is a mere double and necessarily has the same "thesis" as that which receives it. For, in this case, the problematic is no more than one propositional thesis among others, and "neutrality" falls to the other side, being opposed to all theses in general, but only in order to represent yet another manner of conceiving of that which is expressed as the double of the corresponding proposition. Once again we find the alternative of consciousness, according to Husserl, the "model" and the "shadow" constituting the two modes of the double.[2] But it seems, on the contrary, that the problem, as theme or expressed sense, possesses a neutrality which belongs to it essentially, although it is never a model or a shadow, never the double of the propositions which express it.

The problem is neutral with respect to every mode of the proposition. *Animal tantum.* . . . A circle qua circle is neither a particular circle, nor a concept represented in an equation the general terms of which must take on a particular value in each instance; it is rather a differential system to which an emission of singularities corresponds.[3] That the problem does not exist outside of the propositions which, in their senses, express it means, properly speaking, that the problem *is not:* it inheres, subsists, or persists in propositions and blends with this extra-being that we had previously encountered. This nonbeing, however, is not the being of the negative; it is rather the being of the problematic, that we should perhaps write as (non)-being or ?-being. The problem is independent of both the negative and the affirmative; it nevertheless does have a positivity which corresponds to its position as a problem. In the same manner, the pure event gains access to this positivity which transcends affirmation and negation, treating both as instances of a solution to a problem which the event now defines by means of what happens, and by means of singularities which it "poses" or "deposes." *Evenit* . . . "Certain propositions are depositive *(abdicativae):* they deprive an object of, or refuse it, something. Thus, when we say that pleasure is not a good something, we deprive it of the quality of goodness. However, the Stoics thought that even this proposition is positive *(dedicativa),* since they argued that for a pleasure to not be good, amounts to stating what has happened to this pleasure. . . ."[4]

We must, therefore, dissociate the notions of the double and of neutrality. Sense is neutral, but it is never the double of the propositions which express it, nor of the states of affairs in which it occurs and which are denoted by the propositions. This is why, as long as we remain within the circuit of the proposition, sense can be only indirectly inferred. As we have seen, sense may be directly apprehended only by breaking the circuit, in an operation analogous to that of breaking open and unfolding the Möbius strip. We cannot think of the condition in the image of the conditioned. The task of a philosophy which does not wish to fall into the traps of consciousness and the cogito is to purge the transcendental field of all resemblance. In order to remain faithful to this exigency, however, we must have something unconditioned which would be the heterogeneous synthesis of the condition in an autonomous figure binding to itself neutrality and genetic power. But when we spoke earlier of the neutrality of sense and we presented this neutrality as a double, it was not from the point of view of the genesis, to the extent that sense has at its disposal a genetic power inherited from the *quasi-cause;* it was from an entirely different point of view, whereby sense was considered first as the effect produced by corporeal causes: an impassible and sterile surface effect. How can we maintain both that sense produces even the states of affairs in which it is embodied, and that it is itself produced by these states of affairs or the actions and passions of bodies (an immaculate conception)?

The idea itself of a static genesis dissipates the contradiction. When we say that bodies and their mixtures produce sense, it is not by virtue of an individuation which would presuppose it. Individuation in bodies, the measure in their mixtures, the play of persons and concepts in their variations—this entire order presupposes sense and the pre-individual and impersonal neutral field within which it unfolds. It is therefore in a different way that sense is produced by bodies. The question is now about bodies taken in their undifferentiated depth and in their measure-less pulsation. This depth acts in an original way, *by means of its power to organize surfaces and to envelop itself within surfaces.* This pulsation sometimes acts through the formation of a minimum amount of surface for a maximum amount of matter (thus the spherical form), and sometimes through the growth of surfaces and their multiplication in accordance with diverse processes (stretching, fragmenting, crushing, drying and moistening, absorbing, foaming, emulsifying, etc.). All the adventures of Alice must be reread from this perspective—her shrinking and grow-ing, her alimentary and enuretic obsessions, and her encounters with spheres. The surface is neither active nor passive, it is the product of the actions and passions of mixed bodies. It is characteristic of the surface that it skims over its own field, impassible and indivisible, much like the thin strips of which Plotinus speaks, which "when they are of fine continuous texture, moisture is observed wetting them right through, and it flows through to the other side."[5] Being a receptacle of mono-molecular layers, it guarantees the internal and external continuity or lateral cohesion of the two layers without thickness. Being a pure effect, it is nevertheless the locus of a quasi-cause, since a surface energy, without even being *of* the surface, is due *to* every surface formation; and from it a fictitious surface tension arises as a force exerting itself on the plane of the surface. Attributed to this force is the labor spent in order to increase this surface. Being a theater for sudden condensations, fusions, changes in the states of extended layers and for distributions and reshufflings of singularities, the surface may indefinitely increase, as in the case of two liquids dissolving into each other. There is therefore an entire physics of surfaces as the effect of deep mixtures—a physics which endlessly assembles the variations and the pulsations of the entire universe, enveloping them inside these mobile limits. And, to the physics of surfaces a metaphysical surface necessarily corresponds. Metaphysical surface (*transcendental field*) is the name that will be given to the frontier established, on one hand, between bodies taken together as a whole and inside the limits which envelop them, and on the other, propositions in general. This frontier implies, as we shall see, certain properties of sound in relation to the surface, making possible thereby a distinct distribution of language and bodies, or of the corporeal depth and the sonorous *continuum*. In all these respects, the surface is the transcendental field itself, and the locus of sense and expression. Sense is that which is formed and deployed at the surface. Even the frontier is not a separation, but rather the element of an articulation, so that sense is presented both as that which happens to bodies and that which insists in propositions. We must therefore maintain that *sense is a doubling up,* and that *the neutrality of sense is inseparable from its status as a double.* The fact is that the doubling up does not at all signify an evanescent and disembodied resemblance, an image without flesh—like a smile without a cat. It is rather defined by the production of surfaces, their multiplication and consolidation. This doubling up is the continuity of reverse and right sides, the art of establishing this continuity in a way which permits sense, at the surface, to be distributed to both sides at once, as the expressed which subsists in propositions and as the event which occurs in states of bodies. When this production collapses, or when the surface is rent by explosions and by snags, bodies fall back again into their depth; everything falls back again into the anonymous pulsation wherein words are no longer anything but affections of the body—everything falls back into the primary order which grumbles beneath the secondary organization of sense. On the other hand, so long as the surface holds, not only will sense be unfolded upon it as an effect, but it will also partake of the quasi-cause attached to it. It, in turn, brings about individuation and all that ensues in a process of determination of bodies and their measured mixtures; it also produces signification and all that ensues in a process of determination of propositions and their assigned relations. It produces, in other words, the entire tertiary arrangement or the object of the static genesis.

Eighteenth Series of the
Three Images of Philosophers

The popular and the technical images of the philosopher seem to have been set by Platonism: the philosopher is a being of ascents; he is the one who leaves the cave and rises up. The more he rises the more he is purified. Around this "ascensional psychism," morality and philosophy, the ascetic ideal and the idea of thought, have established close links. The popular image of the philosopher with his head in the clouds depends upon it, as well as the scientific image according to which the philosopher's heaven is an intelligible one, which nonetheless does not distract us from the earth since it includes its law. In both cases, however, everything happens in the heights (even if this is the height of the person in the heaven of the moral law). As we ask, "what is it to be oriented in thought?", it appears that thought itself presupposes axes and orientations according to which it develops, that it has a geography before having a history, and that it traces dimensions before constructing systems. Height is the properly Platonic Orient. The philosopher's work is always determined as an ascent and a conversion, that is, as the movement of turning toward the high principle *(principe d'en haut)* from which the movement proceeds, and also of being determined, fulfilled, and known in the guise of such a motion. We are not going to compare philosophies and diseases, but there are properly philosophical diseases.

Idealism is the illness congenital to the Platonic philosophy and, with its litany of ascents and downfalls, it is even philosophy's manic-depressive form. Mania inspires and guides Plato. Dialectics is the flight of ideas, the *Ideenflucht*. As Plato says of the Idea, "it flees or it perishes. . . ." And even in the death of Socrates there is a trace of a depressive suicide.

Nietzsche distrusted the orientation by height and asked whether, far from representing the fulfilment of philosophy, it marked rather, from Socrates onward, its degeneration and wandering. In this manner, Nietzsche reopened the whole problem of the orientation of thought: is it not rather in line with other dimensions that the act of thinking is engendered in thought and the thinker engendered in life? Nietzsche has at his disposal a method of his own invention. We should not be satisfied with either biography or bibliography; we must reach a secret point where the anecdote of life and the aphorism of thought amount to one and the same thing. It is like sense which, on one of its sides, is attributed to states of life and, on the other, inheres in propositions of thought. There are dimensions here, times and places, glacial or torrid zones never moderated, the entire exotic geography which characterizes a mode of thought as well as a style of life. Diogenes Laertius, perhaps, in his best pages, had a foreboding of this method: to find vital Aphorisms which would also be Anecdotes of thought—the gesture of philosophers. The story of Empedocles and Etna, for example, is such a philosophical anecdote. It is as good as the death of Socrates but the point is precisely that it operates in another dimension. The pre-Socratic philosopher does not leave the cave; on the contrary, he thinks that we are not involved enough or sufficiently engulfed therein. In Theseus' story, he rejects the thread: "What does your ascending path matter to us, your thread leading outside, leading to happiness and virtue. . . ? Do you wish to save us with this thread? As for us, we ask you in earnest to hang yourselves with this thread!" The pre-Socratics placed thought inside the caverns and life, in the deep. They sought the secret of water and fire. And, as in the case of Empedocles' smashing the statues, they philosophized with a hammer, the hammer of the geologist and the speleologist. In a deluge of water and fire, the volcano spits up only a single reminder of Empedocles—his lead sandal. To the wings of the Platonic soul the sandal of Empedocles is opposed, proving that he was of the earth, under the earth, and autochthonous. To the beating of the Platonic wings there corresponds the pre-Socratic hammer-blow; to the Platonic conversion there corresponds the pre-Socratic subversion. The encased depths strike Nietzsche as the real orientation of philosophy, the pre-Socratic discovery that must be revived in a philosophy of the future, with all the forces of a life which is also a thought, and of a language which is also a body. "Behind every cave there is another, even deeper; and beyond that another still. There is a vaster, stranger, richer world beneath the surface, an abyss underlying every foundation."[1] In the beginning was schizophrenia; pre-Socratic philosophy is the philosophical schizophrenia *par excellence,* the absolute depth dug out in bodies and in thought which brings Hölderlin to discover Empedocles before Nietzsche. In the famous Empedoclean alternation, in the complementarity of hate and love, we encounter, on the one hand, the body of hatred, the parcelled-out body sieve: "heads without a neck, arms without shoulders, eyes without a face"; but on the other hand, we encounter the glorious body without organs: "formed in one piece," without limbs, with neither voice nor sex. Likewise, Dionysus holds out to us his two faces, his open and lacerated body, and his impassible organless head: Dionysus dismembered, but also Dionysus the impenetrable.

Nietzsche was able to rediscover depth only after conquering the surfaces. But he did not remain at the surface, for the surface struck him as that which had to be assessed from the renewed perspective of an eye peering out from the depths. Nietzsche takes little interest in what happened after · Plato, maintaining that it was necessarily the continuation of a long decadence. We have the impression, however, that there arises, in conformity to this method, a third image of philosophers. In relation to them, Nietzsche's pronouncement is particularly apt: how profound these Greeks were as a consequence of their being superficial![2] These third Greeks are no longer entirely Greek. They no longer expect salvation from the depths of the earth or from autochthony, any more than they expect it from heaven or from the Idea. Rather, they expect it laterally, from the event, from the East—where, as Carroll says, "all that is good. . . , ris(es) with the dawn of Day!" With the Megarians, Cynics, and Stoics, we have the beginning of a new philosopher and a new kind of anecdote. Rereading Diogenes Laertius' most beautiful chapters, those on Diogenes the Cynic and on Chrysippus the Stoic, we witness the development of a curious system of provocations. On one hand, the philosopher eats with great gluttony, he stuffs himself; he masturbates in public, regretting that hunger cannot be so easily relieved; he does not condemn incest with the mother, the sister, or the daughter; he tolerates cannibalism and anthropophagy—but, in fact, he is also supremely sober and chaste. On the other hand, he keeps quiet when people ask him questions or gives them a blow with his staff. If you pose abstract and difficult questions, he will respond by designating some bit of food, or will give you a whole box of food which he will then break over you—always with a blow of his staff. Yet he also holds a new discourse, a new logos animated with paradox and philosophical values and significations which are new. Indeed, we feel that these anecdotes are no longer Platonic or pre-Socratic.

This is a reorientation of all thought and of what it means to think: *there is no longer depth or height*. The Cynical and Stoic sneers against Plato are many. It is always a matter of unseating the Ideas, of showing that the incorporeal is not high above *(en hauteur)*, but is rather at the surface, that it is not the highest cause but the superficial effect par excellence, and that it is not Essence but event. On the other front, it will be argued that depth is a digestive illusion which complements the ideal optical illusion. What, in fact, is signified by this gluttony, this apology for incest and cannibalism? While this latter theme is common to both Chrysippus and Diogenes the Cynic, Laertius offers no explanation of Chrysippus' views. But he does propose a particularly convincing explanation in the case of Diogenes:

... he saw no impropriety ... in eating the flesh of any animal; nor even anything impious in touching human flesh, this, he said, being clear from the custom of some foreign nations. Moreover, according to right reason, as he put it, all elements are contained in all things and pervade everything: since not only is meat a constituent of bread, but bread of vegetables; and all other bodies also, by means of certain invisible passages and particles, find their way in and unite with all substances in the form of vapor. This he makes plain in the *Thyestes,* if the tragedies are really his. . . .

This thesis, which holds for incest as well, establishes that in the depth of bodies everything is mixture. There are no rules, however, according to which one mixture rather than another might be considered bad. Contrary to what Plato believed, there is no measure high above for these mixtures and combinations of Ideas which would allow us to define good and bad mixtures. Or again, contrary to what the pre-Socratics thought, there is no immanent measure either, capable of fixing the order and the progression of a mixture in the depths of Nature *(Physis)*; every mixture is as good as the bodies which pervade one another and the parts which coexist. How could the world of mixtures not be that of a black depth wherein everything is permitted?

Chrysippus used to distinguish two kinds of mixtures: imperfect mixtures which alter bodies; and perfect mixtures which leave bodies intact and make them coexist in all their parts. Undoubtedly, the unity of corporeal causes defines a perfect and liquid mixture wherein everything is exact in the cosmic present. But bodies caught in the particularity of their limited presents do not meet directly in line with the order of their causality, which is good only for the whole, taking into consideration all combinations at once. This is why any mixture can be called good or bad: good in the order of the whole, but imperfect, bad, or even execrable, in the order of partial encounters. How can we condemn incest and cannibalism in this domain, where passions are themselves bodies penetrating other bodies, and where the particular will is a radical evil? Taking our example from Seneca's extraordinary tragedies, we ask: what is the unity between Stoic thought and this tragic thought which stages for the first time beings devoted to evil, prefiguring thereby with such precision Elizabethan theater? A few Stoicizing choirs *(chœurs stoïcisants)* will not suffice to bring about this unity. What is really Stoic here is the discovery of passions-bodies and of the infernal mixtures which they organize or submit to: burning poisons and paedophagous banquets. The tragic supper of Thyestes is not only the lost manuscript of Diogenes. It is Seneca's subject as well, which has happily been conserved. The poisoned tunics begin their deadly work by burning into the skin and by devouring the surface. The deadly work then reaches more deeply, in a trajectory which goes from the pierced body to the fragmented body, *membra discerpta.* Everywhere poisonous mixtures seethe in the depth of the body; abominable necromancies, incests, and feedings are elaborated.

Let us look now for the antidote or the counter-proof: the hero of Seneca's tragedies and of the entire Stoic thought is Hercules. Hercules is always situated relative to the three realms of the infernal abyss, the celestial height and the surface of the earth. Inside the depths, he comes across only frightening combinations and mixtures; in the sky he finds only emptiness and celestial monsters duplicating those of the inferno. As for the earth, he is its pacifier and surveyor, and even treads over the surface of its waters. He always ascends or descends to the surface in every conceivable manner. He brings back the hell-hound and the celestial hound, the serpent of hell and the serpent of the heavens. It is no longer a question of Dionysus down below, or of Apollo up above, but of Hercules of the surface, in his dual battle against both depth and height: reorientation of the entire thought and a new geography.

Stoicism is sometimes presented as enacting a sort of return to the pre-Socratics, beyond Plato—to the Heraclitean world, for example. But it is rather a question of a total reevaluation of the pre-Socratic world. By interpreting this world through a physics of mixtures in depth, the Cynics and the Stoics abandon it partly to all the local disorders which can be reconciled only in the Great mixture, that is, in the unity of causes among themselves. This is a world of terror and cruelty, of incest and anthropophagy. But there is of course another story, namely, the story of that which, from the Heraclitean world, is able to climb to the surface and receive an entirely new status. This is the event in its difference in nature from causes-bodies, the Aion in its difference in nature from the devouring Chronos. In a parallel manner, Platonism undergoes a similar total reorientation. It had aspired to bury the pre-Socratic world even deeper, to repress it even more, and to crush it under the full weight of the heights; but now we see it deprived of its own height, and the Idea again falls to the surface as a simple incorporeal effect. The autonomy of the surface, independent of, and against depth and height; the discovery of incorporeal events, meanings, or effects, which are irreducible to "deep" bodies and to "lofty" Ideas —these are the important Stoic discoveries against the pre-Socratics and Plato. Everything that happens and everything that is said happens or is said at the surface. The surface is no less explorable and unknown than depth and height which are nonsense. For the principal frontier is displaced. It no longer passes, in terms of height, between the universal and the particular; nor, in terms of depth, does it pass between substance and accident. It is perhaps to Antisthenes that credit must be given for the new demarcation: between things and propositions them-selves. It is a frontier drawn between the thing such as it is, denoted by the proposition, and the expressed, which does not exist outside of the proposition. (Substance is no more than a secondary determination of the thing, and the universal no more than a secondary determination of the expressed.)

The Cynics and the Stoics establish themselves and wrap themselves up with the surface, the curtain, the carpet, and the mantle. The double sense of the surface, the continuity of the reverse and right sides, replace height and depth. There is nothing behind the curtain except unnameable mixtures, nothing above the carpet except the empty sky. Sense appears and is played out at the surface (at least if one knows how to mix it properly) in such a way that it forms letters of dust. It is like a fogged-up windowpane on which one can write with one's finger. The staff-blow philosophy *(philosophie à coup de bâton)* of the Cynics and the Stoics replaces the hammer-blow philosophy. The philosopher is no longer the being of the caves, nor Plato's soul or bird, but rather the animal which is on a level with the surface—a tick or louse. The philosophical symbol is no longer the Platonic wing, or Empedocles' lead sandal, but the reversible cloak of Antisthenes and Diogenes: the staff and the mantle, as in the case of Hercules with his club and lion skin. What are we to call this new philosophical operation, insofar as it opposes at once Platonic conversion and pre-Socratic subversion? Perhaps we can call it "perversion," which at least befits the system of provocations of this new type of philosopher—if it is true that perversion implies an extraordinary art of surfaces.

Nineteenth Series
of Humor

It appears at first as though language were incapable of finding a sufficient foundation in the states of the one who expresses herself, or in the denoted sensible things, and that such a foundation were to be located only in the Ideas which offer language a possibility of truth or falsity. It is not clear, however, by what miracle propositions would participate in the Ideas in a more assured manner than bodies which speak or bodies of which we speak, unless the Ideas were "names-in-themselves." And are bodies, at the other extreme, better able to ground language? When sounds fall back on (se rabattent sur) bodies and become the actions and passions of mixed bodies, they are no more than the bearers of agonizing nonsense. One after the other, the impossibility of a Platonic language and a pre-Socratic language, of an idealistic language and a physical language, of a manic language and a schizophrenic language are exposed. The alternative is imposed with no way out: either to say nothing, or to incorporate what one says—that is, to eat one's words. As Chrysippus says, "if you say 'chariot,' a chariot passes through your lips," and it is neither better nor more convenient if this is the Idea of a chariot.

The idealist language is made up of hypostatized significations. But every time we will be asked about signifieds such as "what is Beauty,

Justice, Man?" we will respond by designating a body, by indicating an object which can be imitated or even consumed, and by delivering, if necessary, a blow of the staff (the staff being the instrument of every possible designation). Diogenes the Cynic answers Plato's definition of man as a biped and featherless animal by bringing forth a plucked fowl. And to the person who asks "what is philosophy?" Diogenes responds by carrying about a cod at the end of a string. The fish is indeed the most oral of animals; it poses the problem of muteness, of consumability, and of the consonant in the wet/palatalized element—in short, the problem of language. Plato laughed at those who were satisfied with giving examples, pointing or designating, rather than attaining the Essences: I am not asking you (he used to say) who is just, but what is justice. It is therefore easy to ask Plato to follow down the path which he claimed to have made us climb. Each time we are asked about a signification, we respond with a designation and a pure "monstration." And, in order to persuade the spectator that it is not a question of a simple "example," and that Plato's problem was poorly posed, we are going to imitate what is designated, we are going to eat what is mimicked, we will shatter what is shown. The important thing is to do it quickly: to find quickly something to designate, to eat, or to break, which would replace the signification (the Idea) that you have been invited to look for. All the faster and better since there is no resemblance (nor should there be one) between what one points out and what one has been asked. There is a difficult relation, which rejects the false Platonic duality of the essence and the example. This exercise, which consists in substituting designations, monstrations, consumptions, and pure destructions for significations, requires an odd inspiration—that one know how to "descend." What is required is humor, as opposed to the Socratic irony or to the technique of the ascent.

But where does such a descent throw us? It hurls us into the ground of bodies and the groundlessness of their mixtures. Every denotation is prolonged in consumption, pulverization, and destruction, without there being any chance of arresting this movement, as if the staff shattered everything it singled out. Precisely because of this, it is clear that language can no more be based on denotation than on signification. When significations hurl us into pure denotations, which replace and negate them, we are faced with the absurd as that which is without signification. But when denotations in turn precipitate us into the destructive and digestive ground, we are faced with the non-sense of the depths as sub-sense (sous-sens) or Untersinn. Is there any way out? By the same movement with which language falls from the heights and then plunges below, we must be led back to the surface where there is no longer anything to denote or even to signify, but where pure sense is produced. It is produced in its essential relation to a third element, this time the nonsense of the surface. Once again, what matters here is to act quickly, what matters is speed.

What does the wise man find at the surface? Pure events considered from the perspective of their eternal truth, that is, from the point of view of the substance which sub-tends them, independent of their spatio-temporal actualization in a state of affairs. Or, what amounts to the same thing, one finds pure singularities, an emission of singularities considered from the perspective of their aleatory element, independent of the individuals and persons which embody them or actualize them. This adventure of humor, this two-fold dismissal of height and depth to the advantage of the surface is, in the first instance, the adventure of the Stoic sage. But later on, and in another context, it will also be the adventure of Zen—against the Brahman depths and the Buddhist heights. The famous problems-tests, the questions-answers, the koans, demonstrate the absurdity of significations and show the nonsense of denotations. The staff is the universal instrument, the master of questions; mimicry and consumption are the response. Returned to the surface, the sage discovers objects-events, all of them communicating in the void which constitutes their substance; he discovers the Aion in which they are sketched out and developed without ever filling it up.[1] The event is the identity of form and void. It is not the object as denoted, but the object as expressed or expressible, never present, but always already in the past and yet to come. As in Mallarmé's works, it has the value of its own absence or abolition, since this abolition (abdicatio) is precisely its position in the void as the pure Event (dedicatio). "If you have a cane," says the Zen master, "I am giving you one; if you do not have one, I am taking it away." (Or, as Chrysippus said, "If you never lost something, you have it still; but you never lost horns, ergo you have horns.")[2] The negation no longer expresses anything negative, but rather releases the purely expressible with its two uneven halves. One of the halves is always lacking from the other, since it exceeds by virtue of its own deficiency, even if this means to be deficient by virtue of its excess (word $=$ x for a thing $=$ x). We can see this clearly in the Zen arts: not only in the art of drawing, where the brush controlled by an unsupported wrist balances form and emptiness and distributes the singularities of a pure event in fortuitous strokes and "furry lines"; but also in the arts of gardening and flower arranging, in the tea ceremony, and in the arts of archery and fencing, where the "flourishing of iron" arises from a marvelous vacuity. Across the abolished significations and the lost denotations, the void is the site of sense or of the event which harmonizes with its own nonsense, in the palce where the place only takes place *(là où n'a plus lieu que le lieu)*. The void is itself the paradoxical element, the surface nonsense, or the always displaced aleatory point whence the event bursts forth as sense. "There is no circle of birth and death to escape from, nor any supreme knowledge to attain." The empty sky rejects both the highest thoughts of the spirit and the profound cycles of nature. The question is less that of attaining the immediate than of determining the site where the immediate is "immediately" as not-to-be-attained *(comme non-à-atteindre)*: the surface where the void and every event along with it are made; the frontier as the cutting edge of a sword or the stretched string of the bow. To paint without painting, non-thought, shooting which becomes non-shooting, to speak without speaking: this is not at all the ineffable up above or down below, but rather the frontier and the surface where language becomes possible and, by becoming possible, inspires only a silent and immediate communication, since it could only be spoken in the resuscitation of all the mediate and abolished significations or denotations.

We ask "who speaks?" as much as we ask what makes language possible. Many different answers have been given to this question. We call "classic" response the one which determines the individual as the speaker. That of which the individual speaks is determined rather as a particularity, and the means, that is, language itself, is determined as a conventional generality. It is therefore a matter of disentangling, from a combined threefold operation, a universal form of the individual (reality), and, at the same time, of extracting a pure Idea of what we speak about (necessity), and of confronting language with an ideal model assumed to be primitive, natural, or purely rational (possibility). It is precisely this conception which animates Socratic irony as an ascent, and gives it at once the following tasks: to tear the individual away from his or her immediate existence; to transcend sensible particularity toward the Idea; and to establish laws of language corresponding to the model. Such is the "dialectical" whole of a remembering and speaking subjectivity. For the operation to be complete, however, the individual must be not only a point of departure and a springboard, but to be also recovered at the end of the operation, with the universality of the Idea being like a means of exchange between the two. This closure or perfect circle of irony is still absent from Plato, or it appears only under the guise of the comic and of derision, as in the exchange between Socrates and Alcibiades. Classical irony, on the contrary, reaches this perfect state when it finally determines not only the whole reality, but also the whole of the possible as a supreme originary individuality. Kant, we have seen, anxious to submit the classical world of representation to his critique, begins by describing it with exactitude: "we yet find, on closer scrutiny, that this idea (the idea of the *sum total of all possibility*), as a primordial concept, excludes a number of predicates which as derivative are already given through other predicates or which are incompatible with others; and that it does, indeed, define itself as a concept that is completely determinate a priori. It thus becomes the concept of an individual object."[3] Classical irony acts as the instance which assures the coextensiveness of being and of the individual within the world of representation. Thus, not only the universality of the Idea, but also the model of a pure rational language in relation to the first possible ones, become the means of natural communication between a supremely individuated God and the derived individuals which he created. This God renders possible the ascent of the individual to the universal form.

After the Kantian critique, however, a third figure of irony appears. Romantic irony determines the one who speaks as the person and no longer as the individual. It grounds itself on the finite synthetic unity of the person and no longer on the analytic identity of the individual. It is defined by the coextensiveness of the I and representation. There is much more to this than a mere shifting of terms. To determine its full import, it would be necessary to evaluate, for example, the difference between Montaigne's *Essays,* already inscribed in the classical world insofar as they explore the most diverse figures of individuation, and Rousseau's *Confessions,* announcing Romanticism insofar as they consti-tute the first manifestation of a person, or an I. Not only the universal Idea and the sensible particularity become now the characteristic possi-bilities of the person but also the two extremes of individuality and the worlds corresponding to individuals. These possibilities continue to be distributed into originary and derived possibilities; but "originary" now designates only those predicates of the person which are constant in all possible worlds (categories); and "derived" now designates only the individual variables in accordance with which the person is embodied in different worlds. From this, a profound transformation comes about —of the universality of the Idea, of the form of subjectivity, and of the model of language as function of the possible. The position of the person as an unlimited class, which nevertheless has only one member (I)—such is the Romantic irony. Undoubtedly, there are already precursive elements in the Cartesian cogito and, above all, in the Leibnizian person. But these elements remain subordinate to the demands of individuation, whereas in the Romanticism which follows Kant, they liberate and express themselves for their own sake, overthrowing the subordination.

But this infinite poetic freedom, already suggested by the fact that to become (blive til) nothing at all is itself included, is expressed in a still more positive way, for the ironic individual has most often traversed a multitude of determinations in the form of possibility, poetically lived through them, before he ends in nothingness. For irony, as for the Pythagorean doctrine, the soul is constantly on a pilgrimage, except irony does not require such a long time to complete it. . . . (The ironist) therefore counts on his fingers like a child: rich man, poor man, beggar man, etc. As all these determinations merely have the validity of possibility, he can even run through the whole lot almost as quickly as a child. What costs the ironist time, however, is the care he lavishes on selecting the proper costume for the poetic personage he has poetized himself to be. . . . When the given actuality loses its validity for the ironist, therefore, this is not because it is outlived actuality which shall be displaced by a truer, but because the ironist is the eternal ego for whom no actuality is adequate.[4]

What all the figures of irony have in common is that they confine the signularity within the limits of the individual or the person. Thus, irony only in appearance assumes the role of a vagabond. But this is why all these figures are threatened by an intimate enemy who works on them from within: the undifferentiated ground, the groundless abyss of which we previously spoke, that represents tragic thought and the tragic tone with which irony maintains the most ambivalent relations. It is Dionysus, present beneath Socrates, but it is also the demon who holds up to God and to his creatures the mirror wherein universal individuality dissolves. It is the chaos which brings about the undoing of the person. Classical discourse was held by the individual, Romantic discourse by the person. But beneath these two discourses, overturning them in various ways, the faceless Ground speaks now while rumbling. We have seen that this language of the ground, the language which is confused with the depth of the body, had a two-fold power—that of shattered phonetic elements and that of non-articulated tonic values. The first of these threatens and overturns classical discourse from within; the second threatens and overturns Romantic discourse. In each case and for each type of discourse, three languages must be distinguished. First, a real language corresponding to the quite ordinary assignation of the speaker (the individual, or rather the person . . .). Second, an ideal language representing the model of discourse relative to the form of the one who holds it (the divine model of *Cratylus* in relation to the Socratic subjectivity, for example; or the rational Leibnizian model in relation to classical individuality; or the evolutionist model in relation to the Romantic person). And finally, esoteric language, which in each case represents the subversion, from the ground up, of the ideal language and the dissolution of the one who holds the real language. In each case, moreover, there are internal relations between the ideal model and its esoteric reversal, as between irony and the tragic ground, to the point that it is impossible to know on which side the maximum irony lies. It is for this reason that it is vain to seek a unique formula, a unique concept, which would be applicable to every esoteric language: for the grand literal, syllabic, and phonetic synthesis of Court de Gébelin, for example, with which the classical world comes to a close, as well as for the evolutive tonic synthesis of Jean-Pierre Brisset, with which Romanticism came to an end (we saw also that there is no uniformity in the case of portmanteau words).

To the question "Who is speaking?", we answer sometimes with the individual, sometimes with the person, and sometimes with the ground which dissolves both. "The self of the lyric poet raises its voice from the bottom of the abyss of being; its subjectivity is pure imagination." [5] But a final response yet remains, one which challenges the undifferentiated primitive ground and the forms of the individual and the person, and which rejects their contradiction as well as their complementarity. No, singularities are not imprisoned within individuals and persons; and one does not fall into an undifferentiated ground, into groundless depth, when one undoes the individual and the person. The impersonal and pre-individual are the free nomadic singularities. Deeper than any other ground is the surface and the skin. A new type of esoteric language is formed here which is its own model and reality. Becoming-mad changes shape in its climb to the surface, along the straight line of the Aion, in eternity; and the same thing happens to the dissolved self, the cracked I, the lost identity, when they cease being buried and begin, on the contrary, to liberate the singularities of the surface. Nonsense and sense have done away with their relation of dynamic opposition in order to enter into the co-presence of a static genesis—as the nonsense of the surface and the sense which hovers over it. The tragic and the ironic give way to a new value, that of humor. For if irony is the co-extensiveness of being with the individual, or of the I with representation, humor is the co-extensiveness of sense with nonsense. Humor is the art of the surfaces and of the doubles, of nomad singularities and of the always displaced aleatory point; it is the art of the static genesis, the savoir-faire of the pure event, and the "fourth person singular"—with every signification, denotation, and manifestation suspended, all height and depth abolished.

Twentieth Series on the Moral
Problem in Stoic Philosophy

Diogenes Laertius relates that the Stoics compared philosophy to an egg: "The shell is Logic, next comes the white, Ethics, and the yoke in the center is Physics." We sense that Diogenes rationalizes. We must recover the aphorism-anecdote, that is, the koan. We must imagine a situation in which a disciple is raising a question of signification: O master, what is ethics? The Stoic sage takes then a hard-boiled egg from his reversible cloak and designates the egg with his staff. (Or, having taken out the egg, he strikes the disciple with his staff, giving him to understand that he himself must provide the answer. The disciple, in turn, takes the staff and breaks the egg in such a manner that a little of the white remains attached to the yoke and a little to the shell. Either the master has to do all of this himself, or the disciple will have come to have an understanding only after many years.) At any rate, the place of ethics is clearly displayed between the two poles of the superficial, logical shell and the deep physical yoke. Is not Humpty Dumpty himself the Stoic master? Is not the disciple's adventure Alice's adventure? For her adventure consists of climbing back from the depth of bodies to the surface of words, of having the troubling experience of ethical ambiguity: the ethics of bodies or the morality of words ("the moral of what is said . . ."); an ethics of foodstuff or an ethics of language, of eating or of speaking, of the yoke or of the shell, of states of affairs or of sense.

We must go back to what we said a little while ago, at least in order to be able to introduce some variants. We moved too quickly as we presented the Stoics challenging depth, and finding there only infernal mixtures corresponding to passions-bodies and to evil intentions. The Stoic system contains an entire physics, along with an ethics of this physics. If it is true that passions and evil intentions are bodies, it is true that good will, virtuous actions, true representations, and just consents are also bodies. If it is true that certain bodies form abominable, cannibalistic, and incestuous mixtures, the aggregate of bodies taken as a whole necessarily forms a perfect mixture, which is nothing other than the unity of causes among themselves or the cosmic present, in relation to which evil itself can only be an evil of "consequence." If there are bodies-passions, there are also bodies-actions, unified bodies of the great Cosmos. Stoic ethics is concerned with the event; it consists of willing the event as such, that is, of willing that which occurs insofar as it does occur. We cannot yet evaluate the import of these formulations. But in any case, how could the event be grasped and willed without its being referred to the corporeal cause from which it results and, through this cause, to the unity of causes as *Physics?* Here, *divination* grounds ethics. In fact, the divinatory interpretation consists of the relation between the pure event (not yet actualized) and the depth of bodies, the corporeal actions and passions whence it results. We can state precisely how this interpretation proceeds: it is always a question of cutting into the thickness, of carving out surfaces, of orienting them, of increasing and multiplying them in order to follow out the tracing of lines and of incisions inscribed on them. Thus, the sky is divided into sections and a bird's line of flight is distributed according to them; we follow on the ground the letter traced by a pig's snout; the liver is drawn up to the surface where its lines and fissures are observed. Divination is, in the most general sense, the art of surfaces, lines, and singular points appearing on the surface. This is why two fortune-tellers cannot regard one another without laughing, a laughter which is humorous. (It would, of course, be necessary to distinguish two operations, namely, the production of a physical surface for lines which are still corporeal, for images, imprints, or representations; and the translation of these onto a "metaphysical" surface, where only incorporeal lines of the pure event are played out, which represents the interpreted sense of these images.)

But it is not accidental that Stoic ethics was unable (and had no desire) to trust in physical methods of divination, that it oriented itself toward an entirely different pole, and that it developed itself in accordance with an entirely different method—namely logic. Victor Goldschmidt has clearly shown these two poles between which the Stoic ethics oscillates. One one hand, it would be a question of participating to the greatest possible extent in a divine vision which gathers in depth all the physical causes in the unity of a cosmic present, in order to elicit the divination of events which ensue. On the other hand, however, it is a question of willing the event whatever it may be, without any interpretation, thanks to a "usage of representations" which accompanies the event ever since its first actualization, assigning to it the most limited present possible.[1] In the one case, we move from the cosmic present to the not-yet actualized event; in the other, we go from the pure event to its most limited present actualization. Moreover, in the one case, we link the event to its corporeal causes and to their physical unity; in the other, we link it to its incorporeal quasi-cause, the kind of causality which it gathers and makes resonate in the production of its own actualization. This bipolarity was already comprised in the paradox of double causality and in the two characteristics of the static genesis —impassibility and productivity, indifference and efficacy—the immaculate conception which now characterizes the Stoic sage. The insufficiency of the first pole derives from the fact that events, being incorporeal effects, differ in nature from the corporeal causes from which they result; that they have other laws than they do, and are determined only by their relation with the incorporeal quasi-cause. Cicero put it very well when he said that the passage of time is similar to the unraveling of a thread (explicatio).[2] But events, to be precise, do not exist on the straight line of the unraveled thread (Aion), just as causes do not exist in the circumference of the wound-up thread (Chronos).

What is the logical usage of representations, namely of this art which reached its peak in the works of Epictetus and Marcus Aurelius? The obscurity of the Stoic theory of representation, such as it has been handed down to us, is well known: the role and nature of assent in the sensible corporeal representation, as something borrowed; the manner by which rational representations, which are still corporeal, derive from sensible representations; above all, that which constitutes the character of representation, such that it may or may not be "comprehensible"; and finally, the scope of the difference between representations-bodies, or imprints, and incorporeal events-effects (between *representations* and *expressions*).[3] These last two difficulties concern us here essentially, since sensible representations are denotations and rational representations are significations, while only incorporeal events constitute expressed sense. We have encountered this difference of nature between the expression and the representation at every turn, each time we noted the specificity of sense or of the event, its irreducibility to the denotatum and to the signified, its neutrality in relation to the particular and to the general, or its impersonal and pre-individual singularity. This difference culminates in the opposition between the object $=$ x as the identitarian instance of the representation in common sense, and the thing $=$ x as the nonidentifiable element of expression in the paradox. But, if sense is never an object of possible representation, it does not for this reason intervene any less in representation as that which confers a very special value to the relation that it maintains with its object.

By itself, representation is given up to an extrinsic relation of resemblance or similitude only. But its internal character, by which it is intrinsically "distinct," "adequate," or "comprehensive," comes from the manner in which it encompasses, or envelops an expression, much as it may not be able to represent it. The expression, which differs in nature from the representation, acts no less as that which is enveloped (or not) inside the representation. For example, the perception of death as a state of affairs and as a quality, or the concept "mortal" as a predicate of signification, remain extrinsic (deprived of sense) as long as they do not encompass the event of dying as that which is actualized in the one and expressed in the other. Representation must encompass an expression which it does not represent, but without which it itself would not be "comprehensive," and would have truth only by chance or from outside. To know that we are mortal is an apodeictic knowledge, albeit empty and abstract; effective and successive deaths do not suffice of course in fulfilling this knowledge adequately, so long as one does not come to know death as an impersonal event provided with an always open problematic structure (where and when?). In fact, two types of knowledge *(savoir)* have often been distinguished, one indifferent, remaining external to its object, and the other concrete, seeking its object wherever it is. Representation attains this topical ideal only by means of the hidden expression which it encompasses, that is, by means of the event it envelops. There is thus a "use" of representation, without which representation would remain lifeless and senseless. Wittgenstein and his disciples are right to define meaning by means of use. But such use is not defined through a function of representation in relation to the represented, nor even through representativeness as the form of possibility. Here, as elsewhere, the functional is transcended in the direction of a topology, and use is in the relation between representation and something extra-representative, a nonrepresented and merely expressed entity. Representation envelops the event in another nature, it envelops it at its borders, it stretches until this point, and it brings about this lining or hem. This is the operation which defines living usage, to the extent that representation, when it does not reach this point, remains only a dead letter confronting that which it represents, and stupid in its representiveness.

The Stoic sage "identifies" with the quasi-cause, sets up shop at the surface, on the straight line which traverses it, or at the aleatory point which traces or travels this line. The sage is like the archer. However, this connection with the archer should not be understood as a moral metaphor of intention, as Plutarch suggests, by saying that the Stoic sage is supposed to do everything, for the sake of attaining the end. One rather acts in order to have done all that which depended on one in order to attain the end. Such a rationalization implies a late interpretation, one which is hostile to Stoicism. The relation to the archer is closer to Zen: the bowman must reach the point where the aim is also not the aim, that is to say, the bowman himself; where the arrow flies over its straight line while creating its own target; where the surface of the target is also the line and the point, the bowman, the shooting of the arrow, and what is shot at. This is the oriental Stoic will as *pro-airesis*. The sage waits for the event, that is to say, *understands the pure event* in its eternal truth, independently of its spatio-temporal actualization, as something eternally yet-to-come and always already passed according to the line of the Aion. But, at the same time, the sage also *wills the embodiment* and the actualization of the pure incorporeal event in a state of affairs and in his or her own body and flesh. Identifying with the quasi-cause, the sage wishes to "give a body" to the incorporeal effect, since the effect inherits the cause (Goldschmidt puts it very well, with respect to an event such as going for a walk: "The walk, incorporeal insofar as it is a way of being, acquires a body *(prend corps)* under the effect of the hegemonic principle which is manifested in it."[4] And this applies to the wound and to archery just as much as it applies to the stroll). But how could the sage be the quasi-cause of the incorporeal event, and thereby will its embodiment, if the event were not already in the process of being produced by and in the depth of corporeal causes, or if illness were not prepared at the innermost depth of bodies? The quasi-cause does not create, it "operates," and wills only what comes to pass. Representation and its usage therefore intervene at this point. Corporeal causes act and suffer through a cosmic mixture and a universal present which produces the incorporeal event. But the quasi-cause operates by doubling this physical causality—it embodies the event in the most limited possible present which is the most precise and the most instantaneous, the pure instant grasped at the point at which it divides itself into future and past, and no longer the present of the world which would gather into itself the past and the future. The actor occupies the instant, while the character portrayed hopes or fears in the future and remembers or repents in the past: it is in this sense that the actor "represents." To bring about the correspondence of the minimum time which can occur in the instant with the maximum time which can be thought in accordance with the Aion. To limit the actualization of the event in a present without mixture, to make the instant all the more intense, taut, and instantaneous since it expresses an unlimited future and an unlimited past. This is the use of representation: the mime, and no longer the fortune-teller. One stops going from the greatest present toward a future and past which are said only of a smaller present; on the contrary, one goes from the future and past as unlimited, all the way to the smallest present of a pure instant which is endlessly subdivided. This is how the Stoic sage not only comprehends and wills the event, but also *represents it and, by this, selects it,* and that an ethics of the mime necessarily prolongs the logic of sense. Beginning with a pure event, the mime directs and doubles the actualization, measures the mixtures with the aid of an instant without mixture, and prevents them from overflowing.

Twenty-First Series
of the Event

We are sometimes hesitant to call Stoic a concrete or poetic way of life, as if the name of a doctrine were too bookish or abstract to designate the most personal relation with a wound. But where do doctrines come from, if not from wounds and vital aphorisms which, with their charge of exemplary provocation, are so many speculative anecdotes? Joe Bousquet must be called Stoic. He apprehends the wound that he bears deep within his body in its eternal truth as a pure event. To the extent that events are actualized in us, they wait for us and invite us in. They signal us: "My wound existed before me, I was born to embody it."[1] It is a question of attaining this will that the event creates in us; of becoming the quasi-cause of what is produced within us, the Operator; of producing surfaces and linings in which the event is reflected, finds itself again as incorporeal and manifests in us the neutral splendor which it possesses in itself in its impersonal and pre-individual nature, beyond the general and the particular, the collective and the private. It is a question of becoming a citizen of the world. "Everything was in order with the events of my life before I made them mine; to live them is to find myself tempted to become their equal, as if they had to get from me only that which they have that is best and most perfect."

Either ethics makes no sense at all, or this is what it means and has nothing else to say: not to be unworthy of what happens to us. To grasp whatever happens as unjust and unwarranted (it is always someone else's fault) is, on the contrary, what renders our sores repugnant —veritable *ressentiment*, resentment of the event. There is no other ill will. What is really immoral is the use of moral notions like just or unjust, merit or fault. What does it mean then to will the event? Is it to accept war, wounds, and death when they occur? It is highly probable that resignation is only one more figure of *ressentiment*, since *ressentiment* has many figures. If willing the event is, primarily, to release its eternal truth, like the fire on which it is fed, this will would reach the point at which war is waged against war, the wound would be the living trace and the scar of all wounds, and death turned on itself would be willed against all deaths. We are faced with a volitional intuition and a transmutation. "To my inclination for death," said Bousquet, "which was a failure of the will, I will substitute a longing for death which would be the apotheosis of the will." From this inclination to this longing there is, in a certain respect, no change except a change of the will, a sort of leaping in place *(saut sur place)* of the whole body which exchanges its organic will for a spiritual will. It wills now not exactly what occurs, but something *in* that which occurs, something yet to come which would be consistent with what occurs, in accordance with the laws of an obscure, humorous conformity: the Event. It is in this sense that the *Amor fati* is one with the struggle of free men. My misfortune is present in all events, but also a splendor and brightness which dry up misfortune and which bring about that the event, once willed, is actualized on its most contracted point, on the cutting edge of an operation. All this is the effect of the static genesis and of the immaculate conception. The splendor and the magnificence of the event is sense. The event is not what occurs (an accident), it is rather inside what occurs, the purely expressed. It signals and awaits us. In accordance with the three preceding determinations, it is what must be understood, willed, and represented in that which occurs. Bousquet goes on to say: "Become the man of your misfortunes; learn to embody their perfection and brilliance." Nothing more can be said, and no more has ever been said: to become worthy of what happens to us, and thus to will and release the event, to become the offspring of one's own events, and thereby to be reborn, to have one more birth, and to break with one's carnal birth—to become the offspring of one's events and not of one's actions, for the action is itself produced by the offspring of the event.

The actor is not like a god, but is rather like an "anti-god" *(contre-dieu)*. God and actor are opposed in their readings of time. What men grasp as past and future, God lives it in its eternal present. The God is Chronos: the divine present is the circle in its entirety, whereas past and future are dimensions relative to a particular segment of the circle which leaves the rest outside. The actor's present, on the contrary, is the most narrow, the most contracted, the most instantaneous, and the most punctual. It is the point on a straight line which divides the line endlessly, and is itself divided into past-future. The actor belongs to the Aion: instead of the most profound, the most fully present, the present which spreads out and comprehends the future and the past, an unlimited past-future rises up here reflected in an empty present which has no more thickness than the mirror. The actor or actress represents, but what he or she represents is always still in the future and already in the past, whereas his or her representation is impassible and divided, unfolded without being ruptured, neither acting nor being acted upon. It is in this sense that there is an actor's paradox; the actor maintains himself in the instant in order to act out something perpetually antici-pated and delayed, hoped for and recalled. The role played is never that of a character; it is a theme (the complex theme or sense) constituted by the components of the event, that is, by the communicating singular-ities effectively liberated from the limits of individuals and persons. The actor strains his entire personality in a moment which is always further divisible in order to open himself up to the impersonal and pre-individual role. The actor is always acting out other roles when acting one role. The role has the same relation to the actor as the future and past have to the instantaneous present which corresponds to them on the line of the Aion. The actor thus actualizes the event, but in a way which is entirely different from the actualization of the event in the depth of things. Or rather, the actor redoubles this cosmic, or physical actualization, in his own way, which is singularly superficial—but because of it more distinct, trenchant and pure. Thus, the actor delimits the original, disengages from it an abstract line, and keeps from the event only its contour and its splendor, becoming thereby the actor of one's own events—a *counter-actualization*.

The physical mixture is exact only at the level of the whole, in the full circle of the divine present. But with respect to each part, there are many injustices and ignominies, many parasitic and cannibalistic processes which inspire our terror at what happens to us, and our resentment at what occurs. Humor is inseparable from a selective force: in that which occurs (an accident), it selects the pure event. In eating, it selects speaking. Bousquet listed the characteristics of the humor-actor (de l'humour-acteur): to annihilate his or her tracks whenever necessary; "to hold up among men and works *their being before bitterness,*" "to assign to plagues, tyrannies, and the most frightful wars the comic possibility of having reigned for nothing"; in short, to liberate for each thing "its immaculate portion," language and will, *Amor Fati.*[2]

Why is every event a kind of plague, war, wound, or death? Is this simply to say that there are more unfortunate than fortunate events? No, this is not the case since the question here is about the double structure of every event. With every event, there is indeed the present moment of its actualization, the moment in which the event is embodied in a state of affairs, an individual, or a person, the moment we designate by saying *"here,* the moment has come." The future and the past of the event are evaluated only with respect to this definitive present, and from the point of view of that which embodies it. But on the other hand, there is the future and the past of the event considered in itself, sidestepping each present, being free of the limitations of a state of affairs, impersonal and pre-individual, neutral, neither general nor particular, *eventum tantum.* . . . It has no other present than that of the mobile instant which represents it, always divided into past-future, and forming what must be called the counter-actualization. In one case, it is my life, which seems too weak for me and slips away at a point which, in a determined relation to me, has become present. In the other case, it is I who am too weak for life, it is life which overwhelms me, scattering its singularities all about, in no relation to me, nor to a moment determinable as the present, except an impersonal instant which is divided into still-future and already-past. No one has shown better than Maurice Blanchot that this ambiguity is essentially that of the wound and of death, of the mortal wound. Death has an extreme and definite relation to me and my body and is grounded in me, but it also has no relation to me at all—it is incorporeal and infinitive, impersonal, grounded only in itself. On one side, there is the part of the event which is realized and accomplished; on the other, there is that "part of the event which cannot realize its accomplishment." There are thus two accomplishments, which are like actualization and counter-actualization. It is in this way that death and its wound are not simply events among other events. Every event is like death, double and impersonal in its double. "It is the abyss of the present, the time without present with which I have no relation, toward which I am unable to project myself. For in it *I* do not die. I forfeit the power of dying. In this abyss they *(on)* die—they never cease to die, and they never succeed in dying."[3]

How different this "they" is from that which we encounter in everyday banality. It is the "they" of impersonal and pre-individual singularities, the "they" of the pure event wherein *it* dies in the same way that *it* rains. The splendor of the "they" is the splendor of the event itself or of the fourth person. This is why there are no private or collective events, no more than there are individuals and universals, particularities and generalities. Everything is singular, and thus both collective and private, particular and general, neither individual nor universal. Which war, for example, is not a private affair? Conversely, which wound is not inflicted by war and derived from society as a whole? Which private event does not have all its coordinates, that is, all its impersonal social singularities? There is, nevertheless, a good deal of ignominy in saying that war concerns everybody, for this is not true. It does not concern those who use it or those who serve it—creatures of *ressentiment*. And there is as much ignominy in saying that everyone has his or her own war or particular wound, for this is not true of those who scratch at their sores—the creatures of bitterness and *ressentiment*. It is true only of the free man, who grasps the event, and does not allow it to be actualized as such without enacting, the actor, its counter-actualization. Only the free man, therefore, can comprehend all violence in a single act of violence, and every mortal event *in a single Event* which no longer makes room for the accident, and which denounces and removes the power of *ressentiment* within the individual as well as the power of oppression within society. Only by spreading *ressentiment* the tyrant forms allies, namely slaves and servants. The revolutionary alone is free from the *ressentiment,* by means of which one always participates in, and profits by, an oppressive order. *One and the same Event?* Mixture which extracts and purifies, or measures everything at an instant without mixture, instead of mixing everything together. All forms of violence and oppression gather together in this single event which denounces all by denouncing one (the nearest or final state of the question).

The psychopathology which the poet makes his own is not a sinister little accident of personal destiny, or an individual, unfortunate accident. It is not the milkman's truck which has run over him and left him disabled. It is the horsemen of the Hundred Blacks carrying out their pogroms against their ancestors in the ghettos of Vilna. . . . The blows received to the head did not happen during a street brawl, but when the police charged the demonstrators. . . . If he cries out like a deaf genius, it is because the bombs of Guernica and Hanoi have deafened him. . . .[4]

It is at this mobile and precise point, where all events gather together in one that transmutation happens: this is the point at which death turns against death; where dying is the negation of death, and the impersonality of dying no longer indicates only the moment when I disappear outside of myself, but rather the moment when death loses itself in itself, and also the figure which the most singular life takes on in order to substitute itself for me.[5]

Twenty-Second Series—
Porcelain and Volcano

"Of course all life is a process of breaking down. . . ."[1] Few phrases resonate in our heads with such a hammer blow, few texts possess this final character of a masterpiece, or are able to impose silence or force such terrified acquiescence as Fitzgerald's *The Crack Up*. The entire work of Fitzgerald is the unique development of this proposition—in particular, of the "of course." Here is a man and a woman, there is a couple (and why couples, if not because it is already a question of movement, and of a process defined on the basis of the dyad?) who have, as we say, everything it takes to be happy: looks, charm, riches, superficiality, and lots of talent. And then something happens that shatters them like an old plate or glass. There is a terrible tête-à-tête of the schizophrenic and the alcoholic, unless death takes them both. Is this the notorious self-destruction? What has happened exactly? They have not tried anything special beyond their power, and yet they wake up as if from a *battle* which has been too much for them, their bodies broken, their muscles strained, their souls dead: "a feeling that I was standing at twilight on a deserted range, with an empty rifle in my hands and the targets down. No problem set—simply a silence with only the sound of my own breathing. . . . My self-immolation was something sodden-dark." In fact, a lot has happened, outside as well as inside: the war, the financial crash, a certain growing older, the depression, illness, the flight of talent. But all these noisy accidents already have their outright effects; and they would not be sufficient in themselves had they not dug their way down to something of a wholly different nature which, on the contrary, they reveal only at a distance and when it is too late—the silent crack. "Why have we lost peace, love, and health one after the other?" There was a silent, imperceptible crack, at the surface, a unique surface Event. It is as if it were suspended or hovering over itself, flying over its own field. The real difference is not between the inside and the outside, for the crack is neither internal nor external, but is rather at the frontier. It is imperceptible, incorporeal, and ideational. With what happens inside and outside, it has complex relations of interference and interfacing, of syncopated junctions—a pattern of corresponding beats over two different rhythms. Everything noisy happens at the edge of the crack and would be nothing without it. Conversely, the crack pursues its silent course, changes direction following the lines of least resistance, and extends its web only under the immediate influence of what happens, until sound and silence wed each other intimately and continuously in the shattering and bursting of the end. What this means is that the entire play of the crack has become incarnated in the depth of the body, at the same time that the labor of the inside and the outside has widened the edges.

("By God, if I ever cracked, I'd try to make the world crack with me. Listen! The world only exists through your apprehension of it, and so it's much better to say that it's not you that's cracked—it's the Grand Canyon." What would we say to a friend who consoled us with these words? This kind of consolation, *à l'americaine,* through projection, doesn't wash for those who know that the crack is no more internal than external, and that its projection to the outside marks no less the end's approach than does the purest introjection. Even if it becomes the crack of the Grand Canyon or of a rock in the Sierra Madre, even if the cosmic images of ravine, mountain, and volcano replace the intimate and familiar porcelain, has anything changed? How can we help but experience an unbearable pity for stones, a petrifying identification? As Malcolm Lowry had a member of another couple say:

But granted it had been split, was there no way, before total disintegration should set in, of at least saving the severed halves? . . . Oh, but why—by some fanciful geologic thaumaturgy, couldn't the pieces be welded together again! She (Yvonne) longed to heal the cleft rock. She was one of the rocks and she yearned to save the other, that both might be saved. By a superlapidary effort, she moved herself nearer it, poured out her pleas, her passionate tears, told all her forgiveness: the rock stood unmoved. "That's all very well," it said, "but it happens to be your fault, and as for myself, I propose to disintegrate as I please!")[2]

Though the association may be close, we have here two elements or two processes which differ in nature. There is the crack which extends its straight, incorporeal, and silent line at the surface; and there are external blows or noisy internal pressures which make it deviate, deepen it, and inscribe or actualize it in the thickness of the body. Are these not the two aspects of death that Blanchot distinguished earlier? Death as event, inseparable from the past and future into which it is divided, never present, an impersonal death, the "ungraspable, that which I can not grasp, for it is not bound to me by any sort of relation, which never comes and toward which I do not go." And then personal death, which occurs and is actualized in the most harsh present whose "extreme horizon (is) the freedom to die and to be able to risk oneself mortally." We could mention various ways in which the association of the two may be brought about: suicide or madness, the use of drugs or alcohol. Perhaps the last two are the most perfect, because, rather than bringing the two lines together in a fatal point, they take time. Nevertheless, there is, in all cases, something illusory. When Blanchot thinks of suicide as the wish to bring about the coincidence of the two faces of death—of prolonging impersonal death by means of the most personal act—he clearly shows the inevitability of this coupling or of this attempt at coupling. But he tries also to define the illusion.[3] In fact, an entire difference of nature subsists between what is joined together or what is narrowly extended.

But this is not where the problem resides. For whom does this difference in nature subsist if not for the abstract thinker? And how could this thinker, with respect to this problem, not be ridiculous? The two processes differ in nature; so be it. But what can be done so that one process does not naturally and necessarily prolong the other? How could the silent trace of the incorporeal crack at the surface fail to "deepen" in the thickness of a noisy body? How could the surface gash fail to become a deep *Spaltung,* and the surface nonsense a nonsense of the depths? If to will is to will the event, how could we not also will its full actualization in a corporeal mixture, subject to this tragic will which presides over all ingestions? If the order of the surface is itself cracked, how could it not itself break up, how is it to be prevented from precipitating destruction, even if this meant losing all accompanying benefits—the organization of language and even life itself? How could we not reach the point at which we can only spell letter by letter and cry out in a sort of schizophrenic depth, but no longer speak at all? If there is a crack at the surface, how can we prevent deep life from becoming a demolition job and prevent it from becoming it as a matter "of course"? Is it possible to maintain the inherence of the incorporeal crack while taking care not to bring it into existence, and not to incarnate it in the depth of the body? More precisely, is it possible to limit ourselves to the counter-actualization of an event—to the actor's or dancer's simple, flat representation—while taking care to prevent the full actualization which characterizes the victim or the true patient? All these questions point out the ridiculousness of the thinker: yes, there are always two aspects, and the two processes differ in nature. But when Bousquet speaks of the wound's eternal truth, it is in the name of a personal and abominable wound which he bears within his body. When Fitzgerald or Lowry speak of this incorporeal metaphysical crack and find in it the locus as well as the obstacle of their thought, its source as well as its drying up, sense and nonsense, they speak with all the gallons of alcohol they have drunk which have actualized the crack in the body. When Artaud speaks of the erosion of thought as something both essential and accidental, a radical impotence and never- theless a great power, it is already from the bottom of schizophrenia. Each one risked something and went as far as possible in taking this risk; each one drew from it an irrepressible right. What is left for the abstract thinker once she has given advice of wisdom and distinction? Well then, are we to speak always about Bousquet's wound, about Fitzgerald's and Lowry's alcoholism, Nietzsche's and Artaud's madness while remaining on the shore? Are we to become the professionals who give talks on these topics? Are we to wish only that those who have been struck down do not abuse themselves too much? Are we to take up collections and create special journal issues? Or should we go a short way further to see for ourselves, be a little alcoholic, a little crazy, a little suicidal, a little of a guerilla—just enough to extend the crack, but not enough to deepen it irremediably? Wherever we turn, everything seems dismal. Indeed, how are we to stay at the surface without staying on the shore? How do we save ourselves by saving the surface and every surface organization, including language and life? How is this *politics,* this full *guerilla warfare* to be attained? (How much we have yet to learn from Stoicism. . . .)

Alcoholism does not seem to be a search for pleasure, but a search for an effect which consists mainly in an extraordinary hardening of the present. One lives in two times, at two moments at once, but not at all in the Proustian manner. The other moment may refer to projects as much as to memories of sober life; it nevertheless exists in an entirely different and profoundly modified way, held fast inside the hardened present which surrounds it like a tender pimple surrounded by indurate flesh. In this soft center of the other moment, the alcoholic may identify himself with the objects of his love, or the objects of his "horror and compassion," whereas the lived and willed hardness of the present moment permits him to hold reality at a distance.[4] The alcoholic does not like this rigidity which overtakes him any less than the softness that it surrounds and conceals. One of the moments is inside the other, and the present is hardened and tetanized, to this extent, only in order to invest this soft point which is ready to burst. The two simultaneous moments are strangely organized: the alcoholic does not live at all in the imperfect or the future; the alcoholic has only a *past perfect (passé composé)*—albeit a very special one. In drunkenness, the alcoholic puts together an imaginary past, as if the softness of the past participle came to be combined with the hardness of the present auxiliary: I have-loved, I have-done, I have-seen. The conjunction of the two moments is expressed here, as much as the manner in which the alcoholic experiences one *in* the other, as one enjoys a manic omnipotence. Here the past perfect does not at all express a distance or a completion. The present moment belongs to the verb *"to have,"* whereas all being is "past" in the other *simultaneous* moment, the moment of participation and of the identification of the participle. But what a strange, almost unbearable tension there is here . . . this embrace, this manner in which the present surrounds, invests, and encloses the other moment. The present has become a circle of crystal or of granite, formed about a soft core, a core of lava, of liquid or viscous glass. This tension, however, is unraveled for the sake of something else. For it behooves the past perfect to become an "I have-drunk" (j'ai-bu). The present moment is no longer that of the alcoholic effect, but that of the effect of the effect. The other moment now indifferently embraces the near past—the moment when I was drinking—the system of imaginary identifications concealed by this near past, and the real element of the more or less distanced sober past. In this way, the induration of the present has changed its meaning entirely. In its hardness, the present has lost its hold and faded. It no longer encloses anything; it rather distances every aspect of the other moment. We could say that the near past, as well as the past of identifications which is constituted in it, and finally the sober past which supplied the material, have all fled with outstretched wings. We could say that all these are equally far off, maintained at a distance in the generalized expansion of this faded present, and in the new rigidity of this new present in an expanding desert. The past perfect of the first effect is replaced by the lone "I have-drunk" of the second, wherein the present auxiliary expresses only the infinite distance of every participle and every participation. The hardening of the present (I have) is now related to an effect of the flight of the past (drunk). Everything culminates in a "has been." This effect of the flight of the past, this loss of the object in every sense and direction, constitutes the depressive aspect of alcoholism. And it is perhaps this effect of flight that yields the greatest force in Fitzgerald's work, and that which expresses it most deeply.

It is curious that Fitzgerald rarely, if ever, presents his characters in the act of drinking or looking for a drink. He does not live alcoholism as a lack or a need. Perhaps this is discretion on his part; or he has always been able to have a drink; or there are several forms of alcoholism, one of them even turned toward its most recent past. (The case of Lowry, though, is the opposite. . . . But, when alcoholism is experienced as such an acute need, a no less profound deformation of time appears. This time, every future is experienced as a *future perfect (futur-antérieur)*, with an extraordinary precipitation of this compound future, an effect of the effect which goes on until death).[5] Alcoholism, for Fitzgerald's characters, is a process of demolition even to the extent that it determines the effect of flight of the past: not only the sober past from which they are separated ("My God, drunk for ten years"), but also the near past in which they have just been drinking, and the fantastic past of the first effect. Everything has become equally remote and determines the necessity of drinking anew, or rather of having drunk anew, in order to triumph over this hardened and faded present which alone subsists and signifies death. It is in this regard that alcoholism is exemplary. For other events, in their own way, can bring about this alcohol-effect: loss of money, for example, love, the loss of our native country, or the loss of success. They do so independently of alcohol and in an external way, but they resemble the way of alcohol. Fitzgerald, for example, experiences money as an "I have been rich," which separates him from the moment at which he was not yet rich, from the moment at which he became rich, and from the identifications with the "true rich" to which he used to apply himself. Take, for instance, Gatsby's great love scene: at the very moment he loves and is loved, Gatsby, in his "stupefying sentimentality," behaves as if intoxicated. He hardens this present with all of his might and wishes to bring it to enclose the most tender identification—namely, that with a past perfect in which we would have been loved absolutely, exclusively, and without rival by the same woman (five years absence like ten years drunkenness). It is at this summit of identification—Fitzgerald said of it that it was equivalent "to the death of all realization"—that Gatsby breaks like a glass, that he loses everything, his recent love, his old love, and his fantastic love. What gives alcoholism an exemplary value, however, among all these events of the same type, is that alcohol is at once love and the loss of love, money and the loss of money, the native land and its loss. It is at once *object, loss of object, and the law governing this loss* within an orchestrated process of demolition ("of course").

The problem of knowing whether we can prevent the crack from being incarnated and actualized in the body in a certain form is obviously not subject to general rules. "Crack" remains a word as long as the body is not compromised by it, as long as the liver and brain, the organs, do not present the lines in accordance with which the future is told, and which themselves foretell the future. If one asks why health does not suffice, why the crack is desirable, it is perhaps because only by means of the crack and at its edges thought occurs, that anything that is good and great in humanity enters and exits through it, in people ready to destroy themselves—better death than the health which we are given. Is there some other health, like a body surviving as long as possible its scar, like Lowry dreaming of rewriting a "Crack Up" which would end happily, and never giving up the idea of a new vital conquest? It is true that the crack is nothing if it does not compromise the body, but it does not cease being and having a value when it intertwines its line with the other line, inside the body. We can not foresee, we must take risks and endure the longest possible time, we must not lose sight of grand health. The eternal truth of the event is grasped only if the event is also inscribed in the flesh. But each time we must double this painful actualization by a counter-actualization which limits, moves, and transfigures it. We must accompany ourselves— first, in order to survive, but then even when we die. Counter-actualization is nothing, it belongs to a buffoon when it operates alone and pretends to have the value of *what could have happened*. But, to be the mime of *what effectively occurs,* to double the actualization with a counter-actualization, the identification with a distance, like the true actor and dancer, is to give to the truth of the event the only chance of not being confused with its inevitable actualization. It is to give to the crack the chance of flying over its own incorporeal surface area, without stopping at the bursting within each body; it is, finally, to give us the chance to go farther than we would have believed possible. To the extent that the pure event is each time imprisoned forever in its actualization, counter-actualization liberates it, always for other times. We can not give up the hope that the effects of drugs and alcohol (their "revelations") will be able to be relived and recovered for their own sake at the surface of the world, independently of the use of those substances, provided that the techniques of social alienation which determine this use are reversed into revolutionary means of exploration. Burroughs wrote some strange pages on this point which attest to this quest for the great Health— our own manner of being pious: "Imagine that everything that can be attained by chemical means is accessible by other paths. . . ." A strafing of the surface in order to transmute the stabbing of bodies, oh psychedelia.

Twenty-Third Series
of the Aion

From the start, we have seen how two readings of time—time as Chronos and time as Aion—were opposed: 1) in accordance with Chronos, only the present exists in time. Past, present, and future are not three dimensions of time; only the present fills time, whereas past and future are two dimensions relative to the present in time. In other words, whatever is future or past in relation to a certain present (a certain extension or duration) belongs to a more vast present which has a greater extension or duration. There is always a more vast present which absorbs the past and the future. Thus, the relativity of past and future with respect to the present entails a relativity of presents themselves, in relation to each other. God experiences as present that which for me is future or past, since I live inside more limited presents. Chronos is an encasement, a coiling up of relative presents, with God as the extreme circle or the external envelope. Inspired by the Stoics, Boethius said that the divine present *complicates* or comprehends the future and the past.[1]

2) Inside Chronos, the present is in some manner corporeal. It is the time of mixtures or blendings, the very process of blending: to temper or to temporalize is to mix. The present measures out the action of bodies and causes. The future and past are rather what is left of passion

in a body. But, as it happens, the passion of a body refers to the action of a more powerful body. The greatest present, the divine present, is the great mixture, the unity of corporeal causes among themselves. It measures the activity of the cosmic period in which everything is simultaneous: Zeus is also Dia, the "Through" (l'A-travers) or that which is mixed, the blender.[2] The greatest present is not therefore unlimited. It pertains to the present to delimit, and to be the limit or measure of the action of bodies, even if we are confronted by the greatest of bodies or the unity of all causes (Cosmos). It can, however, be infinite without being unlimited. For example, it could be circular in the sense that it encompasses every present, begins anew, and measures off a new cosmic period after the preceding one, which may be identical to the preceding one. To the relative movement by means of which each present refers to a relatively more vast present, we must add an absolute movement proper to the most vast of presents. This movement contracts and dilates in depth in order to absorb or restore in the play of cosmic periods the relative presents which it surrounds (to encompass—to set aflame (embrasser-embraser)).

3) Chronos is the regulated movement of vast and profound presents. But from where exactly does it draw its measure? Do the bodies which fill it possess enough unity, do their mixtures possess enough justice and perfection, in order for the present to avail a principle of an immanent measure? Perhaps it does, at the level of the cosmic Zeus. But is this the case for bodies at random and for each partial mixture? Is there not a fundamental disturbance of the present, that is, a ground which overthrows and subverts all measure, a becoming-mad of depths which slips away from the present? Is this measureless something merely local and partial, or does it stretch rather little by little to the entire universe, establishing everywhere its poisonous, monstrous mixture, and the subversion of Zeus and Chronos itself? Is there not already in the Stoics this dual attitude of confidence and mistrust, with respect to the world, corresponding to the two types of mixtures—the white mixture which conserves as it spreads, and the black and confused mixture which alters? In the *Meditations* of Marcus Aurelius, the alternative frequently resounds: is this the good or the bad mixture? This question finds an answer only when the two terms end up being indifferent, that is, when the status of virtue (or of health) has to be sought elsewhere, in another direction, in another element—Aion versus Chronos.[3]

The becoming-mad of depth is then a bad Chronos, opposed to the living present of the good Chronos. Saturn grumbles from deep within Zeus. The pure and measureless becoming of qualities threatens the order of qualified bodies from within. Bodies have lost their measure and are now but simulacra. The past and the future, as unleashed forces, take their revenge, in one and the same abyss which threatens the present and everything that exists. We have seen that Plato, at the end of the second hypothesis of *Parmenides,* expressed this becoming as the power to sidestep the present (for to be present would mean to be and no longer to become). Nevertheless, Plato added that "to sidestep the present" is precisely what becoming cannot do (for it is *now* becoming, and hence cannot leap over this "now"). Both expressions are valid: time has only the present with which to express the internal subversion of the present in time, precisely because it is internal and deep; Chronos must still express the revenge taken by future and past on the present in terms of the present, because these are the only terms it comprehends and the only terms that affect it. This is its own way of wanting to die. Thus, it is still a terrifying, measureless present which sidesteps and subverts the other, the good present. Having been a corporeal mixture, Chronos has become a deep break. In this sense the adventures of the present manifest themselves in Chronos, in agreement with the two aspects of the chronic present—absolute and relative movement, global and partial present: in relation to itself, in depth, insofar as it bursts asunder and contracts (the movement of schizophrenia); and in relation to its more or less vast extension, in virtue of a delirious future and a delirious past (the movement of manic depression). Chronos wants to die, but has it not already given way to another reading of time?

1) In accordance with Aion, only the past and future inhere or subsist in time. Instead of a present which absorbs the past and future, a future and past divide the present at every instant and subdivide it ad infinitum into past and future, in both directions at once. Or rather, it is the instant without thickness and without extension, which subdivides each present into past and future, rather than vast and thick presents which comprehend both future and past in relation to one another. What difference is there between this Aion and the becoming-mad of depths which already overturned Chronos within its own domain? At the outset of this study, we were able to proceed as if both were intimately

prolonged: they were both opposed to the corporeal and measured present; both were capable of sidestepping the present; and both developed the same contradictions (of quality, quantity, relation, and modality). At most, there was between them a shift of orientation: in the case of Aion, the becoming-mad of the depths was climbing to the surface, the simulacra in turn were becoming phantasms, the deep break was showing as a crack in the surface. But we learned that this change of orientation and this conquest of the surface implied radical differences in every respect. This is almost the difference between the second and third hypotheses of *Parmenides*—that of the "now" and that of the "instant." It is no longer the future and past which subvert the existing present; it is the instant which perverts the present into inhering future and past. The essential difference is no longer simply between Chronos and Aion, but between the Aion of surfaces and the whole of Chronos together with the becoming-mad of the depths. Between the two becomings, of surface and depth, we can no longer say that they have in common the sidestepping of the present. For if depth evades the present, it is with all the force of a "now" which opposes *its* panic-stricken present to the wise present of measure; and if the surface evades the present, it is with all the power of an "instant," which distinguishes its occurrence from any assignable present subject to division and redivision. Nothing ascends to the surface without changing its nature. Aion no longer belongs to Zeus or Saturn, but to Hercules. Whereas Chronos expressed the action of bodies and the creation of corporeal qualities, Aion is the locus of incorporeal events, and of attributes which are distinct from qualities. Whereas Chronos was inseparable from the bodies which filled it out entirely as causes and matter, Aion is populated by effects which haunt it without ever filling it up. Whereas Chronos was limited and infinite, Aion is unlimited, the way that future and past are unlimited, and finite like the instant. Whereas Chronos was inseparable from circularity and its accidents—such as blockages or precipitations, explosions, disconnections, and indurations—Aion stretches out in a straight line, limitless in either direction. Always already passed and eternally yet to come, Aion is the eternal truth of time: *pure empty form of time,* which has freed itself of its present corporeal content and has thereby unwound its own circle, stretching itself out in a straight line. It is perhaps all the more dangerous, more labyrinthine, and more tortuous for this reason. It is this other movement, of which Marcus Aurelius spoke, which occurs neither up above nor down below, nor in a circular fashion, but only at the surface—the movement of "virtue" . . . If there is also a death wish *(vouloir-mourir)* on the side of the Aion, it would be totally different.

2) It is this new world of incorporeal effects or surface effects which makes language possible. For, as we shall see, it is this world which draws the sounds from their simple state of corporeal actions and passions. It is this new world which distinguishes language, prevents it from being confused with the sound-effects of bodies, and abstracts it from their oral-anal determinations. Pure events ground language because they wait for it as much as they wait for us, and have a pure, singular, impersonal, and pre-individual existence only inside the language which expresses them. It is what is expressed in its independence that grounds language and expression—that is, the metaphysical property that sounds acquire in order to have a sense, and secondarily, to signify, manifest, and denote, rather than to belong to bodies as physical qualities. The most general operation of sense is this: it brings that which expresses it into existence; and from that point on, as pure inherence, it brings itself to exist within that which expresses it. It rests therefore with the Aion, as the milieu of surface effects or events, to trace a frontier between things and propositions; and the Aion traces it with its entire straight line. Without it, sounds would fall back on bodies, and propositions themselves would not be "possible." Language is rendered possible by the frontier which separates it from things and from bodies (including those which speak). We can thus take up again the account of the surface organization as it is determined by the Aion.

First, the entire line of the Aion is run through by the Instant which is endlessly displaced on this line and is always missing from its own place. Plato rightly said that the instant is *atopon,* without place. It is the paradoxical instance or the aleatory point, the nonsense of the surface and the quasi-cause. It is the pure moment of abstraction whose role is, primarily, to divide and subdivide every present in both directions at once, into past-future, upon the line of the Aion. Second, the instant extracts singularities from the present, and from individuals and persons which occupy this present. It extracts singular points twice projected—once into the future and once into the past—forming by this double equation the constitutive elements of the pure event (in the manner of a pod which releases its spores). Third, the straight line which extends simultaneously in two directions traces the frontier between bodies and language, states of affairs and propositions. Language, or the system of propositions, would not exist without this frontier which renders it possible. Language therefore is endlessly born, in the future direction of the Aion where it is established and, somehow, anticipated; and although it must also say the past, it says it as the past of states of affairs which go on appearing and disappearing in the other direction. In short, the straight line is now related to its two environs; and while it separates them, it also articulates the one and the other as two series which are capable of being developed. It brings to them both the instantaneous aleatory point which traverses it and the singular points which are distributed in it. There are two faces therefore which are always unequal and in disequilibrium: one turned toward states of affairs and the other toward propositions. But they are not allowed to be reduced to states of affairs or to propositions. The vent is brought to bear upon states of affairs, but only as the logical attribute of these states. It is entirely different from their physical qualities, despite the fact that it may happen to them, be embodied or actualized in them. Sense and event are the same thing—except that now sense is related to propositions. It is related to propositions as what is expressible or expressed by them, which is entirely different from what they signify, manifest, or denote. It is also entirely different from their sonorous qualities, even though the independence of sonorous qualities from things and bodies may be exclusively guaranteed by the entire organization of the sense-event. The entire organization, in its three abstract moments, runs from the point to the straight line, and from the straight line to the surface: the point which traces the line; the line which forms the frontier; and the surface which is developed and unfolded from both sides.

3) Many movements, with a fragile and delicate mechanism, intersect: that by means of which bodies, states of affairs, and mixtures, considered in their depth, succeed or fail in the production of ideal surfaces; and conversely, that by means of which the events of the surface are actualized in the present of bodies (in accordance with complex rules) by imprisoning first their singularities within the limits of worlds, individuals, and persons. There is also the movement wherein the event implies something excessive in relation to its actualization, something

that overthrows worlds, individuals, and persons, and leaves them to the depth of the ground which works and dissolves them. The notion of the present has therefore several meanings: the measureless or dislocated present as the time of depth and subversion; the variable and measured present as the time of actualization. But there is perhaps yet another present. How could there be a measurable actualization, unless a third present prevented it constantly from falling into subversion and being confused with it? It would seem, no doubt, that the Aion cannot have any present at all, since in it the instant is always dividing into future and past. But this is only an appearance. What is excessive in the event must be accomplished, even though it may not be realized or actualized without ruin. Between the two presents of Chronos—that of the subversion due to the bottom and that of the actualization in forms—there is a third, there must be a third, pertaining to the Aion. In fact, the instant as the paradoxical element or the quasi-cause which runs through the entire straight line must itself be represented. It is even in this sense that representation can envelop an expression on its edges, although the expression itself may be of another nature; and that the sage can "identify" with the quasi-cause, although the quasi-cause itself is missing from its own identity. This present of the Aion representing the instant is not at all like the vast and deep present of Chronos: it is the present without thickness, the present of the actor, dancer, or mime—the pure perverse "moment." It is the present of the pure operation, not of the incorporation. It is not the present of subversion or actualization, but that of the counter-actualization, which keeps the former from overturning the latter, and the latter from being confused with the former, and which comes to duplicate the lining (redoubler la doublure).

Twenty-Fourth Series of the
Communication of Events

One of the boldest moments of the Stoic thought involves the splitting of the causal relation. Causes are referred in depth to a unity which is proper to them, and effects maintain at the surface specific relations of another sort. Destiny is primarily the unity and the link of physical causes among themselves. Incorporeal effects are obviously subject to destiny, to the extent that they are the effect of these causes. But to the extent that they differ in nature from these causes, they enter, with one another, into relations of quasi-causality. Together, they enter into a relation with a quasi-cause which is itself incorporeal and assures them a very special independence, not exactly with respect to destiny, but rather with respect to necessity, which normally would have had to follow destiny. The Stoic paradox is to affirm destiny and to deny necessity.[1] The wise person is free in two ways which conform to the two poles of ethics: free in the first instance because one's soul can attain to the interiority of perfect physical causes; and again because one's mind may enjoy very special relations established between effects in a situation of pure exteriority. It would then seem that incorporeal causes are inseparable from a form of interiority, but that incorporeal effects are inseparable from a form of exteriority. On one hand, events-effects maintain a relation of causality with their physical causes, without this relation being one of necessity; it is rather a relation of expression. On the other hand, they have between them, or with their ideational quasi-cause, no longer a relation of causality, but rather, once again and this time exclusively, a relation of expression.

The question becomes: what are these expressive relations of events? Between events, there seem to be formed extrinsic relations of silent compatibility or incompatibility, of conjunction or disjunction, which are very difficult to apprehend. What makes an event compatible or incompatible with another? We cannot appeal to causality, since it is a question of a relation of effects among themselves. What brings destiny about at the level of events, what brings an event to repeat another in spite of all its difference, what makes it possible that a life is composed of one and the same Event, despite the variety of what might happen, that it be traversed by a single and same fissure, that it play one and the same air over all possible tunes and all possible words—all these are not due to relations between cause and effect; it is rather an aggregate of noncausal correspondences which form a system of echoes, of resumptions and resonances, a system of signs—in short, an expressive quasi-causality, and not at all a necessitating causality. When Chrysippus insists on the transformation of hypothetical propositions into conjunctives or disjunctives, he shows well the impossibility of events expressing their conjunctions and disjunctions in terms of brute causality.[2]

Is it necessary, then, to invoke identity and contradiction? Would two events be incompatible because they were contradictory? Is this not a case, though, of applying rules to events, which apply only to concepts, predicates, and classes? Even with respect to hypothetical propositions (if it is day, it is light), the Stoics noted that contradiction must be defined on a single level. Rather, contradiction must be defined in the space between the principle itself and the negation of the consequence (if it is day, it is not light). This difference of levels in the contradiction, we have seen, assures that contradiction results always from a process of a different nature. Events are not like concepts; it is their alleged contradiction (manifest in the concept) which results from their incompatibility, and not the converse. It is held, for example, that a species of butterfly cannot be at once gray and vigorous. Either the specimens are gray and weak, or they are vigorous and black.[3] We can always assign a causal physical mechanism to explain this incompatibility, a hormone, for example, on which the predicate gray would depend, and which would soften or weaken the corresponding class. And we can conclude from this causal condition that there is a logical contradiction between gray and vigorous. But if we isolate the pure events, we see that *to turn gray* is no less positive than *to turn black:* it expresses an increase in security (to be hidden, to be taken for the bark of a tree), as much as the becoming black is an increase of vigor (to invigorate). Between these two determinations, each one of which has its advantage, there is initially a relation of primary, "eventmental" incompatibility. Physical causality inscribes the incompatibility only secondarily in the depth of the body, and the logical contradiction translates it only in the content of the concept. In short, the relations of events among themselves, from the point of view of an ideational or noematic quasi-causality, first expresses noncausal correspondence— alogical compatibilities or incompatibilities. The Stoics' strength was in committing themselves to this line of thought: according to what criteria are events *copulata, confatalia* (or *inconfatalia), conjuncta,* or *disjuncta?* Astrology was perhaps the first important attempt to establish a theory of alogical incompatibilities and noncausal correspondences.

It seems, however, if we follow the surviving partial and deceiving texts, that the Stoics may not have been able to resist the double temptation of returning to the simple physical causality or to the logical contradiction. The first theoretician of alogical incompatibilities, and for this reason the first important theoretician of the event, was Leibniz. For what Leibniz called "compossible" and "incompossible" cannot be reduced to the identical and the contradictory, which govern only the possible and the impossible. Compossibility does not even presuppose the inherence of predicates in an individual subject or monad. It is rather the inverse; inherent predicates are those which correspond to events from the beginning compossible (the monad of Adam the sinner includes in predicative form only future and past events which are compossible with the sin of Adam). Leibniz was thus extremely conscious of the anteriority and originality of the event in relation to the predicate. Compossibility must be defined in an original manner, at a pre-individual level, by the convergence of series which singularities of events form as they stretch themselves out over lines of ordinary points. Incompossibility must be defined by the divergence of such series: if another Sextus than the one we know is incompossible with our world, it is because he would correspond to a singularity the series of which would diverge from the series of our world, clustered about the Adam, the Judas, the Christ, and the Leibniz that we know. Two events are compossible when the series which are organized around their singularities extend in all directions; they are incompossible when the series diverge in the vicinity of constitutive singularities. Convergence and divergence are entirely original relations which cover the rich domain of alogical compatibilities and incompatibilities, and therefore form an essential component of the theory of sense.

Leibniz though makes use of this rule of incompossibility in order to exclude events from one another. He made a negative use of divergence of disjunction—one of exclusion. This is justified, however, only to the extent that events are already grasped under the hypothesis of a God who calculates and chooses, and from the point of view of their actualization in distinct worlds or individuals. It is no longer justified, however, if we consider the pure events and the ideal play whose principle Leibniz was unable to grasp, hindered as he was by theological exigencies. For, from this other point of view, the divergence of series or the disjunction of members (membra disjuncta) cease to be negative rules of exclusion according to which events would be incompossible or incompatible. Divergence and disjunction are, on the contrary, affirmed as such. But what does it mean to make divergence and disjunction the objects of affirmation? As a general rule, two things are simultaneously affirmed only to the extent that their difference is denied, suppressed from within, even if the level of this suppression is supposed to regulate the production of difference as much as its disappearance. To be sure, the identity here is not that of indifference, but it is generally *through identity* that opposites are affirmed at the same time, whether we accentuate one of the opposites in order to find the other, or whether we create a synthesis of the two. We speak, on the contrary, of an operation according to which two things or two determinations are affirmed *through* their difference, that is to say, that they are the objects of simultaneous affirmation only insofar as their difference is itself affirmed and is itself affirmative. We are no longer faced with an identity of contraries, which would still be inseparable as such from a movement of the negative and of exclusion.[4] We are rather faced with a positive distance of different elements: no longer to identify two contraries with the same, but to affirm their distance as that which relates one to the other insofar as they are "different." The idea of a positive distance as distance (and not as an annulled or overcome distance) appears to us essential, since it permits the measuring of contraries through their finite difference instead of equating difference with a measureless contrariety, and contrariety with an identity which is itself infinite. It is not difference which must "go as far as" contradiction, as Hegel thought in his desire to accommodate the negative; it is the contradiction which must reveal the nature of *its* difference as it follows the distance corresponding to it. The idea of positive distance belongs to topology and to the surface. It excludes all depth and all elevation, which would restore the negative and the identity. Nietzsche provides the example for such a procedure, which must not, under any circumstances, be confused with some unknown identity of contraries (as is commonplace in spiritualist and dolorist philosophy). Nietzsche exhorts us to live health and sickness in such a manner that health be a living perspective on sickness and sickness a living perspective on health; to make of sickness an exploration of health, of health an investigation of sickness: "Looking from the perspective of the sick toward *healthier* concepts and values and, conversely, looking again from the fullness and self-assurance of a *rich* life down into the secret work of the instinct of decadence—in this I have had the longest training, my truest experiences; if in anything, I became master in *this*. Now I know how, have the know-how, to *reverse perspectives*. . . ."[5] We cannot identify contraries, nor can we affirm their entire distance, except as that which relates one to the other. Health affirms sickness when it makes its distance from sickness an object of affirmation. Distance is, at arm's length, the affirmation of that which it distances. This procedure which makes of health an evaluation of sickness and sickness an evaluation of health—is this not the Great Health (or the Gay Science)? Is it not this which permits Nietzsche to experience a superior health at the very moment that he is sick? Conversely, Nietzsche does not lose his health when he is sick, but when he can no longer affirm the distance, when he is no longer able, by means of his health, to establish sickness as a point of view on health (then, as the Stoics say, the role is over, the play has ended). "Point of view" does not signify a theoretical judgment; as for "procedure," it is life itself. From Leibniz, we had already learned that there are no points of view on things, but that things, beings, are themselves points of view. Leibniz, however, subjected the points of view to exclusive rules such that each opened itself onto the others only insofar as they converged: the points of view on the same town. With Nietzsche, on the contrary, the point of view is opened onto a divergence which it affirms: another town corresponds to each point of view, each point of view is another town, the towns are linked only by their distance and resonate only through the divergence of their series, their houses and their streets. There is always another town within the town. Each term becomes the means of going all the way to the end of another, by following the entire distance. Nietzsche's per-spective—his perspectivism—is a much more profound art than Leibniz's point of view; for divergence is no longer a principle of exclusion, and disjunction no longer a means of separation. Incompossibility is now a means of communication.

It is not that the disjunction has become a simple conjunction. Three sorts of synthesis are distinguished: the connective synthesis (if . . . , then), which bears upon the construction of a single series; the conjunc-tive series (and), as a method of constructing convergent series; and the disjunctive series (or), which distributes the divergent series: *conexa, conjuncta, disjuncta*. But the whole question, and rightly so, is to know under what conditions the disjunction is a veritable synthesis, instead of being a procedure of analysis which is satisfied with the exclusion of predicates from one thing in virtue of the identity of its concept (the negative, limitative, or exclusive use of disjunction). The answer is given insofar as the divergence or the decentering determined by the disjunc-tion become objects of affirmation as such. The disjunction is not at all reduced to a conjunction; it is left as a disjunction, since it bears, and continues to bear, upon a divergence as such. But this divergence is affirmed in such a way that the *either* . . . *or* itself becomes a pure affirmation. Instead of a certain number of predicates being excluded from a thing in virtue of the identity of its concept, each "thing" opens itself up to the infinity of predicates through which it passes, as it loses its center, that is, its identity as concept or as self.[6] The communication of events replaces the exclusion of predicates. We have already seen the procedure of this affirmative synthetic disjunction: it consists of the erection of a paradoxical instance, an aleatory point with two uneven faces, which traverses the divergent series as divergent and causes them to resonate through their distance and in their distance. Thus, the ideational center of convergence is by nature perpetually decentered, it serves only to affirm divergence. This is why it seemed that an esoteric, ex-centric path was opened to us, a path altogether different from the ordinary one. For ordinarily the disjunction is not properly speaking a synthesis, but only a regulative analysis at the service of conjunctive syntheses, since it separates the nonconvergent series from one another. As for the conjunctive synthesis, it tends also toward being subordinated to the synthesis of connection, since it organizes the converging series over which it bears as it prolongs them under a condition of continuity. Now, the whole sense of *esoteric words* was to turn this path around: a disjunction which had become a synthesis introduced its *ramifications* everywhere, so that the conjunction was already *coordinating* in a global way divergent, heterogeneous, and disparate series, and that, affecting the details, the connection already *contracted* a multitude of divergent series in the successive appearance of a single one.

This is a new reason for distinguishing the becoming of depths and the Aion of surfaces. For both, at first glance, seemed to dissolve the identity of each thing within infinite identity as the identity of contraries. And from all points of view, whether of quantity, quality, relation, or modality, contraries appeared connected at the surface as much as in depth and to have the same sense no less than the same infra-sense. But, once again, everything changes nature as it climbs to the surface. And it is necessary to distinguish two ways whose personal identity is lost, two ways by means of which the contradiction is developed. In depth, it is through infinite identity that contraries communicate and that the identity of each finds itself broken and divided. This makes each term at once the moment and the whole; the part, the relation, and the whole; the self, the world, and God; the subject, the copula, and the predicate. But the situation is altogether different at the surface where only infinitive events are deployed; each one communicates with the other through the positive characters of its distance and by the affirmative character of the disjunction. The self merges with the very disjunction which it liberates and places outside of itself the divergent series as so many impersonal and pre-individual singularities. Counter-actualization is already infinitive distance instead of infinite identity. Everything happens through the resonance of disparates, point of view on a point of view, displacement of perspective, differentiation of difference, and not through the identity of contraries. It is true that the form of the self ordinarily guarantees the connection of a series; that the form of the world guarantees the convergence of continuous series which can be extended; and that the form of God, as Kant had clearly seen, guarantees disjunction in its exclusive or limitative sense. But when disjunction accedes to the principle which gives to it a synthetic and affirmative value, the self, the world, and God share in a common death, to the advantage of divergent series as such, overflowing now every exclusion, every conjunction, and every connection. It is Klossowski's merit to have shown how the three forms had their fortunes linked, not by a dialectical transformation and the identity of contraries, but by a common dissipation at the surface of things. If the self is the principle of manifestation, in relation to the proposition, the world is the principle of denotation, and God the principle of signification. But sense expressed as an event is of an entirely different nature: it emanates from nonsense as from the always displaced paradoxical instance and from the eternally decentered ex-centric center. It is a pure sign whose coherence excludes merely, and yet supremely, the coherence of the self, world, and God.[7] This quasi-cause, this surface nonsense which traverses the divergent as such, this aleatory point which circulates throughout singularities, and emits them as pre-individual and impersonal, does not allow God to subsist. It does not tolerate the subsistence of God as an original individuality, nor the self as a Person, nor the world as an element of the self and as God's product. The divergence of the affirmed series forms a "chaosmos" and no longer a world; the aleatory point which traverses them forms a counter-self, and no longer a self; the disjunction posed as a synthesis exchanges its theological principle for a diabolic principle. It is the decentered center which traces between the series, and for all disjunctions, the merciless straight line of the Aion, that is, the distance whereupon the castoffs of the self, the world, and God are lined up: the Grand Canyon of the world, the "crack" of the self, and the dismembering of God. Upon this straight line of the Aion, there is also an eternal return, as the most terrible labyrinth of which Borges spoke—one very different from the circular or monocentered return of Chronos: an eternal return which is no longer that of individuals, persons, and worlds, but only of pure events which the instant, displaced over the line, goes on dividing into already past and yet to come. Nothing other than the Event subsists, the Event alone, *Eventum tantum* for all contraries, which communicates with itself through its own distance and resonates across all of its disjuncts.

Twenty-Fifth Series
of Univocity

It seems that our problem, in the course of our investigation, has changed altogether. We were inquiring into the nature of the alogical compatibilities and incompatibilities between events. But, to the extent that divergence is affirmed and disjunction becomes a positive synthesis, it seems that all events, even contraries, are compatible—that they are "inter-expressive" (s'entr' expriment). Incompatibility is born only with individuals, persons, and worlds in which events are actualized, but not between events themselves or between their *a-cosmic, impersonal,* and *pre-individual* singularities. Incompatibility does not exist between two events, but between an event and the world or the individual which actualizes another event as divergent. At this point, there is something which does not allow itself to be reduced to a logical contradiction between predicates and which is nevertheless an incompatibility; but it is an alogical incompatibility, an incompatibility of "humor" to which Leibniz's original criteria must be applied. The person, such as we have defined it in its difference from the individual, pretends to amuse itself ironically with these incompatibilities, precisely because they are alogical. In another manner, we have seen how portmanteau words express, from the point of view of the lexicon, wholly compatible meanings, ramifiable and resonating between themselves, which nonetheless become incompatible with certain syntactical forms.

The problem is therefore one of knowing how the individual would be able to transcend his form and his syntactical link with a world, in order to attain to the universal communication of events, that is, to the affirmation of a disjunctive synthesis beyond logical contradictions, and even beyond alogical incompatibilities. It would be necessary for the individual to grasp herself as event; and that she grasp the event actualized within her as another individual grafted onto her. In this case, she would not understand, want, or represent this event without also understanding and wanting all other events as individuals, and without representing all other individuals as events. Each individual would be like a mirror for the condensation of singularities and each world a distance in the mirror. This is the ultimate sense of counter-actualization. This, moreover, is the Nietzschean discovery of the individual as the *fortuitous case,* as Klossowski takes it up and restores it, in an essential relation to the eternal return. Witness

the vehement oscillations which upset the individual as long as he seeks only his own center and does not see the circle of which he himself is a part; for if these oscillations upset him, it is because each corresponds to an individuality *other* than that which he takes as his own from the point of view of the undiscoverable center. Hence, an identity is essentially fortuitous and a series of individualities must be traversed by each, in order that the fortuity make them completely necessary."[1]

We do not raise contrary qualities to infinity in order to affirm their identity; we raise each event to the power of the eternal return in order that the individual, born of that which comes to pass, affirm her distance with respect to every other event. As the individual affirms the distance, she follows and joins it, passing through all the other individuals implied by the other events, and extracts from it a unique Event which is once again herself, or rather the universal freedom. The eternal return is not a theory of qualities and their circular transformations, but rather the theory of pure events and their linear and superficial condensation. The eternal return has a sense of selection and remains tied to an incompatibility—with the forms which hinder its constitution and its functioning.

Counter-actualizing each event, the actor-dancer extracts the pure event which communicates with all the others and returns to itself through all the others, and with all the others. She makes of the disjunction a synthesis which affirms the disjunct as such and makes each series resonate inside the other. Each series returns to itself as the other series returns to it, and returns outside of itself as the other series returns into itself: to explore all distances, but over a single line; to run very fast in order to remain in the same place. The gray butterfly understands so well the event "*to be hidden*" that, by remaining in the same place, plastered to the trunk of a tree, it covers the whole distance separating it from the "*to invigorate*" of the black butterfly; it also causes the other event to resonate as individual, within its own individuality as an event, and as a fortuitous case. My love is an exploration of distance, a long journey which affirms my hate for the friend in another world and with another individual. It causes the bifurcating and ramified series to resonate within one another. But this is the solution of humor, quite different from the romantic irony of the person still founded upon the identity of contraries.

You come to this house; but in other possible pasts you are my enemy; in others my friend. . . . Time is forever dividing itself toward innumerable futures and in one of them I am your enemy. . . . The future exists now . . . but I am your friend. . . . For a moment his back was again turned to me. I had the revolver ready. I fired with the utmost care.[2]

Philosophy merges with ontology, but ontology merges with the univocity of Being (analogy has always been a theological vision, not a philosophical one, adapted to the forms of God, the world, and the self). The univocity of Being does not mean that there is one and the same Being; on the contrary, beings are multiple and different, they are always produced by a disjunctive synthesis, and they themselves are disjointed and divergent, *membra disjuncta*. The univocity of Being signifies that Being is Voice that it is said, and that it is said in one and the same "sense" of everything about which it is said. That of which it is said is not at all the same, but Being is the same for everything about which it is said. It occurs, therefore, as a unique event for everything that happens to the most diverse things, *Eventum tantum* for all events, the ultimate form for all of the forms which remain disjointed in it, but which bring about the resonance and the ramification of their disjunction. The univocity of Being merges with the positive use of the disjunctive synthesis which is the highest affirmation. It is the eternal return itself, or—as we have seen in the case of the ideal game—the affirmation of all chance in a single moment, the unique cast for all throws, one Being and only for all forms and all times, a single instance for all that exists, a single phantom for all the living, a single voice for every hum of voices and every drop of water in the sea. It would be a mistake to confuse the univocity of Being to the extent that it is said with the pseudo-univocity of everything about which it is said. But at the same time, if Being cannot be said without also occurring, if Being is the unique event in which all events communicate with one another, univocity refers both to what occurs and to what is said. Univocity means that it is the same thing which occurs and is said: the attributable to all bodies or states of affairs and the expressible of every proposition. Univocity means the identity of the noematic attribute and that which is expressed linguistically—event and sense. It does not allow Being to subsist in the vague state that it used to have in the perspectives of the analogy. Univocity raises and extracts Being, in order to distinguish it better from that in which it occurs and from that of which it is said. It wrests Being from beings in order to bring it to all of them at once, and to make it fall upon them for all times. Being pure saying and pure event, univocity brings in contact the inner surface of language (insistence) with the outer surface of Being (extra-Being). Univocal Being inheres in language and happens to things; it measures the internal relation of language with the external relation of Being. Neither active nor passive, univocal Being is neutral. It is *extra-Being,* that is, the minimum of Being common to the real, the possible, and the impossible. A position in the void of all events in one, an expression in the nonsense of all senses in one, univocal Being is the pure form of the Aion, the form of exteriority which relates things and propositions.[3] In short, the univocity of Being has three determinations: one single event for all events; one and the same *aliquid* for that which happens and that which is said; and one and the same Being for the impossible, the possible, and the real.

Twenty-Sixth Series
of Language

Events make language possible. But making possible does not mean causing to begin. We always begin in the order of speech, but not in the order of language, in which everything must be given simultaneously and in a single blow. There is always someone who begins to speak. The one who begins to speak is the one who manifests; what one talks about is the denotatum; what one says are the significations. The event is not any of these things: it speaks no more than it is spoken of or said. Nevertheless, the event does belong to language, and haunts it so much that it does not exist outside of the propositions which express it. But the event is not the same as the proposition; what is expressed is not the same as the expression. It does not preexist it, but pre-inheres in it, thus giving it a foundation and a condition. To render language possible thus signifies assuring that sounds are not confused with the sonorous qualities of things, with the sound effects of bodies, or with their actions and passions. What renders language possible is that which separates sounds from bodies and organizes them into propositions, freeing them for the expressive function. It is always a mouth which speaks; but the sound is no longer the noise of a body which eats—a pure orality—in order to become the manifestation of a subject expressing itself. One speaks always of bodies and their mixtures, but sounds have ceased being qualities attached to these bodies in order that they may enter into a new relation with them, that of denotation, and that they may express this power of speaking and of being spoken. Denotation and manifestation do not found language, they are only made possible with it. They presuppose the expression. The expression is founded on the event, as an entity of the expressible or the expressed. What renders language possible is the event insofar as the event is confused neither with the proposition which expresses it, nor with the state of the one who pronounces it, nor with the state of affairs denoted by the proposition. And in truth, without the event all of this would be only noise—and an indistinct noise. For not only does the event make possible and separate that which it renders possible, it also makes distinctions within what it renders possible (see, for example, the triple distinction in the proposition of denotation, manifestation, and signification).

How does the event make language possible? We have seen that its essence is that of the pure surface effect, or the impassible incorporeal entity. The event results from bodies, their mixtures, their actions, and their passions. But it differs in nature from that of which it is the result. It is, for example, attributed to bodies, to states of affairs, but not at all as a physical quality; rather, it is ascribed to them only as a very special *attribute,* dialectical or, rather, noematic and incorporeal. This attribute does not exist outside of the proposition which expresses it. But it differs in nature from its expression. It exists in the proposition, but not at all as a name of bodies or qualities, and not at all as a subject or predicate. It exists rather only as that which is expressible or expressed by the proposition, enveloped in a *verb.* The event occurring in a state of affairs and the sense inhering in the proposition are the same entity. Consequently, to the extent that the incorporeal event is constituted and constitutes the surface, it raises to this surface the terms of its double reference: the bodies to which it refers as a noematic attribute, and the propositions to which it refers as an expressible entity. It organizes these terms as two series which it separates, since it is by and in this separation that it distinguishes itself from the bodies from which it ensues and from the propositions it renders possible. This separation, this line-frontier between things and propositions (to eat/to speak), enters as well into the "made possible," that is, into the propositions themselves, between nouns and verbs, or, rather, between denotations and expressions. Denotations refer always to bodies and, in principle, to consumable objects; expressions refer to expressible meanings. But this line-frontier would not enact the separation of series at the surface it if did not finally articulate that which it separates. It operates on both sides by means of one and the same incorporeal power, which, on one hand, is defined as that which occurs in a state of affairs and, on the other, as that which insists in propositions. (This is why language has only one power, though it may have several dimensions.)

The line-frontier brings about the convergence of divergent series; but it neither abolishes nor corrects their divergence. For it makes them converge not in themselves (which would be impossible) but around a paradoxical element, a point traversing the line and circulating through-out the series. This is an always displaced center which constitutes a circle of convergence only for that which diverges as such (the power of affirming the disjunction). This element or point is the quasi-cause to which the surface effects are attached, precisely insofar as they differ in nature from their corporeal causes. It is this point which is expressed in language by means of esoteric words of different kinds, guaranteeing the separation, the coordination, and the ramifications of series at once. Thus the entire organization of language presents three figures: the metaphysical or transcendental *surface,* the incorporeal abstract *line,* and the decentered *point.* These figures correspond to surface effects or events; at the surface, the line of sense immanent to the event; and on the line, the point of nonsense, surface nonsense, being co-present with sense.

The two great ancient systems, Epicureanism and Stoicism, at-tempted to locate in things that which renders language possible. But they did so in very different ways. For in order to found not only freedom but also language and its use, the Epicureans created a model based on the *declension* of the atom; the Stoics, on the contrary, created a model based on the *conjugation* of events. It is not surprising therefore that the Epicurean model privileges nouns and adjectives; nouns are like atoms or linguistic bodies which are coordinated through their declen-sion, and adjectives like the qualities of these composites. But the Stoic model comprehends language on the basis of "prouder" terms: verbs and their conjugation, in relation to the links between incorporeal events. The question of knowing whether nouns or verbs are primary in language cannot be resolved according to the general maxim "in the beginning, there is the action," however much one makes of the verb the representative of primary action and of the root the primary state of the verb. For it is not true that the verb represents an action; it expresses an event, which is totally different. Moreover, language is not developed from primary roots; it is organized around formative elements which determine it in its entirety. But if language is not formed progressively following the succession of an external time, we should not believe, for this reason, that its totality is homogeneous. It is true that "phonemes" guarantee every linguistic distinction possible within "morphemes" and "semantemes"; but conversely, the signifying and morphological units determine, in the phonematic distinctions, those which are pertinent in a language under examination. The whole cannot be described by a simple movement, but by a two-way movement of linguistic action and reaction which represents the circle of the proposition.[1] And if phonic action forms an open space for language, semantic reaction forms an internal time without which this space could not be determined in conformity with a specific language. Independently, therefore, of elements and only from the point of view of movement, nouns and their declension incarnate action, whereas verbs and their conjugation incarnate reaction. The verb is not an image of external action, but a process of reaction internal to language. This is why, in its most general notion, it envelops the internal temporality of language. It is the verb which constitutes the ring of the proposition, bringing signification to bear upon denotation and the semanteme upon the phoneme. But it is from the verb as well that we infer what the ring conceals or coils up, or what it reveals once it is split, unrolled, and deployed over a straight line: sense or the event as the expressed of the proposition.

The verb has two poles: the present, which indicates its relation to a denotable state of affairs in view of a physical time characterized by succession; and the infinitive, which indicates its relation to sense or the event in view of the internal time which it envelops. The entire verb oscillates between the infinitive "mood," which represents the circle once unwound from the entire proposition, and the present "time," which, on the contrary, closes the circle over the denotatum of the proposition. Between the two, the verb curves its conjugation in conformity with the relations of denotation, manifestation, and signification — the aggregate of times, persons, and modes. The pure infinitive is the Aion, the straight line, the empty form, and the distance; it permits no distinction of moments, but goes on being divided formally in the double and simultaneous direction of the past and the future. The infinitive does not implicate a time internal to language without expressing the sense or the event, that is to say, the set of problems raised by language. It connects the interiority of language to the exteriority of being. It inherits therefore the communication of events among themselves. As for univocity, it is transmitted from Being to language, from the exteriority of Being to the interiority of language. Equivocity is always the equivocity of nouns. The Verb is the univocity of language, in the form of an undetermined infinitive, without person, without present, without any diversity of voice. It is poetry itself. As it expresses in language all events in one, the infinitive verb expresses the event of language—language being a unique event which merges now with that which renders it possible.

Twenty-Seventh Series
of Orality

Language is rendered possible by that which distinguishes it. What separates sounds from bodies makes sounds into the elements of a language. What separates speaking from eating renders speech possible; what separates propositions from things renders propositions possible. The surface and that which takes place at the surface is what "renders possible"—in other words, the event as that which is expressed. The expressed makes possible the expression. But in this case, we find ourselves confronted with a final task: to retrace the history which liberates sounds and makes them independent of bodies. It is no longer a question of a static genesis which would lead from the presupposed event to its actualization in states of affairs and to its expression in propositions. It is a question of a dynamic genesis which leads directly from states of affairs to events, from mixtures to pure lines, *from depth to the production of surfaces,* which must not implicate at all the other genesis. For, from the point of view of the other genesis, we posit eating and speaking by right as two series already separated at the surface. They are separated and articulated by the event which is the result of one of them, to which it relates as a noematic attribute, and renders the other series possible, to which it relates as an expressible sense. But it is an entirely different question how speaking is effectively disengaged from eating, how the surface itself is produced, or how the incorporeal event results from bodily states. When we say that the sound becomes independent, we mean to say that it ceases to be a specific quality attached to bodies, a noise or a cry, and that it begins to designate qualities, manifest bodies, and signify subjects or predicates. As it happens, sound takes on a conventional value inside denotation, a customary value in manifestation, and an artificial value in signification, only because it establishes its independence at the surface from the higher authority of expressivity. The depth-surface distinction is, in every respect, primary in relation to the distinctions nature-convention, nature-custom, or nature-artifice.

Now, the history of depths begins with what is most terrifying: it begins with the theater of terror whose unforgettable picture Melanie Klein painted. In it, the nursing infant is, beginning with his or her first year, stage, actor, and drama at once. Orality, mouth, and breast are initially bottomless depths. Not only are the breast and the entire body of the mother split apart into a good and a bad object, but they are aggressively emptied, slashed to pieces, broken into crumbs and alimentary morsels. The introjection of these partial objects into the body of the infant is accompanied by a projection of aggressiveness onto these internal objects, and by a re-projection of these objects into the maternal body. Thus, introjected morsels are like poisonous, persecuting, explosive, and toxic substances threatening the child's body from within and being endlessly reconstituted inside the mother's body. The necessity of a perpetual re-introjection is the result of this. The entire system of introjection and projection is a communication of bodies in, and through, depth. Orality is naturally prolonged in cannibalism and anality in the case of which partial objects are excreta, capable of exploding the mother's body, as well as the body of the infant. The bits of one are always the persecutors of the other, and, in this abominable mixture which constitutes the Passion of the nursing infant, persecutor and persecuted are always the same. In this system of mouth-anus or aliment-exrement, bodies burst and cause other bodies to burst *in* a universal cesspool.[1] We call this world of introjected and projected, alimentary and excremental partial internal objects the world of *simulacra*. Melanie Klein describes it as the paranoid-schizoid position of the child. It is succeeded by a depressive position which characterizes a dual progress, since the child strives to reconstitute a complete *good* object and to identify himself with this object. The child strives thus to achieve a corresponding identity, even if in this new drama he has to share the threats, sufferings, and all the passions undergone by the good object. Depressive "identification," with its confirmation of the super-ego and formation of the ego, replaces paranoid and schizoid "introjec-tion-projection." Everything is prepared at last for the access to a sexual position marked by Oedipus, through new dangers. In it, the libidinal impulses tend to be disengaged from destructive impulses and to invest through "symbolization" always better organized objects, interests, and activities.

The comments we will make about certain details of the Kleinian schema are intended to sketch out "orientations" only. For the very theme of positions implies the idea of the orientations of psychic life and of cardinal points; it also implies the idea of the organization of this life in accordance with variable or shifting coordinates and dimensions, an entire geography and geometry of living dimensions. It seems at first as if the paranoid-schizoid position merges with the development of an oral-anal depth—a bottomless depth. Everything starts out in the abyss. But in this respect, in this domain of partial objects and pieces which people the depth, we are not certain whether or not the "good object" (the good breast) can be considered as introjected in the same way as the bad object is. Melanie Klein herself showed that the splitting of the object into good and bad in the case of introjection is duplicated through a fragmentation which the good object is unable to resist, since one can never be sure that the good object does not conceal a bad piece. Furthermore, every piece is bad in principle (that is, persecuting and persecutor), only what is wholesome and complete is good. But introjection, to be precise, does not allow what is wholesome to subsist.[2] This is why the equilibrium proper to the schizoid position and its relation to the subsequent depressive position do not seem capable of coming about from the introjection of a good object as such, and they must be revised. What the schizoid position opposes to bad partial objects—introjected and projected, toxic and excremental, oral and anal—is not a good object, even it if were partial. What is opposed is rather an organism without parts, a body without organs, with neither mouth nor anus, having given up all introjection or projection, and being complete, at this price. At this point, the tension between id and ego is formed. Two depths are opposed: a hollow depth, wherein bits whirl about and explode, and full depth. These are two mixtures: one is made of hard and solid fragments which change; the other is liquid, fluid, and perfect, without parts or alteration because it has the property of melting and welding (all the bones in a mass of blood). It does not seem, in this sense, that the urethral theme can be set on the same plane as the anal theme. Excrements are always organs and morsels, sometimes dreaded as toxic substances and sometimes utilized as weapons to break apart still other morsels. Urine, on the contrary, bears witness to a liquid principle capable of binding all of the morsels together , and of surmounting such a breaking apart in the full depth of a body (finally) without organs.[3] If we assume that the schizophrenic, with all the language he has acquired, regresses to this schizoid position, we should not be surprised to find again in schizophrenic language the duality and complementarity of words-passions, splintered excremental bits, and of words-actions, blocks fused together by a principle of water or fire. Henceforth, everything takes place in depth, beneath the realm of sense, between two nonsenses of pure noise—the nonsense of the body and of the splintered word, and the nonsense of the block of bodies or of inarticulate words (the "that doesn't make sense," *ça n'a pas de sens,* acting as the positive process of both sides). The same duality of complementary poles is found again in schizophrenia between reiterations and perseverations, between jaw-grinding and catatonia, for example. The first bears witness to internal objects and to the bodies they break to pieces—the same bodies which break them to pieces; the second manifests the body without organs.

It seems to us that the good object is not introjected as such, because it belongs from the very start to another dimension. The good object has another "position." It belongs to the heights, it holds itself above, and does not allow itself to fall without also changing its nature. We should not understand height as an inverted depth. It is rather an original dimension distinguished by the nature of the object which occupies it, and by the instance which circulates in it. The superego does not begin with the first introjected objects, as Melanie Klein says, but rather with this good object which holds itself aloft. Freud often insisted on the importance of this transference from depth to height, which indicates, between the id and the superego, a total change of orientation and a central reorganization of psychic life. Depth has an internal tension determined by dynamic categories—container-contained, empty-full, massive-meager, etc. But the tension proper to height is verticality, difference in size, the large and the small. In opposition to partial introjected objects, which do not express the aggressiveness of the infant without also expressing the aggressiveness directed against him or her, and which by the same token are bad and dangerous, the good object as such is a complete object. If it manifests the most venomous cruelty as well as love and protection, it is not because of its partial and divided nature, but as a good and complete object all the manifestations of which emanate from a higher and superior unity. In fact, the good object has taken upon itself the two schizoid poles—that of partial objects from which it extracts its force and that of the body without organs from which it extracts its form, that is, its completeness and integrity. It maintains therefore complex relations with the id as a reservoir of partial objects (introjected and projected into a fragmented body), and with the ego (as a complete body without organs). *Insofar as it is the principle of the depressive position,* the good object is not the successor of the schizoid position, but rather forms itself in the current of this position, with borrowings, blockages, and pressures which attest to a constant communication between the two. At the limit, of course, the schizoid can reinforce the tension of his own position in order to shut himself up to the revelations of height or verticality. But, in any event, the good object of the heights maintains a struggle with the partial objects in which force is at stake in the violent confrontation of two dimensions. The body of the infant is like a den full of introjected savage beasts which endeavour to snap up the good object; the good object, in turn, behaves in their presence like a pitiless bird of prey. Under these circumstances, the ego identifies with the good object, patterning itself after it in a model of love and partaking of its power and its hatred toward the internal objects. But it also partakes of its wounds and its suffering under the blows of these bad objects.[4] On the other hand, it identifies itself with these bad partial objects which endeavor to catch the good object; it offers assistance, alliance, and even pity. Such is the vortex id-ego-superego, in which every one receives as many blows as he metes out and which characterizes the manic-depressive position. In relation to the ego, the good object as superego mobilizes all of its hatred to the extent that the ego has allied itself to the introjected objects. But is does grant it assistance and love, to the extent that the ego crosses over and attempts to identify itself with it.

That love and hate do not refer to partial objects, but express the unity of the good and whole object, must be understood in terms of the "position" of that object—its transcendence in height. Beyond loving and hating, assisting or fighting, there is "escaping" and "withdrawing" in the heights. The good object is by nature a lost object. It only shows itself and appears from the start as already lost, as *having been lost*. Its eminent unity lies here. Only as lost, the good object confers its love on the one who is able to find it for the first time as "found again" *("retrouvé")* (the ego which identifies with it); and it confers its hate on the one who approaches it aggressively as something "discovered" or "exposed," and yet already there (the ego taking the side of internal objects). Coming about in the course of the schizoid position, the good object posits itself as having always preexisted in this other dimension which now interferes with depth. This is why, higher than the movement through which it confers love and blows, there is the essence through which and into which it withdraws and frustrates us. It withdraws covered with its wounds, but it also withdraws into its love and its hate. It gives its love only as a love which was given before *(comme redonné)*, as a pardoning; it confers its hate only as a recalling of threats and warnings which did not take place. It is therefore as a result of frustration that the good object, as a lost object, distributes love and hatred. If it hates, it is as a good object, and no less than it loves. If it loves the ego which identifies with it and hates the ego which identifies with the partial objects, it withdraws even further; it frustrates the ego which hesitates between the two and suspects it of double-dealing. Frustration, in view of which the first time can only be a second time, is the common origin of love and hatred. The good object is cruel (the cruelty of the superego) to the extent that it ties together all these moments of love and hate conferred from on high with an instance which turns its face away and offers its gifts *(dons)* only as gifts offered once before *(redonnés)*. Schizophrenic pre-Socratic philosophy is thus followed by depressive Platonism: the Good is reached only as the object of a reminiscence, uncovered as essentially veiled; the One gives only what it does not have, since it is superior to what it gives, withdrawn into its height; and, as Plato said of the Idea, "it flees or it perishes"—it perishes under the blows of internal objects, but it flees in relation to the ego, since the Idea precedes it; the Idea withdraws as the ego advances, leaving with it only a little love or hate. These, as we have seen, are the characteristics of the depressive past perfect.

The manic-depressive position, being determined by the good object, presents therefore all sorts of new characteristics at the same time that it inserts itself in the paranoid-schizoid position. This is no longer the deep world of the simulacra, but rather that of the *idol* on high. It is no longer a matter of mechanisms of introjection and projection, but of identification. And it is no longer the same *Spaltung* or division of the ego. The schizophrenic split is a split between the explosive, introjected and projected internal objects, or rather the body which is fragmented by these objects, *and* the body without organs and without mechanisms renouncing projection as well as introjection. The depressive split is between the two poles of identification, that is, the identification of the ego with the internal objects and its identification with the object of heights. In the schizophrenic position, "partial" qualifies internal objects and is contrasted with "complete," which qualifies the body without organs reacting to these objects and the fragmentation they make it suffer. In the depressive position, "complete" qualifies the object, and subsumes under it not only the qualifications "unharmed" and "wounded," but also "present" and "absent," as the double movement by means of which this highest object gives outside of itself and withdraws into itself. For this reason, the experience of frustration, that is, the experience of the good object which withdraws into itself or which is essentially lost, belongs to the depressive position. In the case of the schizoid position, everything is aggressiveness exerted or undergone in the mechanisms of introjection and projection; in the strained relation between fragmented parts and the body without organs, *everything is passion and action,* everything is communication of bodies in depth, attack and defense. There is no room for privation or for the frustrating situation, which appears in the course of the schizoid position, although it emanates from the other position. It is for this reason that the depressive position prepares us for something which is *neither action nor passion,* that is, for the impassible withdrawal or contraction. It is for this reason as well that the manic-depressive position seems to have a cruelty which is different from the paranoid-schizoid aggressiveness. Cruelty implies all these moments of a love and hate bestowed from above, by a good but lost object which withdraws and which always gives what it gives for the second time. Masochism belongs to the depressive position, not only with respect to the sufferings which it undergoes, but also with respect to the sufferings that it likes to confer, through identification with the cruelty of the good object as such. Sadism, on the other hand, depends on the schizoid position, not only with respect to the sufferings it inflicts upon others, but also with respect to the sufferings it inflicts upon itself through the projection and internalization of aggressiveness. We have seen, from another point of view, how alcoholism fits the depressive position, playing the role of the highest object, its loss and the law of this loss in the past perfect; we have seen how finally it replaces the liquid principle of schizophrenia in its tragic presents.

And then the first stage of the dynamic genesis appears. The depth is clamorous: clappings, crackings, gnashings, cracklings, explosions, the shattered sounds of internal objects, and also the inarticulate howls-breaths (cris-souffles) of the body without organs which respond to them —all of this forms a sonorous system bearing witness to the oral-anal voracity. This schizoid system is inseparable from the terrible prediction: speaking will be fashioned out of eating and shitting, language and its univocity will be sculpted out of shit . . . (Artaud speaks of the "caca of being and of its language"). But, to be precise, what guarantees the first rough sketch of this sculpture, and the first stage in the formation of a language, is the good object of the depressive position up above. For it is this object that, from among all the sounds of the depth, extracts a Voice. If we take into consideration the characteristics of the good object (of being found only as lost, of appearing for the first time as already there, etc.) it seems that they are necessarily gathered into a voice which speaks and comes from on high.[5] Freud himself stressed the acoustic origin of the superego. For the child, the first approach to language consists in grasping it as the model of that which preexists, as referring to the entire domain of what is already there, and as the familial voice which conveys tradition, it affects the child as a bearer of a name and demands his insertion even before the child begins to understand. In a certain way, this voice has at its disposal all the dimensions of organized language: it denotes the good object as such or, on the contrary, the introjected objects; it signifies something, namely, all the concepts and classes which structure the domain of preexistence; and it manifests the emotional variations of the whole person (the voice that loves and reassures, attacks and scolds, that itself complains about being wounded, or withdraws and keeps quiet). The voice, though, presents the dimensions of an organized language, without yet being able to grasp the organizing principle according to which the voice itself would be a language. And so we are left outside sense, far from it, this time in a *pre-sense (pré-sens)* of heights: the voice does not yet have at its disposal the univocity which would make it a language, and, having unity only in virtue of its eminence, rests entangled in the equivocity of its denotations, the analogy of its significations, and the ambivalence of its manifestations. Truth to tell, to the extent that it denotes the lost object, one does not know what the voice denotes; one does not know what it signifies since it signifies the order of preexisting entities; one does not know what it manifests since it manifests withdrawal into its principle, or silence. It is at once the object, the law of the loss, and the loss itself. Indeed, as the superego, it is the voice of God, that which forbids without our knowing what is forbidden, since we will learn it only through the sanction. This is the paradox of the voice which at the same time marks the insufficiency of all theories of analogy and equivocity: it has the dimensions of a language without having its condition; it awaits the *event* that will make it a language. It is no longer a noise, but is not yet language. We can, at least, measure the progress of the vocal with respect to the oral, or the originality of this depressive voice in relation to the sonorous schizoid system. The voice is no less opposed to noises when it silences them than when it itself groans under their aggression, or keeps the silence. We constantly relive in our dreams the passage from noise to voice; observers have correctly noted how sounds reaching the sleeper were organized in the voice ready to awaken him.[6] We are schizophrenic while sleeping, but manic-depressive when nearing the point of awakening. When the schizoid puts up a defense against the depressive position, when the schizophrenic regresses beyond this position, it is because the voice threatens the whole body, thanks to which it acts, no less than it threatens the internal objects through which it suffers. As in the case of the schizophrenic language student, the maternal voice must be decomposed, without delay, into literal phonetic sounds and recomposed into inarticulate blocks. The thefts of the body, thought and speech experienced by the schizophrenic in his confrontation with the depressive position are but one. It is not necessary to wonder whether echoes, constraints, and thefts are primary or only secondary in relation to automatic phenomena. This is a false problem since what is stolen from the schizophrenic is not the voice; what is stolen by the voice from on high is, rather, the entire sonorous, *prevocal* system that he was able to make into his "spiritual automaton."

Twenty-Eighth Series
of Sexuality

The word "partial" has two senses. First, it designates the state of introjected objects and the corresponding state of the drives attached to these objects. It also designates elective bodily zones and the state of the drives which find in them a "source." These are objects which may themselves be partial: the breast or finger for the oral zone, excrements for the anal zone. The two senses should not, however, be confused. It has often been noted that the two psychoanalytic notions of stage and zone do not coincide. A stage is characterized by a type of activity which assimilates other activities and realizes in a certain mode a mixture of drives—absorption, for example, in the first oral stage, which also assimilates the anus, or excretion during the anal stage, which prolongs it, and which also takes over the mouth. Zones, on the contrary, represent the isolation of a territory, activities which "invest" this territory, and drives which now find in it a distinct source. The partial object of a stage is fragmented by the activities to which it has been submitted; the partial object of a zone, on the other hand, is separated from the whole by the territory which it occupies and which limits it. The organization of zones and the organization of stages occur, of course, almost simultaneously, since all positions are elaborated during the first year of life, each one encroaching on the preceding position and intervening in its course. But the essential difference is that zones are *facts of the surface,* and that their organization implies the constitution, the discovery, and the investment of a third dimension which is no longer either depth or height. One could say that the object of a zone is "projected," but projection no longer signifies a mechanism of depth. It now indicates a surface operation—an operation occurring on the surface.

In conformity with the Freudian theory of erogenous zones and their relation to perversion, a third position, the sexual-perverse, can thus be defined. Its autonomy is based on the dimension which is proper to it: sexual perversion is distinct from the depressive ascent or conversion and from the schizophrenic subversion. The erogenous zones are cut up on the surface of the body, around orifices marked by the presence of mucous membranes. When people note that internal organs are also able to become erogenous zones, it appears that this is conditional upon the spontaneous topology of the body. In accordance with the latter, as Simondon said of membranes, "the entire content of internal space is topologically in contact with the content of external space on the limits of the living." [1] It does not even suffice to say that the erogenous zones are cut up on the surface, since the surface does not preexist them. In fact, each zone is the dynamic formation of a surface space around a singularity constituted by the orifice. It is able to be prolonged in all directions up to the vicinity of another zone depending on another singularity. Our sexual body is initially a Harlequin's cloak. Each erogenous zone is inseparable from one or several singular points, from a serial development articulated around the singularity and from a drive investing this territory. It is inseparable from a partial object "projected" onto the territory as an object of satisfaction *(image),* from an observer or an ego bound to the territory and experiencing satisfaction, and from a mode of joining up with other zones. The entire surface is the product of this connection, and, as we will see, this poses specific problems. Precisely because the entire surface does not preexist, sexuality in its first (pregenital) aspect must be defined as a veritable production of partial surfaces. The auto-eroticism which corresponds to it must be characterized by the object of satisfaction projected onto the surface and by the little narcissistic ego which contemplates it and indulges in it.

How does this production come about? How is this sexual position formed? It is clearly necessary to seek the principle in the preceding positions, and especially in the reaction of the depressive position to the schizoid position. Height, in fact, has a strange power of reaction to depth. It seems, from the point of view of height, that depth turns, orients itself in a new manner, and spreads itself out: from a bird's eye view, it is but a fold more or less easily undone, or rather a local orifice surrounded or hemmed in at the surface. Of course, the fixation or the regression to the schizoid position implies a resistance to the depressive position, such that the surface would not be able to be formed. In this case, each zone is pierced by a thousand orifices which annul it; or, on the contrary, the body without organs is closed on a full depth without limits and without exteriority. Moreover, the depressive position does not itself constitute a surface; rather, it hurls into the orifice anyone who might be careless enough to venture there—as in the case of Nietzsche, who discovered the surface from a height of six thousand feet, only to be engulfed by the subsisting orifice (see the apparently manic-depressive episodes preceding the onset of Nietzsche's madness). The fact is though that height renders possible a constitution of partial surfaces, like many-colored fields unfolding beneath the wings of an airplane. As for the superego, despite all its cruelty, it is not without kindness with respect to the sexual organization of superficial zones, to the extent that it can assume that the libidinal drives *are there separated from the destructive drives of the depths.*[2]

Of course, the sexual or libidinal drives were already at work in the depths. But it is important to understand the state of their mixture— with the drives of preservation, on one hand, and drives of death, on the other. In depth, the drives of preservation which constitute the alimentary system (absorption and even excretion) do indeed have real objects and aims, but thanks to the powerlessness of the nursing child, they do not have at their disposal the means to be satisfied or to possess the real object. This is why the so-called sexual drives are fashioned very much after the drives of conservation, being born together with them and substituting introjected and projected partial objects for objects that are out of reach. A strict complementarity exists between sexual drives and simulacra. Destruction, then, does not designate a certain character of the relation to the formed real object; it qualifies rather the entire mode of the formation of the internal partial object (pieces) and the entire relation to it, since the same thing is destroyed and destroyer, and serves to destroy the ego as much as the other, to the point that destroying/being destroyed covers all internal sensibility. In this sense, all three drives merge together in depth, under such conditions that preservation provides the drive, sexuality provides the substitutive object, and destruction provides the whole reversible relation. But precisely because preservation is, at its foundation, threatened by this system in which it has become involved (wherein *to eat* becomes *to be eaten*), we see the whole system being displaced; death is recovered as a drive inside the body without organs at the same time that this dead body is eternally conserved and nourished while it is sexually born of itself. The world of oral-anal-urethral depth is the world of a revolving mixture which can truly be called bottomless, as it bears witness to a perpetual subversion.

When we link sexuality to the constitution of surfaces or zones, what we mean to say is that the libidinal drives find the occasion for an at least apparent double liberation, which is expressed precisely in auto-eroticism. On one hand, they free themselves from the alimentary model of the drives of preservation, since they find new sources in the erogenous zones and new objects in the images projected onto these zones: thus, for example, sucking *(le suçotement)* which is distinguished from suction *(la succion)*. On the other hand, they free themselves from the constraint of the destructive drives to the extent that they get involved in the productive labor of surfaces and in new relations with these new pellicular objects. It is important, once again, to distinguish, for example, between the oral stage of depths and the oral zone of the surface; between the introjected and projected internal partial object (simulacrum) and the object of the surface, projected over a zone in accordance with an entirely different mechanism (image); or finally between subversion, which depends on depths, and perversion, which is inseparable from surfaces.[3] We must then consider the twice liberated libido as a veritable *superficial energy*. We should not believe, however, that the other drives have disappeared, that they do not continue their work in depth, or especially that they do not find an original position in the new system.

We must again turn to the entire sexual position, with its successive elements which encroach so much upon one another that the element which precedes is determined only through its confrontation with the one which follows, or with the prefiguration of the one which follows.

The pre-genital erogenous zones or surfaces cannot be separated from the problem of their coordination. It is certain, though, that this coordination is enacted in several ways: by contiguity, to the degree that the series which is developed over one zone is extended in another series; at a distance, to the degree that a zone can be turned inward or projected onto another, furnishing the image by which the other is satisfied; and above all, indirectly, as in Lacan's mirror stage. It is nevertheless true that the direct and global function of integration, or of general coordination, is normally vested in the genital zone. It is this zone which must bind all the other partial zones, thanks to the *phallus*. And the phallus, in this respect, does not play the role of an organ, but rather that of a particular image projected, in the case of the little girl as well as the little boy, onto this privileged (genital) zone. The organ penis already has a long history tied to the schizoid and depressive positions. As is the case with all organs, the penis has known the adventure of the depths in which it is fragmented, placed inside the mother's and the child's body, being victim and aggressor, and identified with a poisonous bit of food or with an explosive excrement. But it is no less acquainted with the adventure of height in which, as a whole-some and good organ, it confers love and punishment, while at the same time withdrawing in order to form the whole person or the organ corresponding to the voice, that is, the combined idol of both parents. (In a parallel manner, the parental coitus, which is at first interpreted as pure noise, fury, and aggression, becomes an organized voice, even in its power to be silent and to frustrate the child.) It is from all these points of view that Melanie Klein shows that the schizoid and depressive positions supply the early elements of the Oedipus complex; *that is,* that the transition from the bad penis to the good is the indispensable condition for the arrival of the Oedipus complex in its strict sense, to genital organization and to the corresponding new problems.[4] We know what these new problems consist of: it is a matter of organizing surfaces and bringing about their coordination. In fact, as surfaces imply the disengagement of sexual drives from alimentary and destructive drives, the child may come to think that he abandons nourishment and power to his parents, and in return may hope that the penis, *as complete and good organ,* will come to be posed and projected on his own genital zone. If so, the penis would become the phallus which "doubles" the child's own organ and permits him to have sexual relations with the mother without offending the father.

What is essential is the precaution and modesty, at the beginning, of the Oedipal demands. The phallus, as the image projected on the genital zone, is not at all an aggressive instrument of penetration and eventration. On the contrary, it is an instrument of the surface, meant to *mend* the wounds that the destructive drives, bad internal objects, and the penis of depths have inflicted on the maternal body, and to reassure the good object, to convince it not to turn its face away. (The processes of "reparation" on which Melanie Klein insists seem in this sense to belong to the constitution of a surface which is itself restorative.) Anxiety and guilt are not derived from the Oedipal desire of incest; they are formed well in advance, the former during the schizoid aggressiveness, the latter during the depressive frustration. Oedipal desire would rather invoke them. *Oedipus is a pacifying hero of the Herculean type.* We are confronted with the Theban cycle. Oedipus dispelled the infernal power of depths and the celestial power of heights, and now claims only a third empire, the surface, nothing but the surface. His conviction that he is free of fault and his assurance that he had arranged everything to evade the prediction come from this. This point, which would have to be developed through the interpretation of the entire myth, finds a confirmation in the original nature of the phallus. The phallus should not penetrate, but rather, like a plowshare applied to the thin fertile layer of the earth, it should trace *a line at the surface.* This line, emanating from the genital zone, is the line which ties together all the erogenous zones, thus ensuring their connection or "interfacing" *(doublure),* and bringing all the partial surfaces together into one and the same surface on the body of the child. Moreover, it is supposed to reestablish a surface on the body of the mother herself and bring about the return of the withdrawn father. It is in this oedipal phallic phase that a sharp distinction of the two parents occurs, the mother taking on the aspect of an injured body to be mended, and the father taking on the aspect of a good object to be made to return. Above all, it is here that the child pursues on his own body the constitution of a surface and the integration of the zones, thanks to the well-founded privilege of the genital zone.

Twenty-Ninth Series—Good Intentions Are Inevitably Punished

It is necessary therefore to imagine Oedipus not only as innocent, but as full of zeal and good intentions—a second Hercules who will experience a similarly painful experience. But why do good intentions seem to turn against him? It is first because of the fragility of the enterprise—the fragility characteristic of surfaces. One is never certain that the destructive drives, which continue to act under the sexual drives, are not directing the work of the latter. The phallus as an image at the surface risks constantly being recuperated by the penis of the depths or the penis of the heights. Thus, it risks being castrated as phallus, since the penis of the depths devours and castrates, and the penis of the heights frustrates. There is therefore a double menace of castration through preoedipal regression (castration-devouring, castration-deprivation). The line traced by the phallus risks being swallowed up inside the deep *Spaltung*. Incest risks also returning to the state of eventration of the mother and of the child, or to a cannibalistic mixture where the one who eats is also eaten. In short, the schizoid and even the depressive position—the anxiety of one and the culpability of the other—threaten endlessly the Oedipal complex. As Melanie Klein says, anxiety and culpability are not born of the incestuous affair. They would, rather, prevent its formation and compromise it constantly.

This first response, however, will not suffice. The constitution of surfaces has also as a principle and intention the separation of sexual drives from destructive drives from the depths, and, in this respect, it encounters a certain complacency on the part of the superego or of the good object of the heights. Thus, the dangers of the oedipal affair must also derive from an internal evolution. Moreover, the risks of confusion or of corporeal mixture, invoked by the first response, take on their full meaning only in relation to these new dangers generated by the oedipal enterprise itself. In short, this affair necessarily creates a new anxiety which is proper to it, a new culpability or a new castration which is not reduced to either of the preceding cases—and to which alone the name "castration complex" corresponds in relation to Oedipus. The constitution of surfaces is the most innocent, but "innocent" does not signify "without perversity." We must realize that the superego abandons its original benevolence—at the oedipal moment, *for example*—when we go from the organization of pregenital partial surfaces to their genital integration or coordination under the sign of the phallus. But why is this so?

The surface has a decisive importance in the development of the ego, as Freud clearly demonstrated when he said that the perception-consciousness system is localized on the membrane formed at the surface of the protoplasmic vesicle.[1] The ego, as factor of the "primary narcissism," is initially lodged in the depths, in the vesicle itself or the body without organs. But it is able to attain independence only in the "auto-eroticism" of partial surfaces and all the small egos which haunt them. The real test of the ego then lies in the problem of coordination, and thus of *its own* coordination, when the libido as superficial energy invests it in a "secondary narcissism." And, as we earlier suggested, this phallic coordination of surfaces, and of the ego itself on the surface, is accompanied by operations which are qualified as oedipal. This is what we must analyze. The child receives the phallus as an image that the good ideal penis projects over the genital zone of his body. He receives this gift (narcissistic overinvestment of an organ) as the condition by which he would be able to bring about the integration of all his other zones. But the fact is that he cannot accomplish the production of the surface without introducing elsewhere some very important changes. In the first place, he splits the gift-making idol or good object of the heights. Both parents were combined earlier, in accordance with formulas clearly analyzed by Melanie Klein: the maternal body of the depths comprised a multiplicity of penises as partial internal objects; and especially, the good object of the heights was, as a complete organ, both penis and breast—mother provided with a penis, father provided with a breast. We believe now that the cleavage is achieved as follows: from the two disjunctions subsumed under the good object (unharmed-wounded, present-absent) the child begins by extracting the negative and makes use of it in order to qualify a mother *image* and a father *image*. On one hand, the child identifies the mother with the wounded body, being the primary dimension of the complete, good object (the wounded body must not be confused with the shattered or fragmented body of the depths); and on the other hand, the child identifies the father with the last dimension, that is, with the good object retired into its height. As for the wounded body of the mother, the child wishes to repair it, with his restorative phallus and make it unharmed. He wishes to recreate a surface to this body at the same time that he creates a surface for his own body. As for the withdrawn object, he wishes to bring about its return, to render it present with his evocative phallus.

In the unconscious, everyone is the offspring of divorced parents, dreaming of restoring the mother and bringing about the return of the father, pulling him back from his retreat: it seems to us that this is the basis of what Freud called the "familial romance" and its linkage with the Oedipus complex. Never has the child, in his narcissistic confidence, had better intentions, never again will he feel as good. Far from casting himself into an agonizing and guilt-ridden venture, never, in this position, had he believed himself so close to dispelling the anxiety and culpability of the previous positions. It is true that he assumes the father's place and takes the mother as the object of his incestuous desire. But the incest relationship, almost by proxy, does not imply here violence: neither eventration nor usurpation, but rather a surface relation, a process of restoration and evocation in which the phallus brings about a lining at the surface. We darken and harden the Oedipus complex if we neglect the horror of the preceding stages where the worst has already happened, and we forget that the Oedipal situation is attained only to the extent that the libidinal drives are liberated from the destructive drives. When Freud remarks that the normal person is not only more immoral than he thinks, but more moral than he suspects, this remark is true above all with respect to the Oedipus complex. Oedipus is a tragedy, but we must be able to imagine the tragic hero as gay and innocent, and as starting off on the right foot. Incest with the mother through restoration and the replacement of the father through evocation are not only good intentions (for it is with the Oedipus complex that the intention—the moral notion par excellence —is born). As intentions, they are inseparable extensions of what is apparently the most innocent activity, which, from the point of view of the child, consists of creating a total surface from all his partial surfaces, making use of the phallus projected by the good penis from above, and causing the parental images to benefit from this projection. Oedipus is Herculean because, as peace-maker, he too wishes to form a kingdom of surfaces and of the earth to fit his size. He believed that he had warded off the monsters of the depth and allied himself with the powers from on high. And in his endeavour, the restoration of the mother and the summoning of the father are the targets: this is the true Oedipus complex.

But why does it all turn out so badly? Why is the product of this affair a new anguish and a new culpability? Why does Hercules find in Juno a stepmother filled with hatred, resisting every offer of reparation, and in Zeus a father ever more withdrawn, turning away from his son after having favored him? One could say that the affair of the surfaces (good intention, the kingdom of the earth) encounters not only an expected enemy from the infernal depths, whose defeat was the question at hand, but an unexpected enemy as well—that of the heights which, however, rendered the affair possible and can no longer bail it out. The superego as the good object begins to condemn the libidinal drives themselves. In fact, in his desire for incest-restoration, Oedipus saw. What he saw (once the cleavage has been made), but should not have seen, is that the wounded body of the mother is not only wounded by the internal penises it contains; insofar as its surface is lacking a penis, it is wounded like a castrated body. The phallus as a projected image, which bestowed a new force on the child's penis, designates, on the contrary, a lack in the mother. This discovery threatens the child in an essential manner, for it signifies (on the other side of the cleavage) that the penis is the property of the father. Wishing to summon the father back and to make him present, the child betrays the paternal essence of withdrawal. This essence could not be found but only as if recovered—recovered *in* absence and *in* forgetfulness—but never given in a simple presence of the "thing" which would eliminate forgetting.[2] It becomes therefore true, at this moment, that by wishing to restore the mother, the child has in fact castrated and eventrated her; and that by wishing to bring back the father, the child has betrayed and killed him, transformed him into a cadaver. Castration, death by castration, becomes the child's destiny, reflected by the mother in this anguish he now experiences, and inflicted by the father in this culpability he now submits to as a sign of vengeance.

All this story began with the phallus as an image projected over the genital zone, which gave to the child's penis the force of embarking on the venture. But everything seems to terminate with the image which is dissipated and which carries along with it the disappearance of the child's penis. "Perversity" is the traversal of surfaces, and here, in this traversal, something new and changed is revealed. The line that the phallus traced at the surface, across every partial surface, is now the trace of castration where the phallus is itself dissipated—and the penis along with it. This castration, which alone merits the name "complex," is distinguished in principle from the two other castrations: that of depth, through devouring-absorption; and that of height, through privation-frustration. It is a castration through "adsorption," a surface phenomenon: like, for example, the surface poisons, those of the tunic and the skin which burn Hercules; or the poisons on images which might only have been contemplated, such as the venomous coatings on a mirror or on a painting which so inspired the Elizabethan theater. But, as it happens, it is in virtue of its specificity that this castration recovers the other two. As a surface phenomenon, it marks the failure or illness, the premature mold, the way in which the surface prematurely rots, and the surface line rejoins the deep *Spaltung* or incest rejoins the cannibalistic mixture of the depths—all of this, in conformity with the first reason which we invoked earlier.

The matter, however, does not end here. The release, in the case of Oedipus, of intention as an ethical category, has a considerable positive importance. At first sight only the negative is present in the case of the good intention that has gone awry: the willed action has been denied almost, and suppressed by what is really done; and what is really done is *negated* as well by the one who did it and who rejects responsibility for it (it's not me, I didn't want that—"I have killed unwittingly"). It would be a mistake, however, to think of good intention, and its essential perversity, in the framework of a simple opposition between two determined actions—an intended action and an accomplished action. Indeed, on the one hand, the willed action is an image of action, a projected action; and we do not speak of a psychological project of the will, but of that which renders it possible, that is, of a mechanism of projection tied to physical surfaces. It is in this sense that Oedipus can be understood as the tragedy of Semblance *(Apparence)*. Far from being an agency of the depths, intention is the phenomenon of the entire surface, or the phenomenon which adequately corresponds to the coordination of the physical surfaces. The very notion of Image, after having designated the superficial object of a partial zone, and then the phallus projected on the genital zone, and the pellicular parental images born of a cleavage, comes finally to designate action in general. The latter concerns the surface—not at all a particular action, but any action which spreads itself out at the surface and is able to stay there (to restore and to evoke, to restore the surface and to summon to the surface). But, on the other hand, the action effectively accomplished is no more a determined action which would oppose the other, nor a passion which would be the repercussion of the projected action. Rather it is something that happens, or something which represents all that can happen; better still, it is the necessary result of actions and passions, although of an entirely different nature, and itself neither action nor passion: event, pure event, *Eventum tantum* (to kill the father and castrate the mother, to be castrated and to die). But this amounts to saying that the accomplished action is projected on a surface no less than the other action. This surface, though, is entirely different; it is metaphysical or transcendental. One might say that the entire action is projected on a double screen—one screen constituted by the sexual and physical surface, the other by an already metaphysical or "cerebral" surface. In short, intention as an Oedipal category does not at all oppose a determined action to another, as, for example, a particular willed action to a particular accomplished action. On the contrary, it takes the totality of every possible action and divides it in two, projects it on two screens, as it determines each side according to the necessary exigencies of each screen. On one hand, the entire image of action is projected on a physical surface, where the action itself appears as willed and is found determined in the forms of restoration and evocation; on the other, the entire result of the action is projected on a metaphysical surface, where the action itself appears as produced and not willed, determined by the forms of murder and castration. The famous mechanism of "denegation" (that's not what I wanted . . .), with all its importance with respect to the formation of *thought,* must be interpreted as expressing the passage from one surface to another.

Perhaps we are moving too fast. It is obvious that the murder and the castration which result from the action concern bodies, that they do not by themselves constitute a metaphysical surface and that they do not even belong to it. But nonetheless they are on the way, provided that we acknowledge that this is a long road marked by stages. In fact, along with the "narcissistic wound," that is, when the phallic line is transformed into the trace of castration, the libido, which invested the ego of secondary narcissism at the surface, undergoes a particularly important transmutation—that which Freud called *"desexualization."* Desexualized energy appeared to Freud as nourishing the death instinct and as conditioning the mechanism of thought. We must therefore grant a dual value to the themes of death and castration. We must grant the value they have with respect to the preservation or liquidation of the Oedipus complex and in the organization of the definitive genital sexuality, upon its own surface and in its relations to the previous dimensions (the schizoid and depressive positions). But we must also grant the value which they take on as the origin of desexualized energy and the original manner by which this energy reinvests them on its new metaphysical surface, or surface of pure thought. This second process —which, to a certain extent, is independent of the others, since it is not directly proportional to the success or failure of the liquidation of Oedipus—corresponds in its first aspect to what is called *"sublimation,"* and in its second aspect to what is called *"symbolization."* We must therefore concede that metamorphoses do not end with the transformation of the phallic line into a trace of castration on the physical or corporeal surface. We must also concede that the trace of castration corresponds to a crack marking an entirely different incorporeal and metaphysical surface which brings about transmutation. This change raises all sorts of problems with respect to the desexualized energy which forms the new surface, to the very mechanisms of sublimation and symbolization, to the destiny of the ego on this new plane, and finally to the double belonging of murder and castration in the old and new systems.[3] In this crack of thought, at the incorporeal surface, we recognize the pure line of the Aion and the death instinct in its speculative form. But then the Freudian idea that the death instinct is an affair of speculation must, with good reason, be taken literally. At the same time, we must keep in mind that this last metamorphosis runs the same dangers as the others, and perhaps in a more acute manner: the crack, in a singular fashion, risks breaking up the surface from which it is nevertheless inseparable. It runs the risk of encountering again on the other surface the simple trace of castration. Or even worse, it runs the risk of being swallowed up in the *Spaltung* of depths and heights—carrying with it all the debris of the surface in this generalized debacle where the end finds again the point of departure and the death instinct, the bottomless destructive drives. All this would follow from the confusion we previously noted between the two figures of death: this is the central point of obscurity which raises endlessly the problem of the relations of thought to schizophrenia and depression, to the psychotic *Spaltung* in general as well as to neurotic castration. "For, of course all life is a process of demolition . . . ," including speculative life.

Thirtieth Series of the Phantasm

The phantasm has three main characteristics. 1) It represents neither an action nor a passion, but a result of action and passion, that is, a pure event. The question of whether particular events are real or imaginary is poorly posed. The distinction is not between the imaginary and the real, but between the event as such and the corporeal state of affairs which incites it about or in which it is actualized. Events are effects (thus, for example, the castration "effect," and the parricide "effect" . . .). But insofar as they are effects, they must be tied not only with endogenous causes, but with exogenous causes as well, effective states of affairs, actions really undertaken, and passions or contemplations effectively actualized. Freud was then right to maintain the rights of reality in the production of phantasms, even when he recognized them as products transcending reality.[1] It would be unfortunate if we were to forget or feign to forget that children do observe their parents' bodies and parental coitus; that they really become the object of seduction on the part of adults; that they are subjected to precise and detailed threats of castration, etc. Moreover, parricide, incest, poisoning, and eventration are not exactly absent from public and private histories. The fact is, though, that phantasms, even when they are effects and because they are effects, differ in nature from their real causes. We speak of endogenous causes (hereditary constitution, phylo-genetic heritage, internal evolution of sexuality, introjected actions and passions) no less than we speak of exogenous causes. The phantasm, like the event which it represents, is a "noematic attribute" distin-guished not only from states of affairs and their qualities, but from the psychological lives and from logical concepts as well. It belongs as such to an ideational surface over which it is produced as an effect. It transcends inside and outside, since its topological property is to bring "its" internal and external sides into contact, in order for them to unfold onto a single side. This is why the phantasm-event is submitted to a double causality, referring to the external and internal causes whose result in depth it is, and also to a quasi-cause which "enacts" it at the surface and brings it into communication with all the other event-phantasms. We have already twice seen how the place was prepared for such effects, differing in nature from that whose result they are: the first time, in the case of the depressive position, when the cause withdrew into the heights and left the field free for the develop-ment of a surface yet to come; later on, in the case of the Oedipal situation, when intention left the field free for a result of an entirely different nature, where the phallus plays the role of a quasi-cause.

Neither active nor passive, neither internal nor external, neither imaginary nor real—phantasms have indeed the impassibility and ide-ality of the event. In light of this impassibility, they inspire in us an unbearable waiting—the waiting of that which is going to come about as a result, and also of that which is already in the process of coming about and never stops coming about. What is psychoanalysis talking about with its grand trinity of murder-incest-castration, or of devour-ing-eventration-*ad*sorption, if not about pure events? Isn't this the case of all events in One, as in the wound? *Totem and Taboo* is the great theory of the event, and psychoanalysis in general is the science of events, on the condition that the event should not be treated as something whose sense is to be sought and disentangled. The event is sense itself, insofar as it is disengaged or distinguished from the states of affairs which produce it and in which it is actualized. Over states of affairs and their depth, their mixtures and their actions and passions, psychoanalysis casts the most intense light in order to reach the point of emergence of that which results, that is, the event of another type, as a surface effect. Therefore, whatever may be the importance of the earlier positions, or the necessity of always connecting the event to its causes, psychoanalysis is correct to recall the role of Oedipus as a "nuclear complex"—a formula which has the same importance as Husserl's "noematic core." For it is with Oedipus that the event is disengaged from its causes in depth, spreads itself at the surface and connects itself with its quasi-cause from the point of view of a dynamic genesis. It is the perfect crime, the eternal truth, the royal splendor of the event—each one of which communicates with all the others in the variants of one and the same phantasm. It is as distinct from its actualization as from the causes which produce it, using to its advantage the eternal part of excess over these causes and the part which is left unaccomplished in its actualizations, skimming over its own field, making us its own offspring. And if it is indeed at the point where the actualization cannot accomplish or the cause produce that the entire event resides, it is at the same point also that it offers itself to counter-actualization; it is here that our greatest freedom lies—the freedom by which we develop and lead the event to its completion and transmutation, and finally become masters of actualizations and causes. As the science of pure events, psychoanalysis is also an art of counter-actualizations, sublimations, and symbolizations.

2) The second characteristic of the phantasm is its position in relation to the ego, or rather the situation of the ego in the phantasm itself. It is indeed true that the phantasm finds its point of departure (or its author) in the phallic ego of secondary narcissism. But if the phantasm has the property of turning back on its author, what is the place of the ego in the phantasm, taking account of the unfolding or the development which is inseparable from it? Laplanche and Pontalis in particular have raised this problem, under conditions which caution us about any easy response. Although the ego may appear occasionally in the phantasm as acting, as undergoing an action, or as a third observing party, it is neither active nor passive and does not allow itself at any moment to be fixed in a place, even if this place were reversible. The originary phantasm "would be characterized by an absence of subjectivation accompanying the presence of the subject in the scene"; "any distribution of subject and object finds itself abolished"; "the subject does not aim at the object or its sign, it is included in the sequence of images . . . , it is represented as participating in the setting, without, in the forms closer to the originary phantasm, a place being assigned to it."

These remarks have two advantages: on one hand, they emphasize that the phantasm is not a representation of either action or passion, but rather that it pertains to an entirely different domain; on the other hand, they show that if the ego is dissipated in it, it is not perhaps because of an identity of contraries, or a reversal whereby the active would become passive—like that occurring in the becoming of depths and the infinite identity which it implies.[2]

We cannot, however, follow these authors when they search for this beyond the active and the passive in a pronominal model, which would still make an appeal to the ego and would even refer explicitly to an auto-erotic "this-side." The value of the pronominal—to punish oneself, to punish, or to be punished, or better yet, to see oneself, rather than to see or to be seen—is well attested to in Freud's writings. But it does not seem to go beyond the point of view of an identity of contraries, either by means of a deeper appreciation of one, or by a synthesis of both. That Freud remained attached to such a "Hegelian" position is beyond doubt, as we can see, in the realm of language, from a thesis on *primitive words,* endowed with contradictory sense.[3] In fact, the transcendence of the active and the passive and the dissolution of an ego which corresponds to it do not occur along the lines of an infinite or reflected subjectivity. That which is beyond the active and the passive is not the pronominal, but the result—the result of actions and passions, the surface effect or the event. What appears in the phantasm is the movement by which the ego opens itself to the surface and liberates the a-cosmic, impersonal, and pre-individual singularities which it had imprisoned. It literally releases them like spores and bursts as it gets unburdened. We must interpret the expression "neutral energy" in the following manner: *"neutral"* means pre-individual and impersonal, but does not qualify the state of an energy which would come to join a bottomless abyss. On the contrary, it refers to the singularities liberated from the ego through the narcissistic wound. This neutrality, that is to say, this movement by which singularities are emitted, or rather restored by an ego which is dissolved or *adsorbed* at the surface, belongs essentially to the phantasm. This is the case in *A Child Is Being Beaten* (or better, "A Father Is Seducing His Daughter," following the example invoked by Laplanche and Pontalis). Thus, the individuality of the ego merges with the event of the phantasm itself, even if that which the event represents in the phantasm is understood as another individual, or rather as a series of other individuals through which the dissolved ego passes. The phantasm is inseparable therefore from the toss of the dice or from the fortuitous instances which it enacts. And the famous *grammatical transformations* (such as those of President Schreber or those of sadism or voyeurism) register each time the rising up of singularities distributed in disjunctions, all of them, in each case, communicating in the event and all events communicating in one event, as for example in the case of the throws of the dice in the same cast. We find once again here an illustration of the principle of positive distance, with the singularities which stake it out, and of an affirmative usage of the disjunctive synthesis (and not a synthesis of contradiction).

3) It is not an accident that the development inherent in the phantasm is expressed in a play of grammatical transformations. The phantasm-event is distinguished from the corresponding state of affairs, whether it is real or possible; the phantasm represents the event according to its essence, that is, as a noematic attribute distinct from the actions, passions, and qualities of the state of affairs. But the phantasm represents another and no less essential aspect as well, according to which the event is that which may be expressed by the proposition (Freud pointed this out in saying that the phantasmatic material, in the representation of the parental coitus for example, has an affinity to "verbal images"). It is not the case that the phantasm is said or signified; the event presents as many differences from the propositions which express it as from the state of affairs in which it occurs. The fact is, though, that it does not exist outside of a proposition which is at least possible, even if this proposition has all of the characteristics of a paradox or nonsense; it also inheres in a particular element of the proposition. This element is the *verb* — the infinitive form of the verb. The phantasm is inseparable from the infinitive mode of the verb and bears witness thereby to the pure event. But in light of the relations and complex connections between the expression and the expressed, between the interiority of the expressor *(l'exprimant)* and the exteriority of the expressed, between the verb as it appears in language and the verb as it subsists in Being, we must conceive of an infinitive which is not yet caught up in the play of grammatical determinations — an infinitive independent not only of all persons but of all time, of every mood and every voice (active, passive, or reflective). This would

be a neutral infinitive for the pure event, Distance, Aion, representing the extra-propositional aspect of all possible positions, or the aggregate of ontological problems and questions which correspond to language. From this pure and undetermined infinitive, voices, moods, tenses, and persons will be engendered. Each one of them will be engendered within disjunctions representing in the phantasm a variable combination of singular points, and constructing around these singularities an instance of solution to the specific problem—the problem of birth, of the difference of the sexes, or the problem of death. Luce Irigaray, in a short article, after having noted the essential relation between the phantasm and the infinitive verb, analyzes several examples of such a genesis. Once an infinitive has been determined in a phantasm (for example, "to live," "to absorb," or "to give"), she investigates several types of connection: the subject-object connection, the active-passive conjunction, the affirmation-negation disjunction, or the type of temporalization of which each one of these verbs is capable ("to live," for example, has a subject, but one that is not an agent and that has no differentiated object). She is therefore able to classify these verbs in an order which runs from the least to the most determined, as if a general infinitive which is taken to be pure were progressively specified according to the differentiation of formal grammatical relations.[4] This is how Aion is peopled by events at the level of singularities which are distributed over its infinitive line. We have attempted to show in a similar way that the verb goes from a pure infinitive, opened onto a question as such, to a present indicative closed onto a designation of a state of affairs or a solution case. The former opens and unfolds the ring of the proposition, the latter closes it up, and between the two, all the vocalizations, modalizations, temporalizations, and personalizations are deployed, together with the transformations proper to each case according to a generalized grammatical "perspectivism."

But then a simpler task is imposed, namely, to determine the phantasm's point of birth and, through this, its real relation to language. This question is nominal or terminological to the extent that it is about the use of the word "phantasm." But it engages other things as well, since it fixes this use in relation to a particular moment, allegedly making it necessary in the course of the dynamic genesis. For example, Susan Isaacs, following Melanie Klein, already employs the word "phantasm" in order to indicate the relation of introjected and projected objects in the schizoid position, at a moment in which the sexual drives are in league with the alimentary drives. It is therefore inevitable that phantasms have only an indirect and tardive relation to language and that, when they are verbalized afterward, the verbalization occurs in accordance with ready-made grammatical forms.[5] Laplanche and Pontalis establish the phantasm along with auto-eroticism, and link it to the moment in which the sexual drives disengage themselves from the alimentary model and abandon "every natural object" (hence the importance they attach to the pronominal and the sense they give to the grammatical transformations as such in the non-localizable position of the subject). Finally, Melanie Klein does make an important remark, despite her very extensive use of the word "phantasm." She often says that symbolism is the foundation of every phantasm, and that the development of the phantasmatic life is hindered by the persistence of the schizoid and depressive positions. It seems to us, precisely, that the phantasm, properly speaking, finds its origin only in the ego of the secondary narcissism, along *with* the narcissistic wound, the neutralization, the symbolization, and the sublimation which ensue. In this sense, it is inseparable not only from grammatical transformations, but also from the neutral infinitive as the ideational material of these transformations. The phantasm is a surface phenomenon and, moreover, a phenomenon which is formed at a certain moment in the development of surfaces. For this reason, we have opted for the word *"simulacrum"* in order to designate the objects of depth (which are already no longer "natural objects"), as well as the becoming which corresponds to them and the reversals by which they are characterized. We choose *"idol"* in order to designate the object of the heights and its adventures. We choose *"image"* in order to designate that which pertains to partial, corporeal surfaces, including the initial problem of their phallic coordination (good intention).

Thirty-First Series of
Thought

The extreme mobility of the phantasm and its capacity for "passage" have often been stressed. It is a little like the Epicurean envelopes and emanations which travel in the atmosphere with agility. Two fundamental traits are tied to this capacity. First, the phantasm covers the distance between psychic systems with ease, going from consciousness to the unconscious and vice versa, from the nocturnal to the diurnal dream, from the inner to the outer and conversely, as if it itself belonged to a surface dominating and articulating both the unconscious and the conscious, or to a line connecting and arranging the inner and the outer over two sides. Second, the phantasm returns easily to its own origin and, as an "originary phantasm," it integrates effortlessly the origin of the phantasm (that is, a question, the origin of birth, of sexuality, of the difference of the sexes, or of death . . .).[1] This is because it is inseparable from a displacement, an unfolding, and a development within which it carries along its own origin. Our earlier problem, "where does the phantasm begin, properly speaking?" already implies another problem: "where does the phantasm go, in what direction does it carry its beginning?" Nothing is finalized like the phantasm; nothing finalizes *itself* to such an extent.

We attempted to determine the beginning of the phantasm as the narcissistic wound or the trace of castration. In fact, in conformity with the nature of the event, a *result* of the action appears at this point, which is quite different from the action itself. The (oedipal) intention was to restore, to bring about, and to coordinate its own physical surfaces; but all of this was still located within the domain of Images — with the narcissistic libido and the phallus as a surface projection. The result is to castrate the mother and to be castrated, to kill the father and to be killed, along with the transformation of the phallic line in the trace of castration and the corresponding dissipation of all the images (mother-world, father-god, ego-phallus). But if we make the phantasm begin on the basis of such a result, it is clear that this result would require for its development a different surface from the corporeal surface, where images were developed according to their own law (partial zones with genital coordination). The result will develop on a second screen, and thus the beginning of the phantasm will find its sequence elsewhere. The trace of castration does not by itself constitute or outline this elsewhere or this other surface: it concerns always the physical surface of the body and seems to disqualify it to the advantage of the depths and heights that it itself had conjured up. Thus, the beginning is truly in the void; it is suspended in the void. It is *with-out*. The paradoxical situation of the beginning, here, is that it is itself a result, and that it remains external to that which it causes to begin. This situation would afford no "way out," had not castration transformed the narcissistic libido into desexualized energy. This neutral or desexualized energy constitutes the second screen, the cerebral or metaphysical surface on which the phantasm is going to develop, begin anew with a beginning which now accompanies it at each step, run to its own finality, represent pure events which are like one and the same Result of the second degree.

There is thus a leap. The trace of castration as a deadly furrow becomes this crack of thought, which marks the powerlessness to think, but also the line and the point from which thought invests its new surface. And precisely because castration is somehow between two surfaces, it does not submit to this transmutation without carrying along its share of appurtenance, without folding in a certain manner and projecting the entire corporeal surface of sexuality over the metaphysical surface of thought. The phantasm's formula is this: from the sexual pair to thought via castration. If it is true that the thinker of depths is a bachelor, and that the depressive thinker dreams of lost betrothals, the thinker of surfaces is married or thinks about the "problem" of the couple. No one better than Klossowski has been able to disentangle this slow advance (cheminement) of the phantasm, for it is the process of his entire work. In words which are seemingly odd, Klossowski says that his problem is that of knowing how a couple may "project itself," independently of children, the way we could go from the couple to *the thought constructed in the mode of the couple,* in a mental comedy, or from sexual difference to the difference of intensity constitutive of thought—the primary intensity which marks the zero point of thought's energy, but also from which thought invests its new surface.[2] His problem is always to extract, by means of castration, thought from a couple, in order to bring about, through this crack, a sort of coupling of thought. Klossowski's couple, Roberte-Octave, have in a certain respect their correspondence in Lowry's couple, and also in Fitzgerald's ultimate couple of schizophrenia and alcoholism. For not only is the entirety of the sexual surface (parts and whole) involved in projecting itself over the metaphysical surface of thought, but depth and its objects or height and its phenomena as well. The phantasm returns to its beginning which remained external to it (castration); but to the extent that beginning itself was a result, the phantasm also returns to that from which the beginning had resulted (the sexuality of corporeal surfaces); and finally, little by little, it returns to the absolute origin from which everything proceeds (the depths). One could now say that everything—sexuality, orality, anality—receives a new form on the new surface, which recovers and integrates not only images but even idols and simulacra.

But what does it mean to recover and to integrate? We gave the name "sublimation" to the operation through which the trace of castration becomes the line of thought, and thus to the operation through which the sexual surface and the rest are projected at the surface of thought. We gave the name "symbolization" to the operation through which thought reinvests with its own energy all that which occurs and is projected over the surface. Obviously, the symbol is no less irreducible than the symbolized, sublimation no less irreducible than the sublimated. It has been quite a while since there has been anything comical in supposing a relation between the wound of castration and the crack constitutive of thought, or between sexuality and thought as such.

There is nothing comical (or sad) in the obsessional paths by which a thinker passes. It is not a question of causality, but rather of geography and topology. This does not mean that thought thinks about sexuality, nor that the thinker thinks about marriage. It is thought which is the metamorphosis of sex and the thinker who is the metamorphosis of the couple. From the couple to thought—although thought reinvests the couple as a dyad and coupling. From castration to thought—although thought reinvests castration as the cerebral crack and the abstract line. To be precise, the phantasm goes from the figurative to the abstract; it begins with the figurative, but must be continued in the abstract. The phantasm is the process of the constitution of the incorporeal. It is a machine for the extraction of a little thought, for the distribution of a difference of potential at the edges of the crack, and for the polarization of the cerebral field. As it returns to its external beginning (deadly castration), it is always beginning again its internal beginning (the movement of desexualization). In this way, the phantasm has the property of bringing in contact with each other the inner and the outer and uniting them on a single side. This is why it is the site of the eternal return. It mimics endlessly the birth of a thought, it begins a new desexualization, sublimation, and symbolization, caught in the act of bringing about this birth. Without this intrinsic repetition of beginnings, the phantasm could not integrate its other, extrinsic beginning. The risk is obviously that the phantasm falls back on the poorest thought, on a puerile and redundant diurnal reverie "about" sexuality, each time that it misses its mark and falls short, that is, each time it falls back in the "in-between" of the two surfaces. But the phantasm's path of glory is that which was indicated by Proust. From the question "shall I marry Albertine?" to the problem of the work of art yet to be made—this is the path of enacting the speculative coupling, beginning with a sexual pair, and retracing the path of the divine creation. Why glory? What kind of metamorphosis is it, when thought invests (or reinvests) that which is projected over its surface with its own desexualized energy? The answer is that thought does it in the guise of the Event. It does it with the part of the event that we should call non-actualizable, precisely because it belongs to thought and can be accomplished only by thought and in thought. There arise then aggressions and voracities which transcend what was happening in the depths of bodies; desires, loves, pairings, copulations, and intentions which transcend everything happening at the surface of bodies; and finally, powerlessnesses and deaths which transcend all that could have happened. This is the incorporeal splendor of the event as that entity which addresses itself to thought, and which alone may invest it—extra-Being.

We argued as if it were possible to speak of the event as soon as a result was disengaged, distinguished from the actions and passions from which it resulted, or from the bodies in which it was actualized. This is not accurate; we must wait for the second screen, namely, the metaphysical surface. Earlier, there have been only simulacra, idols and images, but not phantasms, to represent events. Pure events are results, but results of the second degree. It is true that the phantasm reintegrates and retrieves everything in the retrieval of *its own* movement, but everything is changed. It is not that nourishment has become spiritual nourishment, and copulations gestures of the spirit. But each time a proud and shiny verb has been disengaged, distinct from things and bodies, states of affairs and their qualities, their actions and passions: like the verb *"to green,"* distinct from the tree and its greenness, the verb *"to eat"* (or "to be eaten") distinct from food and its consumable qualities, or the verb *"to mate"* distinct from bodies and their sexes— eternal truths. In short, metamorphosis is the liberation of the non-existent entity for each state of affairs, and of the infinitive for each body and quality, each subject and predicate, each action and passion. Metamorphosis (sublimation and symbolization) consists, for each thing, in the liberation of an *aliquid* which is the *noematic attribute* and *that which can noetically be expressed,* eternal truth, and sense which hovers over bodies. Only here to die and to kill, to castrate and to be castrated, to restore and to bring about, to wound and to withdraw, to devour and to be devoured, to introject and to project, become pure events on the metaphysical surface which transforms them, and where their infinitive is drowned out. For the sake of one single language which expresses them, and under a single "Being" in which they are thought, all the events, verbs, and expressible-attributes communicate as one inside this extraction. The phantasm recovers everything on this new plane of the pure event, and in this symbolic and sublimated part of that which cannot be actualized; similarly, it draws from this part the strength to orient its actualization, to duplicate it, and to conduct its concrete counter-actualization. For the event is *properly* inscribed in the flesh and in the body, with the will and the freedom which befit the patient thinker, only in virtue of the incorporeal part containing their secret, that is, the principle, truth, finality, and quasi-cause.

Castration, then, has a very special situation between that of which it is the result and that which it causes to begin. But it is not castration alone which is in the void, caught between the corporeal surface of sexuality and the metaphysical surface of thought. It is, in fact, the entire sexual surface which is intermediary between physical depth and metaphysical surface. Oriented in one direction, sexuality may pull everything down: castration reacts on the sexual surface from which it comes, and to which it still belongs in virtue of its trace; it shatters this surface, causing it to rejoin the fragments of the depth. Further still, it prevents any successful sublimation, any development of the metaphysical surface, and causes the incorporeal crack to be actualized at the most profound depths of the body, to be confused with the *Spaltung* of the depths; it also causes thought to collapse into its point of impotence, or into its line of erosion. But oriented in another direction, sexuality may project everything: castration prefigures the metaphysical surface the beginning of which it brings about and to which it already belongs in virtue of the desexualized energy which it releases; it projects not only the sexual dimension, but the other dimensions of depth and height as well, over this new surface on which the forms of their metamorphosis are inscribed. The first orientation must be determined as the orientation of psychosis, the second as that of the successful sublimation; between the two, one finds all the neuroses, in the ambiguous character of Oedipus and of castration. And it is the same thing with death: the narcissistic self regards it from two sides, according to the two figures described by Blanchot—the personal and present death, which shatters and "contradicts" the ego, as it abandons it to the *destructive drives* of the depths and to blows of the outside; but also the impersonal and infinitive death, which "distances" the ego, causing it to release the singularities which it contains and raising it to the *death instinct* on the other surface, where "one" dies, where one never succeeds in, or finishes, dying. The entire biopsychic life is a question of dimensions, projections, axes, rotations, and foldings. Which way should one take? On which side is everything going to tumble down, to fold or unfold? The erogenous zones are already engaged in combat upon the sexual surface—a combat that the genital zone is supposed to arbitrate and pacify. But the genital zone is itself the arena of a larger context, on the level of species and of the entire humanity: the contest of the mouth and the brain. The mouth is not only a superficial oral zone but also the organ of depths, the mouth-anus, the cesspool introjecting and projecting every morsel. The brain is not only a corporeal organ but also the inductor of another invisible, incorporeal, and metaphysical surface on which all events are inscribed and symbolized.[3] Between this mouth and this brain everything occurs, hesitates, and gets its orientation. Only the victory of the brain, if it takes place, frees the mouth to speak, frees it from excremental food and withdrawn voices, and nourishes it with every possible word.

Thirty-Second Series on the Different Kinds of Series

Melanie Klein remarks that between symptoms and sublimations there must be an intermediary series corresponding to cases of *less successful sublimation.* But the whole of sexuality, in its own right, is a "less successful" sublimation: it is intermediary between the symptoms of corporeal depth and the sublimations of the incorporeal surface; and in this intermediary state it is organized in series on its own intermediary surface. Depth is not organized in series. The fragmentation of its objects and the undifferentiated plentitude of the body that it contrasts to the fragmented objects prevent it from happening in the void. On one hand, it presents blocks of coexistence, bodies without organs or words without articulation; on the other hand, it presents sequences of partial objects bound only by the common property of being detachable and fragmentable, introjectable and projectable, bursting and causing to burst (thus the renowned sequence breast-food-excrement-penis-infant). These two aspects—sequence and block—represent the forms taken on respectively by displacement and condensation in depth, within the schizoid position. It is with sexuality, that is to say, with the release of the sexual drives, that the series begins—because the serial form is a surface organization.

We must therefore distinguish, in the different moments of sexuality previously considered, very different kinds of series. There are, first, the erogenous zones of pregenital sexuality: each one of them is organized in a series which converges around a singularity represented most often by an orifice surrounded by a mucous membrane. The serial form is founded in the erogenous zone of the surface, insofar as the latter is defined by the extension of a singularity or, what amounts to the same thing, by the distribution of a difference of potential or intensity, having a maximum and a minimum (the series ends around points which depend upon another series). The serial form on the erogenous zones, therefore, is founded on a mathematics of singular points and on a physics of intensive quantities. But it is in yet another manner that each erogenous zone supports a series: this time, a series of images is projected over the zone, that is, a series of objects capable of assuring for the zone an auto-erotic satisfaction. Consider, for example, objects of sucking or images of the oral zone. Each one becomes coextensive to the entire range of the partial surface and traverses it, as it explores its orifice and field of intensity, from the maximum to the minimum and vice versa. They are organized into series according to the way in which they are made coextensive (a piece of candy, for example, or chewing gum, the surface of which is multiplied by its being crunched, by being stretched respectively); but they are also organized according to their origin, that is, according to the whole from which they are extracted (another region of the body, another person, external object or reproduction of an object, a plaything, etc.), and according to the degree of their distance from the primitive objects of alimentary and destructive drives from which the sexual drives were just released.[1] In each of these senses, a series linked to an erogenous zone appears to have a simple form, to be *homogeneous,* to give rise to a synthesis of *succession* which may be *contracted* as such, and which in any case constitutes a simple *connection.* But second, it is clear that the problem of the phallic coordination of the erogenous zones comes to complicate the serial form: without doubt, the series prolong one another and converge around the phallus as the image imposed on the genital zone. The genital zone has its own series. It is inseparable, however, from a complex form which subsumes under it *heterogeneous* series, now that a condition of *continuity or convergence* has replaced homogeneity; it gives rise to a synthesis of *coexistence and coordination* and constitutes a *conjunction* of the subsumed series.

Third, we know that the phallic coordination of surfaces is necessarily accompanied by oedipal affairs which in turn emphasize parental images. In the development proper to Oedipus, therefore, these images enter into one or several series—a heterogeneous series with alternating terms, father and mother, or two coexisting series, maternal and paternal: for example, wounded, restored, castrated, and castrating mother; withdrawn, evoked, killed, and killing father. Moreover, this or these Oedipal series enter into relation with the pregenital series, with the images which corresponded to them, and even with the groups and persons wherefrom these images were extracted. It is even in this relation between images of different origin, oedipal and pregenital, that the conditions of a "choice of an external object" are elaborated. The importance of this new moment or relation could not be too greatly stressed, since it animates the Freudian theory of the event, or rather of the two series of events. This theory consists first in showing that a *traumatism* presupposes the existence of at least two independent events, separated in time, one of them infantile and the other post-pubescent, between which a sort of resonance is produced. Under a different aspect the two events are presented as two series, one pregenital and the other oedipal, with their resonance being the process of the *phantasm*.[2] In our terminology, it is therefore not a question of events properly speaking, but rather of two series of independent images, whereby the Event is disengaged only through resonance of the series in the phantasm. The first series does not imply a "comprehension" of the event in question, because it is constructed according to the law of partial pregenital zones, and because only the phantasm, to the extent that it makes both series resonate, attains such a comprehension. The event to be comprehended is no different from the resonance itself (in this capacity it is not confused with either of the two series). In any case, it is the resonance of the two independent and temporally disjointed series that is essential.

Here we find ourselves before a third figure of the serial form. For the series now under consideration are indeed heterogeneous, but they no longer respond at all to the conditions of continuity and convergence which had ensured their conjunction. On one hand, they diverge and resonate only on this condition; on the other, they constitute ramified disjunctions and give rise to a disjunctive synthesis. The reason for this must be sought at the two extremities of the serial form. The fact is that the serial form puts images into play; but, whatever the heterogeneity of images might be, whether pregenital images of partial zones or parental images of Oedipus, we have seen that their common origin is in the idol, or in the good object lost and withdrawn in the heights. It is this object, first of all, that renders possible a conversion of depth into partial surfaces and a release of these surfaces and of the images haunting them. But it is also the same object which, in the guise of the good penis, projects the phallus as an image over the genital zone. And finally, it is the same object which provides the subject matter or the quality of parental Oedipal images. One could therefore say at least that the series under consideration converge toward the good object of the heights. This, however, is not at all the case: the good object (the idol) functions only insofar as it is lost and withdrawn into this height which constitutes its proper dimension. And, in this capacity, it always acts only as the source of disjunctions, the source of the emission or liberation of alternatives, as it has carried off in its retirement the secret of an eminent, superior unity. It was defined earlier in this manner: wounded-unharmed, present-absent. Ever since the manic-depressive position, it is in the same vein that it imposes an alternative on the ego —to model itself after the good object or to identify itself with bad objects. Moreover, when it renders possible the spreading out of partial zones, it establishes them only as disjointed and separate—to the point that they will find their convergence only with the phallus. And when it determines parental images, it is again by dissociating its own aspects, by distributing them in alternatives which supply the alternating terms of the Oedipal series, and by arranging them around the image of the mother (wounded and to be healed), and the image of the father (withdrawn and to be made present). Only the phallus would then be left as an agent of convergence and coordination; the problem is that it itself gets involved in Oedipal dissociations. We can clearly see, above all, that it evades its role, if we refer to the other end of the chain, no longer to the origin of images but rather to their common dissipation during the evolution of Oedipus.

This is because, in its evolution and in the line which it traces, the phallus marks always an excess and a lack, oscillating between one and the other and even being both at once. It is essentially an excess, as it projects itself over the genital zone of the child, duplicating its penis, and inspiring it with the Oedipal affair. But it is essentially lack and deficiency when it designates, at the heart of the affair, the absence of the penis in the case of the mother. It is in relation to itself that the phallus is both a defect and an excess, *when the phallic line merges with the trace of castration,* and the excessive image no longer designates anything other than its own lack, as it takes away the child's penis. We are not going to repeat the characteristics of the phallus that Lacan has analyzed in several well-known texts. It is the paradoxical element or object = x, missing always its own equilibrium, at once excess and deficiency, never equal, missing its own resemblance, its own identity, its own origin, its own *place,* and always displaced in relation to itself. It is floating signifier and floated signified, place without occupant and occupant without place, the empty square (which can also create an excess through this void) and a supernumerary object (which can also create a lack by being this excess number). It is the phallus which brings about the resonance of the two series that we earlier called pregenital and oedipal, and which can also receive different qualifications, provided that, through all possible qualifications, the one is determined as signified and the other as signifying.[3] It is the phallus which is surface nonsense, twice nonsense, as we have seen, and which distributes sense to the two series, as something *happening* to the one and as something *insisting* in the other (it is thus inevitable that the first series does not yet imply a comprehension of what is in question).

But the whole problem is this: how does the phallus, as the object = x, that is, as the agent of castration, cause the series to resonate? It is no longer a question of a convergence and a continuity at all, as it was when we were considering the pregenital series for themselves, insofar as the still intact phallus was coordinating them around the genital zone. Now, the pregenital forms one series, with a pre-comprehension of infantile parental images; and the oedipal forms another series, with other and otherwise formed parental images. The two series are discontinuous and divergent. The phallus no longer ensures a role of convergence, but on the contrary, being excess and lack, it ensures a role of resonance for series which diverge. For, however much the two series may resemble one another, they do not resonate *by* their resemblance, but rather *by* their difference. This difference is regulated each time by the relative displacement of terms, and this displacement is itself regulated by the absolute displacement of the object = x in the two series. At least in its beginning, the phantasm is nothing else but the internal resonance of two independent sexual series, insofar as this resonance prepares the emergence of the event and signals its comprehension. This is why, in its third species, the serial form is presented in a form irreducible to the previous ones, that is, as a *disjunctive* synthesis of the heterogeneous series, since these heterogeneous series now diverge. This is also a *positive and affirmative use* (no longer negative and limitative) of the disjunction, since the divergent series *resonate* as such; it is a continuous *ramification* of these series, relative to the object = x which does not cease to be displaced and to traverse them.[4] If we consider all three serial kinds—the connective synthesis on a single series, the conjunctive synthesis of convergence, and the disjunctive synthesis of resonance, we see that the third proves to be the truth and the destination of the others, to the degree that the disjunction attains its positive and affirmative use. The conjunction of zones makes visible therefore the divergence already present in the series which it coordinated globally, and the connection of a zone makes visible the wealth of details already contained in the series which it apparently homogenizes.

The theory of a sexual origin of language (Sperber) is well known. But, more precisely, we must consider the sexual position as intermediary, insofar as it produces under its different aspects (erogenous zones, phallic stage, castration complex) different types of series. What is its incidence, or what is their incidence in the dynamic genesis and the evolution of sounds? Further, is it not the case that the serial organization presupposes a certain state of language? We have seen that the first step of the genesis, from the schizoid to the depressive position, went from noises to the voice: from noises as qualities, actions, and passions of bodies in depth, to the voice as an entity of the heights, withdrawn into heights, expressing itself in the name of that which preexists, or rather posing itself as preexisting. The child, of course, comes to a language that she cannot yet understand as language, but only as a voice, or as a familial hum of voices which already speaks of her. This factor is of considerable importance for the evaluation of the following fact: that, in the series of sexuality, something begins by being grasped as a premonition before being understood. This pre-understanding relates to what is already there. We ask, therefore, about that which, in language, corresponds to the second stage of the dynamic genesis, about that which founds the different aspects of the sexual position—and which is also founded by them. Although Lacan's work has a much more extensive import, and has completely renewed the general problem of the relations between sexuality and language, it also includes suggestions which are applicable to the complexity of this second stage —indications pursued and developed in an original manner by certain of his disciples. If the child comes to a preexisting language which she cannot yet understand, perhaps conversely, she grasps that which we no longer know how to grasp in our own language, namely, the phonemic relations, the differential relations of phonemes.[5] The child's extreme sensitivity to phonemic distinctions of the mother tongue and her indifference to sometimes more pronounced variations belonging to another system have often been noted. This is what gives each system a circular form and a retroactive movement by right, since phonemes depend no less on morphemes and semantemes than morphemes and semantemes depend on them. This is, indeed, what the child extricates from the voice upon leaving the depressive position: an apprenticeship of formative elements before any understanding of formed linguistic units. In the continuous flow of the voice which comes from above, the child cuts out elements of different orders, free to give them a function which is still prelinguistic in relation to the whole and to the different aspects of the sexual position.

Although the three elements may playfully circulate, it is tempting to make each one correspond to an aspect of the sexual position, as if the wheel were to stop three times in different fashions. But to what extent can we link phonemes to the erogenous zones, morphemes to the phallic stage, and semantemes to the evolution of Oedipus and the castration complex? As to the first point, Serge Leclaire's recent book, *Psychanalyser,* proposes an extremely interesting thesis: an erogenous zone (that is, a libidinal movement of the body insofar as it happens at the surface, distinguishing itself from drives of conservation and destruction) would be marked essentially by a "letter" which, at the same time, would trace its limit and subsume under it images or objects of satisfaction. "Letter" at this point assumes no mastery of language and still less a possession of writing. It is rather a question of a phonemic difference in relation to the difference of intensity which characterizes the erogenous zone. The precise example invoked by Leclaire, however, that of the letter V in the case of the Wolf Man, does not seem to go in this direction: in fact, the letter V in this example marks rather a very general movement of openness, common to several zones (to open one's eyes, one's ears, one's mouth), and connotes several dramatic scenes rather than objects of satisfaction.[6] Should we rather think, to the extent that the phoneme itself is a *cluster of distinctive traits* or differential relations, that each zone would rather be analogous to one of these traits and determined by them in relation to another zone? In this case, there would be reason for a new heralding of the body founded on phonology; the oral zone would necessarily enjoy an essential privilege, insofar as the child would make an active apprenticeship of phonemes at the same time that she would extract them from the voice.

The fact is now that the oral zone would pursue its liberation and its progress in the acquisition of language only to the extent that a global integration of zones could be produced, or even an alignment of clusters and an entry of phonemes into more complex elements—what linguistics sometimes call a "concatenation of successive entities." Here we encounter the second point, and with it the problem of the phallic coordination as the second aspect of the sexual position. It is in this sense that Leclaire defines the surface of the entire body as an aggregate or sequence of letters, while the image of the phallus assures their convergence and continuity. We thus find ourselves inside a new domain. It is no longer at all a question of a simple addition of the preceding phonemes, but rather of the construction of the first *esoteric words,* which integrate phonemes into a conjunctive synthesis of heterogeneous, convergent, and continuous series—thus, in an example analyzed by Leclaire, the secret name "Poord'jeli," that a child creates. It seems to us at this level that the esoteric word in its entirety plays not the role of a phoneme or of an element of articulation but that of a morpheme or of an element of grammatical construction represented by the conjunctive character. It refers to the phallus as an agent of coordination. Only afterward, such an esoteric word takes on another value, or another function: as the conjunction forms an entire series, this series enters into a relation of resonance with another divergent and independent series—*"joli corps de Lili"* (Lili's beautiful body). The new series corresponds to the third aspect of the sexual position, that is, to the development of Oedipus, the castration complex and the concomitant transformation of the phallus which has now become object = x. Then, and only then, the esoteric word becomes a *portmanteau word* insofar as it enacts a disjunctive synthesis of the two series (the pregenital and the oedipal, that of the proper name of the subject and that of Lili), causes the two divergent series to resonate as such and ramifies them.[7] The entire esoteric word, in line with Lacan's thesis, plays now the role of a semanteme. According to this thesis, the phallus of Oedipus and of castration is a signifier which does not animate the correponding series without cropping up suddenly in the preceding series, in which it also circulates, since it "conditions the effects of the signified by its presence as signifier." We thus go from the phonemic letter to the esoteric word as morpheme, and then from this to the portmanteau word as semanteme.

In the transition from schizoid position of depth to the depressive position of the heights, we went from noises to the voice. But in the surface sexual position, we go from voice to speech. The organization of the physical sexual surface has three moments which produce three types of syntheses or series: the erogenous zones and connective syntheses bearing on a homogeneous series; the phallic coordination of zones and the conjunctive synthesis bearing on heterogeneous, yet convergent and continuous series; and the evolution of Oedipus, the transformation of the phallic line into the trace of castration, and the disjunctive synthesis, bearing on divergent and resonating series. Now, these series or moments condition the three formative elements of language—phonemes, morphemes, and semantemes—as much as they are conditioned by them in a circular reaction. Nevertheless, there is still no language; we are still in a prelinguistic domain. These elements are not organized into formed linguistic units which would be able to denote things, manifest persons, and signify concepts.[8] This is why these elements have not yet a reference other than a sexual one, as if the child was learning to speak on his own body—with phonemes referring to the erogenous zones, morphemes to the phallus of coordination, and semantemes to the phallus of castration. This reference must not be interpreted as a denotation (phonemes do not "denote" erogenous zones), as a manifestation, nor even as a signification. It is rather a question of a "conditioning-conditioned" structure, of a surface effect, under its double sonorous and sexual aspect or, if one prefers, under the aspects of resonance and mirror. At this level, speech begins: *it begins when the formative elements of language are extracted at the surface, from the current of voice which comes from above.* This is the paradox of speech. On one hand, it refers to language as to something withdrawn which preexists in the voice from above; on the other hand, it refers to language as to something which must result, but which shall come to pass only with formed units. Speech is never equal to language. It still awaits the result, that is, the event which will make the formation effective. It masters the formative elements but without purpose, and the history which it relates, the sexual history, is nothing other than itself, or its own double. We are not yet therefore in the realm of sense. The noise of the depths was an infra-sense, an under-sense, *Untersinn;* the voice from the heights was a pre-sense. One could now come to believe, with the organization of the surface, that nonsense has reached that point at which it becomes sense, or takes on sense: is not precisely the phallus as object $= x$, this surface nonsense which distributes sense to the series which it traverses, ramifies, and makes them resonate, determining one as signifying and the other as signified? In us, though, the advice and the rule of method resound: do not hasten to eliminate nonsense and to give it a sense. Nonsense would keep its secret of the real manner by which it creates sense. The organization of the physical surface is not yet sense; it is, or rather will be, a co-sense. That is to say, when sense is produced over another surface, there will *also* be this sense. Sexuality, according to the Freudian dualism, is that which also is—everywhere and always. There is nothing the sense of which is not *also* sexual, in accordance with the law of the double surface. But it is still necessary to await this result which never ends, this other surface, for sexuality to be made the concomitant, and the co-sense of sense, so that one might say "everywhere," "for all times," and "eternal truth."

Thirty-Third Series
of Alice's Adventures

The three types of esoteric words that we encountered in Lewis Carroll's works correspond to the three kinds of series: the "unpronounceable monosyllable" brings about the connective synthesis of a series; the "phlizz" or "snark" guarantees the convergence of two series and brings about the conjunctive series; and finally, the portmanteau word, the "Jabberwock," the word = x whose presence we discover already at work in the two others, brings about the disjunctive synthesis of divergent series, as it makes them resonate and ramify. But how many adventures can we find under this organization?

Alice has three parts, which are marked by changes of location. The first part (chapters 1-3), starting with Alice's interminable fall, is completely immersed in the schizoid element of depth. Everything is food, excrement, simulacrum, partial internal object, and poisonous mixture. Alice herself is one of these objects when she is little; when large, she is identified with their receptacle. The oral, anal, and urethral character of this part has often been stressed. But the second part (chapters 4-7) seems to display a change of orientation. To be sure, there is still, and with renewed force, the theme of the house filled by Alice, her preventing the rabbit from entering and her expelling violently the lizard from it (the schizoid sequence child-penis-excrement). But we notice considerable modifications. First, it is in being too large that Alice now plays the role of the internal object. Moreover, to grow and to shrink no longer occur only in relation to a third term in depth (the key to be reached or the door to pass through in the first part), but rather act of their own accord in a free style, one in relation to the other—that is, they act on high. Carroll has taken pains to indicate that there has been a change, since now it is drinking which brings about growth and eating which causes one to shrink (the reverse was the case in the first part). In particular, causing to grow and causing to shrink are linked to a single object, namely, the mushroom which founds the alternative on its own circularity (chapter 5). Obviously, this impression would be confirmed only if the ambiguous mushroom gives way to a good object, presented explicitly as an object of the heights. The caterpillar, though he sits on top of the mushroom, is insufficient in this regard. It is rather the Cheshire Cat who plays this role: he is the good object, the good penis, the idol or voice of the heights. He incarnates the disjunctions of this new position: unharmed or wounded, since he sometimes presents his entire body, sometimes only his cut off head; present or absent, since he disappears, leaving only his smile, or forms itself from the smile of the good object (provisional complacency with respect to the liberation of sexual drives). In his essence, the cat is he who withdraws and diverts himself. The new alternative or disjunction which he imposes on Alice, in conformity with this essence, appears twice: first, a question of being a baby or a pig, as in the Duchess' kitchen; and then as the sleeping Dormouse seated between the Hare and the Hatter, that is, between an animal who lives in burrows and an artisan who deals with the head, a matter of either taking the side of internal objects or of identifying with the good object of heights. In short, it is a question of choosing between depth and height.[1] In the third part (chapters 8-12), there is again a change of element. Having found again briefly the first location, Alice enters a garden which is inhabited by playing cards without thickness and by flat figures. It is as if Alice, having sufficiently identified herself with the Cheshire Cat, whom she declares to be her friend, sees the old depth spread out in front of her, and the animals which occupied it become slaves or inoffensive instruments. It is on this surface that she distributes her images of the father—the image of the father in the course of a trial: "They told me you had been to her,/And mentioned me to him. . . ." But Alice has a foreboding of the dangers of this new element: the manner in which good intentions run the risk of producing abominable results, and the phallus, represented by the Queen, risks turning into castration (" 'Off with her head!' the Queen shouted at the top of her voice"). The surface is burst, ". . . the whole pack rose up into the air, and came flying down upon her. . . ."

One could say that *Through The Looking-Glass* takes up this same story, this same undertaking, but that things here have been displaced or shifted, the first moment being suppressed and the third greatly developed. Instead of the Cheshire Cat being the good voice for Alice, it is Alice who is the good voice for her own, real cats—a scolding voice, loving and withdrawn. Alice, from her height, apprehends the mirror as a pure surface, a continuity of the outside and the inside, of above and below, of reverse and right sides, where "Jabberwocky" spreads itself out in both directions at once. After having behaved briefly once again as the good object or the withdrawn voice vis-à-vis the chess pieces (with all the terrifying attributes of this object or this voice), Alice herself enters the game: she belongs to the surface of the chessboard, which has replaced the mirror, and takes up the task of becoming queen. The squares of the chessboard which must be crossed clearly represent erogenous zones, and becoming-queen refers to the phallus as the agency of coordination. It soon appears that the corresponding problem is no longer that of the unique and withdrawn voice, and that it has rather become the problem of multiple discourses: what must one pay, how much must one pay in order to be able to speak? This question appears in almost every chapter, with the word sometimes referring to a single series (as in the case of the proper name so contracted that it is no longer remembered); sometimes to two convergent series (as in the case of Tweedledum and Tweedledee, so much convergent and continuous as to be indistinguishable); and sometimes to divergent and ramified series (as in the case of Humpty Dumpty, the master of semantemes and paymaster of words, making them ramify and resonate to such a degree as to be incomprehensible, so that their reverse and right sides are no longer distinguishable). But in this simultaneous organization of words and surfaces, the danger already indicated in *Alice* is specified and developed. Again, Alice has distributed her parental images on the surface: the White Queen, the plaintive and wounded mother; the Red King, the withdrawn father, asleep from the fourth chapter onward. But, traversing all depth and height, it is the

Red Queen who arrives — the phallus become the agent of castration. It is the final debacle again, this time finished off voluntarily by Alice herself. Something is going to happen, she declares. But what? Would it be a regression to the oral-anal depths, to the point that everything would begin anew, or rather the liberation of another glorious and neutralized surface?

The psychoanalytic diagnosis often formulated with respect to Lewis Carroll notes the following: the impossibility of confronting the Oedipal situation; flight before the father and renunciation of the mother; projection onto the little girl, identified with the phallus but also deprived of a penis; and the oral-anal regression which follows. Such diagnoses, however, have very little interest, and it is well known that the encounter between psychoanalysis and the work of art (or the literary-speculative work) cannot be achieved in this manner. It is not achieved certainly by treating authors, through their work, as possible or real patients, even if they are accorded the benefit of sublimation; it is not achieved by "psychoanalyzing" the work. For authors, if they are great, are more like doctors than patients. We mean that they are themselves astonishing diagnosticians or symptomatologists. There is always a great deal of art involved in the grouping of symptoms, in the organization of a *table* where a particular symptom is dissociated from another, juxtaposed to a third, and forms the new figure of a disorder or illness. Clinicians who are able to renew a symptomatological table produce a work of art; conversely, artists are clinicians, not with respect to their own case, nor even with respect to a case in general; rather, they are clinicians of civilization. In this regard, we cannot follow those who think that Sade has nothing essential to say on sadism, nor Masoch on masochism. It seems, moreover, that an evaluation of symptoms might be achieved only through a *novel*. It is not by chance that the neurotic creates a "familial romance," and that the Oedipus complex must be found in the meanderings of it. From the perspective of Freud's genius, it is not the complex which provides us with information about Oedipus and Hamlet, but rather Oedipus and Hamlet who provide us with information about the complex. It will be objected that the artist is, in fact, not necessary; the patient himself provides the romance and the doctor evaluates it. But this would be to neglect the specificity of the artist both as patient and as doctor of civilization; it would be to neglect the difference between the artist's novel as a work of art and the neurotic's novel. The neurotic can only actualize the terms and the story of his novel: the symptoms are this actualization, and the novel has no other meaning. On the contrary, to extract the non-actualizable part of the pure event from symptoms (or, as Blanchot says, to raise the visible to the invisible), to raise everyday actions and passions (like eating, shitting, loving, speaking, or dying) to their noematic attribute and their corresponding pure Event, to go from the physical surface on which symptoms are played out and actualizations decided to the metaphysical surface on which the pure event stands and is played out, to go from the cause of the symptoms to the quasi-cause of the *œuvre* —this is the object of the novel as a work of art, and what distinguishes it from the familial novel.[2] In other words, the positive, highly affirmative character of desexualization consists in the *replacement of psychic regression by speculative investment.* This does not prevent the speculative investment from bearing upon a sexual object—since the investment disengages the event from it and poses the object as concomitant of the corresponding event: what is a little girl? An entire *œuvre* is needed, not in order to answer this question but in order to evoke and to compose the unique event which makes it into a question. The artist is not only the patient and doctor of civilization, but is also its pervert.

Of this process of desexualization and this leap from one surface to another, we have said almost nothing. Only its power appears in Carroll's work: it appears in the very force with which the basic series (those that esoteric words subsume) are desexualized to the benefit of the alternative to eat/to speak; but also in the force with which the sexual object, the little girl, is maintained. Indeed, the mystery lies in this leap, in this passage from one surface to another, and in what the first surface becomes, skirted over by the second. From the physical chessboard to the logical diagram, or rather from the sensitive surface to the ultra-sensitive plate—it is in this leap that Carroll, a renowned photographer, experiences a pleasure that we might assume to be perverse, and that he innocently declares (as he says to Amelia in an "uncontrollable excitement": "Miss Amelia, I hope to do myself the honor of coming to *you* for a negative. . . . Amelia, thou are mine!").

Thirty-Fourth Series of Primary Order
and Secondary Organization

If it is true that the phantasm is constructed upon at least two diverging sexual series and that it merges with their *resonance,* it is nevertheless the case that the two basic series (along with the object = x which traverses them and causes them to resonate) constitute only the extrinsic beginning of the phantasm. Let us call the resonance "intrinsic beginning." The phantasm develops to the extent that the resonance induces a *forced movement* that goes beyond and sweeps away the basic series. It has a pendular structure: the basic series traversed by the movement of the object = x, the resonance, and the forced movement of an amplitude greater than the initial movement. This initial movement is, as we have seen, the movement of Eros, which operates on the intermediary physical surface, the sexual surface, or the liberated area of sexual drives. But the forced movement which represents desexualization is Thanatos and "compulsion"; it operates between the two extremes of the original depth and the metaphysical surface, the destructive cannibalistic drives of depth and the speculative death instinct. We know that the greatest danger associated with this forced movement is the merging of the extremes or, rather, the loss of everything in the bottomless depth, at the price of a generalized debacle of surfaces. But, conversely, the greatest potentiality of the forced movement lies in the constitution, beyond the physical surface, of a metaphysical surface of great range, on which even the devouring-devoured objects of the depths are projected. We can therefore name the entire forced movement "death instinct," and name its full amplitude "metaphysical surface." At any rate, the forced movement is not established between the basic sexual series, but rather between the two new and infinitely larger series—eating, on the one hand, and thinking, on the other, where the second always risks disappearing into the first, and the first, on the contrary, risks being projected onto the second.[1] Thus, the phantasm requires four series and two movements. The movement of resonance of the two sexual series induces a forced movement which extends beyond the base and the limits of life, plunging into the abyss of bodies. But it also opens onto a mental surface, giving birth thereby to the two new series between which the entire struggle that we attempted to describe is waged.

What happens if the mental or metaphysical surface has the upper hand in this pendular movement? In this case, the verb is inscribed on this surface—that is, the glorious event enters a symbolic relation with a state of affairs, rather than merging with it; the shining, noematic attribute, rather than being confused with a quality, sublimates it; the proud Result, rather than being confused with an action or passion, extracts an eternal truth from them. What Carroll calls "Impenetrability," and also "Radiancy," is actualized. This is the verb which, in its univocity, conjugates devouring and thinking: it projects eating on the metaphysical surface and sketches out thinking on it. And because to eat is no longer an action nor to be eaten a passion, but rather the noematic attribute which corresponds to them in the verb, the mouth is somehow liberated for thought, which fills it with all possible words. The verb is, therefore, *"to speak"*; it means *to eat/to think,* on the metaphysical surface, and causes the event, as that which can be expressed by language, to happen to consumable things, and sense, as the expression of thought, to insist in language. Thus, *"to think"* also means *to eat/to speak*—to eat as the "result," to speak as "made possible." The struggle between the mouth and the brain comes to an end here. We have seen this struggle for the independence of sounds go on, ever since the excremental and alimentary noises which occupied the mouth-anus in depth; we followed it to the disengagement of a voice high above; and finally we traced it to the primary formation of surfaces and words. Speaking, in the complete sense of the word, presupposes the verb and passes through the verb, which projects the mouth onto the metaphysical surface, filling it with the ideal events of this surface. The verb is the "verbal representation" in its entirety, as well as the highest affirmative power of the disjunction (univocity, with respect to that which diverges). The verb, however, is silent; and we must take literally the idea that Eros is sonorous and that the death instinct is silence. In the verb, the secondary organization is brought about, and from this organization the entire ordering of language proceeds. Nonsense functions as the zero point of thought, the aleatory point of desexualized energy or the punctual Instinct of death; Aion or empty form and pure Infinitive is the line traced by this point, that is, a cerebral crack at the limits of which the event appears; and the event taken in the univocity of this infinitive is distributed in the two series of amplitude which constitute the metaphysical surface. The event is related to one of these series as a noematic attribute, and to the other as a noetic sense, so that both series, to eat/to speak, form the disjunct for an affirmative synthesis, or the equivocity of what there is for and in univocal Being. It is this whole system, point-line-surface, that represents the organization of sense and nonsense. Sense occurs to states of affairs and insists in propositions, varying its pure univocal infinitive according to the series of the states of affairs which it subli- mates and from which it results, and the series of propositions which it symbolizes and makes possible. We have seen the way in which the order of language with its formed units comes about—that is, with denotations and their fulfillments in things, manifestations and their actualizations in persons, signification and their accomplishments in concepts; it was precisely the entire subject matter of the static genesis. But, in order to get to that point, it was necessary to go through all the stages of the dynamic genesis. For the voice gave us only denotations, empty manifestations and denotations, or pure intentions suspended in tonality. The first words gave us only formative elements, without reaching formed units. In order that there be language, together with the full use of speech conforming to the three dimensions of language, it was necessary to pass through the verb and its silence, and through the entire organization of sense and nonsense on the metaphysical surface—the last stage of the dynamic genesis.

It is certain that sexual organization is a prefiguration of the organization of language, just as the physical surface was a preparation for the metaphysical surface. The phallus plays an important role in the stages of the conflict between mouth and brain. Sexuality is in between eating and speaking and, at the same time that the sexual drives are detached from the destructive alimentary drives, they inspire the first words made up of phonemes, morphemes, and semantemes. Sexual organization already presents us with an entire point-line-surface system; and the phallus, as object = x and word = x, has the role of nonsense, distributing sense to the two basic sexual series, the pregenital and the Oedipal. This entire intermediary domain, however, seems to be neutralized by the movement of desexualization, just as the basic series of the phantasm have been by the series of amplitude. The reason is that phonemes, morphemes, and semantemes, in their original relation to sexuality, do not yet form units of denotation, manifestation, or signification. Sexuality is neither denoted, nor manifested, nor signified by them; rather, sexuality is the surface that they double, and they themselves are the doubling up which builds the surface. It is a question of a dual surface effect, of reverse and right sides, which precedes all relations between states of affairs and propositions. This is why when another surface is developed with different effects which at last found denotations, manifestations, and significations as ordered linguistic units, elements like phonemes, morphemes, and semantemes seem to turn up on this new plane, but seem to lose their sexual resonance. This sexual resonance is repressed or neutralized, while the basic series are swept aside by the new series of amplitude. Sexuality exists only as an allusion, as vapor or dust, showing a path along which language has passed, but which it continues to jolt and to erase like so many extremely disturbing childhood memories.

The matter is, however, still more complicated. For if it is true that the phantasm is not content with oscillating between the extreme of alimentary depth and the other extreme represented by the metaphysical surface, if it strives to project onto this metaphysical surface the event corresponding to nourishment, how would it not *also* release the events of sexuality? How would it not release them, in a very particular manner? As we have seen, the phantasm does not eternally recommence its intrinsic movement of desexualization without turning back on its extrinsic sexual beginning. This paradox has no equivalent in the other instances of projection on the metaphysical surface: a desexualized energy invests or reinvests an object of sexual interest as such and is thereby re-sexualized in a new way. Such is the most general mechanism of perversion, on the condition that perversion be distinguished as an art of the surface from subversion as a technique of depth. According to Paula Heimann, most "sexual" crimes are wrongly said to be perverse; they should be attributed to the subversion of depths, where the sexual drives are still directly woven into the devouring and destructive drives. But perversion as a surface dimension bound to the erogenous zones, to the phallus of coordination and castration and to the relation of the physical and metaphysical surfaces, raises only the problem of the investment of a sexual object by a desexualized energy as such. Perversion is a surface structure which expresses itself as such, without being necessarily actualized in criminal behaviors of a subversive nature. Crimes may undoubtedly follow, but only through a regression from perversion to subversion. The real problem of perversion is shown correctly in the essential mechanism which corresponds to it, that of *Verleugnung*. For if *Verleugnung* is a question of maintaining the image of the phallus in spite of the absense of a penis, in the case of women, this operation presupposes a desexualization as the consequence of castration, but also a reinvestment of the sexual object insofar as it is sexual by means of desexualized energy: *Verleugnung* is not an hallucination, but rather an esoteric knowledge.[2] Thus Carroll, perverse but without crime, perverse but nonsubversive, stuttering and left-handed, uses the desexualized energy of the photographic apparatus as a frightfully speculative eye, in order to invest the sexual object par excellence, namely, the little girl-phallus.

Caught up in the system of language, there is thus a co-system of sexuality which mimics sense, nonsense, and their organization: a simulacrum for a phantasm. Furthermore, throughout all of that which language will designate, manifest, or signify, there will be a sexual history that will never be designated, manifested, or signified in itself, but which will coexist with all the operations of language, recalling the sexual appurtenance of the formative linguistic elements. This status of sexuality accounts for repression. It does not suffice to say that the concept of repression in general is topical: it is topological. Repression is always the repression of one dimension by another. Height—that is, the superego, whose precocious formation we have seen—represses the depth where sexual and destructive drives are closely linked together.

It is even on this link, or on the internal objects which represent it, that the so-called primary repression comes to bear. Repression then signifies that depth is almost covered up by the new dimension, and that the drive takes on a new figure in conformity with the repressing instance—at least in the beginning (in this case, the liberation of sexual drives from the destructive drives and the pious intentions of Oedipus). That the surface may be in turn the object of the so-called secondary repression, and that it is not therefore the least bit identical to consciousness, is explained in a complex manner: first, in accordance with Freud's hypothesis, the play of two distinct series forms an essential condition of the repression of sexuality and of the retroactive character of this repression. Moreover, even when it puts into play only a partial homogeneous series, or a continuous global series, sexuality does not have the conditions which would render possible its being maintained in consciousness (namely, the possibility of being denoted, manifested, and signified by linguistic elements corresponding to it). The third reason must be sought on the side of the metaphysical surface, in the manner in which this surface represses the sexual surface at the same time that it imposes on the energy of the drive the new figure of desexualization. It should not be surprising that the metaphysical surface, in turn, is not at all identical to a consciousness. It should be enough to recall that the series of amplitude which characterize it essentially transcend whatever may be conscious and form an impersonal and pre-individual transcendental field. Finally, consciousness, or rather the preconscious, has no other field than that of possible denotations, manifestations, and significations—that is, the order of language which arises from all that which has preceded. But the play of sense and nonsense, and surface effects, on the metaphysical as well as on the physical surface, do not belong to consciousness any more than do actions and passions of the most deeply buried depth. The return of the repressed occurs in accordance with the general mechanism of regression: there is regression as soon as one dimension falls back on another. Without doubt, the mechanisms of regression are very different depending on the accidents proper to particular dimensions (the drop from the heights, for example, or the holes in the surface). But what is essential is the threat that depth brings to bear on all other dimensions; thus, it is the locus of primitive repression and of "fixations"—the ultimate terms of regressions. As a general rule, there is a difference in nature between surface zones and stages of depth, and thus between a regression to the erogenous anal zone, for example, and a regression to the anal stage as a digestive-destructive stage. But the points of fixation, which are like beacons attracting the regressive processes, always strive to assure that regression itself regresses, as it changes nature by changing dimensions, and finally returns to the depth of stages into which all dimensions descend. One final distinction is left between regression as the movement by which a dimension falls back on those which preceded it and this other movement by which a dimension reinvests, in its own way, the one preceding it. Alongside repression and the return of the repressed, we must save a place for these complex processes through which an element characteristic of a certain dimension is invested as such with the very different energy corresponding to another dimension: for example, subversive criminal conduct is inseparable from the function of the voice from above, which reinvests the destructive process of depth as if it were an obligation that is forever *fixed,* and orders it in the guise of the superego or of the good object (see the story of Lord Arthur Savile).[3] Perverse conduct is also inseparable from a movement of the metaphysical surface which, instead of repressing sexuality, uses desexualized energy in order to invest a sexual element as such and to *fix* it with unbearable attention (the second sense of fixation).

The aggregate of surfaces constitutes the organization which is called secondary, and which is defined by "verbal representation." Verbal representation must be carefully distinguished from "object representation," because it concerns an incorporeal event and not a body, an action, a passion, or a quality of bodies. Verbal representation is, as we have seen, the representation which enveloped an expression. It is made of what is expressed and what is expressing, and conforms itself to the twisting of the one into the other. It represents the event as expressed, brings it to exist in the elements of language, and, conversely, confers on these elements an expressive value and a function as "representatives" which they did not have by themselves. The whole order of language is the result of it, with its code of tertiary determinations founded in turn on "objectal" representations (denotation, manifestation, signification; individual, person, concept; world, self, and God).

But what matters here is the preliminary, founding, or poetic organization—that is, this play of surfaces in which only an a-cosmic, impersonal, and pre-individual field is deployed, this exercise of nonsense and sense, and this deployment of series which precede the elaborate products of the *static* genesis. From the tertiary order, we must move again up to the secondary organization, and then to the primary order, in accordance with the *dynamic* requirement. Take, for example, the table of categories of the dynamic genesis in relation to the moments of language: passion-action (noise); possession-privation (voice); intention-result (speech). Secondary organization (the verb or verbal representation) is itself the result of this long itinerary; it emerges when the event knows how to raise the result to a second power, and when the verb knows how to grant elementary words the expressive value of which they were still deprived. But the entire itinerary is indicated by the primary order, where words are directly actions and passions of the body, or even withdrawn voices. They are demonic possessions or divine privations. Obscenities and insults afford an idea, by way of regression, of this chaos in which bottomless depth and unlimited height are respectively combined. For, however intimate their liaison may be, the obscene word illustrates the direct action of one body on another which is acted upon, whereas the insult pursues all at once the one who withdraws, dispossesses this one of all voice, and is itself a voice which withdraws.[4] This strict combination of obscene and abusive words testifies to the properly satiric values of language. We call *"satiric"* the process by which regression regresses itself; that is, it is never a sexual regression at the surface without its also being a digestive alimentary regression in depth, stopping only at the cesspool and pursuing the withdrawn voice as it uncovers the excremental soil that this voice leaves behind. Making a thousand noises and withdrawing his voice, the satiric poet, or the great pre-Socratic of one and the same movement of the world, pursues God with insults and sinks into the excrement. Satire is a prodigious art of regressions.

Height, however, prepares new values for language and affirms in it its independence and its radical difference from depth. *Irony* appears each time language deploys itself in accordance with relations of eminence, equivocity, or analogy. These three great concepts of the tradition are the source from which all the figures of rhetoric proceed. Thus, irony will find a natural application in the tertiary order of language, in the case of the analogy of significations, the equivocity of denotations, and the eminence of the one who manifests himself—the whole comparative play of self, world, and God, in the relation of being and the individual, representation and person, which constitute the classical and romantic forms of irony. But even in the primary process, the voice from high above liberates properly ironic values; it withdraws behind its eminent unity and utilizes the equivocity of its tone and the analogy of its objects. In short, it has at its disposal the dimensions of a language before having at its disposal the corresponding principle of organization. There is, for example, a primordial form of Platonic irony, redressing height, disengaging it from depth, repressing and hemming in satire or the satirist, and employing all its "irony" in asking whether, by chance, there could be an Idea of mud, hair, filth, or excrement. Nevertheless, what silences irony is not a return of satiric values in the manner of an ascent from bottomless depths. Besides, nothing ascends except to the surface—in which case a surface is still necessary. Once height makes the constitution of surfaces possible, along with the corresponding release of sexual drives, we believe that something happens, something capable of vanquishing irony on its own terrain—that is, on the terrain of equivocity, eminence, and analogy. It is as if there were an eminence in excess, an exaggerated equivocation, and a supernumerary analogy which, rather than being added to the others, would on the contrary ensure their closure. An equivocation such that "afterward" there can be no other equivocation—this is the sense of the expression *"there is also sexuality."* It is as with Dostoevsky's characters who keep on saying: please consider, dear sir, there is still this matter, and again that matter. . . . But with sexuality, one arrives at an *"again"* which ends every "again," one reaches an equivocation which renders the pursuit of equivocities or the continuation of ulterior analogies impossible. This is why, at the same time that sexuality is deployed over the physical surface, it makes us go from voice to speech and gathers together every word into an esoteric whole and in a sexual history which will not be designated, manifested, or signified by these words, but which rather will be strictly coextensive and co-substantial with them. This is what words represent; all the formative elements of language which exist only in relation (or in reaction) to one another—phonemes, morphemes, and semantemes—form their totality from the point of view of this immanent history with which they are identical. There is therefore an excessive equivocation from the point of view of the voice and in relation to voice: an equivocation which ends equivocity and makes language ripe for something else. This something else is that which comes from the *other,* desexualized and metaphysical surface, when we finally go from speech to the verb, or when we compose a unique verb in the pure infinitive—along with the assembled words. This something else is the revelation of the univocal, the advent of Univocity—that is, the Event which communicates the univocity of being to language.

The univocity of sense grasps language in its complete system, as the total expresser of a unique expressed—the event. The values of humor are distinguished from those of irony: *humor* is the art of surfaces and of the complex relation between the two surfaces. Beginning with one excessive equivocation, humor constructs all univocity; beginning with the properly sexual equivocation which ends all equivocity, humor releases a desexualized Univocity—a speculative univocity of Being and language—the entire secondary organization in one word.[5] It is necessary to imagine someone, one-third Stoic, one-third Zen, and one-third Carroll: with one hand, he masturbates in an excessive gesture, with the other, he writes in the sand the magic words of the pure event open to the univocal: "Mind—I believe—is Essence—Ent—Abstract —that is—an Accident—which we—that is to say—I meant—." Thus, he makes the energy of sexuality pass into the pure asexual, without, however, ceasing to ask "What is a little girl?"—even if this question must be replaced with the problem of a work of art yet to come, which alone would give an answer. See, for example, Bloom on the beach. . . . Equivocity, analogy, and eminence will no doubt recover their rights with the tertiary order, in the denotations, significations, and manifestations of everyday language submitted to the rules of good sense and common sense. As we then consider the perpetual entwining which constitutes the logic of sense, it seems that this final ordering recovers the voice of the heights of the primary process, but also that the secondary organization at the surface recovers something of the most profound noises, blocks, and elements for the Univocity of sense —a brief instant for a poem without figures. What can the work of art do but follow again the path which goes from noise to the voice, from voice to speech, and from speech to the verb, constructing this *Musik für ein Haus,* in order always to recover the independence of sounds and to fix the thunderbolt of the univocal. This event is, of course, quickly covered over by everyday banality or, on the contrary, by the sufferings of madness.

Appendixes

I. The Simulacrum and
Ancient Philosophy

1. PLATO AND THE SIMULACRUM

What does it mean "to reverse Platonism"? This is how Nietzsche defined the task of his philosophy or, more generally, the task of the philosophy of the future. The formula seems to mean the abolition of the world of essences *and* of the world of appearances. Such a project, however, would not be peculiar to Nietzsche. The dual denunciation of essences and appearances dates back to Hegel or, better yet, to Kant. It is doubtful that Nietzsche meant the same thing. Moreover, this formula of reversal has the disadvantage of being abstract; it leaves the motivation of Platonism in the shadows. On the contrary, "to reserve Platonism" must mean to bring this motivation out into the light of the day, to "track it down"—the way Plato tracks down the Sophist.

In very general terms, the motive of the theory of Ideas must be sought in a will to select and to choose. It is a question of "making a difference," of distinguishing the "thing" itself from its images, the original from the copy, the model from the simulacrum. But are all these expressions equivalent? The Platonic project comes to light only when we turn back to the method of division, for this method is not just one dialectical procedure among others. It assembles the whole

253

power of the dialectic in order to combine with it another power, and represents thus the entire system. One might at first want to say that this method amounts to the division of a genus into contrary species in order to subsume the thing investigated under the appropriate species: this would explain the process of specification, in the *Sophist,* undertaken for the sake of a definition of the angler. But this is only the superficial aspect of division, its ironic aspect. If one takes this aspect seriously, Aristotle's objection would clearly be in order: division would be a bad and illicit syllogism, since the middle term is lacking, and this would make us conclude, for example, that angling is on the side of the arts of acquisition, of acquisition by capture, etc.

The real purpose of division must be sought elsewhere. In the *Statesman,* a preliminary definition is attained according to which the statesman is the shepherd of men. But all sorts of rivals spring up, the doctor, the merchant, the laborer, and say: "I am the shepherd of men." Again, in the *Phaedrus,* the question is about the definition of delirium and, more precisely, about the discernment of the well-founded delirium or true love. Once again, many pretenders rise up to say, "I am the inspired one, the lover." The purpose of division then is not at all to divide a genus into species, but, more profoundly, to select lineages: to distinguish pretenders; to distinguish the pure from the impure, the authentic from the inauthentic. This explains the constancy of the metaphor assimilating division to the testing of gold. Platonism is the philosophical *Odyssey* and the Platonic dialectic is neither a dialectic of contradiction nor of contrariety, but a dialectic of rivalry *(amphisbetesis),* a dialectic of rivals and suitors. The essence of division does not appear in its breadth, in the determination of the species of a genus, but in its depth, in the selection of the lineage. It is to screen the claims *(pretensions)* and to distinguish the true pretender from the false one.

To achieve this end, Plato proceeds once again by means of irony. For when division gets down to the actual task of selection, it all happens as though division renounces its task, letting itself be carried along by a myth. Thus, in the *Phaedrus,* the myth of the circulation of the souls seems to interrupt the effort of division. The same thing happens in the *Statesman* with the myth of archaic ages. This flight, this appearance of flight or renunciation, is the second snare of division, its second irony. In fact, myth interrupts nothing. On the contrary, it is an integral element of division. The characteristic of division is to sur-mount the duality of myth and dialectic, and to reunite in itself dialectical and mythic power. Myth, with its always circular structure, is indeed the story of a foundation. It permits the construction of a model according to which the different pretenders can be judged. What needs a foundation, in fact, is always a pretension or a claim. It is the pretender who appeals to a foundation, whose claim may be judged well-founded, ill-founded, or unfounded. Thus, in the *Phaedrus,* the myth of circulation explains that before their incarnation souls had been able to see the Ideas. At the same time, it gives us a criterion of selection according to which the well-founded delirium or true love belongs only to souls which have seen many things, and which have within them many slumbering but revivable memories. The souls which are sensual, forgetful, and full of petty purposes, are, on the contrary, denounced as false pretenders. It is the same in the *Statesman:* the circular myth shows that the definition of the statesman as "shepherd of men" literally applies only to the ancient god; but a criterion of selection is extracted from the myth, according to which the different men of the city participate unequally in the mythic model. In short, an elective partici-pation is the response to the problem of a method of selection.

To participate is, at best, to rank second. The celebrated Neoplatonic triad of the "Unparticipated," the participated, and the participant follows from this. One could express it in the following manner as well: the foundation, the object aspired to, and the pretender; the father, the daughter, and the fiancé. The foundation is that which possesses some-thing in a primary way; it relinquishes it to be participated in, giving it to the suitor, who possesses only secondarily and insofar as he has been able to pass the test of the foundation. The participated is what the unparticipated possesses primarily. The unparticipated gives it out for participation, it offers the participated to the participants: Justice, the quality of being just, and the just men. Undoubtedly, one must distin-guish all sorts of degrees, an entire hierarchy, in this elective participa-tion. Is there not a possessor of the third or the fourth rank, and on to an infinity of degradation culminating in the one who possesses no more than a simulacrum, a mirage—the one who is himself a mirage and simulacrum? In fact, the *Statesman* distinguishes such a hierarchy in detail: the true statesman or the well-founded aspirer, then relatives, auxiliaries, and slaves, down to simulacra and counterfeits. Malediction weighs heavily on these last—they incarnate the evil power of the false pretender.

Thus myth constructs the immanent model or the foundation-test according to which the pretenders should be judged and their pretensions measured. Only on this condition does division pursue and attain its end, which is not the specification of the concept but the authentication of the Idea, not the determination of species but the selection of lineage. How are we to explain, however, that of the three important texts dealing with division—the *Phaedrus,* the *Statesman,* and the *Sophist* —the last one contains no founding myth? The reason for this is simple. In the *Sophist,* the method of division is employed paradoxically, not in order to evaluate the just pretenders, but, on the contrary, in order to track down the false pretender as such, in order to define the being (or rather the nonbeing) of the simulacrum. The Sophist himself is the being of the simulacrum, the satyr or centaur, the Proteus who meddles and insinuates himself everywhere. For this reason, it may be that the end of the *Sophist* contains the most extraordinary adventure of Platonism: as a consequence of searching in the direction of the simulacrum and of leaning over its abyss, Plato discovers, in the flash of an instant, that the simulacrum is not simply a false copy, but that it places in question the very notations of copy and model. The final definition of the Sophist leads us to the point where we can no longer distinguish him from Socrates himself—the ironist working in private by means of brief arguments. Was it not necessary to push irony to that extreme? Was it not Plato himself who pointed out the direction for the reversal of Platonism?

We started with an initial determination of the Platonic motivation: to distinguish essence from appearance, intelligible from sensible, Idea from image, original from copy, and model from simulacrum. But we already see that these expressions are not equivalent. The distinction wavers between two sorts of images. *Copies* are secondary possessors. They are well-founded pretenders, guaranteed by resemblance; *simulacra* are like false pretenders, built upon a dissimilarity, implying an essential perversion or a deviation. It is in this sense that Plato divides in two the domain of images-idols: on one hand there are *copies-icons,* on the other there are *simulacra-phantasms.*[1] We are now in a better position to define the totality of the Platonic motivation: it has to do with selecting among the pretenders, distinguishing good and bad copies or, rather, copies (always well-founded) and simulacra (always engulfed in dissimilarity). It is a question of assuring the triumph of the copies over simulacra, of repressing simulacra, keeping them completely submerged, preventing them from climbing to the surface, and "insinuating themselves" everywhere.

The great manifest duality of Idea and image is present only in this goal: to assure the latent distinction between the two sorts of images and to give a concrete criterion. For if copies or icons are good images and are well-founded, it is because they are endowed with resemblance. But resemblance should not be understood as an external relation. It goes less from one thing to another than from one thing to an Idea, since it is the Idea which comprehends the relations and proportions constitutive of the internal essence. Being both internal and spiritual, resemblance is the measure of any pretension. The copy truly resembles something only to the degree that it resembles the Idea of that thing. The pretender conforms to the object only insofar as he is modeled (internally and spiritually) on the Idea. He merits the quality (the quality of being just, for example) only insofar as he has founded himself on the essence (justice). In short, it is the superior identity of the Idea which founds the good pretension of the copies, as it bases it on an internal or derived resemblance. Consider now the other species of images, namely, the simulacra. That to which they pretend (the object, the quality, etc.), they pretend to underhandedly, under cover of an aggression, an insinuation, a subversion, "against the father," and without passing through the Idea.[2] Theirs is an unfounded pretension, concealing a dissimilarity which is an internal unbalance.

If we say of the simulacrum that it is a copy of a copy, an infinitely degraded icon, an infinitely loose resemblance, we then miss the essential, that is, the difference in nature between simulacrum and copy, or the aspect by which they form the two halves of a single division. The copy is an image endowed with resemblance, the simulacrum is an image without resemblance. The catechism, so much inspired by Platonism, has familiarized us with this notion. God made man in his image and resemblance. Through sin, however, man lost the resemblance while maintaining the image. We have become simulacra. We have forsaken moral existence in order to enter into aesthetic existence. This remark about the catechism has the advantage of emphasizing the demonic character of the simulacrum. Without doubt, it still produces an *effect* of resemblance; but this is an effect of the whole, completely external and produced by totally different means than those at work within the model. The simulacrum is built upon a disparity or upon a difference. It internalizes a dissimilarity. This is why we can no longer define it in relation to a model imposed on the copies, a model of the Same from which the copies' resemblance derives. If the simulacrum still has a model, it is another model, a model of the Other *(l'Autre)* from which there flows an internalized dissemblance.[3]

Take for instance the great Platonic trinity of the user, the producer, and the imitator. If the user is placed at the top of the hierarchical ladder, it is because he evaluates ends and has at his disposal true *knowledge (savoir)*, which is knowledge of the model or Idea. The copy can be called an imitation, to the degree that it reproduces the model; since this imitation is noetic, spiritual, and internal, however, it is a veritable production ruled by the relations and proportions constitutive of the essence. There is always a productive operation in the good copy and, corresponding to this operation, a *right opinion,* if not knowledge. We see, then, that imitation is destined to take on a pejorative sense to the extent that it is now only a simulation, that is applies to the simulacrum and designates only the external and nonproductive effect of resemblance, that is, an effect obtained by ruse or subversion. There is no longer even right opinion, but rather a sort of ironic encounter which takes the place of a mode of knowledge, an art of encounter that is outside knowledge and opinion.[4] Plato specifies how this nonproductive effect is obtained: the simulacrum implies huge dimensions, depths, and distances that the observer cannot master. It is precisely because he cannot master them that he experiences an impression of resemblance. This simulacrum includes the differential point of view; and the observer becomes a part of the simulacrum itself, which is transformed and deformed by his point of view.[5] In short, there is in the simulacrum a becoming-mad, or a becoming unlimited, as in the *Philebus* where "more and less are always going a point further," a becoming always other, a becoming subversive of the depths, able to evade the equal, the limit, the Same, or the Similar: always more and less at once, but never equal. To impose a limit on this becoming, to order it according to the same, to render it similar—and, for that part which remains rebellious, to repress it as deeply as possible, to shut it up in a cavern at the bottom of the Ocean—such is the aim of Platonism in its will to bring about the triumph of icons over simulacra.

Platonism thus founds the entire domain that philosophy will later recognize as its own: the domain of representation filled by copies-icons, and defined not by an extrinsic relation to an object, but by an intrinsic relation to the model or foundation. The Platonic model is the Same, in the sense that Plato says that Justice is nothing more than just, Courage nothing other than courageous, etc.—the abstract determination of the foundation as that which possesses in a primary way *(en premier)*. The Platonic copy is the Similar: the pretender who possesses in a secondary way. To the pure identity of the model or original there corresponds an exemplary similitude; to the pure resemblance of the copy there corresponds the similitude called imitative. We should not think, however, that Platonism develops this power of representation only for itself: it is satisfied with staking out this domain, that is, founding it, selecting it, and excluding from it everything that might come to blur its limits. The deployment of representation as a well-founded, limited, and finite representation is rather Aristotle's object: representation runs through and covers over the entire domain, extending from the highest genera to the smallest species, and the method of division takes on its traditional fascination with specification which it did not yet have in Plato. We may also determine a third moment when, under the influence of Christianity, one no longer seeks only to establish a foundation for representation or to make it possible, nor to specify or determine it as finite. Now one tries to *render it infinite,* to endow it with a valid claim to the unlimited, to make it conquer the infinitely great as well as the infinitely small, opening it up to Being beyond the highest genera and to the singular beneath the smallest species.

Leibniz and Hegel marked this attempt with their genius. But they too do not get beyond the element of representation, since the double exigency of the Same and the Similar is retained. Simply put, the Same had found an unconditioned principle capable of making it the ruler of the unlimited: sufficient reason; and the Similar has found a condition capable of being applied to the unlimited: convergence or continuity. In fact, a notion like the Leibnizian *"compossibility"* means that, with the monads being assimilated to singular points, each series which converges around one of these points is extended in other series which converge around other points; another world begins in the vicinity of points which would bring about the divergence of the obtained series. We see therefore how Leibniz *excludes* divergence by distributing it into "incompossibles," and by retaining maximum convergence or continuity as the criterion of the best possible world, that is, of the real world (Leibniz presents the other worlds as less well-founded "pretenders"). The same applies to Hegel. It has recently been pointed out to what extent the circles of dialectics revolve around a single center, to what extent they rely on a single center.[6] Whether in monocentric circles or in converging series, philosophy does not free itself from the element of representation when it embarks upon the conquest of the infinite. Its intoxication is a false appearance. It always pursues the same task, Iconology, and adapts it to the speculative needs of Christianity (the infinitely small and the infinitely large). Always the selection among pretenders, the exclusion of the eccentric and the divergent, in the name of a superior finality, an essential reality, or even a meaning of history.

Aesthetics suffers from a wrenching duality. On one hand, it designates the theory of sensibility as the form of possible experience; on the other hand, it designates the theory of art as the reflection of real experience. For these two meanings to be tied together, the conditions of experience in general must become conditions of real experience; in this case, the work of art would really appear as experimentation. We know, for example, that certain literary procedures (the same holds for other arts) permit several stories to be told at once. This is, without doubt, the essential characteristic of the modern work of art. It is not at all a question of different points of view on one story supposedly the same; for points of view would still be submitted to a rule of convergence. It is rather a question of different and divergent stories, as if an absolutely distinct landscape corresponded to each point of view. There is indeed a unity of divergent series insofar as they are divergent, but it is always a chaos perpetually thrown off center which becomes one only in the Great Work. This unformed chaos, the great letter of *Finnegans Wake,* is not just any chaos: it is the power of affirmation, the power to affirm all the heterogeneous series—it "complicates" within itself all the series (hence the interest of Joyce in Bruno as the theoretician of the *complicatio*). Between these basic series, a sort of *internal resonance* is produced; and this resonance induces a *forced movement,* which goes beyond the series themselves. These are the characteristics of the simulacrum, when it breaks its chains and rises to the surface: it then affirms its phantasmatic power, that is, its repressed power. Freud has already shown how the phantasm results from at least two series, one infantile and the other post-pubescent. The affective charge associated with the phantasm is explained by the internal resonance whose bearers are the simulacra. The impression of death, of the rupture or dismembering of life, is explained by the amplitude of the forced movement which carries them along. Thus the conditions of real experience and the structures of the work of art are reunited: divergence of series, decentering of circles, constitution of the chaos which envelops them, internal resonance and movement of amplitude, aggression of the simulacra.[7]

Such systems, constituted by placing disparate elements or heterogeneous series in communication, are in a sense quite common. They are signal-sign systems. The signal is a structure in which differences of potential are distributed, assuring the communication of disparate components: the sign is what flashes across the boundary of two levels, between two communicating series. Indeed, it seems that all phenomena respond to these conditions inasmuch as they find their ground in a constitutive dissymmetry, difference, or inequality. All physical systems are signals; all qualities are signs. It is true, however, that the series which border them remain external. By the same token, the conditions of their reproduction remain external to phenomena. In order to speak of simulacra, it is necessary for the heterogeneous series to be really internalized in the system, comprised or complicated in the chaos. Their differences must be *inclusive*. There is always, no doubt, a resemblance between resonating series, but this is not the problem. The problem is rather in the status and the position of this resemblance. Let us consider the two formulas: "only that which resembles differs" and "only differences can resemble each other." These are two distinct readings of the world: one invites us to think difference from the standpoint of a previous similitude or identity; whereas the other invites us to think similitude and even identity as the product of a deep disparity. The first reading precisely defines the world of copies or representations; it posits the world as icon. The second, contrary to the first, defines the world of simulacra; it posits the world itself as phantasm. From the point of view of this second formula, therefore, it matters little whether the original disparity, upon which the simulacrum is built, it great or small; it may happen that the basic series have only a slight difference between them. It suffices that the constitutive disparity be judged in itself, not prejuding any previous identity, and that the *disparate (le dispars)* be the unity of measure and communication. Resemblance then can be thought only as the product of this internal difference. It matters little whether the system has great external and slight internal difference, or whether the opposite is the case, provided that resemblance be produced on a curve, and that difference, whether great or small, always occupy the center of the thus decentered system.

So "to reverse Platonism" means to make the simulacra rise and to affirm their rights among icons and copies. The problem no longer has to do with the distinction Essence-Appearance or Model-Copy. This distinction operates completely within the world of representation. Rather, it has to do with undertaking the subversion of this world—the "twilight of the idols." The simulacrum is not a degraded copy. It harbors a positive power which denies *the original and the copy, the model and the reproduction*. At least two divergent series are internalized in the simulacrum—neither can be assigned as the original, neither as the copy.[8] It is not even enough to invoke a model of the Other, for no model can resist the vertigo of the simulacrum. There is no longer any privileged point of view except that of the object common to all points of view. There is no possible hierarchy, no second, no third. . . . Resemblance subsists, but it is produced as the external effect of the simulacrum, inasmuch as it is built upon divergent series and makes them resonate. Identity subsists, but it is produced as the law which complicates all the series and makes them all return to each one in the course of the forced movement. In the reversal of Platonism, resemblance is said of internalized difference, and identity of the Different as primary power. The same and the similar no longer have an essence except as *simulated,* that is as expressing the functioning of the simulacrum. There is no longer any possible selection. The non-hierarchized work is a condensation of coexistences and a simultaneity of events. It is the triumph of the false pretender. It simulates at once the father, the pretender, and the fiancé in a superimposition of masks. But the false pretender cannot be called false in relation to a presupposed model of truth, no more than simulation can be called an appearance or an illusion. Simulation is the phantasm itself, that is, the effect of the functioning of the simulacrum as machinery—a Dionysian machine. It involves the false as power, *Pseudos,* in the sense in which Nietzsche speaks of the highest power of the false. By rising to the surface, the simulacrum makes the Same and the Similar, the model and the copy, fall under the power of the false (phantasm). It renders the order of participation, the fixity of distribution, the determination of the hierarchy impossible. It establishes the world of nomadic distributions and crowned anarchies. Far from being a new foundation, it engulfs all foundations, it assures a universal breakdown (*effondrement),* but as a joyful and positive event, as an un-founding (*effondement):* "behind each cave another that opens still more deeply, and beyond each surface a subterranean world yet more vast, more strange. Richer still . . . and under all foundations, under every ground, a subsoil still more profound."[9] How would Socrates be recognized in these caverns, which are no longer his? With what thread, since the thread is lost? How would he exit from them, and how could he still distinguish himself from the Sophist?

That the Same and the Similar may be simulated does not mean that they are appearances or illusions. Simulation designates the power of producing an *effect.* But this is not intended only in a causal sense, since causality would remain completely hypothetical and indeterminate without the intervention of other meanings. It is intended rather in the sense of a "sign" issued from a process of signalization; it is in the sense of a "costume," or rather a mask, expressing a process of disguising, where, behind each mask, there is yet another. . . . Simulation understood in this way is inseparable from the eternal return, for it is in the eternal return that the reversal of the icons or the subversion of the world of representation is decided. Everything happens here as if a latent content were opposed to a manifest content. The manifest content of the eternal return can be determined in conformity to Platonism in general. It represents then the manner in which chaos is organized by the action of the demiurge, and on the model of the Idea which imposes the same and the similar on him. The eternal return, in this sense, is becoming-mad, which is mastered, monocentric, and determined to copy the eternal. Indeed, this is how it appears in the founding myth. It establishes the copy in the image and subordinates the image to resemblance.

Far from representing the truth of the eternal return, however, this manifest content marks rather the utilization and survival of the myth in an ideology which no longer supports it, and which has lost its secret. We would do well to recall to what extent the Greek soul in general, and Platonism in particular, loathed the eternal return in its latent signification.[10] Nietzsche was right when he treated the eternal return as his own vertiginous idea, an idea nourished only by esoteric Dionysian sources, ignored or repressed by Platonism. To be sure, Nietzsche a few times made statements that remained at the level of the manifest content: the eternal return as the Same which brings about the return of the Similar. But how can one not see the disproportion between this flat, natural truth, which does not go beyond a generalized order of the seasons, and Zarathustra's emotion? Furthermore, the manifest statement exists only to be refuted dryly by Zarathustra. Once to the dwarf and again to his animals, Zarathustra reproaches their transforming into a platitude what is otherwise profound, what belongs to another music into an "old refrain," and what would otherwise be tortuous into circular simplicity. In the eternal return, one must pass through the manifest content, but only in order to reach the latent content situated a thousand feet below (the cave behind every cave . . .). Thus, what appeared to Plato to be only a sterile effect reveals in itself the intractability of masks and the impassibility of signs.

The secret of the eternal return is that it does not express an order opposed to the chaos engulfing it. On the contrary, it is nothing other than chaos itself, or the power of affirming chaos. There is a point where Joyce is Nietzschean when he shows that the *vicus of recirculation* can not affect and cause a "chaosmos" to revolve. To the coherence of representation, the eternal return substitutes something else entirely— its own chaodyssey *(chao-errance)*. Between the eternal return and the simulacrum, there is such a profound link that the one cannot be understood except through the other. Only the divergent series, insofar as they are divergent, return: that is, each series insofar as it displaces its difference along with all the others, and all series insofar as they complicate their difference within the chaos which is without beginning or end. The circle of the eternal return is a circle which is always ex-centric in relation to an always decentered center. Klossowski is right to say of the eternal return that it is a "simulacrum of a doctrine": it is indeed Being *(Être)*, but only when "being" *(étant)* is the simulacrum.[11]

The simulacrum functions in such a way that a certain resemblance is necessarily thrown back onto its basic series and a certain identity necessarily projected on the forced movement. Thus, the eternal return is, in fact, the Same and the Similar, but only insofar as they are simulated, produced by the simulation, through the functioning of the simulacrum (will to power). It is in this sense that it reverses representation and destroys the icons. It does not presuppose the Same and the Similar; on the contrary, it constitutes the only Same—the Same of that which differs, and the only resemblance—the resemblance of the unmatched. It is the unique phantasm of all simulacra (the Being of all beings). It is the power to affirm divergence and decentering and makes this power the object of a superior affirmation. It is under the power of the false pretender causing that which *is* to happen again and again. And it does not make *everything* come back. It is still selective, it "makes a difference," but not at all in the manner of Plato. What is selected are all the procedures opposed to selection; what is excluded, what is *made not to* return, is that which presupposes the Same and the Similar, that which pretends to correct divergence, to recenter the circles or order the chaos, and to provide a model or make a copy. For all its long history, Platonism happened only once, and Socrates fell under the blade. For the Same and the Similar become simple illusions when they cease to be simulated.

Modernity is defined by the power of the simulacrum. It behooves philosophy not to be modern at any cost, no more than to be nontemporal, but to extract from modernity something that Nietzsche designated as the untimely, which pertains to modernity, but which must also be turned against it—"in favor, I hope, of a time to come." It is not in the great forests and woodpaths that philosophy is elaborated, but rather in the towns and in the streets—even in the most artificial *(factice)* in them. The untimely is attained in relation to the most distant past, by the reversal of Platonism; in relation to the present, by the simulacrum conceived as the edge of critical modernity; in relation to the future, it is attained by the phantasm of the eternal return as belief in the future. The artificial and the simulacrum are not the same thing. They are even opposed to each other. The artificial is always a copy of a copy, which should be pushed *to the point where it changes its nature and is reversed into the simulacrum* (the moment of Pop Art). Artifice and simulacrum are opposed at the heart of modernity, at the point where modernity settles all of its accounts, as two modes of destruction: the two nihilisms. For there is a vast difference between destroying in order to conserve and perpetuate the established order of representations, models, and copies, and destroying the models and copies in order to institute the chaos which creates, making the simulacra function and raising a phantasm—the most innocent of all destructions, the destruction of Platonism.

2. LUCRETIUS AND THE SIMULACRUM

Following Epicurus, Lucretius was able to determine as "naturalism" the speculative and practical object of philosophy. His importance in philosophy is tied to this double determination.

The products of Nature are inseparable from a diversity which is essential to them. But to think the diverse as diverse is a difficult task on which, according to Lucretius, all previous philosophies had run aground.[1] In our world, natural diversity appears in three intertwined aspects: the diversity of species; the diversity of individuals which are members of the same species; and the diversity of the parts which together compose an individual. Specificity, individuality, and heterogeneity. There is no world which is not manifest in the variety of its parts, places, rivers, and the species which inhabit it. There is no individual absolutely identical to another individual; no calf which is not recognizable to its mother; no two shellfish or grains of wheat which are indiscernible. There is no body composed of homogeneous parts— neither plant nor stream which does not imply a diversity of matter or a heterogeneity of elements, where each animal species, in turn, may find the nourishment appropriate to it. From these three points of view, we can deduce the diversity of worlds themselves: worlds are innumerable, often of different species, sometimes similar, and always composed of heterogeneous elements.

What right have we to make this inference? Nature must be thought of as the principle of the diverse and its production. But a principle of the production of the diverse makes sense only if it does *not* assemble its own elements into a whole. We should not read this demand as circular, as if Epicurus and Lucretius had meant to say that the principle of the diverse had itself to be diverse. The Epicurean thesis is entirely different: Nature as the production of the diverse can only be an infinite sum, that is, a sum which does not totalize its own elements. There is no combination capable of encompassing all the elements of Nature at once, there is no unique world or total universe. *Physis* is not a determination of the One, of Being, or of the Whole. Nature is not collective, but rather distributive, to the extent that the laws of Nature *(foedera naturae,* as opposed to the so-called *foedera fati)* distribute parts which cannot be totalized. Nature is not attributive, but rather conjunctive: it expresses itself through "and," and not through "is." This *and* that— alternations and entwinings, resemblances and differences, attractions and distractions, nuance and abruptness. Nature is Harlequin's cloak, made entirely of solid patches and empty spaces; she is made of plenitude and void, beings and nonbeings, with each one of the two posing itself as unlimited while limiting the other. Being an addition of indivisibles, sometimes similar and sometimes different, Nature is indeed a sum, but not a whole. With Epicurus and Lucretius the real noble acts of philosophical pluralism begin. We shall find no contradiction between the hymn to Venus-Nature and to the pluralism which was essential to this philosophy of Nature. Nature, to be precise, is power. In the name of this power things exist *one by one,* without any possibility of their being gathered together *all at once.* Nor is there any possibility of their being united in a combination adequate to Nature, which would express all of it *at one time.* Lucretius reproached Epicurus' predecessors for having believed in Being, the One and the Whole. These concepts are the obsessions of the mind, speculative forms of belief in the *fatum,* and the theological forms of a false philosophy.

Epicurus' predecessors identified the principle with the One or the Whole. But what is the one if not a particular perishable and corruptible object which we consider arbitrarily in isolation from every other object? And what forms a whole if not a particular finite combination, filled with holes, which we arbitrarily believe to join all the elements of the sum? In both cases, we do not understand diversity and its production. We may generate the diverse out of the One only if we presuppose that anything may be born out of anything, and thus that something may arise from nothing. We may generate the diverse out of the whole, only if we presuppose that the elements which form this whole are contraries capable of being transformed into one another. This is but another way of saying that one thing produces another by changing its nature, and that something is born out of nothing. Because antinatural-ist philosophers did not want to consider the void, the void encom-passed everything. Their Being, their One and their Whole are artificial and unnatural, always corruptible, fleeting, porous, friable, or brittle. They would rather say that "being is nothing" than recognize that there are beings *and* there is void—that there are simple beings within the void and that there is void within compound beings.[2] For the diversity of the diverse, philosophers have substituted the identical or the contra-dictory, and often both at once. However, the Nature of things is coordination *and* disjunction. Neither identity nor contradiction, it is a matter of resemblances and differences, compositions and decomposi-tions, "everything is formed out of connections, densities, shocks, encounters, concurrences, and motions."[3]

Naturalism requires a highly structured principle of causality to account for the production of the diverse inside different and non-totalizable compositions and combinations of the elements of Nature.

1) The atom is that which must be thought, and that which can only be thought. The atom is to thought what the sensible object is to the senses: it is the object which is essentially addressed to thought, the object which gives food to thought, just as the sensible object is that which is given to the senses. The atom is the absolute reality of what is perceived. That the atom is not, and cannot be perceived, that it is essentially hidden, is the effect of its own nature and not the imperfec-tion of our sensibility. In the first place, the Epicurean method is a method of analogy: the sensible object is endowed with sensible parts, but there is a minimum sensible which represents the smallest part of the object; similarly, the atom is endowed with parts that are thought, but there is a minimum thought which represents the smallest part of the atom. The indivisible atom is formed of thought minima, as the divisible object is composed of sensible minima.[4] In the second place, the Epicurean method is a method of passage or transition: guided by analogy, and, as the sensible is composed and decomposed, we go from the sensible to the thought and from the thought to the sensible by means of transitions. We go from the noetic to the sensible analogue, and conversely, through a series of steps conceived and established according to a process of exhaustion.

2) The sum of atoms is infinite, precisely because atoms are elements which do not form a totality. But this sum would not be infinite if the void were not also infinite. The void and the plenum are interlaced and distributed in such a manner that the sum of the void and the atoms is itself infinite. This third infinity expresses the fundamental correlation between the atoms and the void. Up and down in the void result from the correlation between the void itself and the atoms; the weight of atoms (movement from top to bottom) results from the correlation of the atoms with the void.

3) In their fall the atoms collide, not because of their differing weights, but because of the *clinamen*. The *clinamen* is the reason for the collision, it relates one atom to another. It is tied in a fundamental manner to the Epicurean theory of time and is an essential part of the system. In the void, all atoms fall with equal velocity: an atom is no more or less rapid with respect to its weight than other atoms which more or less hinder its fall. In the void, the velocity of the atom is equal to its movement *in a unique direction in a minimum of continuous time*. This minimum expresses the smallest possible term during which an atom moves in a given direction, before being able to take another direction as the result of a collision with another atom. There is therefore a minimum of time, no less than a minimum of matter or a minimum of the atom. In agreement with the nature of the atom, this minimum of continuous time refers to the apprehension of thought. It expresses the most rapid or briefest thought: the atom moves "as swiftly as thought."[5] But, as a result, we must conceive of an originary direction for each atom, as a synthesis which would give to the movement of the atom its initial direction, without which there would be no collision. This synthesis is necessarily accomplished in a time smaller than the minimum of continuous time. This is the *clinamen*. The *clinamen* or swerve has nothing to do with an oblique movement which would come accidentally to modify a vertical fall.[6] It has always been present: it is not a secondary movement, nor a secondary determination of the movement, which would be produced at any time, at any place. The *clinamen* is the original determination of the direction of the movement of the atom. It is a kind of *conatus*—a differential of matter and, by the same token, a differential of thought, based on the method of exhaustion. The meanings of the terms which qualify it have in fact this origin:

"incertus" does not mean indeterminate, but rather unassignable; *"paulum," "incerto tempore," "intervallo minimo"* mean "in a time smaller than the minimum of continuous, thinkable time."

4) This is why the *clinamen* manifests neither contingency nor indetermination. It manifests something entirely different, the *lex atomi,* that is, the irreducible plurality of causes or of causal series, and the impossibility of bringing causes together into a whole. In fact, the *clinamen* is the determination of the meaning of causal series, where each causal series is constituted by the movement of an atom and conserves in the encounter its full independence. In the well-known discussion which set the Epicureans and Stoics against each other, the problem was not directly relating to contingency and necessity, but rather to causality and destiny. Epicureans and Stoics alike affirm causality (no motion without a cause); but the Stoics wish also to affirm destiny, that is, the unity of causes "among themselves." To this, the Epicureans object that one cannot affirm destiny without also introducing necessity, that is, the absolute linking up of effects with one another. It is true that the Stoics retort that they are not at all introducing necessity, but that the Epicureans, for their part, cannot refuse the unity of causes without falling into contingency and chance.[7] Thus, the true problem is whether there is a unity of causes *among themselves.* Must the thought of Nature bring causes together into a whole? The big difference between the Epicureans and the Stoics is that they do not enact the same cleavage of the causal relation. The Stoics affirm a difference of nature between corporeal causes and their incorporeal effects. As a result, effects refer to effects and form a *conjugation,* whereas causes refer to causes and form a *unity.* The Epicureans, on the contrary, affirm the independence of the *plurality* of the material causal series, in virtue of a *swerve* which affects each; and it is only in this objective sense that the *clinamen* may be called "chance."

5) Atoms have various sizes and shapes. But the atom cannot have just any size whatsoever, since it would in this case reach and overtake the sensible minimum. Nor can it have an infinity of shapes, since every diversity in shape implies either a permutation of the minima of atoms or a multiplication of these minima which could not be pursued to infinity without the atom, again, becoming sensible.[8] The sizes and shapes of atoms are not infinite in number, there is however an infinity of atoms of the same size and shape.

6) Not every atom combines with another as they meet; otherwise atoms would form an infinite combination. The shock, in fact, repels as much as it combines. Atoms combine as long as their shapes allow it. Battered by other atoms which break apart their hold, their combinations come undone, losing their elements which go on to join other compounds. If atoms are said to be "specific seeds" or sperms, it is because atoms cannot be joined together in every possible manner.

7) Every combination being finite, there is an infinity of combinations, but no combination is formed of a single species of atoms. Thus, atoms are specific seeds in a second sense—they constitute the heterogeneity of the diverse in a single body. Nevertheless, different atoms in the body tend, in virtue of their weight, to be distributed in accordance with their shapes. In our world, atoms with the same shape group together, forming thereby vast compounds. Our world distributes its elements in a way which allows the earth to occupy the center, "expressing" those elements which go on to form the sea, the air, and the ether *(magnae res).*[9] The philosophy of Nature presents to us the heterogeneity of the diverse with itself, *and also* the resemblance of the diverse with itself.

8) There is the power of the diverse and its production, but there is also the power of the reproduction of the diverse: it is important to see how this second power is derived from the first. Resemblance proceeds from the diverse as such and from its diversity. There is no world or body that loses elements at every moment and then finds new of the same shape. There are no worlds or bodies which do not have their similar in space and time. The production of any composite entity presupposes that the different elements capable of forming it be themselves infinite in number. They would have no chance of coming together, if each one of them, in the void, were the only member of its kind or limited in number. But since each one of them has an infinite number of similar elements, they do not produce a composite entity, without their equivalents having the same chance of renewing their parts, and even of reproducing a similar complex entity.[10] This argument of probability holds especially for worlds. Intra-worldly bodies have also at their disposal a principle of reproduction. They are born, in fact, into already complex settings, each one of which gathers a maximum number of elements of the same shape: earth, sea, air, ether, the *magnae res* or great strata which constitute our world and are

connected to one another through imperceptible transitions. A determined body has its place in one of these realms.[11] As this body loses endlessly the elements of its composition, the realm in which it is immersed offers it new ones—whether it offers these elements to it directly, or whether it transmits them to it in a determined order from the point of the other realms with which it communicates. Moreover, a body will itself have bodies similar to it in other places, or in the element which produces and nourishes it.[12] It is for this reason that Lucretius acknowledges a final aspect of the principle of causality: a body is born not only of determined elements, which are like the seeds producing it; it is born also into a determined setting, which is like a mother suited for its reproduction. The heterogeneity of the diverse forms a sort of vitalism of seeds, but the resemblance of the diverse forms a sort of pantheism of mothers.[13]

Physics is Naturalism from the speculative point of view. What is essential to physics is to be found in the theory of the infinite, and of the spatial and temporal minima. The first two books of Lucretius conform to this fundamental object of physics: *to determine what is really infinite and what is not,* and to distinguish the true from the false infinite. What is truly infinite is the sum of atoms, the void, the sum of atoms and the void, the number of atoms of the same shape and size, and the number of combinations or worlds which are similar to (or different from) ours. What is not infinite are the parts of the body and of the atom, the sizes and shapes of the atom, and above all, every worldly or intra-worldly combination. We must observe that, in this determination of the true and the false infinite, physics operates in an apodeictic manner; and it is here at the same time that it discloses its subordination to practice and ethics. (When physics proceeds hypothetically, on the other hand, as in the explication of a finite phenomenon, it has little bearing on ethics).[14] We must therefore ask why the apodeictic determination of the true and the false infinite is, speculatively, the necessary means of ethics and practice.

The goal or object of practice is pleasure. Hence practice, in this sense, only recommends to us the means of suppressing and avoiding pain. But our pleasures have much more formidable obstacles than our pains: phantoms, superstitions, terrors, the fear of death—everything that tends to disturb the soul.[15] The picture of humanity is one of a troubled humanity, more terrified than in pain (even the plague is defined not only by the pain and suffering it transmits, but by the disturbance of the spirit which it institutes). It is this disturbance of the soul which increases suffering, renders it invincible—although its origin is more profound and is to be found elsewhere. It is composed of two elements: an illusion which arises from the body of an infinite capacity for pleasure; then a second illusion, cast in the mind, of an infinite duration of the soul itself, which is given over without restraint to the idea of an infinity of possible sufferings following death.[16] And the two illusions are linked: the fear of infinite punishment is the natural price to be paid for having unlimited desires. It is on this ground that one must seek out Sisyphus and Tityos; "the fool's life at length becomes a hell on earth."[17] Epicurus goes so far as to say that if injustice is an evil, if greed, ambition, and even debauchery are evils, it is because they deliver us up to the idea of a punishment which may occur at any instant.[18] To be delivered without defense to this turmoil of the soul is, precisely, the condition of man, or the product of this double illusion. ". . . As it is, there is no way of resistance and no power, because everlasting punishment is to be feared after death."[19] This is why, for Lucretius as for Spinoza later on, the religious man displays two aspects: avidity and anguish, covetousness and culpability—a strange complex that generates crimes. The spirit's disquietude is therefore brought about by the fear of dying when we are not yet dead, and also by the fear of not yet being dead once we already are. The entire problem is that of the source of this disturbance or of these two illusions.

It is at this point that we note the intervention of a brilliant, though difficult, Epicurean theory. Bodies or atomic compounds never cease to emit particularly subtle, fluid, and tenuous elements. These second-degree compounds are of two sorts: either they emanate from the depth of bodies, or they detach themselves from the surface of things (skins, tunics, or wrappings, envelopes or barks—what Lucretius calls simulacra and Epicurus calls idols). Insofar as they affect the *animus* and the *anima,* they account for sensible qualities. Sounds, smells, tastes, and temperatures refer especially to the emissions from the depths, whereas visual determinations, forms, and colors refer to the simulacra of the surface. But the situation is even more complicated than this, since each sense seems to combine information of the depth with information of the surface. Emissions arising from the depths pass through the surface, and the superficial envelopes, as they detach themselves from the object, are replaced by formerly concealed strata. Noises from the depth, for example, become voices when they find in certain perforated surfaces (the mouth) the conditions of their articulation. Conversely, the simulacra of the surface are able to provide colors and forms only if there is light, which is emitted from the depths. In any case, emissions and simulacra are obviously understood, not as atomic compounds, but as qualities apprehended at a distance on and in the object. Distance is given by the stream of air that emissions and simulacra push before them, as it passes through the sensory organ.[20] This is why the object is perceived as it must be perceived, relative to the state of simulacra and emissions, the distance they have to cross over, the obstacles they encounter, the distortions to which they submit, or the explosions of which they are the center. At the end of a long journey, the visual envelopes do not strike us with the same vigor; shouts lose their distinction. But always, the property of being related to an object subsists. And, in the case of touch—the only sense which grasps the object without an intermediary—the surface element is related to depth, and what is apprehended when we touch the surface of the object is perceived as residing in its innermost depth.[21]

What is the origin of this appurtenance to the object, whose emissions and simulacra are nevertheless detached? It seems to us that their status, in the Epicurean philosophy, is inseparable from the theory of time. Their essential characteristic, in fact, is the speed with which they traverse space. It is for this reason that Epicurus uses the same formula for the simulacrum and the atom (though perhaps not in the same sense): it moves "as swiftly as thought." On the basis of the analogy, there is a *minimum of sensible time* no less than there is a minimum of thinkable time. *Just as* the swerve of the atom occurs in a time smaller than the minimum thinkable time, so that it has already happened within the smallest time that can be thought, *likewise* the emission of simulacra occurs in a time smaller than the minimum sensible time, so that they are already there in the smallest time that can be sensed and seem to be still within the object after they have reached us. ". . . In one moment of time perceived by us, that is, while one word is being uttered, many times are lurking which reason understands to be there, that is why in any given moment all these various images are present, ready in every place. . . ."[22] The simulacrum is thus imperceptible. The image alone is sensible, which conveys quality, and which is made up of this very rapid succession, and the summation of many identical simulacra. What we have said with respect to the speed of the formation of simulacra applies also, although to a lesser degree, to emanations from the depths: simulacra are swifter than emanations, as if there were, in the case of sensible time, differentials of diverse orders.[23] We are thus able to see on what the originality of the Epicurean method is founded, insofar as it combines the resources of analogy and gradation. The theory of time and its "exhaustive" character assure the unity of the two aspects of the method. For there is a minimum of sensible time as well as a minimum of thinkable time, and in both cases a time smaller than the minimum. But, finally, the analogous times, or their analogous determinations, are organized in a gradation, a gradation, which causes us to pass from the thinkable to the sensible, and vice versa: 1) a time smaller than the minimum of thinkable time (an *incertum tempus* brought about by the *clinamen*); 2) a minimum of continuous thinkable time (the speed of the atom traveling in a single direction); 3) a time smaller than the minimum of sensible time *(punctum temporis,* occupied by the *simulacrum);* and 4) a minimum of continuous sensible time (to which the *image* corresponds, which assures the perception of the object).[24]

There is yet a third species, distinct from the emanations issued from the depth and from the simulations detached from the surface of things. These are phantasms, which enjoy a high degree of independence with respect to objects and an extreme mobility, or an extreme inconstancy in the images which they form (since they are not renewed by the constant supplies emitted by the object). It seems that here the image stands for the object itself. There are three main varieties of this new species of simulacra: theological, oneiric, and erotic. Theological phantasms are made up of simulacra which intersect spontaneously in the sky, forming immense images out of the clouds—high mountains and figures of giants.[25] In any case, simulacra are everywhere. We do not cease to be immersed in them, and to be battered by them as if by waves. Being very far from the objects from which they emanate, and having lost with them any direct connection, they form these grand autonomous figures. Their independence makes them all the more subject to change; one might say that they dance, that they speak, that they modify ad infinitum their tones and gestures. It is true, therefore, as Hume will later recall, that at the origin of the belief in gods there is not permanence, but rather whim and the variability of passions.[26] The second genre of phantasms is constituted by simulacra which are particularly subtle and agile, coming from different objects. They are apt to merge together, to condense and dissipate, and are too swift and too tenuous to offer themselves to sight. But they are capable of supplying the *animus* with visions which pertain to it in its own right: centaurs, Cerberus-like creatures, and ghosts; all of the images which correspond to desire or, again and especially, dream images. Not that desire is creative here; rather, it renders the mind attentive and makes it choose the most suitable phantasm from among all of the subtle phantasms in which we are immersed. The mind, moreover, isolated from the external world and collected or repressed when the body lies dormant, is open to these phantasms.[27] And as for the third genre, the erotic phantasms, they too are constituted of simulacra issuing from very diverse objects and are apt to be condensed ("what was before a woman seems to be changed into a man in our grasp"). The image constituted by these simulacra is doubtless connected with the actual love object; but, unlike what happens in the case of the other needs, the love object cannot be either absorbed or possessed. The image alone inspires and resuscitates desire, a mirage which no longer signals a consistent reality: "But from man's aspect and beautiful bloom nothing comes into the body to be enjoyed except thin images; and this poor hope is often snatched away by the wind."[28]

Time itself is affirmed in relation to movement. This is why we speak of a time of thought in relation to the movement of the atom in the void, and of a sensible time in relation to the mobile image which we perceive, and which causes us to perceive the qualities of atomic compounds. And we speak of a time smaller than the minimum of thinkable time, in relation to the *clinamen* as the determination of the movement of the atom; and of a time smaller than the minimum of sensible time, in relation to simulacra as components of the image (for these components, there are even differential orders of swiftness—profound emanations being less swift than surface simulacra, and surface simulacra being less rapid than the third species). Perhaps movement, in all of these senses, is constitutive of "events" *(eventa,* what Epicurus calls *symptoms),* in contrast with attributes or properties *(conjuncta),* so that time must be called the event of events, and the "symptom of symptoms," which is entailed by movement.[29] For attributes are properties which cannot be abstracted or separated from bodies: for example, the form, dimension, or weight of the atom; or the qualities of a compound which express the atomic disposition without which it would cease to be what it is (the warmth of the fire or the liquidity of water). But the event expresses rather what is happening, without destroying the nature of the thing—thus, a degree of movement compatible with its order (the movement of compounds and their simulacra, or the movements and collisions of each atom). And if birth and death, composition and decomposition are events, this is so in relation to elements of an order inferior to the order of compounds, whose existence is compatible with the variation of movements in a passage at the limit of the corresponding times.

We are thus able to provide an answer to the question of the false infinite. Simulacra are not perceived in themselves; what is perceived is their aggregate in a minimum of sensible time (image). The movement of the atom in a minimum of continuous thinkable time bears witness to the declination, which nevertheless occurs in a time smaller than this minimum. Similarly, the image bears witness to the succession and summation of simulacra, which occur in a time smaller than the minimum of continuous sensible time. And, in the same way that the *clinamen* leads thought to false conceptions of freedom, the simulacra lead the sensibility to a false impression of will and desire. In virtue of their speed, which causes them to be and to act below the sensible minimum, *simulacra produce the mirage of a false infinite in the images which they form.* They give birth to the double illusion of an infinite capacity for pleasure and an infinite possibility of torment—this mixture of avidity and anguish, of cupidity and culpability, which is so characteristic of the man of religion. It is particularly with the third and swiftest species, the phantasms, that one witnesses the development of the illusion and the *myths* which accompany it. In a mixture of theology, eroticism, and oneirism, amorous desire possesses only those simulacra which lead it to know bitterness and torment, even into the pleasure which it wishes were infinite. Our belief in gods rests upon simulacra which seem to dance, to change their gestures, and to shout at us promising eternal punishment—in short, to represent the infinite.

How are we to prevent illusion, if not by means of the rigorous distinction of the true infinite and the correct appreciation of times nested one within the other, and of the passages to the limit which they imply? Such is the meaning of Naturalism. Phantasms then become objects of pleasure, even in the effect which they produce, and which finally appears such as it is: an effect of swiftness or lightness which is attached to the external interference of very diverse objects—as a condensation of successions and simultaneities. The false infinite is the principle of the disturbance of spirit. The speculative object and the practical object of philosophy as Naturalism, science and pleasure, coincide on this point: it is always a matter of denouncing the illusion, the false infinite, the infinity of religion and all of the theologico-erotic-oneiric myths in which it is expressed. To the question "what is the use of philosophy?" the answer must be: what other object would have an interest in holding forth the image of a free man, and in denouncing all of the forces which need myth and troubled spirit in order to establish their power? Nature is not opposed to custom, for there are natural customs. Nature is not opposed to convention: that the law depends upon conventions does not exclude the existence of natural law, that is, a natural function of law which measures the illegitimacy of desires against the disturbance of spirit which accompanies them. Nature is not opposed to invention, inventions being discoveries of Nature itself. But Nature is opposed to myth. Describing the history of humanity, Lucretius offers us a sort of law of compensation: man's unhappiness comes not from his customs, conventions, inventions, or industry, but from the side of myth which is mixed with them, and from the false infinite which it introduces into his feelings and his works. To the origins of language, the discovery of fire, and the first metals royalty, wealth, and property are added, which are mythical in their principle; to the conventions of law and justice, the belief in gods; to the use of bronze and iron, the development of war; to the inventions of art and industry, luxury and frenzy. The events which bring about the unhappiness of humanity are inseparable from the myths which render them possible. To distinguish in men what amounts to myth and what amounts to Nature, and in Nature itself, to distinguish what is truly infinite from what is not—such is the practical and speculative object of Naturalism. The first philosopher is a naturalist: he speaks about nature, rather than speaking about the gods. His condition is that his discourse shall not introduce into philosophy new myths that would deprive Nature of all its positivity. Active gods are the myth of religion, as destiny is the myth of a false physics, and Being, the One and the Whole are the myth of a false philosophy totally impregnated by theology.

Never has the enterprise of "demystification" been carried further. The myth is always the expression of the false infinite and of the disturbance of spirit. One of the most profound constants of Naturalism is to denounce everything that is sadness, everything that is the cause of sadness, and everything that needs sadness to exercise its power.[30] From Lucretius to Nietzsche, the same end is pursued and attained. Naturalism makes of thought and sensibility an affirmation. It directs its attack against the prestige of the negative; it deprives the negative of all its power; it refuses to the spirit of the negative the right to speak in the name of philosophy. The spirit of the negative made an appearance out of the sensible; and linked the intelligible to the One or the Whole. But this Whole, this One, was but a nothingness of thought, just as the appearance was a nothingness of sensation. Naturalism, according to Lucretius, is the thought of an infinite sum, all of the elements of which are not composed at once; but, conversely as well, it is the sensation of finite compounds which are not added up as such with one another. In these two ways, the multiple is affirmed. The multiple as multiple is the object of affirmation, just as the diverse as diverse is the object of joy. The infinite is the absolute intelligible determination (perfection) of a sum which does not form its elements into a whole. But the finite itself is the absolute sensible determination (perfection) of everything which is composed. The pure positivity of the finite is the object of the senses, and the positivity of the veritable infinite is the object of thought. There is no opposition between these two points of view, but rather a correlation. Lucretius established for a long time to come the implications of naturalism: the positivity of Nature; Naturalism as the philosophy of affirmation; pluralism linked with multiple affirmation; sensualism connected with the joy of the diverse; and the practical critique of all mystifications.

II. Phantasm and
Modern Literature

Klossowski's work is built upon an astonishing parallelism between body and language, or rather on a reflection of one in the other. Reasoning is the operation of language, but pantomime is the operation of the body. On the basis of motives yet to be determined, Klossowski thinks that reasoning has a theological essence and the form of the disjunctive syllogism. At the other extreme, the body's pantomime is essentially perverse and has the form of a disjunctive articulation. Fortunately, we have at our disposal a guiding thread in order to understand better this point of departure. Biologists, for example, teach us that the development of the body proceeds by fits and starts: a butt of a limb is determined to be a paw before it is determined to be the right paw, etc. It is possible to say that the animal body "hesitates," and that it proceeds by way of dilemmas. Similarly, reasoning proceeds by fits and starts, hesitates and bifurcates at each level. The body is a disjunctive syllogism; language is an egg on the road to differentiation. The body seals and conceals a hidden language, and language forms a glorious body. The most abstract argumentation is a mimicry, but the body's pantomime is a sequence of syllogisms. One no longer knows whether it is the pantomime which reasons, or reasoning which mimics.

In a certain respect, it is our epoch which has discovered perversion.

It does not need to describe behaviors or undertake abominable accounts. Sade needed to do so, but he is now taken for granted. We, on the other hand, look for the "structure," that is, the form which may be filled by these descriptions and accounts (since it makes them possible), but the structure does not need to be filled in order to be called perverse. What is perverse is precisely this objective power of hesitation in the body: this paw which is neither left nor right; this determination by fits and starts; this differentiation never suppressing the undifferentiated which is divided in it; this suspense which marks each moment of difference; and this immobilization which marks each moment of the fall. Gombrowicz entitles *Pornographia* a perverse novel which contains no obscene tales, but only shows young suspended bodies which hesitate and fall in a frozen movement. In Klossowski, who makes use of a completely different technique, sexual descriptions appear with great force, but only in order to "fulfill" the hesitation of bodies and to distribute it into the parts of the disjunctive syllogism. The presence of such descriptions assumes therefore a linguistic function: being no longer a question of speaking of bodies such as they are prior to, or outside of, language, they form, on the contrary, with words a "glorious body" for pure minds. There is no obscene in itself, says Klossowski; that is, the obscene is not the intrusion of bodies into language, but rather their mutual reflection and the act of language which fabricates a body for the mind. This is the act by which language transcends itself as it reflects a body. "There is nothing more verbal than the excesses of the flesh. ... The reiterated description of the carnal act not only reviews the transgression, it is itself a transgression of language by language." [1]

In another respect, it is our epoch which has discovered theology. One no longer needs to believe in God. We seek rather the "structure," that is, the form which may be filled with beliefs, but the structure has no need to be filled in order to be called "theological." Theology is now the science of nonexisting entities, the manner in which these entities —divine or anti-divine, Christ or Antichrist—animate language and make for it this glorious body which is divided into disjunctions. Nietzsche's prediction about the link between God and grammar has been realized; but this time it is a recognized link, willed, acted out, mimed, "hesitated," developed in the full sense of the disjunction, and placed in the service of the Antichrist—Dionysus crucified. If perversion is the power befitting the body, equivocity is the power of theology; they are reflected in one another. If one is the pantomime par excellence, the other is reasoning par excellence.

That which accounts for the surprising character of Klossowski's work derives from this: the unity of theology and pornography in this very particular sense. We must call it a superior pornology. It is his own way of transcending metaphysics: mimetic argumentation and syllogistic pantomime, the dilemma in the body and the disjunction in the syllogism. The rapes of Roberte punctuate reasoning and alternatives; conversely, syllogisms and dilemmas are reflected in the postures and the ambiguities of the body.[2] The bond of reasoning and description has always been the foremost logical problem—its most noble form. We can see it clearly in the work of logicians who cannot get rid of this problem, perhaps because they raise it in very general conditions. The difficult and decisive conditions are those in which the description concerns the perversion of bodies in pathology (the disjunctive organic cascade), and reasoning concerns the equivocity of language in theology (the disjunctive spiritual syllogism). The problem of the relation between reasoning and description had found a first solution in the work of Sade, which was of the greatest theoretical and technical, philosophical and literary importance. Klossowski opens up some very new paths, to the extent that he poses the conditions of our modern conception of perversion, theology or anti-theology. Everything begins with this blazon, and this reflection of the body and language.

The parallelism presents itself in the first instance between *seeing* and *speaking*. Already in the Des Forêts' novel and its gossip-voyeur, "seeing" designated a very special operation or contemplation. It designated a pure vision of reflections which multiply that which they reflect. These reflections offer the voyeur a more intense participation than if he had himself experienced these passions, the double or the reflection of which he now surveys in the faces of others. This is the case in Klossowski's works, when Octave establishes the law of hospitality according to which he "gives" his wife Roberte to the guests. He attempts to multiply Roberte's essence, to create as many simulacra and reflections of Roberte as there are persons establishing relations with her, and to inspire Roberte to emulate somehow her own doubles, thanks to which Octave, the voyeur, possesses and is able to know her better than if he had kept her, quite simply, for himself. "It was necessary that Roberte begin to appreciate herself, that she be interested in finding herself again in the one whom I elaborated with her own elements, and that little by little she might wish, through a sort of emulation of her own double, to surpass even those aspects which drew themselves in my mind. Hence it was important that she be constantly surrounded by idle young men in quest of opportunities."[3] Such is visual possession: we possess thoroughly only that which is already possessed; not simply possessed by another, for the other here is but an intermediary and, in the last analysis, has no existence—but rather possessed by a dead other, or by spirits. We possess thoroughly only what is expropriated, placed outside of itself, split into two, reflected in the gaze, and multiplied by possessive minds. This is why Roberte, in *Le Souffleur,* is the object of an important problem: can there be "one and the same deceased for two widows?" To possess is thus to give over to possession and to *see* the given multiplied in the gift. "Such common partaking of a dear but living being is not without analogy to the devoted gaze of an artist"[4] (this strange theme of theft and gift, it will be recalled, appears also in Joyce's *Exiles*).

The function of sight consists in doubling, dividing, and multiplying, whereas the function of the ear consists in resonating, in bringing about resonance. Klossowski's entire work moves toward a single goal: to assure the loss of personal identity and to dissolve the self. This is the shining trophy that Klossowski's characters bring back from a voyage to the edge of madness. But as it happens, the dissolution of the self ceases to be a pathological determination in order to become the mightiest power, rich in positive and salutary promises. The self is "corrupted" only because, in the first instance, it is dissolved. This happens, not only to the self which is observed and loses its identity under the gaze, but to the observer also, who is set outside of herself and is multiplied in her own gaze. Octave announces his perverse project with respect to Roberte: "To bring her to anticipate that she is seen . . . , to encourage her to free the gestures from this sentiment of self without ever losing sight of herself . . . , to attribute them to her reflection, to the point of mimicking herself in some manner."[5] But he also knows well that, as a result of his observation, he loses his own identity, sets himself outside of himself, and is multiplied in the gaze as much as the other is multiplied under the gaze—and that this is the most profound content of the idea of Evil. The essential relation, that is, the complicity of sight with speech appears. For what can one do, vis-à-vis doubles, simulacra, or reflections, other than speak? With respect to that which can only be seen and heard, which is never confirmed by another organ and is the object of Forgetting in memory, of an Unimaginable in imagination, and of an Unthinkable in thought—what else can one do, other than speak of it? Language is itself the ultimate double which expresses all doubles—the highest of simulacra.

Freud elaborated some active-passive couples concerning the voyeur-ist and exhibitionist modes. This schema, however, does not satisfy Klossowski, who thinks that speech is the only activity corresponding to the passivity of sight, and the only action corresponding to the passion of sight. Speech is our active conduct with respect to reflec-tions, echoes, and doubles—for the sake of bringing them together and also of eliciting them. If sight is perverse, so too is speech. For clearly it is not a matter, as in the case of a child, of speaking *to* doubles and *to* simulacra. It is a matter of speaking of them. To whom? Once again, to spirits. As soon as we "name" or "designate" something or someone, on the condition that this be done with the necessary precision and above all the necessary style, we "denounce" as well: we remove the name, or rather cause the multiplicity of the denominated to rise up under the name; we divide, we reflect the thing, we give, under the same name, many objects to see, just as seeing gives, in a glance, so much to speak about. One never speaks to someone, but *of* someone to a power apt to reflect and divide it. This is why one does not name something without also denouncing it to a spirit, which serves as a strange mirror. Octave, in his splendid conceit, says: I did not speak to Roberte, I did not name 'a spirit' for her. On the contrary, I named Roberte to the spirit and, in this way, 'denounced' her—in order that the spirit might reveal what she hid, and in order that she finally liberate what was gathered under her name.[6] Sometimes sight induces speech, and sometimes speech leads sight. But there is always the multiplication and the reflection of what is seen and spoken—as well as of the person who sees and speaks: the speaker participates in the grand dissolution of selves, and even commands or provokes it. Michel Foucault has written a fine article on Klossowski, in which he analyzes the play of doubles and simulacra, of sight and language. He attributes Klossowskian categories of sight to them: simulacrum, similitude, and simulation.[7] Categories of language correspond to them: evocation, provocation, and revocation. Sight splits what it sees into two and multiplies the voyeur; likewise, language denounces what it says and multiplies the speaker (thus the multiplicity of superimposed voices in *Le Souffleur*).

That bodies speak has been known for a long time. Klossowski, however, designates a point which is almost the center at which language is formed. Being a Latinist, he invokes Quintillian: the body is capable of gestures which prompt an understanding contrary to what they indicate. In language, the equivalents of such gestures are called *"solecisms."*[8] For example, one arm may be used to hold off an aggressor while the other is held open to him, in seeming welcome. Or the same hand may be used to hold off, but is incapable of doing so without also offering an open palm. And there is also this play of the fingers, some being held open, and others, closed. Thus, Octave has a collection of secret paintings by the imaginary painter Tonnerre, who is close to Ingres, Chasseriau, and Courbet, and knows that painting is in the solecism of bodies, as, for example, in Lucrezia's ambiguous gesture. His imaginary descriptions are like shining stereotypes punctuating *La Révocation*. And in his own drawings—canvasses of great beauty— Klossowski willfully leaves the sexual organ indeterminate, provided that he overdetermines the hand as the organ of solecisms. But what, precisely, is the positivity of the hand, its ambiguous gesture, or its "suspended gesture"? Such a gesture is the incarnation of a power which is also internal to language: dilemma, disjunction, and disjunctive syllogism. With regard to the painting representing Lucrezia, Octave writes:

If she yields, she obviously betrays; if she does not yield, she will still be considered as having betrayed since, killed by her aggressor, she will be slandered on top. Do we see her yield, because she is resolved to be done away with, as soon as she makes her downfall known? Or did she first make up her mind to yield, ready to disappear, after having spoken? No doubt, she yields because she reflects; if she did not reflect, she would kill herself or would have herself killed immediately. Now, as she reflects herself in her death project, she throws herself into the arms of Tarquin and, as Saint Augustine insinuates, urged perhaps by her own covetousness, she punishes herself for this confusion and this solecism. As Ovid said, the thing amounts to succumbing to the fear of dishonor. I would say that she succumbs to her own covetousness, which splits into two: the covertousness of her own modesty abandons modesty in order to rediscover itself carnal.[9]

Here, in their identity, the proliferating dilemma and the suspended gesture represent both the determination of the body and the movement of language. But the fact that the common element is *reflection* indicates something else besides.

The body is language because it is essentially "flexion." In reflection, the corporeal flexion seems to be divided, split in two, opposed to itself and reflected in itself; it appears finally for itself, liberated from everything that ordinarily conceals it. In an excellent scene of *La Révocation,* Roberte, thrusting her hands into the tabernacle, feels them grasped by two long hands, similar to her own. . . . In *Le Souffleur,* the two Robertes fight, clasp hands, and lock fingers while an invited guest "prompts": make *her* separate! And *Robert ce soir* ends with Roberte's gesture—her holding out "a pair of keys to Victor, which he touches though never takes." This is a suspended scene, a genuinely frozen cascade, which reflects all the dilemmas and syllogisms with which "the spirits" had assailed Roberte during her rape. But if the body is flexion, so too is language. An entire reflection of words, or a reflection in words, is necessary for the flexional character of language to appear, finally liberated of everything that covers it up and conceals it. In an admirable translation of the *Aeneid,* Klossowski makes this point obvious: stylistic research must bring forth the image out of a flexion reflected in two words—a flexion that would be opposed to itself and reflected on itself in words. Such is the positive power of a superior "solecism," or the force of poetry constituted in the clash and copulation of words. If language *imitates* bodies, it is not through onomatopoeia, but through flexion. And if bodies imitate language, it is not through organs, but through flexion. There is an entire pantomime, internal to language, as a discourse or a story within the body. If gestures speak, it is first of all because words mimic gestures: "Virgil's epic poem is, in fact, a theater where words mimic the gestures and the mental states of the characters. . . . Words, not bodies, strike a pose; words, not garments, are woven; words, not armors, sparkle. . . ."[10] There would be a great deal to say about Klossowski's syntax, which is itself made of cascades, suspense, and reflected flexions. In flexion, according to Klossowski, there is a double "transgression"—of language by the flesh and of the flesh by language.[11] He was able to derive from this a style and a mimicry—a particular language and a particular body at once.

What is the role of these suspended scenes? It is less a question of grasping in them a perseveration or a continuation than of grasping them as the object of a fundamental repetition: "Life reiterating itself in order to recover its hold on itself during its fall—as if holding its breath in an instantaneous apprehension of its origin; but the reiteration of life by itself would be hopeless without the simulacrum of the artist who, by reproducing this spectacle, succeeds in delivering himself from reiteration."[12] This is the strange theme of a saving repetition, that saves us first and foremost from repetition. Psychoanalysis, it is true, taught us that we are ill from repetition, but it also taught us that we are healed through repetition. *Le Souffleur* is, precisely, the account of a salvation or a "cure." This cure, however, owes less to the attention of the disturbing Doctor Ygdrasil than to theater rehearsals and to theatrical repetition. But what must theatrical repetition be for it to be capable of securing salvation? The Roberte of *Le Souffleur* plays *Roberte ce soir* and she divides herself into two Robertes. If she repeats too exactly, if she acts the role too naturally, repetition misses its mark, no less than if she played the role badly and reproduced it awkwardly. Is this a new insoluble dilemma? Or should we rather imagine two sorts of repetition, one false and the other true, one hopeless and the other salutary, one constraining and the other liberating; one which would have exactness as its contradictory criterion, and another which would respond to other criteria?

One theme runs through the entire work of Klossowski: the opposition between exchange and true repetition. For exchange implies only resemblance, even if the resemblance is extreme. Exactness is its criterion, along with the equivalence of exchanged products. This is the false repetition which causes our illness. True repetition, on the other hand, appears as a singular behavior that we display in relation to that which cannot be exchanged, replaced, or substituted—like a poem that is repeated on the condition that no word may be changed. It is no longer a matter of an equivalence between similar things, it is not even a matter of an identity of the Same. True repetition addresses something singular, unchangeable, and different, without "identity." Instead of exchanging the similar and identifying the Same, *it authenticates the different.* The opposition is developed by Klossowski in the following manner: Théodore, in *Le Souffleur,* takes up again Octave's "laws of hospitality," which consist of multiplying Roberte by *giving* her to the guests. Now, in this resumption, Théodore comes up against an odd circumstance: the hôtel de Longchamp is a state institution where each spouse must be "declared," in accordance with financial rules and norms of equivalence, in order to serve as the object of exchange and contribute to the sharing of men and women.[13] Théodore however comes to see, in the institution of Longchamp, the caricature of, and the contrary to, the laws of hospitality. Doctor Ygdrasil tells him:

You insist absolutely upon giving without return and never receiving! You cannot live without submitting to the universal law of exchange. . . . The practice of hospitality, such as you conceive it, cannot be unilateral. Like any hospitality, this (and especially this) requires an absolute reciprocity in order to be viable; that's the hurdle you don't want to overcome—the sharing of women by men and men by women. You have to carry it through to the end, to consent to exchange Roberte for other women, to accept being unfaithful to Roberte as you persist in desiring that she be unfaithful to you.[14]

Théodore doesn't listen. He knows that the true repetition is in the gift, in the economy of the gift which is opposed to the mercantile economy of exchange (. . . homage to Georges Bataille). He knows that the host and his reflection, in both senses of the word, are opposed to the hôtel; and that in the host and the gift, repetition surges forth as the highest power of the unexchangeable: "the wife, prostituted by her husband, nevertheless remains his spouse, and the husband's un-ex-changeable possession."[15]

How is it that Théodore gets better following his trip to the edge of madness? He was ill and we are now concerned with his recovery. To be precise, he was ill so long as the risk of an exchange had come to compromise and gnaw away at his attempt at a pure repetition. Were not Roberte and K's wife exchanged to the point that one could not be distinguished from the other, even in the struggle in which they clasped hands? And was not K himself exchanged with Théodore, in order to take everything from him and to divert the laws of hospitality? Théodore (or K?) gets well, when he understands that repetition is not to be found in an extreme resemblance, nor in the exactness of the exchanged, nor even in a reproduction of the identical. Being neither the identity of the Same nor the equivalence of the similar, repetition is found in the intensity of the Different. There are no two women who look alike, and who can be taken for Roberte; there are not two beings inside Roberte—inside the same woman. But Roberte designates an "intensity" in herself; she comprises a difference in itself, an inequality, the characteristic of which is to return or to be repeated. In short, the double, the reflection, or the simulacrum opens up at last to surrender its secret: repetition does not presuppose the Same or the Similar— these are not its prerequisites. It is repetition, on the contrary, which produces the only "same" of that which differs, and the only resemblance of the different. The convalescent K (or Théodore?) echoes Nietzsche's convalescent Zarathustra. All "designations" are brought down and are "denounced" in order to make room for the rich system of intensities. The couple Octave-Roberte refers to a pure difference of intensity in thought; the names "Octave" and "Roberte" no longer designate things; they now express pure intensities, risings and falls.[16]

This is the relation between frozen scenes and repetition. A "fall," a "difference," a "suspension" are reflected in the resumption, or in repetition. In this sense, the body is reflected in language: the characterisitic of language is *to take back into* itself the frozen scene, to make a "spiritual" event out of it, or rather an advent of "spirits." In language —at the heart of language—the mind grasps the body, and the gestures of the body, as the object of a fundamental repetition. Difference gives things to be seen and multiplies bodies; but it is repetition which offers things to be spoken, authenticates the multiple, and makes of it a spiritual event. Klossowski says: "In Sade, language, intolerable to itself, does not reach exhaustion, despite being unleashed on the same victim for days on end. . . . There can be no transgression in the carnal act, if it is not lived as a spiritual event; but in order to cease the object, it is necessary to look for, and reproduce the event, in a reiterated description of the carnal act."[17] After all, what is a Pornographer? A Pornographer is one who repeats and iterates. That an author is essentially an iterator must tell us something about the relation between language and body, of the mutual limit and transgression that each one finds in the other. In Gombrowicz's novel *Pornographia,* the central scenes are the frozen scenes: those which the hero (or heroes?) —voyeur-speaker-man of letters, man of the theater—impose(s) on two young people; scenes which derive their perversity from the mutual indifference only of the young people; but also scenes which culminate with a downfall or a difference of level, resumed in a repetition of language and vision; scenes of possession, properly speaking, since the young people have their minds possessed, being fated and denounced by the voyeur-speaker.

No, no, the whole scene would not have been so shocking had it not been so incompatible with their natural rhythm, so set, motionless, and alien. . . . Over their heads, their hands touched "accidentally." And as they touched, they pulled them down abruptly and violently. For some time they both gazed attentively at their joined hands. Then they suddenly fell down—it was impossible to tell who had been pushed by whom—it looked as though their hands had pushed them over.[18]

It is good that two authors, so new, so important, and yet so different, encounter each other on the theme of body-language, of pornography-repetition, pornographer-repeater, and writer-iterator (littérateur-itérateur).

What is the dilemma? How is the disjunctive syllogism, which expresses the dilemma, made up? The body is language; but it may conceal the speech that it is—it can hide it. The body may, and ordinarily does, wish for silence with respect to its works. In this case, repressed by the body but also projected, delegated, and alienated, speech becomes the discourse of a beautiful soul that speaks of laws and virtues while keeping silent over the body. It is clear, in this case, that speech itself is pure, so to speak, but that the silence on which it rests is impure. By holding its silence, at once covering up and delegating its speech, the body delivers us over to silent imaginings. In the scene of her rape by the Colossus and the Hunchback (that is, by spirits which in themselves mark a difference of levels as the ultimate reality), we hear Roberte say: "What are you going to do with us, and what are we going to do with your flesh? Shall we eat it since it is still able to speak? Or shall we treat it as if it had to maintain silence forever? . . . How could (your body) be so delicious if not by virtue of the speech which it conceals?"[19] And Octave says to Roberte: "You have a body with which to cover your speech."[20] In fact, Roberte is the president of the censorship commission; she speaks of virtues and of laws; she is not without austerity, she has not killed the "beautiful soul" within herself. . . . Her words are pure, though her silence is impure. For in this silence she imitates the spirits; thus she provokes them, she provokes their aggression. They act on her body, inside her body, having taken on the form of "undesirable thoughts," at once colossal and dwarfish. Such is the first term of the dilemma: *either* Roberte keeps quiet but provokes the aggression of spirits, her silence being all the more impure as her speech is ever more so. . . . *Or* there must be an impure, obscene, and impious language in order for silence to be pure, for language to be a pure language which resides in this silence. "Speak and we disappear," say the spirits to Roberte.[21]

Does Klossowski simply mean that speaking prevents us from thinking about nasty things? No; the pure language which produces an impure silence is a *provocation* of the mind by the body; similarly, the impure language which produces a pure silence is a *revocation* of the body by the mind. As Sade's heroes say, it is not the bodies which are present that excite the libertine, but rather the great idea of what is not there. In Sade, "pornography is a form of the battle of the mind against the flesh." More precisely, what is revoked in the body? Klossowski's answer is that it is the integrity of the body, and that because of this the identity of the person is somewhat suspended and volatilized. This answer is undoubtedly very complex. It suffices, however, to make us sense that the body-language dilemma is established between two relations of the body and language. The couple "pure language/impure silence" designates a certain relation, in which language brings the identity of a person and the integrity of a body together in a responsible self, but maintains a silence about all the forces which cause the dissolution of this self. Or language itself becomes one of these forces and takes charge of all these forces, giving thereby to the disintegrated body and the dissolved self access to a silence which is that of innocence. In this case, we have the other term of the dilemma: "impure language/pure silence." In other words, the alternative is between two purities, the false and the true, the purity of responsibility and the purity of innocence, the purity of Memory and the purity of Forgetfulness. Posing the problem from a linguistic point of view, *Le Baphomet* says: *either* the words are recalled but their sense remains obscure; *or* the sense appears when the memory of the words disappears.

More profoundly still, the nature of the dilemma is theological. Octave is a professor of theology. *Le Baphomet* is in its entirety a theological novel, which opposes the system of God and the system of the Antichrist as the two terms of a fundamental disjunction.[22] The order of divine creation in fact depends on bodies, is suspended from them. In the order of God, in the order of existence, bodies give to minds (or rather impose on them) two properties: identity and immortality, personality and resurrectibility, incommunicability and integrity. Says the docile nephew Antoine with regard to Octave's seductive theology: "What is incommunicability—It is the principle according to which the being of an individual would not be attributable to several individuals, and which constitutes properly the self-identical person. What is the privative function of the person?—It is that of rendering our substance incapable of being assumed by a nature either inferior or superior to our own."[23] It is insofar as it is tied to a body and is incarnated that the mind acquires personality: separated from the body, in death, it recovers its equivocal and multiple power. And it is insofar as it is brought back to its body that the mind acquires immortality, the resurrection of bodies being the condition of the survival of the mind. Liberated from its body, declining or revoking its body, the spirit would cease to exist—rather, it would "subsist" in its disquieting power. Death and duplicity, death and multiplicity are therefore the true spiritual determinations, or the true spiritual events. We must understand that God is the enemy of spirits, that the order of God runs counter to the order of spirits; in order to establish immortality and personality, in order to impose it forcefully on spirits, God must depend upon the body. He submits the spirits to the privative function of the person and to the privative function of resurrection. The outcome of God's way is "the life of the flesh."[24] God is essentially the Traitor: he commits treason against spirits, treason against breath itself, and, in order to thwart their riposte, doubles the treason by incarnating himself.[25] "In the beginning was treason."

The order of God includes the following elements: the identity of God as the ultimate foundation; the identity of the world as the ambient environment; the identity of the person as a well-founded agency; the identity of bodies as the base; and finally, the identity of language as the power of *denoting* everything else. But this order of God is constructed against another order, and this order subsists in God and weakens him little by little. It is at this point that the story of Baphomet begins: in the service of God, the great master of the Templars has as his mission the sorting out of spirits and the prevention of their mixing together while awaiting the day of resurrection. Thus, there is already in dead souls a certain rebellious intention, an intention to escape from God's judgment: "The most ancient souls lie in wait for the most recently arrived, and merging by means of affinities, each agrees to efface within the others his own responsibility."[26] One day, the grand master recognizes a spirit which has wormed its way into his presence—that of Saint Theresa! Dazzled by his prestigious guest, the master complains to her about the "complication" of his task, and about the ill will of the spirits. Rather than indulge him, however, Theresa begins an extraordinary discourse: the number of the elect is closed; no longer is anyone damnable or sanctifiable; spirits are somehow liberated from God's order; they feel themselves released from resurrection; and they are prepared to penetrate up to six or seven of them in a single embryonic body in order to unburden themselves of their person and their responsibility. Theresa herself is a rebel, a prophet of rebellion. She announces the death of God, His overthrow. "I am excluded from the number of the elect." For a young theologian whom she loved, she was able to obtain a new existence in another body, then a third. . . . Was this not proof that God had abandoned His order, that He had abandoned the myths of the incommunicable person and the definitive resurrection, as well as the theme of "once and for all" implied in these myths? Indeed, an order of perversity had exploded the divine order of integrity: a perversity in the lower world where an exuberant, stormy nature reigns, full of raping, shameful debauchery and travesty, since several souls enter together into the same body, and the same soul may possess several bodies; a perversity up above, since spirits are already mingled together. God can no longer guarantee any identity! This is the great "pornography," the revenge taken by spirits on both God and bodies. And Theresa announces to the grand master his destiny: he himself will no longer have the capacity to sort out spirits! Then, seized by a sort of rage and jealousy, but also by a mad temptation and a dual desire to chastise Theresa and to try her, and finally by the dizziness of the dilemmas which trouble his thoughts (for his consciousness had sunk into "disconcerting syllogisms"), the grand master "insufflated" the breath/spirit (insuffle le souffle) of Theresa into the ambiguous body of a young man, a young page who had once troubled the Templars and had been hung during an initiation scene. His body, suspended and rotating, marked by hanging, miraculously conserved, and reserved for a function which is going to overthrow God's order, received Theresa's breath—an anal insufflation which elicits in the page's body a strong genital reaction.

This is the other term of the dilemma, the system of breaths/spirits, the order of the Antichrist, which is opposed point for point to the divine order. It is characterized by the death of God, the destruction of the world, the dissolution of the person, the disintegration of bodies, and the shifting function of language which now expresses only intensities. It is frequently said that philosophy throughout its history has changed its center of perspective, substituting the point of view of the finite self for that of the infinite divine substance. Kant would stand at the turning point. Is this change, however, as important as it is claimed to be? Is this where the important difference is to be found? As long as we maintain the formal identity of the self, doesn't the self remain subject to a divine order, and to a unique God who is its foundation? Klossowski insists that God is the sole guarantor of the identity of the self and of its substantive base, that is, of the integrity of the body. One cannot conserve the self without also holding on to God. The death of God essentially signifies, and essentially entails, the dissolution of the self: God's tomb is also the tomb of the self.[27] Thus, the dilemma finds perhaps its most acute expression: the identity of the self always refers to the identity of something outside of us; therefore, "if it is God, our identity is pure grace; if it is the ambient world where everything begins and ends by denotation, our identity is but a pure grammatical joke."[28] In his own way, Kant had foreseen this when he subjected to a common, at least speculative, death rational psychology, rational cosmology, and rational theology alike.

As it happens, it is with regard to one of Kant's theses on theology, an odd and particularly ironic thesis, that the problem of the *disjunctive syllogism* takes on its full import: God is presented as the principle or master of the disjunctive syllogism. To understand this thesis, we must recall the link that Kant poses in general between Ideas and syllogism. Reason is not defined initially by special notions which one might call "Ideas." It is rather defined by a certain way of treating the concepts of the understanding: a concept being given, reason seeks another which, taken in the totality of its extension, conditions the attribution of the first to the object to which it refers. This is the nature of the syllogism. For example, "mortal" being a concept attributed to Socrates, one seeks the concept which, taken in the full range of its extension, conditions this attribution *(all men)*. Thus, the deployment of reason would pose no particular problem if it did not run up against a difficulty—namely, that the understanding makes use of original concepts called "categories." These are already attributed to *all* objects of possible experience. So, when reason encounters a category, how is it going to be able to find another concept capable, in all its extension, to condition the attribution of the category to *all* objects of possible experience? It is at this point that reason is forced to invent supra-conditioning notions, which will be called "Ideas." It is therefore in a secondary way that reason is defined as the faculty of Ideas. We will call *"Idea"* a notion taken in all its extension which conditions the attribution of a category of relation (substance, causality, community) to all objects of possible experience. Kant's genius lies in his showing that the self is the Idea which corresponds to the category of substance. Indeed, the self conditions not only the attribution of this category to phenomena of inner sense, but to those of outer sense as well, in virtue of their no less great immediacy. Thus, the self is revealed as the universal prinicple of the categorical syllogism, insofar as this relates a phenomenon determined as a predicate to a subject determined as substance. Kant shows also that the world is the Idea which conditions the attribution of the category of causality to all phenomena. In this way, the world is the universal principle of the hypothetical syllogism. This extraordinary theory of the syllogism, which consists in discovering the ontological implications of the latter, will thus find itself faced with a third and final task, a task which is by far the most delicate: there is no choice, it is left for God as the third Idea to ensure the attribution of the category of community, that is, the *mastery of the disjunctive syllogism*. God is here, at least provisionally, deprived of his traditional claims—to have created subjects or made a world—and now has what is but an apparently humble task, namely, to enact disjunctions, or at least to found them.

How is this possible? At this point the irony comes through: Kant is going to show that, under the name of the philosophical Christian God, nothing but this has ever been understood. In fact, God is defined by the sum total of all possibility, insofar as this sum constitutes an "originary" material or the whole of reality. The reality of each thing "is derived" from it: it rests in effect on the limitation of this totality, "inasmuch as part of it (reality) is ascribed to the thing, and the rest is excluded—a procedure which is in agreement with the 'either-or' of the disjunctive major premise and with the determination of the object, in the minor premise, through one of the members of the division."[29] In short, the sum total of the possible is an originary material from which the exclusive and complete determination of the concept of each thing is derived through disjunction. God has no other sense than that of founding this treatment of the disjunctive syllogism, since distributive unity does not allow us to conclude that his Idea represents a collective or singular unity of a being in itself which would be represented by the Idea.

In Kant, therefore, we see that God is revealed as the master of the disjunctive syllogism only inasmuch as the disjunction is tied to exclusions in the reality which is derived from it, and thus to a *negative and limitative use.* Klossowski's thesis, with the new critique of reason that it implies, takes on therefore its full significance: it is not God but rather the Antichrist who is the master of the disjunctive syllogism. This is because the anti-God determines the *passage* of each thing through all of its possible predicates. God, as the Being of beings, is replaced by the Baphomet, the "prince of all modifications," and himself modification of all modifications. There is no longer any originary reality. The disjunction is always a disjunction; the "either-or" is always an "either-or." Rather than signifying that a certain number of predicates are excluded from a thing in virtue of the identity of the corresponding concept, the disjunction now signifies that each thing is opened up to the infinity of predicates through which it passes, on the condition that it lose its identity as concept and as self. The disjunctive syllogism accedes to a diabolical principle and use, and simultaneously the disjunction is affirmed for itself without ceasing to be a disjunction; divergence or difference becomes objects of pure affirmation, and "either-or" becomes the power of affirmation, outside the conceptual conditions of the identity of a God, a world, or a self. Dilemma and solecism acquire as such a superior positivity. *We have seen, however, how often negative or exclusive disjunctions still subsist in Klossowski's work: between exchange and repetition; between language concealed by the body and the glorious body formed by language; and finally, between God's order and the order of the Antichrist.* But it is precisely inside God's order, and only there, that disjunctions have the negative value of exclusion. And it is on the other side, inside the order of the Antichrist, that the disjunction (difference, divergence, decentering) becomes as such an affirmative and affirmed power.

What is this other side, this Baphomet system of pure breaths or mortal spirits? They do not have the person's identity; they have deposed and revoked it. But they nevertheless have a singularity, or even multiple singularities; they have fluctuations forming figures on the crests of waves. We reach here the point at which the Klossowskian myth of breaths/spirits becomes also a philosophy. It seems that breaths, in themselves and in ourselves, must be conceived of as pure intensities. In this form of intensive quantities or degrees, dead spirits have "subsistence," despite the fact that they have lost the "existence" or extension of the body. In this form they are singular, though they have lost the identity of the self. Intensities comprehend in themselves the unequal or the different—each one is already difference in itself—so that all of them are comprehended in the manifestation of every one. This is a world of pure intentions, as Baphomet explains: "no self-esteem prevails"; "every intention may yet be permeated by other intentions"; "only the most senseless intention of the past hoping for the future could triumph over another intention"; "were another breath to come to encounter it, they would then presuppose each other, but each one according to a *variable intensity of intention*." These are pre-individual and impersonal singularities—the splendor of the indefinite pronoun— mobile, communicating, penetrating one another across an infinity of degrees and an infinity of modifications. Fascinating world where the identity of the self is lost, not to the benefit of the identity of the One or the unity of the Whole, but to the advantage of an intense multiplicity and a power of metamorphosis, where relations of force play within one another. It is the state of what must be called *"complicatio,"* as opposed to the Christian *simplificatio*. *Roberte ce soir* had already displayed Octave's effort to work his way into Roberte, to insert his own intention (his intensive intentionality), and to give her thereby over to other intentions—even if this were by "denouncing" her to the spirits who rape her.[30] And in *Le Baphomet*, Theresa is "insufflated" into the body of the young page, in order to form the androgynous or Prince of modification who is offered up to the intentions of others and gives

PHANTASM AND MODERN LITERATURE   297

himself to other spirits for participation: "I am not a creator who enslaves being to what he creates, his creation in a single self, and this self in a single body. . . ." The system of the Antichrist is the system of simulacra opposed to the world of identities. But, as the simulacrum dismisses identity, speaks and is spoken, it takes hold at the same time of both seeing and speaking and inspires both light and sound. It opens up to its difference and to all other differences. All simulacra rise to the surface, forming this mobile figure at the crest of the waves of intensity —an intense phantasm.

One can see how Klossowski goes from one sense of the word *"intentio"* to another—corporeal intensity and spoken intentionality. The simulacrum becomes phantasm, intensity becomes intentionality to the extent that it takes as its object another intensity which it comprehends and is itself comprehended, itself taken as its object, on to the infinity of intensities through which it passes. This is to say that there is in Klossowski an entire "phenomenology," which borrows from scholastic philosophy as much as Husserl did, but which traces its own paths. As for the passage from intensity to intentionality, it is the passage from sign to sense. In a fine analysis of Nietzsche, Klossowski interprets the "sign" as the trace of a fluctuation, of an intensity, and "sense" as the movement by which intensity aims at itself in aiming at the other, modifies itself in modifying the other, and returns finally onto its own trace.[31] The dissolved self opens up to a series of roles, since it gives rise to an intensity which already comprehends difference in itself, the unequal in itself, and which penetrates all others, across and within multiple bodies. There is always another breath in my breath, another thought in my thought, another possession in what I possess, a thousand things and a thousand beings implicated in my complicatons: every true thought is an aggression. It is not a question of our undergoing influences, but of being "insufflations" and fluctuations, or merging with them. That everything is so "complicated," that *I* may be an other, that something else thinks in us in an aggression which is the aggression of thought, in a multiplication which is the multiplication of the body, or in a violence which is the violence of language—this is the joyful message. For we are so sure of living again (without resurrection) only because so many beings and things think in us: because "we still do not know exactly if it is not others who continue to think within us (but who are these others who form the outside in relation to this inside which we believe ourselves to be?)—everything is brought back to a single discourse, to fluctuations of intensity, for instance, which correspond to the thought of everyone and no one."[32] At the same time that bodies lose their unity and the self its identity, language loses its denoting function (its distinct sort of integrity) in order to discover a value that is purely expressive or, as Klossowski says, "emotional." It discovers this value, not with respect to someone who expresses himself and who would be moved, but with respct to something that is purely expressed, pure motion or pure "spirit"—*sense* as a pre-individual singularity, or an intensity which comes back to itself through others. This is how the name "Roberte" did not designate a person, but rather expressed a primary intensity, or that Baphomet emits the difference of intensity that constitutes his name, B-A BA ("no proper name subsists in the hyperbolic breath of my name, any more than the elevated idea that each one has of himself is able to withstand the dizziness of my stature").[33] The values of expressive or expressionist language are provocation, revocation, and evocation. Evoked (expressed) are the singular and complicated spirits, which do not possess a body without multiplying it inside the system of reflections, and which do not inspire language without projecting it into the intensive system of resonances. Revoked (denounced) are corporeal unicity, personal identity, and the false simplicity of language insofar as it is supposed to denote bodies and to manifest a self. As the spirits say to Roberte, "we can be evoked; but your body can also be revoked."[34]

From intensity to intentionality: every intensity wills itself, intends itself, returns on its own trace, repeats and imitates itself through all the others. This is a movement of sense which must be determined as the eternal return. *Le Souffleur,* a novel of malady and convalescence, already ended with a revelation of the eternal return; and with *Le Baphomet,* Klossowski creates in his work a grandiose sequel to Zarathustra. The difficulty, however, lies with the interpretation of the phrase *"the eternal return of the Same."* For no form of identity is here entertained, since each dissolved self returns through itself only by passing into the others, and wills itself only through a series of roles which are not its own. Intensity, being already difference in itself, opens onto disjoint or divergent series. But since the series are not subject to the condition of the identity of a concept in general, no more than the entity which traverses them is subject to the identity of a self as individual, the disjunctions stay disjunctions. Their synthesis, however, is no longer exclusive or negative, and they take on, to the contrary, an affirmative sense by means of which the mobile entity passes through all the disjoint series. In short, divergence and disjunction as such become the object of affirmation. The true subject of the eternal return is the intensity and singularity; the relation between the eternal return as actualized intentionality and the will to power as open intensity derives from this fact. As soon as the singularity is apprehended as pre-individual, outside of the identity of a self, that is, as *fortuitous,* it communicates with all the other singularities, without ceasing to form disjunctions with them. It does so, however, by passing through all of the disjoint terms that it simultaneously affirms, rather than by distributing them in exclusions. "Thus, all I have to do is to will myself again, no longer as the outcome of previous possibilities, not as one accomplishment out of a thousand, but as a fortuitous moment, the very fortuity of which implies the necessity of the integral return of the whole series."[35]

What the eternal return expresses is this new sense of the disjunctive synthesis. It follows that the eternal return is not said *of* the Same ("it destroys identities"). On the contrary, it is the only Same, which is said of that which differs in itself—the intense, the unequal, or the disjoint (will to power). It is indeed the Whole, which is said of that which remains unequal; it is Necessity, which is said of the fortuitous alone. It is itself univocal: univocal Being, language or silence. However, univocal Being is said of beings which are not univocal, univocal language is applied to bodies which are not univocal, "pure" silence surrounds words which are not "pure." One could thus search in vain within the eternal return for the simplicity of a circle and the convergence of series around a center. If there is a circle, it is the *circulus vitiosus deus:* difference here is at the center, and the circumference is the eternal passage through the divergent series. It is an always decentered circle for an ex-centric circumference. The eternal return is indeed Coherence, but it is a coherence which does not allow my coherence, the coherence of the world and the coherence of God to subsist.[36] The Nietzschean repetition has nothing to do with the Kierkegaardian repetition; or, more generally, repetition in the eternal return has nothing to do with the Christian repetition. For what the Christian repetition brings back, it brings back once, and only once: the wealth of Job and the child of Abraham, the resurrected body and the recovered self. There is a difference in nature between what returns "once and for all" and what returns for each and every time, or for an infinite number of times. The eternal return is indeed the Whole, but it is the Whole which is said of disjoint members or divergent series: it does not bring everything back, it does not bring about the return of that which returns but once, namely, that which aspires to recenter the circle, to render the series convergent, and to restore the self, the world, and God. In the circle of Dionysus, Christ will not return; the order of the Antichrist chases the other order away. *All of that which is founded on God and makes a negative or exclusive use of the disjunction is denied and excluded by the eternal return.* All of that which comes once and for all is referred back to the order of God. The phantasm of Being (eternal return) brings about the return only of simulacra (will to power as simulation). Being a coherence which does not allow mine to subsist, the eternal return is the nonsense which distributes sense into divergent series over the entire circumference of the decentered circle—for "madness is the loss of the world and of oneself in view of a knowledge with neither beginning nor end." [37]

4. MICHEL TOURNIER AND THE WORLD WITHOUT OTHERS

The goat abruptly stopped grazing and looked up with a stalk of grass hanging from its lips. Then it seemed to grin and reared up on its hind legs; in this position it took several steps toward Friday, waving its forefeet and nodding its immense horns as though acknowledging a throng of spectators. This astonishing performance turned Friday rigid with amazement. When it was within a few yards of him the goat dropped its forefeet to the ground and suddenly charged like a battering-ram—or a great arrow feathered with fur —its head lowered and its horns aimed at Friday's chest. Friday flung himself sideways a fraction of a second too late. A musky smell filled his nostrils. . . . [1]

This beautiful passage relates Friday's battle with the goat, in which Friday will be wounded, but the goat will die: "The great goat is dead." [2] Then Friday announces his mysterious project: the dead goat will fly and sing—it will be a flying and musical goat. In the first stage of the project, he makes use of the skin. The hair is removed, the skin is washed, pumiced, and spread out on a wooden structure. Bound to a fishing pole, the goat amplifies the least movement of the line, assumes the role of a gigantic celestial bobber, and transcribes the waters onto the sky. As for the second stage, Friday makes use of the head and the gut and fashions from them an instrument; he places it in a dead tree in order to produce an instantaneous symphony whose sole performer must be the wind. This is how the din of the earth is in turn transported to the heavens and becomes an organized, celestial sound—pansonority —a "music that was truly of the elements."[3] In these two ways, the great goat frees the Elements. It will be noted that the earth and air act less as particular elements than as two complete and opposed figures, each one, for its part, gathering the four elements. The earth, however, holds and subsumes them, contains them within the depth of bodies, whereas the sky, with the light and the sun, sets them in a free and pure state, delivered from their limits, in order to form cosmic surface energy—being one and yet characteristic of each element. There is therefore a terrestrial fire, water, air, and earth, but there is also an aerial or celestial earth, water, fire, and air. There is a struggle between earth and sky, with the imprisonment or liberation of all four elements at stake. The isle is the frontier or field of this struggle. This is why it is so important to know which way the struggle will swing, and whether it is capable of pouring out into the sky its fire, earth, and water—or of becoming solar. The isle is as much the hero of the novel as Robinson or Friday. It changes shape in the course of a series of divisions, no less than Robinson himself changes his form in the course of a series of metamorphoses. Robinson's subjective series is inseparable from the series of the states of the island.

The end result is Robinson becoming elemental on his isle, with the isle itself rendered to the elements: a Robinson of the sun on the solar isle—a Uranian on Uranus. It is not the origin then which matters here, but on the contrary, the outcome or the final result, which is reached through all sorts of avatars. This is the first important difference with Defoe's Robinson. It has often been said that the theme of Robinson in Defoe's work was not only a story, but an "instrument of research"—a research which starts out from the desert island and aspires to reconstitute the origins and the rigorous order of works and conquests which happen with time. But it is clear that the research is twice falsified. On one hand, the image of the origins presupposes that which it tries to generate (see, for example, all that Robinson has pulled from the wreck). On the other hand, the world which is reproduced on the basis of this origin is the equivalent of the *real*—that is, economic —world, or of the world as it would be, as it would have to be if there were no sexuality (see the elimination of all sexuality in Defoe's Robinson).[4] Must we conclude that sexuality is the only fantastic principle able to bring about the deviation of the world from the rigorous economic order assigned by the origin? Defoe's work was, in short, well-intentioned: what becomes of a man who is alone, without Others, on a desert island? But the problem was poorly posed. For, instead of bringing an asexual Robinson to an origin which reproduces an economic world similar to our own, or to an archetype of our own, one should have led an asexual Robinson to *ends quite different and divergent* from ours, in a fantastic world which has itself deviated. By raising the problem in terms of end, and not in terms of origin, Tournier makes it impossible for him to allow Robinson to leave the island. The end, that is, Robinson's final goal, is "dehumanization," the coming together of the libido and of the free elements, the discovery of a cosmic energy or of a great elemental Health which can surge only on the isle—and only to the extent that the isle has become aerial or solar. Henry Miller spoke of the wailing of the fundamental elements helium, oxygen, silica, and iron. Undoubtedly, there is something of Miller and even Lawrence in this Robinson of helium and oxygen: the dead goat already organizes the wailings of the fundamental elements.

But the reader also has the impression that this great Health of Tournier's Robinson conceals something, which is not at all like Miller or Lawrence. Could it not be that the essential *deviation* which this Health implies is inseparable from desert sexuality? Tournier's Robinson is opposed to Defoe's in virtue of three strictly related characteristics: he is related to ends and goals rather than to origins; he is sexual; and these ends represent a fantastic deviation from our world, under the influence of a transformed sexuality, rather than an economic reproduction of our world, under the impact of a continuous effort. This Robinson does nothing perverse, properly speaking. Yet, how are we to free ourselves from the impression that he is himself perverse, according to Freud's definition of the one who deviates with respect to aims? For Defoe it was the same thing to relate Robinson to the origin and to have him produce a world consistent with our own; it is the same thing for Tournier to relate him to aims and have him deviate or diverge with respect to the aims. Related to origins, Robinson must necessarily reproduce our world, but related to ends, he must deviate. This is an odd deviation, although it is not one of those of which Freud spoke, since it is solar and takes elements as its objects: such is the sense of Uranus. "If this [solar coition] is to be translated into human language, I must consider myself feminine and the bride of the sky. But that kind of anthropomorphism is meaningless. The truth is that at the height to which Friday and I have soared, difference of sex is left behind. Friday may be identified with Venus, just as I may be said, in human terms, to open my body to the embrace of the sun."[5] If it is true that neurosis is the negative of perversion, would not perversion, for its part, be the *elemental* aspect of neurosis?

The concept of perversion is a bastard concept—half juridical, half medical. But neither medicine nor law are entirely suited to it. With regard to today's renewed interest in this concept, it seems that we seek the reason for its quite ambiguous and contingent connection with law as well as with medicine in the very structure of perversion. The point of departure is as follows: perversion is not defined by the force of a certain desire in the system of drives; the pervert is not someone who desires, but someone who introduces desire into an entirely differ-ent system and makes it play, within this system, the role of an internal limit, a virtual center or zero point (the well-known Sadean apathy). The pervert is no more a desiring self than the Other is, for him, a desired object endowed with real existence. Tournier's novel is never-theless not a thesis on perversion. It is not a novel with a thesis *(roman à thèse)*. It is neither a novel of characters *(roman à personnages),* since there are no Others, nor a novel of internal analysis, since Robinson has very little interiority. It is an amazing novel of comic adventures and of cosmic avatars. Rather than being a thesis on perversion, it is a novel which develops the very thesis of Robinson: the man without Others on his island. The "thesis," however, makes that much more sense since, instead of referring to a presupposed origin, it announces adven-tures: what is going to happen in the insular world without Others? We will initially try to find out what the term "Others" means on the basis of the *effects* of the others: we will seek the effects on the island of the absence of Others, we will infer the effects of the presence of Others in our habitual world, and we will conclude what the Other is, and what it means for the Other to be absent. The effects of the absence of Others are the real adventures of the spirit: this is an experimental, inductive novel. Under the circumstances, philosophical reflection can garner what the novel reveals with so much force and life.

The first effect of Others is that around each object that I perceive or each idea that I think there is the organization of a marginal world, a mantle or background, where other objects and other ideas may come forth in accordance with laws of transition which regulate the passage from one to another. I regard an object, then I divert my attention, letting it fall into the background. At the same time, there comes forth from the background a new object of my attention. If this new object does not injure me, if it does not collide with me with the violence of a projectile (as when one bumps against something unseen), it is because the first object had already at its disposal a complete margin where I had already felt the preexistence of objects yet to come, and of an entire field of virtualities and potentialities which I already knew were capable of being actualized. Now, such a knowledge or sentiment of marginal existence is possible only through other people. ". . . For all of us the presence of other people is a powerful element of distraction, not only because they constantly break into our activities and interrupt our train of thought, but because the mere possibility of their doing so illumines a world of concerns situated at the edge of our consciousness but capable at any moment of becoming its center."[6] The part of the object that I do not see I posit as visible to Others, so that when I will have walked around to reach this hidden part, I will have joined the Others behind the object, and I will have totalized it in the way that I had already anticipated. As for the objects behind my back, I sense them coming together and forming a world, precisely because they are visible to, and are seen by, Others. And what is *depth,* for me, in accordance with which objects encroach upon one another and hide behind one another, I also live through as being *possible width* for Others, a width upon which they are aligned and pacified (from the point of view of another depth). In short, the Other assures the margins and transitions in the world. He is the sweetness of contiguities and resemblances. He regulates the transformations of form and background and the variations of depth. He prevents assaults from behind. He fills the world with a benevolent murmuring. He makes things incline toward one another and find their natural complements in one another. When one complains about the meanness of Others, one forgets this other and even more frightening meanness—namely, the meanness of things were there no Other. The latter relativizes the not-known and the non-perceived, because Others, from my point of view, introduce the sign of the unseen in what I do see, making me grasp what I do not perceive as what is perceptible to an Other. In all these respects, my desire passes through Others, and through Others it receives an object. I desire nothing that cannot be seen, thought, or possessed by a possible Other. That is the basis of my desire. It is always Others who relate my desire to an object.

What happens when Others are missing from the structure of the world? In that case, there reigns alone the brutal opposition of the sun and earth, of an unbearable light and an obscure abyss: the "summary law of all or nothing." The known and the unknown, the perceived and unperceived confront one another absolutely in a battle with nuances. "My vision of the island is reduced to that of my own eyes, and what I do not see of it is to me a total unknown. Everywhere I am not total darkness reigns."[7] A harsh and black world, without potentialities or virtualities: the category of the possible has collapsed. Instead of relatively harmonious forms surging forth from, and going back to, a background in accordance with an order of space and time, only abstract lines now exist, luminous and harmful—only a groundless abyss, rebellious and devouring. Nothing but Elements. The abyss and the abstract line have replaced the relief and the background. Everything is implacable. Having ceased to stretch out and bend toward one another, objects rise threateningly; we discover then wickedness which is no longer that of man. One might say that each thing, having been rid of its relief and reduced to its harshest lines, slaps us in the face or strikes us from behind. The absence of the Other is felt when we bang against things, and when the stupefying swiftness of our actions is revealed to us. "Nakedness is a luxury in which a man may indulge himself without danger only when he is warmly surrounded by his fellow man. For Robinson, while his soul had not yet undergone any change, it was a trial of desperate temerity. Stripped of its threadbare garments—worn, tattered, and sullied, but the fruit of civilized millennia, and impregnated with human associations—his vulnerable body was at the mercy of every hostile element."[8] There are no longer any transitions; gone is the sweetness of contiguities and resemblances which allowed us to inhabit the world. Nothing subsists but insuperable depths, absolute distances and differences or, on the contrary, unbearable repetitions, looking like precisely superimposed lengths.

By comparing the primary effects of the Other's presence and those of his absence, we are in a position to say what the Other is. The error of philosophical theories is to reduce the Other sometimes to a particular object, and sometimes to another subject. (Even a conception like Sartre's, in *Being and Nothingness,* was satisfied with the union of the two determinations, making of the Other an object of my gaze, even if he in turn gazes at me and transforms me into an object.) But the Other is neither an object in the field of my perception nor a subject who perceives me: the Other is initially a structure of the perceptual field, without which the entire field could not function as it does. That this structure may be actualized by real characters, by variable subjects— me for you and you for me—does not prevent its preexistence, as the condition of organization in general, to the terms which actualize it in each organized perceptual field—yours and mine. Thus the *a priori Other,* as the absolute structure, establishes the relativity of others as terms actualizing the structure within each field. But what is this structure? It is the structure of the possible. A frightened countenance is the expression of a frightening possible world, or of something frightening in the world—something I do not yet see. Let it be understood that the possible is not here an abstract category designating something which does not exist: the expressed possible world certainly exists, but it does not exist (actually) outside of that which expresses it. The terrified countenance bears no resemblance to the terrifying thing. It implicates it, it envelops it as something else, in a kind of torsion which situates what is expressed in the expressing. When I, in turn and for my part, grasp the reality of what the Other was expressing, I do nothing but explicate the Other, as I develop and realize the corresponding possible world. It is true that the Other already bestows a certain reality on the possibilities which he encompasses—especially by speaking. The other is the existence of the encompassed possible. Language is the reality of the possible as such. The self is the development and the explication of what is possible, the process of its realization in the actual. Proust says of the perceived Albertine that she encompasses or expresses the beach and the breaking of the waves: "If she had seen me, what could I have represented for her? At the heart of what universe was she perceiving me?" Love and jealousy will be the attempt to develop and to unfold this possible world named "Albertine." In short, the Other, as structure, is *the expression of a possible world;* it is the expressed, grasped as not yet existing outside of that which expresses it.

Each of these men was a *possible* world, having its own coherence, its values, its sources of attraction and repulsion, its center of gravity. And with all the differences between them, each of these possible worlds at that moment shared a vision, casual and superficial, of the island of Speranza, which caused them to act in common, and which incidentally contained a shipwrecked man called Robinson and his half-caste servant. For the present this picture occupied their minds, but for each of them it was purely temporary, destined very soon to be returned to the limbo from which it had been briefly plucked by the accident of the *Whitebird*'s getting off course. And each of these possible worlds naively proclaimed itself the reality. That was what other people were: the possible obstinately passing for the real.[9]

And we can go even further in our understanding of the effects of the presence of Others. Modern psychology has elaborated a rich series of categories to account for the functioning of the perceptual field and the variations of the object within this field: form-background; depth-length; theme-potentiality; profiles-unity of the object; fringe-center; text-context; thetic-nonthetic; transitive states-substantive parts; etc. But the corresponding philosophical problem is perhaps not very well raised: one asks whether these categories belong to the perceptual field itself being immanent to it (monism), or whether they refer to subjective syntheses operating on the subject matter of perception (dualism). It would be wrong to take exception to the dualist interpretation on the pretext that perception does not occur through a judgmental intellectual synthesis; one can certainly conceive of passive sensible syntheses of an entirely different sort operating on this material (in this sense, Husserl never renounced a certain dualism). Even so, we doubt that dualism is correctly defined as long as it is established between the matter of the perceptual field and the pre-reflective syntheses of the ego. The true dualism lies elsewhere; it lies between the effects of the "structure Other" of the perceptual field and the effects of its absence (what perception would be were there no Others). We must understand that the Other is not one structure among others in the field of perception (in the sense, for example, that one would recognize in it a difference of nature from objects). *It is the structure which conditions the entire field* and its functioning, by rendering possible the constitution and application of the preceding categories. It is not the ego but the Other as structure which renders perception possible. Thus, the authors who interpret dualism poorly are also the authors who cannot extricate themselves from the alternative according to which the Other would be either a particular object in the field or another subject of the field. In defining the Other, together with Tournier, as the expression of a possible world, we make of it, on the contrary, the a priori principle of the organization of every perceptual field in accordance with the categories; we make of it the structure which allows this functioning as the "categorization" of this field. Real dualism then appears with the absence of the Other. But what is happening, in this case, to the perceptual field? Is it structured according to other categories? Or does it, on the contrary, open onto a very special subject matter, allowing us to penetrate into a particular informal realm? This is Robinson's adventure.

The thesis—the Robinson hypothesis—has a great advantage: the disappearance of the structure-Other is presented as the result of circumstances on the desert isle. To be sure, the structure continues to survive and function long after Robinson on the island encounters any actual terms or characters to actualize it. But there comes the moment when this is over: "Those lights have vanished from my consciousness. For a long time, fed by my fantasy, they continued to reach me. Now it is over, and the darkness has closed in."[10] And, as we shall see, when Robinson encounters Friday, he will no longer apprehend him as an Other. And when a ship finally approaches, Robinson knows that he can no longer restore men to their function as Others, since the structure they would thereby fill has itself disappeared: "That was what other people were: the possible obstinately passing for the real. All Robinson's upbringing had taught him that to reject their affirmation was cruel, egotistical, and immoral; but this was an attitude of mind that he had lost during the years, and now he wondered if he could ever recover it."[11] Is not this progressive though irreversible dissolution of the structure what the pervert, on his interior "isle," attains by other means? To put it in Lacanian terms, the "forclusion" of Others brings it about that others *(les autres)* are no longer apprehended as Others *(des autruis),* since the structure which would give them this place and this function is missing. But is it not then the whole of our perceived world that collapses in the interest of something else. . . ?

Let us return to the effects of the presence of Others, such as they follow from the definition "Other = an expression of a possible world." The fundamental effect is the distinction of my consciousness and its object. This distinction is in fact the result of the structure-Other. Filling the world with possibilities, backgrounds, fringes, and transitions; inscribing the possibility of a frightening world when I am not yet afraid, or, on the contrary, the possibility of a reassuring world when I am really frightened by the world; encompassing in different respects the world which presents itself before me developed otherwise; constituting inside the world so many blisters which contain so many possible worlds — this is the Other.[12] Henceforth, the Other causes my consciousness to tip necessarily into an "I was," into a past which no longer coincides with the object. Before the appearance of the Other, there was, for example, a reassuring world from which my consciousness could not be distinguished. The Other then makes its appearance, expressing the possibility of a frightening world which cannot be developed without the one preceding it passing away. For my part, I am nothing other than my past objects, and my self is made up of a past world, the passing away of which was brought about precisely by the Other. If the Other is a possible world, I am a past world. The mistake of theories of knowledge is that they postulate the contemporaneity of subject and object, whereas one is constituted only through the annihilation of the other.

Then suddenly there is a click. The subject breaks away from the object, divesting it of a part of its color and substance. There is a rift in the scheme of things, and a whole range of objects crumbles in becoming *me,* each object transferring its quality to an appropriate subject. The light becomes the eye and as such no longer exists: it is simply the stimulation of the retina. The smell becomes the nostril — and the world declares itself odorless. The song of the wind in the trees is disavowed: it was nothing but a quivering of the timpani. . . . The subject is the disqualified object. My eye is the corpse of light and color. My nose is all that remains of odors when their unreality has been demonstrated. My hand refutes the thing it holds. Thus the problem of awareness is born of anachronism. It implies the simultaneous existence of the subject with the object, whose mysterious relationship to himself he seeks to define. But subject and object cannot exist apart from one another since they are one and the same thing, at first integrated into the real world and then cast out by it.[13]

The Other thus assures the distinction of consciousness and its object as a temporal distinction. The first effect of its presence concerned space and the distribution of categories; but the second effect, which is perhaps the more profound, concerns time and the distribution of its dimensions—what comes before and what comes after in time. How could there still be a past when the Other no longer functions?

In the Other's absence, consciousness and its object are one. There is no longer any possibility of error, not only because the Other is no longer there to be the tribunal of all reality—to debate, falsify, or verify that which I think I see; but also because, lacking in its structure, it allows consciousness to cling to, and to coincide with, the object in an eternal present. "And it is as though, in consequence, my days had rearranged themselves. No longer do they jostle on each other's heels. Each stands separate and upright, proudly affirming its own worth. And since they are no longer to be distinguished as the stages of a plan in process of execution, they so resemble each other as to be superimposed in my memory, so that I seem to be ceaselessly reliving the same day."[14] Consciousness ceases to be a light cast upon objects in order to become a pure phosphorescence of things in themselves. Robinson is but the consciousness of the island, but the consciousness of the island is the consciousness the island has of itself—it is the island in itself. We understand thus the paradox of the desert isle: the one who is shipwrecked, if he is alone, if he has lost the structure-Other, disturbs nothing of the desert isle; rather he consecrates it. The island is named Speranza, but who is the "I"? "The question is far from an idle one, nor is it even unanswerable. Because if it is not *him* then it must be *Speranza.*"[15] Thus Robinson progressively nears a revelation: initially he experienced the loss of Others as a fundamental disorder of the world; nothing subsisted but the opposition of light and night. Everything became harmful, and the world had lost its transitions and virtuality. But he discovers (slowly) that it is the Other who disturbs the world. The Other was the trouble. Having disappeared, it is no longer only the days which are redressed. Things are also, no longer being pulled down by Others one on top of the other. So too is desire, no longer being drawn down on top of a possible object or a possible world expressed by Others. The desert isle initiates a straightening out and a generalized erection.

Consciousness has become not only a phosphorescence internal to things but a fire in their heads, a light over each one, and a "soaring *I.*" In this light, *something else* appears, an ethereal double of each thing. "I seemed to glimpse *another island.* . . . Now I have been transported to that other Speranza, I live perpetually in a moment of innocence."[16] It is this extraordinary birth of the erect double that the novel excels in describing. But what exactly is the difference between the thing such as it appears in the presence of Others and the double which tends to detach itself in their absence? The Other presides over the organization of the world into objects and over the transitive relations of these objects. These objects exist only through the possibilities with which Others filled up the world; each one was closed onto itself, or opened onto other objects, only in relation to possible worlds expressed by Others. In short, it is the Other who has imprisoned the elements within the limits of bodies and, further still, within the limits of the earth. For the earth itself is but a great body which retains the elements; it is earth only to the extent that it is peopled by Others. The Other fabricates bodies out of the elements and objects out of bodies, just as it fabricates its own countenance out of the worlds it expresses. Thus, the liberated double, when the Other collapses, is not a replica of things. It is, on the contrary, the new upright image in which the elements are released and renewed, having become celestial and forming a thousand capricious elemental figures. To begin with, there is the figure of a solar and dehumanized Robinson: "Sun, are you pleased with me? Look at me. Is my transformation sufficiently in the manner of your own radiance? My beard, which pointed earthward like a cluster of earthbound roots, has vanished, and now my head carries its glowing locks like a flame reaching upward to the sky. I am an arrow aimed at your heart. . . ."[17] It is as if the entire earth were trying to escape by way of the island, not only restoring the other elements which it unduly kept under the influence of Others, but also tracing by itself its own ethereal double which renders it celestial and makes it converge with the other elements in the sky for the sake of solar figures. In short, the Other, as it encompasses the possible worlds, prevents the doubles from standing erect. The Other is the grand leveler, and consequently the de-structuration of the Other is not a disorganization of the world, but an upright organization as opposed to the recumbent organization; it is the new uprightness, and the detachment of an image which is vertical at last and without thickness; it is the detachment of a pure element which at last is liberated.

Catastrophes have been necessary for this production of doubles and elements: not only the rites of the great dead goat, but a formidable explosion in which the island gave up all of its fire and vomited itself out through one of its grottos. Through the catastrophes, however, the newly erected desire learns the nature of its true object. Isn't it the case that nature and the earth had already told us that the object of desire is neither the body nor the thing, but only the Image? When we desire Others, are not our desires brought to bear upon this expressed small possible world which the Other wrongly envelops, instead of allowing it to float and fly above the world, developed onto a glorious double? And when we observe a butterfly pillaging a flower that exactly resembles the abdomen of the female of the species and then leaving the flower carrying on its head two horns of pollen, we are tempted to conclude that bodies are but detours to the attainment of Images, and that sexuality reaches its goal much better and much more promptly to the extent that it economizes this detour and addresses itself directly to Images and to the Elements freed from bodies.[18] Robinson's deviation is the conjunction of the libido and the elements; but the full story of this deviation, so far as ends are concerned, encompasses the straightening up of things, the earth, and desire.

How many efforts and fabulous adventures were necessary for him to arrive at that point. For Robinson's first reaction was despair, and this reaction expresses the precise moment of neurosis at which the structure-Other is still functioning, though there is no longer anyone to fill it out or to actualize it. In a certain manner, and since it is no longer occupied by real beings, it functions all the more rigorously. The others *(les autres)* are no longer attached to the structure; the structure functions in a vacuum, without being any less exacting because of this. It endlessly drives Robinson back into an unrecognized personal past, into the snares of memory and the pains of hallucination. This moment of neurosis (in which Robinson is wholly "repressed") is embodied in the *wallowing-place* that Robinson shares with the peccaries: "Only his eyes, nose, and mouth were active, alert for edible weed and toad spawn drifting on the surface. Rid of all terrestrial bonds, his thoughts in a half stupor pursued vestiges of memory which emerged like phantoms from the past to dance in the blue gaps between motionless foliage."[19]

The second moment, however, reveals that the structure-Other begins to crumble. Pulling himself from the wallowing-place, Robinson seeks a substitute for Others, something capable of maintaining, in spite of everything, the fold that Others granted to things—namely, order and work. The ordering of time by means of the clepsydra, the establishment of an overabundant production, or of a code of laws, and the multiplicity of official titles and functions that Robinson takes on—all of this bears witness to an effort to repopulate the world with Others (who would still be himself), and to maintain the effects of the presence of Others when the structure has failed. But the anomaly makes itself felt: Defoe's Robinson does not allow himself to produce beyond his need, thinking that evil begins with surplus production; Tournier's Robinson, however, throws himself into a "frenetic" production, the sole evil being that of consuming, since one always consumes alone and for oneself. In line with this work activity, and as a necessary correlate to it, a strange passion for relaxation and sexuality is developed. Sometimes stopping his clepsydra, getting used to the bottomless night of a grotto, or coating his body with milk, Robinson moves deep into the inner center of the island and finds an alveolus to curl up in, as in a larval envelope of his own body. This is a regression much more fantastic than the regression of neurosis inasmuch as it reaches back to the Earth-Mother—the primordial Mother: "He himself was that supple dough, caught in a hand of all-powerful stone. He was the bean, caught in the massive indestructible flesh of Speranza."[20] Whereas work used to conserve the form of objects as so many accumulated vestiges, involution gives up every formed object for the sake of an inside of the Earth and a principle of burying things in it. The impression one has, however, is that these two very different behaviors are singularly complementary. In both cases, there is frenzy—a double frenzy defining the moment of psychosis—which appears clearly in the return to the Earth and the cosmic genealogy of the schizophrenic, but no less in work, in the production of nonconsumable schizophrenic objects which proceeds by way of piling up and accumulation.[21] At this point, it is the structure-Other which tends to dissolve: the psychotic attempts to compensate for the absence of real Others by establishing an order of human vestiges, and for the dissolution of structure by organizing a superhuman filiation.

Neurosis and psychosis—this is the adventure of depth. The structure-Other organizes and pacifies depth. It renders it livable. This is why the agitations of this structure imply a disorder, a disturbance of depth, as an aggressive return of the bottomless abyss that can no longer be conjured away. Everything has lost its sense, everything becomes *simulacrum and vestige*—even the object of work, the loved one, the world in itself or the self in the world. . .; that is, unless there be some sort of salvation for Robinson; unless he invents a new dimension or a third sense for the expression "loss of Others"; unless the absence of the Other and the dissolution of its structure do not simply disorganize the world but, on the contrary, open up a possibility of salvation. Robinson must return to the surface and discover surfaces. The pure surface is perhaps what Others were hiding from us. It is perhaps at the surface, like a mist, that an unknown image of things is detached and, from the earth, a new surface energy without possible others. For the sky does not at all signify a height which would merely be the inverse image of depth. In opposition to the deep earth, air and sky describe a pure surface, and the surveying of the field of this surface. The solipsist sky has no depth: "It is a strange prejudice which sets a higher value on depth than on breadth, and which accepts 'superficial' as meaning not 'of wide extent' but 'of little depth,' whereas 'deep,' on the other hand, signifies 'of great depth' and not 'of small surface.' Yet it seems to me that a feeling such as love is better measured, if it can be measured at all, by the extent of its surface than by its degree of depth."[22] It is at the surface that doubles and ethereal Images first rise up; then the pure and free Elements arise in the celestial surveying of the field. The generalized erection is the erection of surfaces, their rectification—the disappearance of the Others. At the surface of the isle and the overarching sky, simulacra ascend and become *phantasms*. Doubles without resemblance and elements without constraint—these are the two aspects of the phantasm. This restructuring of the world is Robinson's great Health—the conquest of the great Health, or the third sense of the "loss of Others."

It is here that Friday intervenes. For the main character, as the title indicates, is the young boy, Friday. He alone is able to guide and complete the metamorphosis that Robinson began and to reveal to him its sense and its aim. He will accomplish all of this innocently and superficially. It is Friday who destroys the economic and moral order that Robinson had established on the island. It is he who brings Robinson to dislike the coomb, having grown for his own pleasure another species of Mandrake. It is he who blows up the island as he smokes the forbidden tobacco near a powder keg, and restores the earth, but also water and fire, to the sky. It is he who makes the dead goat (= Robinson) fly and sing. But it is he, above all, who presents to Robinson the image of the personal double as the necessary complement of the iamge of the island: "Robinson turned the question over in his mind. For the first time he was clearly envisaging the possibility that within the crude and brutish half-caste who so exasperated him another Friday might be concealed—just as he had once suspected, before exploring the cave or discovering the coomb, that another Speranza might be hidden beneath his cultivated island." [23] Finally, it is he who leads Robinson to the discovery of the free Elements, which are more radical than Images or Doubles since these latter are formed by them. What is to be said of Friday, if not that he is a mischievous child, wholly at the surface? Robinson will always have ambivalent feelings about Friday, since he saved him only accidentally, having missed when he shot at him wanting to kill him.

What is essential, however, is that Friday does not function at all like a rediscovered Other. It is too late for that, the structure has disappeared. Sometimes he functions as a bizarre object, sometimes as a strange accomplice. Robinson treats him sometimes as a slave and tries to integrate him into the economic order of the island—that is, as a poor simulacrum—and sometimes as the keeper of a new secret which threatens that order—that is, as a mysterious phantasm. Sometimes he treats him almost like an object or an animal, sometimes as if Friday were a "beyond" with respect to himself, a "beyond" Friday, his own double or image. Sometimes he treats him as if he were falling short of the Other, sometimes as if he were transcending the Other. The difference is essential. For the Other, in its normal functioning, ex-presses a possible world. But this possible world exists in our world, and, if it is not developed or realized without changing the quality of our world, it is at least developed in accordance with laws which constitute the order of the real in general and the succession of time.

But Friday functions in an entirely different way—he indicates *another*, supposedly true world, an irreducible double which alone is genuine, and in this other world, a double of the Other who no longer is and cannot be. Not an Other, but something wholly other *(un tout-autre)* than the Other; not a replica, but a Double: one who reveals pure elements and dissolves objects, bodies, and the earth. "It seemed, indeed, that (Friday) belonged to an entirely different realm, wholly opposed to his master's order of earth and husbandry, on which he could have only a disruptive effect if anyone tried to imprison him within it."[24] It is for this reason that he is not even an object of desire for Robinson. Though Robinson embraces his knees and looks into his eyes, it is only in order to grasp the luminous double which now barely retains the free elements which have escaped from his body. "As to my sexuality, I may note that at no time has Friday inspired me with any sodomite desire. For one thing, he came too late, when my sexuality had already become elemental and was directed toward Speranza. . . . It was not a matter of turning me back to human loves but, while leaving me still an elemental, of causing me to change my element."[25] The Other *pulls down (rabat):* it draws the elements into the earth, earth into bodies, and bodies into objects. But Friday innocently makes objects and bodies stand up again. He carries the earth into the sky. He frees the elements. But to straighten up or to rectify is also to shorten. The Other is a strange detour—it brings my desires down to objects, and my love to worlds. Sexuality is linked to generation only in a detour which first channels the difference of sexes through the Other. It is initially in the Other and through the Other that the difference of the sexes is founded. To establish the world without Others, to lift the world up (as Friday does, or rather as Robinson perceives that Friday does) is to avoid the detour. It is to separate desire from its *object,* from its detour through the body, in order to relate it to a pure *cause:* the Elements. ". . . So also has perished the framework of institutions and myths that permits desire to become *embodied,* in the twofold sense of the word—that is to say, to assume a positive form and to expend itself in the body of a woman."[26] Robinson can no longer apprehend himself, or Friday, from the point of view of a differentiated sex. Psychoanalysis may well see in this abolition of the detour, in this separation of the cause of desire from its object, and in this return to the elements, the sign of a death instinct—an instinct which has become solar.

Everything here is fictitious *(romanesque)*, including theory, which merges with a necessary fiction—namely, a certain theory of the Other. First, we must attach a great importance to the notion of the Other as structure: not at all a particular "form" inside a perceptual field (distinct from the form "object" or the form "animal"), but rather a system which conditions the functioning of the entire perceptual field in general. We must therefore distinguish the *a priori Other,* which designates this structure, and the *concrete Other,* which designates real terms actualizing the structure in concrete fields. If this *concrete Other* is always someone—I for you and you for me—that is, in each perceptual field the subject of another field—the a priori Other, on the other hand, is no one since structure is transcendent with respect to the terms which actualize it. How then is it to be defined? The expressiveness which defines the structure-Other is constituted by the category of the possible. The a priori Other is the *existence* of the possible in general, insofar as the possible exists only as expressed—that is, in something expressing it which does not resemble what is expressed (a torsion of the expressed in that which expresses it). When Kierkegaard's hero demands "the possible, the possible or I shall suffocate," when James longs for the "oxygen of possibility," they are only invoking the a priori Other. We have tried to show in this sense how the Other conditions the entire perceptual field, the application to this field of the categories of the perceived object and the dimensions of the perceiving subject, and finally, the distribution of concrete Others in each field. In fact, perceptual laws affecting the constitution of objects (form-background, etc.), the temporal determination of the subject, and the successive development of worlds, seemed to us to depend on the possible as the structure-Other. Even desire, whether it be desire for the object or desire for Others, depends on this structure. I desire an object only as expressed by the Other in the mode of the possible; I desire in the Other only the possible worlds the Other expresses. The Other appears as that which organizes Elements into Earth, and earth into bodies, bodies into objects, and which regulates and measures object, perception, and desire all at once.

What is the sense of the "Robinson" fiction? What is a Robinsonade?

A world without Others. Tournier assumes that Robinson, through much suffering, discovers and conquers a great Health, to the extent that things end up being organized in a manner quite different than their organization in the presence of the Others. They liberate an image without resemblance, or their own double which is normally repressed. This double in turn liberates pure elements which are ordinarily held prisoner. The world is not disturbed by the absence of the Other; on the contrary, it is the glorious double of the world which is found to be hidden by its presence. This is Robinson's discovery: the discovery of the surface, of the elemental beyond, of the "otherwise-Other" *(de l'Autre qu'autrui)*. Why then do we have the impression that this great Health is perverse, and that this "rectification" of the world and of desire is also a deviation and a perversion? Robinson exhibits no perverse behavior. But every study or every novel of perversion strives to manifest the existence of a "perverse structure" as the principle from which perverse behavior eventually proceeds. In this sense, the perverse structure may be specified as that which is opposed to the structure-Other and takes its place. And just as concrete Others are actual and variable terms actualizing this structure-Other, the pervert's behaviors, always presupposing a fundamental absence of the Others, are but variable terms actualizing the perverse structure.

Why does the pervert have the tendency to imagine himself as a radiant angel, an angel of helium and fire? Why does he have—against the *earth,* fertilization, and the objects of desire—the kind of hatred which is already found systematized in Sade? Tournier's novel does not intend to explain—it shows. In this manner, it rejoins, by very different ways, recent psychoanalytic studies which may renew the status of the concept of perversion and disentangle it from the moralizing uncertainty in which it was maintained by the combined forces of psychiatry and the law. Lacan and his school insist profoundly on the necessity of understanding perverse behavior on the basis of a *structure,* and of defining this structure which conditions behavior. They also insist on the manner in which desire undergoes a sort of *displacement* in this structure, and the manner by which the *Cause* of desire is thus detached from the *object;* on the way in which the *difference of sexes* is disavowed by the pervert, in the interest of an androgynous world of *doubles;* on the annulment of the Other inside perversion, on the position of a "beyond the Other" *(un au-delà de l'Autre)* or of an "otherwise Other" *(un Autre qu'autrui)*, as if the Other disengaged in the eyes of the pervert his own *metaphor;* finally, they insist on perverse "desubjectivation"— for it is certain that neither the victim nor the accomplice function as Others.[27] For example, it is not because he has a need or a desire to make the other suffer that the sadist strips him of his quality of being an Other. The converse is rather the case: it is because he is lacking the structure-Other and lives within a completely different structure, as a condition for his living world, that he apprehends others sometimes as victims and sometimes as accomplices, but in neither case does he apprehend them as Others. On the contrary, he always apprehends them as "otherwise Others" *(Autres qu'autrui)*. It is striking to see in Sade's work to what extent victims and accomplices, with their necessary reversibility, are not at all grasped as Others. Rather, they are grasped sometimes as detestable bodies and sometimes as doubles, or allied elements (certainly not as doubles of the hero, but as their own doubles, always outside of their bodies in the pursuit of atomic elements).[28]

The fundamental misinterpretation of perversion, based on a hasty phenomenology of perverse behavior and on certain legal exigencies, consists in bringing perversion to bear upon certain offenses committed against Others. Everything persuades us, from the point of view of behavior, that perversion is nothing without the presence of the Other: voyeurism, exhibitionism, etc. But from the point of view of the structure, the contrary must be asserted: it is because the structure-Other is missing, and is replaced by a completely different structure, that the real "others" are no longer able to play the role of terms actualizing the lost primary structure. Real "others" can only play now, in the second structure, the role of bodies-victims (in the very particular sense that the pervert attributes to bodies), or the role of accomplices-doubles, and accomplices-elements (again, in the very particular sense of the pervert). The world of the pervert is a world without Others, and thus a world without the possible. The Other is that which renders possible. The perverse world is a world in which the category of the necessary has completely replaced that of the possible. This is a strange Spinozism from which "oxygen" is lacking, to the benefit of a more elementary energy and a more rarefied air (Sky-Necessity). All perversion is an "Other-cide," and an "altrucide," and therefore a murder of the possible. But altrucide is not committed through perverse behavior, it is presupposed in the perverse structure. This does not keep the pervert from being a pervert, not constitutionally, but at the end of an adventure which surely has passed through neurosis and brushed up against psychosis. This is what Tournier suggests in this extraordinary novel: we must imagine Robinson as perverse; the only Robinsonade possible is perversion itself.

5. ZOLA AND THE CRACK-UP

In *La Bête humaine* the following celebrated passage can be found:

The family was really not quite normal, and many of them had some flaw. At certain times, he could clearly feel this hereditary taint, not that his health was bad, for it was only nervousness and shame about his attacks that had made him lose weight in his early days. But there were attacks of instability in his being, losses of equilibrium like cracks or holes through which his personality seemed to leak away, amid a sort of thick vapour that deformed everything. . . .[1]

Here Zola launches an important theme, one that will be taken up in other forms and by other means in modern literature and one always found to have a privileged relationship with alcoholism: the theme of the crack-up (Fitzgerald, Lowry).

It is important that Jacques Lantier, the hero of *La Bête humaine,* be sound, vigorous, and in good health, for the crack does not designate a route along which morbid ancestral elements will pass, marking the body. Zola in fact happens to express himself in this manner, but this is only a matter of convenience. It may even be the case for certain characters—the weak and the jittery. But to be precise, they are not the ones who carry the crack—or it is not by virtue of this alone that they carry it. Heredity is not that which passes through the crack, it is the crack itself—the imperceptible rift or the hole. In its true sense, the crack is not a crossing for morbid heredity; it alone is the hereditary and the morbid in its entirety. From one healthy Rougon-Macquart body to another it transmits nothing other than itself. Everything rests on the paradox, that is, the confusion of this heredity with its vehicle or means, or the confusion of what is transmitted with its transmission —the paradox of this transmission which transmits nothing other than itself: the cerebral crack in a vigorous body or the crevice of thought. With the exception of accidents, as we shall see, the *"soma"* is vigorous and healthy. But the *"germen"* is the crack—nothing but the crack. Under these conditions, the crack takes on the appearance of an epic destiny, going from one story or one body to another, forming the red thread of the Rougon-Macquart.

What is distributed around the crack? What is it that swarms at its edges? It is what Zola calls the temperaments, the instincts, "the big appetites." But "temperament" or "instinct" does not designate a psycho-physiological entity. It is a notion far more rich and concrete— a "novelistic" notion. The instincts designate the conditions of life and survival in general—the conditions of the conservation of a kind of life determined in a historical and social milieu (here, the Second Empire). This is why Zola's bourgeois can easily name their vices, their lack of generosity and their ignominies as virtues; conversely, this is why the poor are often reduced to "instincts" like alcoholism, which epxress the historical conditions of their lives and their only way of putting up with a historically determined life. Zola's "naturalism" is always historical and social. Instinct, or appetite, has therefore diverse faces. Sometimes it expresses the manner by which the body conserves itself in a given favorable environment; in this sense, instinct is itself vigor and health. Sometimes it expresses the kind of life that a body invents in order to turn to its own advantage what the environment gives, even if it has to destroy other bodies. In this case, instinct is an ambiguous power. Sometimes it expresses the kind of life without which a body could not support its historically determined existence in an unfavorable environment, even if this means the destruction of itself; in this sense, alcoholism, perversions, illnesses, and even senility are instincts. Instincts tend to conserve, insofar as they always express the effort of perpetuating a way of life. But this *way of life,* and the instinct itself, may be no less destructive than "conservative" in the strict sense of the word. Instincts manifest degeneration, the sudden arrival of an illness—the loss of health no less than health itself. No matter what form it takes, instinct is never confused with the crack. Rather, it maintains strict though variable relations with the crack: sometimes, and thanks to the health of the body, it covers it over and mends it, as best it can, for a greater or shorter length of time; sometimes the instinct widens the crack, providing it with another orientation which causes the pieces to splinter, provoking thereby an accident in the decrepit state of the body. In *L'Assomoir,* for example, in the house of Gervaise, the alcoholic instinct comes to double the original defect of the crack. We leave aside for the moment the question of knowing whether there are any evolutive or ideal instincts capable of transforming the crack.

Through the crack, instincts seek the object which corresponds to them, in the historical and social circumstances of their kind of life: wine, money, power, women. . . . One of the feminine types preferred by Zola is the nervous woman, crushed under an abundance of black hair, passive, hidden to herself, someone who will unleash herself in the romantic encounter (such is the case with Thérèse in *Thérèse Raquin,* written before the Rougon series, and also with Séverine in *La Bête humaine*). A terrible encounter between nerves and blood, an encounter between nervous and sanguine temperaments reproduces the Rougon's origin. The encounter causes the crack to resonate. The characters who are not of the Rougon family (like Séverine, for example) may intervene as objects to which the instinct of a Rougon is fastened, but also as being themselves provided with instincts and temperament, and finally as accomplices or enemies who provide evidence of a secret crack affecting them and linking up with the other. The spider-like crack: in the Rougon-Macquart family, everything culminates with Nana, a healthy and nice girl basically, with a vigorous body, who makes herself into an object in order to fascinate the others and to communicate her crack or to reveal the crack of others—a foul *germen.* The privileged role of alcohol also belongs here: it is under cover of this "object" that the instinct brings about its most profound linkage with the crack itself.

The meeting of instinct and object forms a fixed idea, not a feeling. If Zola the novelist intervenes in his novels, it is primarily in order to say to his readers: look out, don't think that it is a question of feelings here. We know well the insistence with which Zola, in *La Bête humaine* as well as in *Thérèse Raquin,* explains that criminals have no remorse. And there is no love for lovers—except when the instinct is truly able "to patch over" (the crack) and to become evolutive. It is not a question of love or remorse, but of torsions and breakings or, on the contrary, of lulls and appeasements, in relations between temperaments which are always stretched out over the crack. Zola excels in the description of the brief calm coming before the grand decomposition ("it is now certain; there was a progressive disorganization, like a criminal infiltration . . ."). There are obviously several reasons in Zola's work for this refusal of feeling in the interest of the fixed idea. First, we must recall the style of the period and the importance of the physiological schema. "Physiology," since Balzac, had played the literary role that is today vested in psychoanalysis (the physiology of a country or region, of a profession, etc.). Moreover, it is true that, since Flaubert, feeling has been inseparable from a failure, a bankruptcy, or mystification, and that what the novel relates is the impotence of a character to constitute an inner life. In this sense, naturalism introduced into the novel three sorts of characters: the man marked by an inner bankruptcy, that is, the failure; the man living artificial lives, that is, the pervert; and the man possessed by rudimentary sensations and fixed ideas, that is, the beast. But in Zola's work, if the encounter of instinct and its object does not succeed in forming a feeling, it is always because it occurs over the crack, from one edge to the other. It is due to the existence of the crack, the great internal Void. The entire naturalism therefore acquires a new dimension.

In Zola, therefore, two unequal coexisting cycles interfere with each other: *small heredity and grand heredity,* a small historical heredity and a great epical heredity, a somatic heredity and a germinal heredity, a heredity of instincts and a heredity of the crack. No matter how strong or constant the connection between the two may be, they are not confused. The small heredity is the heredity of instincts, in the sense that the conditions or kinds of life led by the ancestors or parents may take root in the descendant—sometimes several generations later— and act in her as nature. A healthy foundation, for example, is rediscovered; alcoholic degradation is passed from one body to the other; or instinct-object syntheses are transmitted at the same time that life-styles are reconstituted. Whatever leaps it may undertake, this heredity of instincts transmits something well-determined. It "reproduces" whatever it transmits; it is a heredity of the Same. But this is not at all the case with the other heredity—the heredity of the crack—for, as we have seen, the crack transmits nothing other than itself. It is not tied to a certain instinct, to an internal, organic determination, or to an external event that could fix an object. It transcends life-styles; it therefore runs its course in a continuous, *imperceptible, and silent* way, forming the complete unity of the Rougon-Macquart. The crack transmits only the crack. That which it transmits does not allow itself to be determined, being necessarily vague and diffuse. Transmitting only itself, it does not reproduce that which it transmits. It does not reproduce the "same." It reproduces nothing, being content to advance in silence and to follow the lines of least resistance. As the perpetual heredity of the Other, it always takes an oblique line, being ready to change directions and to alter its canvas.

Zola's scientific inspiration has often been noted. But what was the import of this inspiration which was derived from the medical research of his time? It bears precisely on the distinction between the two heredities, which was elaborated in the contemporary medical thought: a homologous and well-determined heredity and a "dissimilar or trans-formational" heredity, with a diffuse character, which is defining a "neuropathological family."[2] Now, this distinction is interesting because it easily replaces the dualism of the hereditary and the acquired, or even because it renders this dualism impossible. Indeed, the small homologous heredity of the instincts may very well transmit acquired characteristics. This may even be inevitable to the extent that the formation of the instinct is inseparable from historical and social conditions. As for the grand, dissimilar heredity, it has with the acquired characteristics an entirely different, though no less essential, relationship: it is a question here of a diffuse potentiality which is not actualized unless a transmissible acquired property, whether internal or external, were to give it some particular determination. In other words, if it is true that the instincts are formed and find their object only at the edge of the crack, the crack conversely pursues its course, spreads out its web, changes direction, and is actualized in each body in relation to the instincts which open a way for it, sometimes mending it a little, sometimes widening it, up to the final shattering—which is always assured by the work of the instincts. The correlation between the two orders is thus constant and reaches its highest point when the instinct has become alcoholic and the crack a definitive break. The two orders are tightly joined together, like a ring within a larger ring, but they are never confused.

Now, if it is fair to note the influence of scientific and medical theories on Zola, how unfair would it be not to emphasize the transformation to which he submitted them, the way in which he recreated the notion of the two heredities, and the poetic force which he gave to this notion in order to make of it the new structure of the "familial romance." In this case, the novel integrates two basic elements which were previously foreign to it: Drama, with the historic heredity of instincts; and Epos, with the epical heredity of the crack. As they cross each other, they form the rhythm of the work, that is, they assure the distribution of sounds and silence. Zola's novels are filled with the sounds of the instincts, and the "big appetites" of the characters which form a prodigious din. As for the silence which runs from one novel to the other and beneath each novel, it essentially belongs to the crack; beneath the noise of the instincts, the crack silently extends and transmits itself.

The crack designates, and this emptiness is, Death—the death Instinct. The instincts may speak loud, make noise, or swarm, but they are unable to cover up this more profound silence, or hide that from which they come forth and into which they return: the death instinct, *not merely one instinct among others,* but the crack itself around which all of the instincts congregate. In his homage to Zola, at once profound and reticent, Céline finds Freudian tones to mark the universal presence, beneath the noisy instincts, of the silent death instinct:

The sadism which is today everywhere springs from a desire for nothingness which is established deep within man, especially in the mass of men—a sort of amorous, almost irresistible and unanimous impatience for death. . . . *Our words reach the instincts and sometimes touch them; but at the same time we learn that at this point and forever, our power comes to a halt.* . . . In the play of man, the death Instinct, the silent instinct, is decidedly well placed, perhaps alongside egoism.[3]

But whatever Céline thinks of it, Zola had already discovered how the big appetites gravitate around the death instinct; how they swarm through a crack which is the crack of the death instinct; how death appears beneath every fixed idea; how the death instinct comes to be recognized beneath every instinct; how it alone constitutes the grand heredity of the crack. Our words reach only as far as the instincts, but it is from the other agency, that is, from the death Instinct, that they receive their sense, nonsense, and combinations thereof. Underlying every history of the instincts is the epos of death. We could say initially that the instincts cover over death and cause it to retreat; but this is temporary, and even their noise is fed by death. *La Bête humaine,* with regard to Roubaud, states that ". . . in the troubled darkness of his flesh, in his desire that had been sullied and was bleeding, there suddenly rose up the necessity of death." Misard's fixed idea is the discovery of his wife's savings; but he is unable to pursue this idea without the murder of his wife and the demolition of the house in a silent face-to-face struggle.

In *La Bête humaine,* the essential is the death instinct of the main character, the cerebral crack of Jacques Lantier, the train conductor. As a young man, he has a clear premonition of the manner in which the death instinct is disguised beneath every appetite, the Idea of death beneath every fixed idea, the grand heredity beneath the small, which is held at bay—women, at first, but also wine, money—that is, ambitions which he could quite legitimately have. He has given up the instincts; his sole object is the machine. He knows that the crack brings death into every instinct, that it pursues its work in and through the instincts; he knows that at the beginning and the end of every instinct there is a question of killing, and perhaps of being killed as well. But the silence which Lantier created within himself, in order to oppose it to the deeper silence of the crack, is suddenly interrupted: Lantier has seen in the flash of an instant a murder committed on a passing train and has seen the victim thrown onto the track; he has guessed the assassins, Roubaud and his wife, Séverine. And as he begins to love Séverine and to discover the realm of the instinct, death spreads out within him—for this love has come from death and must return to death.

Beginning with the crime that the Roubauds committed, an entire system of identifications and repetitions is developed which forms the rhythm of the book. Initially, Lantier identifies immediately with the criminal: "The other, the man who held the knife in his fist, had dared! Oh to have the nerve, satisfy himself and thrust the knife in! It was he that the desire had tortured for ten years!" Roubaud killed the President out of jealousy, having understood that the latter had raped Séverine when she was a child and made him marry a tainted woman. But after the crime he identifies in a certain manner with the President. It is his turn to give Lantier his wife tainted and criminal. Lantier begins to love Séverine, because she has participated in the crime: "It was as though she were the dream which had harbored within his flesh." At this point, the triple calm makes its appearance: the calm of torpor falling over the marriage of the Roubauds; the calmness of Séverine, rediscovering her innocence in her love for Lantier; and especially, the calmness of Lantier, rediscovering with Séverine the sphere of instincts and imagining that he has filled in the crack; he believes that he will never desire to kill Séverine—the one who killed ("to possess her was to possess a powerful charm, and she had cured him . . ."). But there is already a triple disorganization coming to take the place of the calm, and following unequal cadences. Roubaud, after the crime, has replaced Séverine with alcohol as the object of his instinct. Séverine has found an instinctive love which gives her innocence; but she cannot help getting it tangled up with the need for an explicit confession to her lover who has nonetheless guessed everything. And, in the scene in which Séverine had been waiting for Lantier, just as Roubaud had been waiting for her before the crime, she tells her lover the whole story; she details her confession and thrusts her desire in the remembrance of death ("the thrill of desire lost itself in another shudder, that of death which had come back to her").[4] Freely, she confesses the crime to Lantier, just as, under constraint, she had confessed to Roubaud her relations with the President, provoking thereby the crime. She is no longer able to conjure away and to divert the image of death which she caused to raise, except by projecting it onto Roubaud and by urging Lantier to kill him ("(Lantier) saw himself with the knife in his hand, plunging it into Roubaud's throat as Roubaud had done to the throat of the President . . .").[5]

As for Lantier, Séverine's confession did not tell him anything new, yet it terrified him. She should not have spoken. The woman he loved, and who was "sacred" to him to the extent that she enveloped within herself the image of death, lost her power as she confessed, and designated another possible victim. Lantier does not succeed in killing Roubaud. He knows that he will be able to kill only the object of his instinct. This paradoxical situation—in which those about him (Roubaud, Séverine, Misard, Flore) kill for reasons drawn from other instincts, but Lantier (who nevertheless bears the pure death instinct) cannot kill—can be resolved only through the murder of Séverine. Lantier learns that the voice of the instincts had deceived him, that his "instinctive" love for Séverine had only seemed to fill in the crack, and that the noise produced by the instincts covered over the silent Instinct of death only for a moment. He learns that it is Séverine whom he must kill in order for the small heredity to link up with the grand, and for all the instincts to enter the crack: To have her dead, like the earth!; "the same kind of stab as for President Grandmorin, in the same place, with the same savagery . . . the two murders were coupled together. Was not one the logical outcome of the other?"[6] Séverine senses a danger all around her, but she interprets it as a barrier between herself and Lantier, due to Roubaud's existence. It is, however, not a barrier between the two of them, but the spider-like crack in Lantier's brain —its silent working. After murdering Séverine, Lantier will have no remorse: always this health, this sound body—"He had never felt better, had no remorse and seemed relieved of a burden, happy and at peace"; ". . . ever since the murder he had felt calm and balanced and had enjoyed perfect health."[7] But this health is even more ludicrous than if the body had fallen ill, undermined by alcohol or by another instinct. This peaceful, healthy body is no more than a terrain ripe for the crack and food for the spider. He will have to kill other women. With all of this health, "he had finished living, there was no longer anything before him except this profound night, a limitless despair in which he fled." And when his old friend, Pecqueux, attempts to throw him off the train, even his bodily protest, his reflexes, his instinct for preservation, his struggle against Pecqueux, are ludicrous reactions which offer Lantier up to the great Instinct all the more clearly than if he had committed suicide, and carry him away, along with Pecqueux, toward a common death.

The force of Zola's work is in scenes with different partners which echo one another. But what is it that assures the distribution of scenes, the range of characters, and the logic of the Instinct? The answer is clearly the train. The novel opens with a sort of ballet of engines in the station. In particular, the fleeting sight of the President's murder is, in the case of Lantier, preceded, glimpsed at, and followed by, passing trains which assume diverse functions (ch. 2). The train appears first as that which rushes by, a mobile spectacle linking the whole earth and men of every origin or every country: yet it is already the spectacle spread out before a dying woman—an immobile crossing guard being murdered slowly by her husband. Then a second train appears, seemingly this time forming a giant body, tracing a crack on it, and communicating this crack to the earth and to the houses—and "on either side . . . eternal passion and eternal crime."[8] A third and fourth train show the elements of the track: deep trenches, embankments-barricades, and tunnels. A fifth, with its lights and headlamps, carries crime within it, since the Roubauds are committing their murder inside it. Finally, a sixth train links together the forces of the unconscious, indifference, and menace, grazing on one side the head of the murdered man and on the other the body of the voyeur—a pure death Instinct, blind and deaf. However clamorous the train may be, it is deaf—and in this way, silent.

The real meaning of the train appears with Lison, the locomotive driven by Lantier. Initially, it had taken the place of all the instinctual objects that Lantier had renounced. It is itself presented as having an instinct and a temperament: ". . . she needed too much oiling, the cylinders in particular consumed quite unreasonable quantities of oil, an insatiable thirst, a real debauch."[9] Now, what applies to the locomotive applies also to humanity, where the din of the instincts refers to a secret crack—the human Beast. In the chapter which tells of the trip undertaken during the snowstorm, Lison plunges headlong over the track as if into a narrow crack in which it can no longer advance. And when it finally frees itself, it is the engine that has cracked, "stricken somewhere by a mortal blow." The journey dug out the crack that the instinct—the appetite for oil—had concealed. Beyond the lost instinct, the machine is revealed more and more as the image of death or as the pure death Instinct. And when Flore provokes the derailment, it is no longer clear whether it is the machine that is assassinated or whether it is the machine that kills. And in the final scene of the novel, the new machine, without a conductor, carries its cargo of drunken, singing soldiers toward death.

The locomotive is not an object, but an epic symbol, a great Phantasm, like the ones which often appear in Zola's work, reflecting all of the themes and situations of the book. In all of the Rougon-Macquart novels there is an enormous fantasized object that plays the roles of place, witness, and agent. The epic character of Zola's genius has often been emphasized, visible as it is in the structure of the work and in the succession of planes, each one of which exhausts a theme. This is evident if one compares La Bête humaine with Thérèse Raquin, a novel preceding the Rougon-Macquart series. The two books share many similarities: the murder which ties the couple; the progression of death and the process of disorganization; the resemblance of Thérèse and

Séverine; and the absence of remorse or the denial of interiority. But *Thérèse Raquin* is the tragic version, whereas *La Bête Humaine* is the epic version. What really takes center stage in *Thérèse Raquin* is instinct, temperament, and the opposition of the temperaments of Thérèse and Laurent. And if there is a transcendence, it is only that of a judge or of an inexorable witness who symbolizes the tragic destiny. This is why the role of the symbol or of the tragic god is held by Madame Raquin, the mute and paralyzed mother of the murder victim, present throughout the decomposition of the lovers. The *drama,* the adventure of the instincts, is reflected only in the *logos* represented by the muteness of the old woman and by her expressive fixity. In the care lavished upon her by Laurent and the theatrical declarations made by Thérèse on her behalf, there is a tragic intensity which has rarely been equalled. But to be precise, this is only the tragic prefiguration of *La Bête humaine.* In *Thérèse Raquin,* Zola does not yet make use of the epic method which animates the Rougon-Macquart enterprise.

What is essential in the epic is a double register in which the gods actively play out, in their own way and on another plane, the adventure of men and of their instincts. The *drama* in this case is reflected in an *epos*—the small genealogy is reflected in a grand genealogy, the small heredity in a big heredity, and a *small maneuver* in a *large maneuver.* All sorts of consequences follow from this: the pagan character of the epic; the opposition between epic and tragic destiny; the open space of the *epos* as opposed to the closed space of tragedy; and especially, the difference of the symbol in the epic and the tragic. In *La Bête humaine,* it is no longer a mere witness or a judge, but rather an agent or a field of action (the train), which plays the role of the symbol with respect to the story and enacts the large maneuver. It traces therefore an open space on the scale of a nation and a civilization, in contrast to the closed space of *Thérèse Raquin,* which is dominated solely by the old woman's gaze. "So many men and women were rushing past in the thunder of trains . . . It was a fact that all the world went by, . . . But they went by in a flash and she was never quite sure she really had seen them." [10] The double register, in *La Bête humaine,* consists of noisy instincts and the crack—the silent death Instinct. As a result, everything that happens occurs on two levels: the levels of love and death, of *soma* and *germen,* of the two heredities. The story is duplicated by an *epos.* The instincts or temperaments no longer occupy the essential position. They swarm about and within the train, but the train itself is the epic representation of the death Instinct. Civilization is evaluated from two perspectives, from the point of view of the instincts which it determines and from the point of view of the crack which determines it.

In the world of his time, Zola discovered the possibility of restoring the epic. Filth as an element of his literature—"putrid literature"—is the history of the instinct against the background of death. The crack is the epic god in the history of the instincts and the condition that renders this history possible. In response to those who accuse him of exaggeration, the writer has no *logos,* but only an *epos,* which states that one can never go too far in the description of decomposition, since it is necessary to go as far as the crack leads. Could it be the case that the death Instinct, by going as far as possible, would turn back on itself? Is it not perhaps the case that the crack, which is only apparently and for a short time filled over by the big appetites, transcends itself in the direction it itself created? Is it possible, since it absorbs every instinct, that it could also enact the transmutation of the instincts, turning death against itself? Would it not thereby create instincts which would be evolutive rather than alcoholic, erotic, or financial, that is, either conserving or destroying? Zola's final optimism, his rose-colored novels among the black, have frequently been noted. It would be a mistake, however, to interpret them by invoking some sort of alternation; in fact, Zola's optimistic literature is not anything other than his putrid literature. It is in one and the same movement—the movement of the epic—that the basest instincts are reflected in the terrible death Instinct, but also that the death Instinct is reflected inside an open space, perhaps even against itself. What Zola's socialist optimism means is that the proletariat already makes its way through the crack. The train as an epic symbol, with the instincts it transports and the death Instinct it represents, is always endowed with a future. The final sentences of *La Bête humaine* are also a hymn to the future—Pecqueux and Lantier are thrown off the train, as the deaf and blind machine carries the soldiers, "already silly with fatigue, drunk and bawling," toward death. It is as if the crack runs through and alienates thought in order to be also the possibility of thought, in other words, that from the vantage point of which thought is developed and recovered. It is the obstacle to thought, but also the abode and power of thought—its field and agent. *Le Docteur Pascal,* the final novel of the series, shows this epic point of the turning back of death upon itself, of the transmutation of instincts and of the idealization of the crack, in the pure element of "scientific" and "progressivist" thought wherein the genealogical tree of the Rougon-Macquart burns.

Notes

FIRST SERIES OF PARADOXES OF PURE BECOMING

1. Plato, *Philebus,* 24, d., trans. R. Hackforth; *Parmenides,* 154–155, trans. F. M. Cornforth; in E. Hamilton and H. Cairns, eds. *Plato: The Collected Dialogues* (Princeton: Princeton University Press, 1961).
2. Plato, *Cratylus,* 437ff. With respect to the preceding, see appendix 1.

SECOND SERIES OF PARADOXES OF SURFACE EFFECTS

1. Émile Bréhier, *La Théorie des incorporels dans l'ancien stoïcisme* (Paris: Vrin, 1928), pp. 11–13.
2. On this example, see the commentary of Bréhier, p. 20.
3. On the distinction between real internal causes and external causes entering into limited relations of "confatality," see Cicero, *De Fato,* 9, 13, 15, and 16.
4. The Epicurean notion of the event is very similar to that of the Stoics: Epicurus, *To Herodotus,* 39–40, 68–73; and Lucretius, *De Rerum Natura,* 1:449ff. As he analyzes the event, "the rape of Tyndareus' daughter . . . ," Lucretius contrasts *eventa* (servitude-liberty), poverty-wealth, war-peace) with *conjuncta* (real qualities which are inseparable from bodies). Events are not exactly incorporeal entities. They are presented nevertheless as not existing by themselves—impassible, pure results of the movements of matter, or actions and passions of bodies. It does not seem likely

though that the Epicureans developed this theory of the event—perhaps because they bent it to the demands of a homogeneous causality and subsumed it under their own conception of the *simulacrum*. See appendix 2.

5. On the account of Stoic categories, see Plotinus, 6:1.25. See also Bréhier, p. 43.

6. This description of the purse comprises some of Carroll's best writing: *Sylvie and Bruno Concluded,* ch. 7.

7. This discovery of the surface and this critique of depth represent a constant in modern literature. They inspire the work of Robbe-Grillet. In another form, we find them again in Klossowski, in the relation between Roberte's epidermis and her glove: see Klossowski's remarks to this effect in the postface to *Lois de l'hospitalité,* pp. 135, 344; see also Michel Tournier's *Friday,* trans. Norman Denny (New York: Pantheon Books, 1985, by arrangement with Doubleday), p. 67: "It is a strange prejudice which sets a higher value on depth than on breadth, and which accepts 'superficial' as meaning not 'of wide extent' but 'of little depth,' whereas 'deep,' on the other hand, signifies 'of great depth,' and not 'of small surface.' Yet it seems to me that a feeling such as love is better measured, if it can be measured at all, by the extent of its surface than by its degree of depth." See appendixes 3 and 4.

THIRD SERIES OF THE PROPOSITION

1. See the theory of "connectors" *(embrayeurs)* as presented by Benveniste in *Problémes de linguistique général* (Paris: Gallimard, 1966), ch. 20. We separate "tomorrow" from yesterday or today, since "tomorrow" is first of all an expression of belief and has only a secondary indicative value.

2. For example, when Brice Parain opposes denomination (denotation) and demonstration (signification), he understands "demonstration" in a manner that encompasses the moral sense of a program to be fulfilled, a promise to be kept, a possibility to be realized—as, for example, in a "demonstration of love" or a phrase such as "I will love you always." See *Recherches sur la nature et les fonctions du langage* (Paris: Gallimard, 1972), ch. 5.

3. Descartes, *Principes,* 1:10.

4. See Lewis Carroll, *Logique sans peine,* trans. Gattegno and Coumet (Paris: Hermann, 1972). For the abundant literary, logical, and scientific bibliography concerning this paradox, refer to Ernest Coumet's commentaries, pp. 281–288.

5. Brice Parain, ch. 3.

6. Bertrand Russell, *An Inquiry Into Meaning and Truth* (London: George Allen and Unwin, 1940).

7. *Ibid.*, p. 179: "We may say that whatever is asserted by a significant sentence has a certain kind of possibility."

8. Hubert Elie, in an excellent book, *La Complexe significabile* (Paris: Vrin, 1936), exposes and comments on the doctrines of Gregory of Rimini and Nicolas d'Autrecourt. He points out the extreme resemblance to Meinong's theories, and how a similar polemic was repeated in both the nineteenth and fourteenth centuries. He does not, however, indicate the Stoic origin of the problem.

9. On the Stoic differentiation of incorporeal entities and rational representations, composed of corporeal traces, see E. Bréhier, pp. 16–18.

10. See Albert Lautman's remarks on the subject of the Möbius strip: it has "but a single side, which is essentially an extrinsic property, since in order to give an account of it the strip must be broken and untwisted. This presupposes of course a rotation around an axis external to the surface of the strip. Yet it is also possible to characterize this unilaterality by means of a purely intrinsic property. . . ." *Essai sur les notions de structure et d'existence en mathématiques* (Paris: Hermann, 1938), 1:51.

11. We do not have in mind here the particular use Husserl makes of "signification" in his terminology, either to identify it or to bind it to "sense."

12. These terms, *"inherence"* and *"extra-Being,"* have their correlates in Meinong's terminology as well as in that of the Stoics.

13. *Logique sans peine,* preface, pp. 19–20.

FOURTH SERIES OF DUALITIES

1. The Gardener's song, in *Sylvie and Bruno,* is formed of nine stanzas, of which eight are dispersed in the first book, the ninth appearing in *Sylvie and Bruno Concluded* (ch. 20). A (French) translation of the whole is given by Henri Parisot in *Lewis Carroll* (Paris: Seghers, 1952), and by Robert Benayoun in his *Anthologie du Nonsense* (Paris: Pauvert, 1957), pp. 180–182.

FIFTH SERIES OF SENSE

1. See G. Frege, *Über Sinn und Bedeutung,* Zeitschrift f. Ph. und ph. Kr., 1892. This principle of an infinite proliferation of entities has evoked little

justified resistance on the part of many contemporary logicians: see R. Carnap, *Meaning and Necessity* (Chicago: University of Chicago Press, 1947), pp. 130–138.

2. The translation here omits a clause of the original text. The original text is as follows: "This passage, which was translated very inelegantly in order to be faithful to Carroll's terminology, distinguishes a series of nominal entities." Tr. note.

3. Husserl, *Ideas,* trans. W. R. Boyce Gibson (New York: Collier, 1962), Section 124.

4. See Hubert Elie, *Le Complexe Significabile.* And Maurice de Gandillac, *Le Mouvement doctrinal du IXe au XIVe siècle* (Paris: Bloud et Gay, 1951).

5. On the paradox of contingent futures and its importance in Stoic thought, see P. M. Schuhl, *Le Dominateur et les possibles* (Paris: P.U.F., 1960).

6. See Étienne Gilson's commentaries, in *L'Être et l'essence* (Paris: Vrin, 1948), pp. 120–123.

SIXTH SERIES ON SERIALIZATION

1. Jacques Lacan, *Écrits* (Paris: Seuil, 1966), "Le Seminaire sur *la lettre volée.*"

2. See Michel Foucault, *Raymond Roussel* (Paris: Gallimard, 1963), ch. 2; with respect to series, see in particular pp. 78ff.

3. Pierre Klossowski, *Les Lois de l'hospitalité* (Paris: Gallimard, 1965), Avertissement, p. 7.

4. Witold Gombrowicz, *Cosmos* (New York: Grove Press, 1970). With respect to the preceding discussion, see appendix 1.

5. See Lacan's "Le Mythe individuel du Névrosé," (Paris: C.D.U., 1953). This test is essential to the serial method, but is not reprinted in *Écrits.*

6. *Écrits,* p. 25. The paradox here described must be named Lacan's paradox. A Carrollian inspiration is often in evidence in Lacan's writings.

SEVENTH SERIES OF ESOTERIC WORDS

1. On the procedures followed by Rabelais and Swift, see Emile Pons' classification in Swift's *Oeuvres* (Paris: Gallimard, Pléiade, 1965), pp. 9–12.

2. Both Henri Parisot and Jacques B. Brunius have produced fine (French) translations of "Jabberwocky." Parisot's is reproduced in his *Lewis Carroll;* Brunius', along with a commentary on the words in the poem, can be found in the *Cahiers du Sud* (1948), no. 287. Both authors also cite versions

of "Jabberwocky" in diverse languages. We borrow the terms that we use sometimes from Parisot, sometimes from Brunius. Antonin Artaud's translation of the first stanza of the poem will be considered later, as this admirable text poses problems which no longer pertain to Carroll.

3. Michel Butor, *Introduction aux fragments de "Finnegans Wake"* (Paris: Gallimard, 1962), p. 12.

EIGHTH SERIES OF STRUCTURE

1. C. Lévi-Strauss, "Introduction à l'oeuvre de Marcel Mauss," in M. Mauss, *Sociologie et anthropologie* (Paris: P.U.F., 1950), pp. 48–49.

2. The parallel with differential calculus may seem both arbitrary and old-fashioned. But what is old-fashioned is only the infinitist interpretation of calculus. Already at the end of the nineteenth century, Weirstrass gave a finite interpretation, *ordinal and static,* very close to a mathematical structuralism. The theme of singularities remains an essential piece of the theory of differential equations. The best study of the history of the differential calculus and its modern structural interpretation is C. B. Boyer's *The History of the Calculus and Its Conceptual Development* (New York: Dover, 1959).

NINTH SERIES OF THE PROBLEMATIC

1. Earlier, "neutral" sense seemed to us to be opposed to the singular no less than to the other modalities. For singularity was defined only in relation to denotation and manifestation; the singular was defined as individual or personal, not as punctual. Now, however, singularity belongs to the neutral domain.

2. Péguy, *Clio* (Paris: Gallimard, 1932), p. 269.

3. Novalis, *L'Encyclopédie,* trans. Maurice de Gandillac (Paris: Minuit, n.d.), p. 396.

4. Proclus, *Commentaires sur le premier livre des Éléments d'Euclide,* trans. Ver Eecke (Paris: Desclée de Brouwer, 1948), pp. 68ff; trans. in English with introduction and notes by Glenn R. Morrow, *A Commentary on the First Book of Euclid's Elements* (Princeton: Princeton University Press, 1970), pp. 63–67.

5. See Albert Lautman, *Essai sur les notions de structure et d'existence en mathématiques* (Paris: Hermann, 1938), 2:148–149; and *Nouvelles recherches sur la*

structure dialectique des mathématiques (Paris: Hermann, 1939), pp. 13–15. On the role of singularities, *Essai,* 2:138–139; and *Le Problème du temps* (Paris: Hermann, 1946), pp. 41–42.

Péguy, in his own way, had seen the essential relation of the event or singularity with the categories of problem and solution: see Péguy, p. 269: ". . . and a problem whose end we could not see, a problem without a way out . . ." etc.

6. *The Dynamics of a Parti-cle.*

TENTH SERIES OF THE IDEAL GAME

1. On the idea of a time smaller than the minimum of continuous time, see appendix 2.
2. J. L. Borges, *Ficciones* (New York: Grove Press, 1962), pp. 69–70. The parable of the tortoise and the hare seems to be an allusion not only to Zeno's paradox but to Carroll's as well, which we have already considered, and which Borges takes up anew in *Other Inquisitions* (Austin: University of Texas Press, 1964).
3. J. L. Borges, *Ficciones,* p. 141. In his *Historia de la eternidad,* Borges does not go so far and seems to conceive of the labyrinth as only circular or cyclical.

   Among the commentators of Stoic thought, Victor Goldschmidt in particular has analyzed the coexistence of these two conceptions of time: the first, of variable presents; the second, of unlimited subdivision into past and future. *Le Système stoïcien et l'idée de temps* (Paris: Vrin, 1953), pp. 36–40. He also demonstrates that there exist for the Stoics two methods and two moral attitudes. But whether these two attitudes correspond to the two times is still obscure: it does not seem so, according to the author's comments. Moreover, the question of two very different eternal returns, themselves corresponding to the two times, does not appear (at least directly) in Stoic thought. We shall return to these points.
4. Mallarmé, "Mimique," *Oeuvres* (Paris: Gallimard, Pléiade, 1945), p. 310.
5. *Le "Livre" de Mallarmé* (Paris: Gallimard, 1978): see Jacques Scherer's study of the "book's" structure, and notably his comments on the four fragments (pp. 130–138). It does not seem, however, in spite of the places at which the two works meet and in spite of certain common problems, that Mallarmé knew Lewis Carroll: even Mallarmé's *Nursery Rhymes,* which relate the story of Humpty Dumpty, depend upon other sources.

1. See Sextus Empiricus, *Adversus Logicos,* 8:133. *"Blituri"* is an onomatopoeia which expresses a sound like that of the lyre; *"skindapsos"* designates the machine or instrument.

2. This distinction corresponds to the two forms of nonsense proposed by Russell. See Franz Crahay, *Le Formalisme logico-mathématique et le problème de non-sens* (Paris: Belles-Lettres, 1957). The Russellian distinction seems to be preferable to the very general distinction proposed by Husserl in his *Logical Investigations* between "nonsense" and "counter-sense," and which inspires Koyré in *Epiménide le menteur* (Paris: Hermann, n.d.), pp. 9ff.

3. See Lévi-Strauss' remarks with respect to the "zero phoneme" in "Introduction à l'oeuvre de Marcel Mauss" in M. Mauss, *Sociologie et anthropologie,* p. 50.

4. In pages which harmonize with the principal theses of Louis Althusser, J.-P. Osier proposes a distinction between those for whom meaning is to be recovered in a more or less lost origin (whether it be divine or human, ontological or anthropological), and those for whom the origin is a sort of nonsense, for whom meaning is always produced as an epistemological surface effect. Applying this criteria to Marx and Freud, Osier estimates that the problem of interpretation is not at all the problem of going from the "derived" to the "originary," but in comprehending the mechanisms of the production of sense in two series: sense is always an "effect." See preface to Feuerbach's *L'Essence du christianisme* (Paris: Maspero, 1968), especially pp. 15–19.

TWELFTH SERIES OF THE PARADOX

1. Boltzmann, *Lecture on Gas Theory,* trans. S. G. Brush (Berkeley: University of California Press, 1964).

2. See Cicero, *Academica,* section 29. See also Kierkegaard's remarks in the *Philosophical Fragments,* which arbitrarily lend support to Carneades.

THIRTEENTH SERIES OF THE SCHIZOPHRENIC AND THE LITTLE GIRL

1. "Perspendicace" is a schizophrenic portmanteau word designating spirits which are held above the subject's head (*perpendiculaire,* perpendicular),

and which are very *perspicacious* (perspicaces). Cited by George Dumas, *Le Surnaturel et les dieux d'après les maladies mentales* (Paris: P.U.F., 1946), p. 303.

2. Antonin Artaud, "L'Arve et l'Aume, tentative antigrammaticale contre Lewis Carroll," *L'Arbalète* (1947), no. 12:

> "Il était roparant, et les vliqueux tarands
> Allaient en gibroyant et en brimbulkdriquant
> Jusque là lò la rourghe est à rouarghe a rangmbde
> et rangmbde a rouarghambde:
> Tous les falomitards étaient les chats-huants
> Et les Ghoré Uk'hatis dans le Grabugeument."

3. Letter to Henri Parisot, *Lettres de Rodez* (Paris: G.L.M., 1946).

4. Louis Wolfson, "Le Schizo et les langues ou la phonétique chez le psychotique," *Les Temps Modernes* (July 1964), no. 218.

5. Freud, "The Unconscious," in *Metapsychology* (1915). Citing the cases of two patients, one of whom perceives his skin, and the other his sock, as systems of little holes which are in perpetual danger of becoming enlarged, Freud shows that this is a properly schizophrenic symptom which could not fit either a hysteric or an obsessed.

6. Antonin Artaud, in *La Tour de feu,* April 1961.

7. With respect to letters-organs, see Antonin Artaud, "Le Rite du peyotl," in *Les Tarahumaras* (Paris: Arbalète, 1963), pp. 26–32.

8. See in *84,* 1948: "No mouth No tongue No teeth No larynx No esophagus No stomach No intestine No anus I shall reconstruct the man that I am." (The body without organs is fashioned of bone and blood alone.)

9. See Wolfson, p. 53: in *"derev'ya,"* "the apostrophe between the palatalized *v* and the *y* represents what is called the soft sign, which in this word functions in such a manner that a complete consonant *y* is pronounced after the (palatalized) *v;* this phoneme would be palatalized in a certain manner without the soft sign, and as a result of the following soft vowel —here represented phonetically by *ya* and being written in Russian by a single character, having the form of a capital *R* back to front (pronounced *dire'vya:* the accent of intensity falls of course on the second syllable; the *i* open and brief; the *d, r,* and *v* palatalized or as if fused with a yod)." See also on p. 73 the schizophrenic's commentary on the Russian word *louD'Mi.*

10. In a very fine study, *Structuration dynamique dans la schizophrénie* (Bern: Verlag Hans Huber, 1956), Gisela Pankow has taken the examination of signs in schizophrenia very far. In connection with the cases related by Mrs. Pankow, special notice should be made of the analysis of fixed alimentary words which explode into phonetic bits: the word "CARAMELS," for

example, on p. 22. Also of particular interest is the dialectic of the container and contained, the discovery of polar opposition, and the theme of water and fire which is tied to it (pp. 57–60, 64, 67, 70); the curious invocation of fish as the sign of active revolt and of hot water as a sign of liberation (pp. 74–79); and the distinction of two bodies—the open and dissociated body of the man-flower, and the head without organs which serves as its complement (pp. 69–72).

It seems to us, however, that Mrs. Pankow's interpretation minimizes the role of the head without organs. It also seems to us that the regime of signs lived in schizophrenia is comprehended, at the level beneath sense, only through the distinction between bodily signs-passions and corporeal signs-actions.

11. It is in this sense that, in Carroll, invention is essentially vocabular, rather than syntactical or grammatical. As a consequence, portmanteau words can open up an infinity of possible interpretations by ramifying the series; nevertheless, syntactical rigor eliminates a certain number of these possibilities. The same holds true in Joyce, as Jean Paris has shown in *Tel Quel* (1967), no. 30, p. 64. The opposite is the case with Artaud, but only because there is no longer a problem of sense properly speaking.

FOURTEENTH SERIES OF DOUBLE CAUSALITY

1. Clement of Alexandria, *Stromateis*, 8:9: "The Stoics say that the body is a cause in the literal sense; but the incorporeal, in a metaphysical fashion, poses in the manner of a cause."

2. Paul Ricœur, *Idées directrices pour une phenoménologie* (Paris: Gallimard, 1950), pp. 431–432.

3. Husserl, *Ideas* (New York: Collier Books, 1972), p. 348: "The X in the different acts or act-noemata furnished with a differing 'determining content' is necessarily known as the same . . ."; p. 365: *"To every object 'that truly is'* there intrinsically corresponds (in the a priori of the unconditioned generality of the essence) the *idea of a possible consciousness* in which the object itself can be grasped in a *primordial* and also *perfectly adequate* way . . ."; p. 366: "This continuum is more closely defined as infinite in all directions, consisting in all its phases of appearances of the same determinable X. . . ."

4. Husserl, sections 100–101, and 102ff.

5. See J.-P. Sartre, *The Transcendence of the Ego* (New York: Noonday Press, 1957). The idea of an "impersonal or pre-personal" transcendental field, producing the I and the Ego, is of great importance. What hinders this

thesis from developing all its consequences in Sartre's work is that the impersonal transcendental field is still determined as the field of a consciousness, and as such it must then be unified by itself through a play of intentionalities or pure retentions.

6. In the *Cartesian Meditations,* monads, centers of vision or points of view, take a very important place on the side of the I as the synthetic unity of apperception. Among Husserl's commentators, it was to Gaston Berger's merit that he insisted on this sliding; he was therefore able to object to Sartre that the pre-personal consciousness perhaps had no need of the I, but that it was not able to do without points of view or centers of individuation. See G. Berger, *Le Cogito dans la philosophie de Husserl* (Paris: Aubier, 1941), p. 154; trans. K. McLaughlin, *The Cogito in Husserl's Philosophy* (Evanston: Northwestern University Press, 1972). See also *Recherches sur les conditions de la connaissance* (Paris: P.U.F., 1941), pp. 190–193. The objection holds, insofar as the transcendental field is still determined as that of a constituting "consciousness."

FIFTEENTH SERIES OF SINGULARITIES

1. George Gurvitch employed the expression "volitional intuition" to designate an intuition whose "given" does not limit the activity; he applied it to Duns Scotus' and Descartes' God, to Kant's will and to Fichte's pure act. See *Morale théorique et science des mœurs* (Paris: P.U.F., 1948), pp. 54ff. It seems to us that the expression is in the first instance suited to a Stoic will, to a willing *of* the event, in the two-fold sense of the genitive.

2. See, in the *Ideas,* the extraordinary section 114 (and with regard to the jurisdiction of reason, section 111).

3. Gilbert Simondon, *L'Individu et sa genèse physico-biologique* (Paris: P.U.F., 1964), pp. 260–264. This entire book, it seems to us, has special importance, since it presents the first thought-out theory of impersonal and pre-individual singularities. It proposes explicitly, beginning with these singularities, to work out the genesis of the living individual and the knowing subject. It is therefore a new conception of the transcendental. The five characteristics through which we have tried to define the transcendental field — *the potential energy of the field, the internal resonance of series, the topological surface of membranes, the organization of sense, and the status of the problematic* — are all analyzed by Simondon. Thus the material of this, and of the following paragraph, depends directly on this book, with which we part company only in drawing conclusions.

4. See Albert Lautman, *Le Problème du temps* (Paris: Hermann, 1946), pp. 41–

42: "The geometrical interpretation of the theory of differential equations clearly places in evidence two absolutely distinct realities: there is the field of directions and the topological accidents which may suddenly crop up in it, as for example the existence of the plane of *singular points to which no direction has been attached;* and there are the integral curves with the form they take on in the vicinity of the singularities of the field of directions. . . . *The existence and distribution* of singularities are notions relative to the field of vectors defined by the differential equation. The form of the integral curves is relative to the solution of this equation. The two problems are assuredly complementary, since the *nature* of the singularities of the field is defined by the form of the curves in their vicinity. But it is no less true that the field of vectors on one hand and the integral curves on the other are two essentially distinct mathematical realities."

5. The best didactic exposition of traditional metaphysics is presented by Kant in "The Transcendental Idea" of the *Critique of Pure Reason.* Kant shows how the idea of a sum total of all possibility excludes all but "originary" predicates and in this way constitutes the completely determined concept of an individual Being: "For only in this one case is a concept a thing—a concept which is in itself universal—completely determined in and through itself, and known as the representation of an individual." *Critique of Pure Reason,* trans. N. Kemp-Smith (London: Macmillan, 1929; New York: St. Martin's Press), p. 491. Thus, the universal is but the form of communication in thought between this supreme individuality and the finite individualities: the thought universal in any case refers to the individual.

6. *Nietzsche* (Kroner, vol. 15, section 83).

SIXTEENTH SERIES OF THE STATIC ONTOLOGICAL GENESIS

1. A constant theme of Leibniz's correspondence with Arnault: God did not create a sinning Adam exactly, but the world in which Adam has sinned.

2. See *Cartesian Meditations,* section 48. Husserl immediately orients this problem toward a transcendental theory of the Other. With regard to the role of the Other in a static genesis, see appendix 4.

3. *Ideas,* section 143.

4. We thus distinguish three selections in conformity with the Leibnizian theme: one which defines a world by means of convergence; another which defines complete individuals in this world; and finally, one which defines incomplete, or rather ambiguous, elements, common to several worlds and to the corresponding individuals.

With regard to this third selection, or with regard to the "vague" Adam constituted by a small number of predicates (being the first man, etc.) which must be completed differently in different worlds, see Leibniz, "Remarks upon M. Arnauld's letter," *The Leibniz-Arnault Correspondence,* ed. and trans. by H. T. Mason (New York: Barnes and Noble, 1967), pp. 39–40. It is true, in this text, that the vague Adam has no existence; he exists only in connection with our finite understanding, and his predicates are only generalities. In the famous text of the *Theodicy,* on the other hand (sections 414–441), the different Sextuses in the diverse worlds have a very special objective unity which rests on the ambiguous nature of the notion of singularity and on the category of the problem from the point of view of an infinite calculus. Very early on, Leibniz had elaborated a theory of "ambiguous signs" in connection with singular points, taking as an example the conic sections: see "De la méthode de l'Universalité," *Opuscules et fragments inédits de Leibniz,* ed. by L. Couturat (Paris: Presses Universitaires de France, 1903).

5. Borges, *Ficciones* (New York: Grove Press, 1962), p. 98.

6. One should, however, note Husserl's curious allusions to a *fiat* or an originary mobile point in the transcendental field determined as the Ego: see *Ideas,* section 122.

SEVENTEENTH SERIES OF THE STATIC LOGICAL GENESIS

1. In the preface to the *Phenomenology,* Hegel clearly demonstrated that philosophical (or scientific) truth is not a proposition taken as a response to a simple question of the sort "when was Caesar born?" With regard to the difference between the problem or theme and the proposition, see Leibniz, *New Essays,* Book 4, ch. 1.

2. *Ideas,* sections 114, 124.

3. In a very fine book entitled *Le Cartésianisme ou la véritable rénovation des sciences* (Paris: Gauthier-Villars, 1843), Bordas-Demoulin shows clearly the difference between these two expressions of circumference: $x^2 + y^2 - R^2 = O$, and $y\, dy + x\, dx = o$. In the first, I am doubtless able to attribute diverse values to each term, but I must attribute to them one value in particular for each case. In the second, dy and dx are independent of any particular value, and their relation refers only to the singularities which define the trigonometric tangent of the angle which the tangent to the curve makes with the axis of the abscisses ($dy/dx = -x/y$).

4. Apuleius, *On Interpretation* (for the terminological couple *abdicativus-dedicativus*).
5. Plotinus, 2:7.1.

EIGHTEENTH SERIES OF THE THREE IMAGES
OF PHILOSOPHERS

1. It is strange that Bachelard, seeking to characterize the Nietzschean imagination, presents it as an "ascensional psychism." *L'Air et les songes* (Paris: Corti, 1943), ch. 5. Not only does he reduce to the minimum the role of earth and surface in Nietzsche, but he interprets Nietzschean "verticality" as being, first of all, height and ascent. But it is indeed rather depth and descent. The bird of prey does not rise, save by accident; rather, it hovers above and drops down upon it. It is even necessary to say that, for Nietzsche, depth serves the purpose of denouncing the idea of height and the ideal of ascent; height is but a mystification, a surface effect, which does not fool the eye of the depths and is undone under its gaze. See Michel Foucault's comments to this effect in "Nietzsche, Freud, Marx," *Nietzsche* (Paris: Cahiers de Royaumont, Minuit, 1967), pp. 186–187.
2. *Nietzsche Contra Wagner,* epilogue, section 2.

NINETEENTH SERIES OF HUMOR

1. The Stoics had already elaborated a very elegant theory of the Void, as at once *extra-Being* and *insistence.* If incorporeal events are the logical attributes of beings and bodies, the void is like the substance of these attributes; it differs in nature from corporeal substance, to the point that it cannot even be said that the world is "in" the void. See Bréhier, *La Théorie des incorporels dans l'ancien stoïcisme,* ch. 3.
2. Diogenes Laertius, *Lives of Eminent Philosophers* (Cambridge: Harvard University Press, 1975), p. 297.
3. Kant, *Critique of Pure Reason,* "The Transcendental Ideal."
4. Kierkegaard, *The Concept of Irony* (Bloomington: Indiana University Press, by arrangement with Harper and Row, 1968), pp. 298–300.
5. Nietzsche, *The Birth of Tragedy,* section 5.

1. See Victor Goldschmidt, *Le Système stoïcien et l'idée de temps* (Paris: Vrin, 1953).
2. Cicero, *On Divination,* 56.
3. On the irreducibility of the incorporeal "expressible" to an even rational representation, see Bréhier's definitive pages, *La Théorie des incorporels dans l'ancien stoïcisme* (Paris: Vrin, 1928), pp. 16-19.
4. Victor Goldschmidt, p. 107.

TWENTY-FIRST SERIES OF THE EVENT

1. With respect to Joe Bousquet's work, which is in its entirety a meditation on the wound, the event, and language, see two essential articles in *Cahiers du Sud* (1950), no. 303: René Nelli, "Joe Bousquet et son double"; and Ferdinand Alquié, "Joe Bousquet et la morale du langage."
2. See Joe Bousquet, *Les Capitales* (Paris: Le Cercle du Livre, 1955), p. 103.
3. Maurice Blanchot, *L'Espace littéraire* (Paris: Gallimard, 1955), p. 160.
4. Essay by Claude Roy on Ginsbert, *Nouvel Observateur,* 1968.
5. See Maurice Blanchot, p. 155: "This attempt to elevate death to itself, to bring about the coincidence of the point at which it disappears in itself and that at which I disappear outside of myself, is not a simple internal affair, but implies an immense responsibility with regard to things and is possible only through their mediation. . . ."

TWENTY-SECOND SERIES — PORCELAIN AND VOLCANO

1. F. Scott Fitzgerald, *The Crack Up* (1936; New York: New Directions, 1945), p. 69.
2. Malcom Lowry, *Under the Volcano* (New York: Lippincott, 1965), p. 55.
3. M. Blanchot, *L'Espace littéraire;* pp. 104–105: "By way of suicide I desire to kill myself at a determinate moment; I connect death to now: yes . . . now, now. But nothing shows the illusion, and the madness of this *I want,* for death is never present. . . . Suicide, in this respect, is not a welcoming of death. It is rather a wishing to abolish it as the future, to deprive it of

that part of the future which is its essence. .... We cannot *project* killing ourselves; we prepare ourselves for it; we act with an eye toward the ultimate gesture, which nevertheless still belongs to the normal category of things to do. But this gesture is not within sight of death, it does not concern it, it does not hold it up in its presence. ..."

4. Fitzgerald, pp. 80–81: "I only wanted absolute quiet to think out why I had developed a sad attitude toward sadness, a melancholy attitude toward melancholy and a tragic attitude toward tragedy—*why I had become identified with the objects of my horror or compassion.* .... Identification such as this spells the death of accomplishment. It is something like this that keeps insane people from working. Lenin did not willingly endure the sufferings of his proletariat, nor Washington of his troops, nor Dickens of his London poor. And when Tolstoy tried some such merging of himself with the objects of his attention, it was a fake and a failure. ..." This passage is a remarkable illustration of psychoanalytic theories (especially those of Klein) of manic-depressive states. As we shall see in what follows, however, there are two points which create problems for these theories. In the first instance, mania is most often presented as a reaction to the depressive state, whereas it seems on the contrary to determine it, at least within the structure of alcoholism. On the other hand, identification is most often presented as a reaction to the loss of the object, whereas it too seems to determine this loss, to entail it and even to "will" it.

5. In Lowry as well, alcoholism is inseparable from the identifications it renders possible and from the bankruptcy of these identifications. Lowry's lost novel, *In Ballast to the White Sea,* had identification, and the possibility of health and salvation through identification, as its theme: see *Selected Letters of Malcom Lowry* (New York: Lippincott, 1965). In any case, one could find in the future perfect a precipitation analogous to the one we have seen in connection with the past perfect.

   In a very interesting article, Gunther Stein has analyzed the figures of the future perfect. The extended future, like the past perfect, ceases to belong to man. "To this time, not even the specific direction of time applies—its positive sense or direction. It is reduced to something that will no longer be of the future, to an Aion irrelevant to the self. Man may indeed still think and point out the existence of this Aion, but in a sterile manner, without comprehending it or realizing it. .... The '*I will be*' *(je serais)* is henceforth changed into a '*what will be, I will not be*' *(ce qui sera, je ne sera pas).* The positive expression of this form is the future perfect: *I will have been (j'aurai été)."* "Pathologie de la liberté, essai sur la nonidentification," *Recherches philosophiques* (1936–1937), vol. 6.

TWENTY-THIRD SERIES OF THE AION

1. Boethius, *Consolation of Philosophy,* 4.
2. See Diogenes Laertius, 7:147.
3. Marcus Aurelius, *The Meditations of Marcus Aurelius,* trans. George Long (New York: P. F. Collier, 1909) 12:14: "Above, below, all around are the movements of the elements. But the motion of virtue is in none of these; it is something more divine, and advancing by a way hardly observed it goes happily on its road" (Meditation 6:17; p. 237). We find here the double negation of the cycle and of a superior knowledge.

TWENTY-FOURTH SERIES OF THE COMMUNICATION
OF EVENTS

1. A general theme of Cicero's *De Fato.*
2. *De Fato,* 8.
3. See Georges Canguilhem, *Le Normal et le pathologique* (Paris: P.U.F., 1966), p. 90.
4. On the role of exclusion and expulsion, see the chapter on "contradiction" in Hegel's *Logic.*
5. Nietzsche, *Ecce Homo,* trans. Walter Kaufmann in *On the Genealogy of Morals and Ecce Homo* (New York: Vintage Books, 1969), p. 223.
6. On the conditions under which the disjunction becomes an affirmative synthesis through a changing of principle, see appendix 3.
7. See appendix 3. Klossowski speaks of "this thought so perfectly coherent that it excludes me at the very instant I think it," "Oubli et anamnèse dans l'expérience vécue de l'éternel retour du même," *Nietzsche* (Paris: Cahiers de Royaumont, Minuit, 1967), p. 234. See also the postface to *Lois de l'hospitalité.* In these texts, Klossowski develops a theory of the sign, sense, and nonsense, and a profoundly original interpretation of the Nietzschean eternal return, conceived of as an ex-centric power of affirming divergence and disjunction, and which allows neither the identity of the self, nor of the world, nor of God to subsist.

TWENTY-FIFTH SERIES OF UNIVOCITY

1. Klossowski, "La Période turinoise de Nietzsche," *L'Ephémère,* no. 5.
2. Borges, *Ficciones* (New York: Grove Press, 1962), pp. 89–101.

3. On the importance of "empty time" in the elaboration of the event, see B. Groethuysen, "De quelques aspects du temps," *Recherches philosophiques* (1935–1936), vol. 5: "Every event is, so to speak, in time where nothing is happening"; and there is a permanence of empty time spanning everything that happens. The profound interest of Joe Bousquet's book, *Les Capitales,* is that it raised the problem of language in relation to the univocity of Being, beginning with a meditation on Duns Scotus.

TWENTY-SIXTH SERIES OF LANGUAGE

1. With respect to this process of return or reaction and the internal temporality that it implies, see the work of Gustave Guillaume and the analysis of this work carried out by E. Ortigues in *Le Discours et le symbole* (Paris: Aubier, 1962). Guillaume derives from it an original conception of the infinitive in "Epoques et niveaux temporels dans le système de la conjugaison française" (*Cahiers de linguistique structurale,* no. 4, Université de Laval).

TWENTY-SEVENTH SERIES OF ORALITY

1. See Melanie Klein, *The Psycho-Analysis of Children,* trans. Alix Strachey (London: Hogarth Press, 1932).
2. See Melanie Klein's remarks along these lines and her references to W. R. D. Fairbairn's thesis, according to which "in the beginning, only the bad object is internalized . . ." (a thesis rejected by Klein): *Developments in Psycho-Analysis* (London: Hogarth Press, 1970), p. 295.
3. Melanie Klein does not establish a difference of natures between anal and urethral sadism and abides by her principle in accordance with which "the unconscious does not distinguish between the body's diverse substances." More generally, it seems to us that the psychoanalytic theory of schizophrenia has a tendency to neglect the importance and dynamism of the theme of the *body without organs.* We said the same thing earlier in the case of Mrs. Pankow. It is, however, much more evident in Melanie Klein. See *Developments in Psycho-Analysis,* p. 311, in which a dream involving blindness and a frock which is buttoned up to the patient's throat is interpreted as a simple sign of closing off, without the theme of the body without organs being disengaged from it. In fact, body without organs and liquid specificity are bound together, in the sense that the liquid

principle ensures the soldering of the pieces into one block, even if this were a mass of water.

4. The division wounded-unharmed is not to be confused with the division partial-complete, but is itself applied to the complete object of the depressive position: see Klein, *Developments in Psycho-Analysis,* p. 201. It should not be surprising that the superego is "good" and nevertheless cruel, vulnerable, etc. Freud has already spoken of a good and consoling superego in connection with humor, adding that there remained much for us to learn with regard to the essence of the superego.

5. Robert Pujol remarks, in Lacan's terminology: "The lost object can only be signified and not recovered. . . ." "Approche théorique du fantasme," *La Psychanalyse* (1964), no. 8, p. 15.

6. See Bergson, *L'Energie spirituelle* (Paris: P.U.F., 1976), pp. 101–102.

TWENTY-EIGHTH SERIES OF SEXUALITY

1. Gilbert Simondon, *L'Individu et sa genèse physico-biologique,* p. 263.

2. This forms a constant theme in Melanie Klein's work: *at first,* the superego reserves its repression not for the libidinal drives but only for the destructive drives which accompany them. See, for example, *The Psycho-analysis of Children,* p. 134. It is for this reason that anxiety and guilt do not find their origin in the libidinal drives, even incestuous ones, but in destructive drives and their repression: "not only would it be the incestuous trends which give rise in the first instance to a sene of guilt, but horror of incest itself would ultimately be derived from the destructive impulses which are bound up permanently with the child's earliest incestuous desires."

3. The first point—that the sexual drives are freed from the impulses of conservation or feeding—is clearly indicated by J. Laplanche and J. B. Pontalis: *Vocabulaire de la psychanalyse* (Paris: P.U.F., 1967), p. 43; and "Fantasme originaire, fantasmes des origines, origine du fantasme," *Les Temps Modernes* (1964), no. 215, pp. 1866–1867. But it does not suffice to define this liberation by saying that the drives of conservation have an external object, and that this object is abandoned by the sexual impulses for something "pronominal." In fact, the liberated sexual drives do still have an object projected at the surface: thus, for example, a sucked-on finger as a projection of the breast (at the limit, a projection of one erogenous zone over another). All of this is recognized perfectly by Laplanche and Pontalis. But, above all, the sexual drives, insofar as they have been connected in depth with the alimentary drives, already have

particular objects distinct from the objects of these drives—namely, partial internal objects. What must be separated are two states of the sexual drives, two sorts of objects of these drives, and two mechanisms of projection. And what must be made the subject of a critique are notions like that of the hallucinatory object, which is indistinctly applied to the internal object, the lost object, and the object of the surface.

The importance of the second point follows: the sexual drives are disengaged from the destructive drives. Melanie Klein insists on this constantly. The entire Kleinean school makes a justified attempt to exonerate sexuality and to free it from the destructive drives to which it is bound only in depth. It is in this sense that the notion of the sexual crime is discussed by Paula Heimann (*Developments in Psycho-Analysis,* pp. 328–329). It is indeed true that sexuality is perverse, but perversion is defined first of all by the role of the partial erogenous zones of the surface. The "sex crime" belongs to another domain, in which sexuality acts only in a depth mixture with the destructive drives (subversion rather than perversion). In any case, we should not confuse the two very different types of regression under the very general theme of a return to the "pregenital" (the regression to an oral stage of depths or the regression to the oral zone of the surface, for example).

4. On the "bad" and the "good" penis, see Melanie Klein, *The Psycho-Analysis of Children,* pp. 233 and 265. Klein notes forcefully that the Oedipus complex implies the previous position of a "good penis," as well as the liberation of libidinal drives with respect to the destructive drives: "For only if the boy has a strong enough belief in the 'goodness' of male genitals—his father's as well as his own—can he allow himself to experience his genital desires towards his mother . . . , he can face his Oedipus hatred and rivalry." *Contributions to Psycho-Analysis 1921–1945* (London: Hogarth Press, 1948), pp. 381–382. This does not mean, as we shall see, that the sexual position and the oedipal situation do not have their new anxieties and dangers—for example, a specific fear of castration. And if it is true, in the early stages of Oedipus, that the superego directs its severity first of all against the destructive drives, "it is only in the later stages of the Oedipus conflict that the defense against the libidinal impulses makes its appearance . . ." (*The Psycho-Analysis of Children,* p. 134, n.).

1. See Freud, *Beyond the Pleasure Principle,* ch. 4. This entire chapter is essential to the bio-psychic theory of surfaces.
2. All of the great interpretations of Oedipus necessarily integrate elements borrowed from the preceding positions, the schizoid and the depressive: thus, Hölderlin's insistence on withdrawal and turning away refers to a preoedipal position.
3. The theory of desexualized energy is outlined by Freud in *The Ego and the Id,* ch. 4. We diverge from the Freudian account on two points. First, Freud often expresses himself as if the narcissistic libido could as such imply a desexualization of energy. This cannot be maintained to the extent that the phallic ego of secondary narcissism still makes use of object relations with parental images (restoration, summoning). In this case, desexualization comes about only with the castration complex defined in its specificity. Second, Freud calls this desexualized energy "neutral"; he means that this energy is able to be displaced and is capable of passing from Eros to Thanatos. But if it is the case that it is not content with joining Thanatos or the death instinct, if it is the case that it constitutes it, at least in the speculative form that the instinct assumes at the surface, then "neutral" must have a completely different meaning, as we shall see in the following paragraphs.

THIRTIETH SERIES OF THE PHANTASM

1. See Freud, *The Wolf Man,* Section 5.
2. See J. Laplanche and J. B. Pontalis, "Fantasme originaire, fantasme des origines, origine du fantasme," *Les Temps Modernes* (1964), no. 215, pp. 1861–1868: "A father seduces a daughter — such would be, for example, the concise formula of the fantasm of seduction. The mark of the primary process is not here the absence of organization, as is occasionally said, but rather the particular character of the structure: it is a scenario with multiple entrances, where nothing says that the subject will find her position straight away in the term "daughter" *(fille);* we may also see it revolve around the term "father" or even the term "seduces." This is an essential point of the critique which Laplanche and Pontalis address to the thesis of Susan Isaacs, "The Nature and Function of Phantasy," in *Developments in Psycho-Analysis.* Isaacs, modeling the phantasm on the drive,

gives to the subject a determined active place, even if the active reverts back to the passive, and conversely. To this Laplanche and Pontalis object: "Does it suffice to recognize in the fantasm of incorporation the equivalence between eating and being eaten? Insofar as the idea of the subject's position is maintained, even if it is passive, have we reached the most fundamental structure of the fantasm?"

3. On the link between the reversal of contraries and the turning back on oneself, as well as on the value of the pronominal in this respect, see Freud, "The Instincts and Their Vicissitudes," in *Metapsychology*.

   Freud's text on *contradictory meanings in primitive words* has been criticized by Emile Benveniste, "Remarques sur la fonction du langage dans la decouverte freudienne," *Problèmes de linguistique générale*. Benveniste shows that although a language might not carry a certain category, it cannot grant it a contradictory expression. Reading Benveniste, however, one has the impression that language *(langue)* is necessarily confused with pure processes of rationalization. But does not language *(langage)* nevertheless imply paradoxical procedures with respect to its manifest organization, even though these procedures are not at all reducible to the identification of contraries?

4. Luce Irigaray, "Du Fantasme et du verbe," *L'Arc* (1968), no. 34. Such an attempt must of course rely on a linguistic genesis of grammatical relations in the verb (voice, mood, tense, person). Examples of such geneses are to be found in the work of Gustave Guillaume, *Epoques et niveaux temporels dans le système de la conjugaison française,* and in the work of Damourette and Pichon, *Essai de grammaire française,* vol. 5. Pichon himself underlines the importance of such studies for pathology.

5. Susan Isaacs, "The Nature and Function of Phantasy," in *Developments in Psycho-Analysis.*

THIRTY-FIRST SERIES OF THOUGHT

1. See Laplanche and Pontalis, "Fantasme originaire, fantasme des origines, origine du fantasme," *Les Temps Modernes* (1964), no. 215, p. 1853; *Vocabulaire de la psychanalyse,* pp. 158–159.

2. Pierre Klossowski, avertissement and postface to *Lois de l'hospitalité.*

3. It was Edmond Perrier who, from an evolutionist perspective, clearly articulated a theory of the "conflict between the mouth and the brain." He demonstrated how the development of the nervous system in vertebrates brings the cerebral extremity to take on the position occupied by the mouth in the annelids. He elaborated the concept of *attitude* in order

to account for these orientations and these changes in position and dimension. He employed a method inherited from Geoffroy Saint-Hilaire —the method of ideal foldings—combining in a complex manner space and time. See "L'Origine des embranchements du règne animal," *Scientia,* May 1918.

The biological theory of the brain has always borne in mind its essentially superficial character (its ectodermic origin, nature, and function of the surface). Freud reasserts this and draws a great deal from it in *Beyond the Pleasure Principle,* ch. 4. Modern studies insist on the relation between areas of cortical projection and topological space. "The projection in fact converts a Euclidean space into a topological space, so that the cortex cannot be adequately represented in a Euclidean manner. In a strict sense, it should not be necessary to speak of projection with respect to the cortex, although there may be a geometrical sense of the term which is applicable to minor regions. It would rather be necessary to say: a conversion of Euclidean space into topological space . . ." a mediate system of relations restoring the Euclidean structures. Simondon, *L'Individu et sa genèse physico-biologique,* p. 262. It is in this sense that we speak of the conversion of the physical surface into a metaphysical surface, or of an induction of the latter by the former. We can thus identify the cerebral and metaphysical surfaces: it is less a question of bringing about the materialization of the metaphysical surface than of following out the projection, conversion, and induction of the brain itself.

THIRTY-SECOND SERIES ON THE DIFFERENT
KINDS OF SERIES

1. The object may apparently be the same: the breast for example. It may also seem to be the same with respect to different zones, as is the case, for example, of the finger. In any case, the breast as an internal partial object (sucking, *succion*) will not be confused with the breast as a surface image (suckling, *suçotement*); nor will we confuse the finger as an image projected over the oral zone or over the anal zone, etc.

2. We must notice Freud's use of the word "series," either with respect to his presentation of the complete Oedipus complex, in its four elements (*The Ego and the Id,* ch. 3), or with respect to his theory of object choice (*Three Essays on the Theory of Sexuality,* Essay 3).

   With respect to the conception of two events or two series, refer to the commentaries of Laplanche and Pontalis, "Fantasme originaire, fantasme des origines, origine du fantasme," *Les Temps Modernes* (1964), no.

215, pp. 1839–1842, 1848–1849. It is essential that the first or pregenital stage (the observation of coitus at the age of one and a half in the case of the Wolf Man, for example) should not be understood as such. As Laplanche and Pontalis say, the first stage and corresponding pregenital images are fragmented "in the series of moments of the transition to auto-eroticism."

3. These series may be quite variable but they are always discontinuous. Above all, the pregenital series puts into play not only partial erogenous zones and their images; it also sets in motion pre-Oedipal parental images fabricated in an entirely different manner than they will be later on, and fragmented according to the zones. This series therefore necessarily implicates adults in relation to the child, without the child's being able to "comprehend" what is in question *(parental series)*. In the second series, on the other hand, it is the child or young man who conducts himself as an adult *(filial series)*. For example, in Lacan's analysis of the Rat Man there is the series of the father who affected the child very early on and belongs to the familial legend (debt-friend-rich woman-poor woman); and there is also another series with the same terms, disguised and shifted, that the subject later on recovers for his own account (the debt playing the role of the object $= x$, bringing about the resonance of the two series). See Jacques Lacan, *Le Mythe individuel du névrosé* (Paris: C.D.U., 1953). Or another example: in Proust's *Remembrance,* the hero undergoes a series of amorous experiences of the pregenital sort with his mother; he then undergoes another series with Albertine. But the pregenital series has already put into play, in a mysterious noncomprehensive or pre-comprehensive mode, the adult model of Swann's love for Odette (the common theme of *The Captive* indicating the object $= x$).

4. At the chain's origin, on the contrary, when the disjunctions are related only to the good object of the depressive position, the disjunctive synthesis has but a limitative and negative use.

5. See Robert Pujol, "Approche théorique du fantasme," *La Psychanalyse,* no. 8, p. 20: the basic unit, the phoneme as it functions in relation to another phoneme, "escapes the adult inasmuch as his understanding is henceforth attuned to the sense which comes from sonority and no longer to the sonority itself. We suggest that the subject *infans* does not hear this with the same ear; he is sensitive only to the phonemic opposition of the signifying chain."

6. Serge Leclaire, *Psychanalyser* (Paris: Seuil, 1968), especially pp. 90–95.

7. With respect to the word "Poord'jeli," its first aspect or the first series it subsumes, see S. Leclaire, pp. 112–115. With respect to the second aspect or second series, see pp. 151–153. Leclaire correctly insists on the neces-

sity of considering initially the first aspect in its own right, without yet discussing sense, which emerges only with the second. In this respect, he reminds us of an essential Lacanian rule, that of not being in a hurry to eliminate nonsense from a mixture of series which would want to be prematurely significant. Moreover, the distinctions which are to be made belong to several domains—not only between the surface series of sexuality but between a series of the surface and a sequence of the depths. For example, phonemes tied to the erogenous zones and complex words tied to their coordination could be confused respectively with the literal values of the fragmented word and with the tonic values of the schizo-phrenic "block" word (letters-organs and inarticulate word). In this case, however, there is only a remote correspondence between a surface orga-nization and the order of depth which it summons, or between the nonsense of the surface and the infra-sense. Leclaire himself, in another text, gives an example of this genre: take, for instance, an oral noise of the depth like *"krog"*; it is very different from the verbal representation *"croque"* (crunch or crackle). This representation necessarily forms part of a surface series linked to the oral zone and capable of being associated with other series, whereas the oral sound is inserted into a schizoid sequence of the sort *"croque, trotte, crotte . . ."* See "Note sur l'objet de la psychanalyse," *Cahiers pour l'Analyse,* no. 2, p. 165.

8. The voice from above, on the contrary, has at its disposal designations, manifestations, and significations, without formative elements, distributed and lost in simple intonation.

THIRTY-THIRD SERIES OF ALICE'S ADVENTURES

1. In both cases the cat is present, since he appears initially in the Duchess' kitchen and then counsels Alice to go to see the hare "or" the hatter. The Cheshire Cat's position in the tree or in the sky, all of his traits, including the terrifying ones, identify him with the superego as the "good" object of the heights (idol): "(The Cat) looked good-natured, (Alice) thought: still it had *very* long claws and a great many teeth, so she felt that it ought to be treated with respect." The theme of the entity of the heights, which slips away or withdraws, but which also fights and captures internal objects, is a constant in Carroll's work—it will be found in all of its curelty in the poems and narratives in which angling occurs (see, for example, the poem "The Two Brothers," in which the younger brother serves as bait). In *Sylvie and Bruno,* the good father, withdrawn to the

kingdom of fairies and hidden behind the voice of a dog, is essential; this masterpiece, which also puts into play the theme of the two surfaces—the common surface and the magic or fairy surface—would require a lengthy commentary. Finally, in relation to the whole of Carroll's work, the tragic poem "The Three Voices" is of particular importance. The first "voice" is that of a severe and boisterous woman who creates a terror-filled scene of nourishment; the second voice is terrifying as well, but has all of the characteristics of the good Voice from above which causes the hero to stammer and stutter; the third is an Oedipal voice of guilt, which sings the terror of the result in spite of the purity of the intentions ("And when at *Eve* the unpitying sun/ Smiled grimly on the solemn fun,/ 'Alack,' he sighed, 'what *have* I done?' ").

2. We would like to cite an example which appears to us important in dealing with such an obscure problem. Ch. Laségue was a psychiatrist who, in 1877, "isolated" exhibitionism (and created the word); in this manner, he did the work of a clinician and a symptomologist: see *Études médicales,* 1:692–700. Now, when he presented his discovery in a brief article, he did not begin by citing cases of manifest exhibitionism. He began rather with the case of a man who daily places himself in the path of a woman and follows her everywhere without a word, without a gesture ("his role restrained to acting as a shadow"). Laségue thus starts out by implicitly giving the reader to understand that this man is altogether identified with a penis. It is only then that he cites manifest cases. Laségue's method is the method of an artist: he begins with a novel. It is, without doubt, a story initially created by the subject; but it took a clinician to recognize it. It is a neurotic novel, since the subject is satisfied with embodying a partial object that he actualizes in his whole person. What then is the difference between such a lived, neurotic, and "familial" novel and a novel as a work of art? The symptom is always taken up in a novel; but the novel sometimes determines the *actualization* of the symptom, sometimes, on the contrary, disengages the *event* which it counter-actualizes in fictive characters. (What is important is not the fictive nature of the characters, but what explains the fiction, namely, the nature of the pure event and the mechanism of counter-actualization.) For example, Sade or Masoch make a novel-work of art out of what sadists or masochists transform into a neurotic and "familial" novel—even if they write it.

1. Depth is not by itself constituted in series, but it is under the conditions of the phantasm that it accedes to the serial form. On the structure of the phantasm, see appendix 1.

2. It is indeed in terms of "knowledge" *(savoir)* that Lacan and certain of his disciples pose the problem of perversion: see the collection *Le Désir et la perversion* (Paris: Seuil, 1967). See also appendix 4.

3. Freud demonstrated the existence of crimes inspired by the superego. But it is not, it seems to us, inevitably or necessarily through the intermediary of a sentiment of guilt preexisting the crime.

4. In fact, the abuser demands the expulsion of the victim, forbids any response—but also withdraws by feigning the maximum disgust. All of this bears witness to the appurtenance of abuse to the manic depressive position (frustration), whereas obscenity refers to the excremental schizoid position (hallucinated action-passion). The intimate union of insult and obscenity is therefore not explained, as Ferenczi believed, solely by means of the repression of objects of infantile pleasure which would return "in the form of swearing and maledictions"; it requires rather the direct fusion of the two fundamental positions.

5. We cannot here follow Lacan's thesis, at least insofar as we understand it as related by Laplanche and Leclaire in "L'Inconscient," *Les Temps Modernes* (July 1961), pp. 111ff. According to this thesis, the primary order of language would be defined through a perpetual slippage of the signifier over the signified, and each word would have a single sense and would refer to other words through a series of equivalents that this single sense opens to it. On the contrary, as soon as a word possesses several senses, organized according to the law of metaphor, it is in a certain manner stabilized. At the same time, language abandons the primary process and founds the secondary process. Univocity, therefore, defines the primary, and equivocity the possibility of the secondary (p. 112). But univocity is here considered as the univocity of the *word,* and not as the univocity of Being which is said of all things in one and the same sense—nor of the language which says it. It is thought that what is univocal is the word, at the risk of concluding that such a word does not exist, having no stability and being a "fiction." It seems to us, on the contrary, that equivocity characterizes accurately the voice in the primary process; and if there is an essential relation between sexuality and equivocity, it takes the form of a limit of the equivocal and of a totalization which is going to render the

univocal possible—as the veritable characteristic of the unconscious secondary organization.

APPENDIXES

I. SIMULACRUM AND ANCIENT PHILOSOPHY

1. PLATO AND THE SIMULACRUM

1. *Sophist*, 236b, 264c.
2. Jacques Derrida has recoverd this Platonic figure in his analysis of the relation between writing and logos: the father of the logos, logos itself, and writing. Writing is a simulacrum, a false suitor, insofar as it claims to take hold of the logos by violence and by ruse, or even to supplant it without passing through the father. See "La Pharmacie de Platon," *Tel Quel*, no. 32, pp. 12ff., and no. 33, pp. 38ff; trans. B. Johnson in *Dissemination* (Chicago: University of Chicago Press, 1981). The same figure is also found in the *Statesman*: the Good, as father of the law, the law itself, and various constitutions. Good constitutions are copies; but they become simulacra as soon as they violate or usurp the law by evading the Good.
3. The Other, in fact, is not only a defect which affects images; it itself appears as a possible model, which is opposed to the good model of the Same: see *Theaetetus*, 176e; *Timaeus*, 28b.
4. See *Republic*, 10:602a. And *Sophist*, 268a.
5. X. Audouard has shown that simulacra "are constructions which include the angle of the observer, so that illusion is produced at the very point at which the observer is found. . . . It is not really on the status of nonbeing that the accent is placed, but rather on this slight gap, this slight distortion of the real image, which happens at the point of view occupied by the observer, and makes possible the constitution of the simulacrum—the work of the sophist." "Le Simulacre," *Cahiers pour l'Analyse*, no. 3.
6. With respect to Hegel, Althusser writes: "A circle of circles, consciousness has but one center which alone determines it: there would have to be circles with other centers, decentered circles, in order that the center of consciousness be affected by their efficacy—briefly, that its essence be overdetermined by them . . ." *Pour Marx* (Paris: Maspero, 1970), p. 101.
7. On the modern work of art, and on Joyce in particular, see Umberto Eco, *L'Oeuvre ouverte* (Paris: Seuil, 1965). On the constitution of divergent series

and the manner in which they resonate and communicate at the heart of a chaos, see the profound comments made by W. Gombrowicz in the preface to his novel *Cosmos.*

8. See Blanchot, "Le Rire des dieux," *La Nouvelle Revue Française,* July 1965: "A universe in which the image ceases to be secondary in relation to the model, in which imposture lays claim to truth, and in which, finally, there is no longer any original, but only an eternal scintillation where the absence of origin, in the splendor of diversion and reversion, is dispersed" (p. 103).

9. *Beyond Good and Evil,* section 289. English translation by R. J. Hollingdale.

10. On the reticence of the Greeks, and notably of Plato, with respect to the eternal return, see Charles Mugler, *Deux thèmes de la cosmologie grecque* (Paris: Klincksieck, 1953).

11. Pierre Klossowski, *Un si funeste désir* (Paris: Gallimard, 1963), p. 226. See also pp. 216–218, where Klossowski comments on section 361 of the *Gay Science:* "The pleasure of simulation, exploding as power, driving back the so-called character, submerging it at times to the point of extinguishing it."

2. LUCRETIUS AND THE SIMULACRUM

1. In the entire critical part of Book 1, Lucretius does not cease to demand a reason for the diverse. The different aspects of diversity are described in Book 2, 342–376, 581–588, 661–681, and 1052–1066. *Translators' note:* passages of the *De Rerum Natura* cited are from Rouse and Smits' translation (Cambridge: Loeb Classical Library, Harvard University Press, 1975).

2. See Book 1, the critique of Heraclitus, Empedocles, and Anaxagoras; on the nothingness which eats into these pre-Epicurean conceptions, see 1:657–669, and 753–762.

3. 1:633–634.

4. 1:599–634, 749–752.

5. See Epicurus, *Letter to Herodotus,* 61–62 (on the minimum of continuous time).

6. 2:243–250.

7. This is one of the principal themes of Cicero's *De Fato.*

8. 2:483–499.

9. 5:449–454.

10. 2:541–568.

11. 5:128–131.

12. 2:1068: *"cum locus est praesto."*

13. 1:168. And 2:708: *"seminibus certis certa genetrice."*

14. See Epicurus, *Letter to Herodotus,* 79.

15. The introduction to Book 2 is built upon the following opposition: to avoid pain as much as possible, a few things will suffice; but to overcome the soul's agitation requires a more profound art.

16. Lucretius insists sometimes on one, sometimes on the other of these aspects: 1:110–119; 3:41–73; 3:978–1023; 6:12–16. On the infinite capacity of pleasures, see Epicurus, *Meditations,* 20.

17. 3:1023.

18. Epicurus, *Meditations,* 7, 10, 34, 35.

19. 1:110–111.

20. 4:245–260.

21. 4:265–270.

22. 4:794–798.

23. Visual simulacra have two advantages over deep emanations: precisely because they detach themselves from the surface, they do not have to modify their order or their shape, and consequently are representative; on the other hand, they move with much greater velocity, since they encounter fewer obstacles. See 4:67–71, 199–209.

24. The analogy of this gradation is clearly seen when Epicurus says of simulacra, and of atoms, that they are "as swift as thought" (*Letter to Herodotus,* 48); it is also apparent when Lucretius applies to the swiftness of simulacra the same expressions as those he uses when speaking of the swiftness of atoms in the void (4:206–208 and 2:162–164).

25. 4:130–142.

26. 5:1169ff. In fact, Lucretius appeals to two coexisting elements—the mobility of the phantasm and the permanence of the celestial order.

27. 4:772ff, 962ff.

28. 4:1094–1096.

29. See Sextus Empiricus, *Adversus Mathematicos,* 10:219. The theory of the event, such as it is given to us in Epicurus's text (*Letter to Herodotus,* 68–73), and in Lucretius (1:440–482), is at once rich and obscure. It is also too brief. Insofar as the void alone is an incorporeal entity, the event does not properly speaking have the status of an incorporeal entity. Certainly, it does have an essential relation to the simulacrum and, in the last analysis, with the movement of the atom (471–477). The Stoics grant the event a well determined status because they cleave causality, so that effects differ in nature from causes; this cannot be the case for the Epicureans, who divide the causal relation in accordance with series which conserve a homogeneity of cause and effect.

30. Obviously, we should not consider the tragic description of the plague as

the end of the poem. It coincides too neatly with the legend of madness and suicide, which Christians propagated in order to demonstrate the unhappy personal end of an Epicurean. It is possible of course that Lucretius, at the end of his life, had become mad. But it is equally vain to invoke the so-called facts of life in order to draw a conclusion about the poem, and to treat the poem as an ensemble of symptoms from which one could draw conclusions about the "personal" case of the author (brute psychoanalysis). It is certainly not in this manner that the problem of the relation of psychoanalysis and art is to be posed—see Thirty-Third Series of Alice's Adventures.

II. PHANTASM AND MODERN LITERATURE

3. KLOSSOWSKI OR BODIES-LANGUAGE

1. *Un si funeste désir* (Paris: Gallimard, 1963), pp. 126–127.
2. In *Le Bain de Diane* (Paris: Pauvert, 1956), the disjunctive syllogism becomes a general method for the interpretation of myth and for the reconstitution of the corporeal in myth.
3. *La Révocation de l'Édit de Nantes* (Paris: Minuit, 1954), p. 59. This book forms, with *Roberte ce soir* (Paris: Minuit, 1953) and *Le Souffleur* (Paris: Pauvert, 1960), a trilogy which was reissued under the title *Les Lois de l'hospitalité* (Paris: Gallimard, 1965).
4. *La Révocation*, p. 48.
5. *La Révocation*, p. 58.
6. *Roberte*, p. 31 (this chapter is entitled "La Denonciation").
7. Michel Foucault, "La Prose d'Actéon," *Nouvelle Revue Française,* March 1964.
8. *La Révocation*, pp. 11–12.
9. *La Révocation*, pp. 28–29.
10. Introduction to the (French) translation of the *Aeneid*.
11. *Un si funeste désir*, p. 126.
12. *La Révocation*, p. 15.
13. *Le Souffleur*, pp. 51ff, 71ff.
14. *Le Souffleur*, pp. 211, 212, 218.
15. *Le Souffleur*, p. 214.
16. See postface to *Lois de l'hospitalité:* "A name, Roberte, has been a specific enough designation of the first intensity"; in the same manner, the couple, as well as the epidermis and the glove, do not designate things—rather, they stand for intensities (pp. 334–336).

17. *Un si funeste désir,* pp. 126–127.
18. W. Gombrowicz, *Pornografia,* trans. Alastair Hamilton (New York: Grove Press, 1968), pp. 121, 131.
19. *Roberte,* pp. 73, 85.
20. *Roberte,* p. 133.
21. *Roberte,* p. 85. With respect to this movement of the pure and the impure, see *Un si funeste désir,* pp. 123–125.
22. *Le Baphomet* (Paris: Mercure de France, 1965).
23. *Roberte,* pp. 43–44.
24. *Roberte,* p. 73.
25. *Roberte,* p. 81.
26. *Le Baphomet,* p. 54.
27. *Un si funeste désir,* pp. 220–221: "When Nietzsche announces the death of God, this amounts to saying that Nietzsche must necessarily lose his identity. . . . The absolute guarantor of the identity of the responsible self disappears on the horizon of Nietzsche's consciousness, which in turn merges with this disappearance."
28. *Les Lois de l'hospitalité,* postface, p. 337.
29. Kant, "The Ideal of Pure Reason" in *Critique of Pure Reason,* trans. Kemp-Smith (London: Macmillan, 1929), p. 491.
30. *Roberte,* p. 53.
31. "Oubli et anamnèse dans l'expérience vécue de l'éternel retour de Même," in *Nietzsche,* Cahiers de Royaumont (Paris: Minuit, 1967).
32. "Oubli et anamnèse," p. 233.
33. *Le Baphomet,* p. 137. On purely expressive or "emotional" language, in relation to the notion of *Stimmung* and in opposition to the function of designation, see "La Periode turinoise de Nietzsche," *L'Ephémère* (1968), no. 5, pp. 62–64.
34. *Roberte,* p. 84.
35. "Oubli et anamnèse," p. 229. See also "La Periode turinoise de Nietzsche," pp. 66–67, 83.
36. *Les Lois de l'hospitalité,* postface. See also "Oubli et anamnèse," p. 233. "Is this to say that the thinking subject will lose its identity with a coherent thought which would exclude it from itself?"
37. *Les Lois de l'hospitalité,* postface, p. 346.

4. MICHEL TOURNIER AND THE WORLD WITHOUT OTHERS

1. *Vendredi ou les limbes du Pacifique* (Paris: Gallimard, 1967). English translation, *Friday,* trans. Norman Denny (New York: Pantheon Books, 1985, by

arrangement with Doubleday), pp. 186–187. *Translators' note:* references
are to the English translation.

2. P. 190.

3. P. 198.

4. On Defoe's Robinson, see Pierre Macherey's remarks, which show how
the theme of origin is tied to an economic reproduction of the world and
to the elimination of the fantastic in the interest of an alleged "reality" of
this world. *Pour une théorie de la production littéraire* (Paris: Maspero, 1970),
pp. 266–275.

5. P. 212.

6. P. 38.

7. P. 55.

8. P. 32.

9. P. 220.

10. P. 55.

11. P. 220.

12. Tournier's conception clearly contains Leibnizian echoes (the monad as
expression of the world); it also contains Sartrean echoes. Sartre's theory
in *Being and Nothingness* is the first great theory of the Other, because it
transcends the alternative: is the Other an object (even if it is a particular
object inside the perceptual field), or rather a subject (even if it is another
subject for another perceptual field)? Sartre is here the precursor of
structuralism, for he is the first to have considered the Other as a real
structure or a specificity irreducible to the object and the subject. But,
since he defined this structure by means of the "look," he fell back into
the categories of object and subject, making of the Other the one who
constitutes me as an object when he looks at me, even if this means that
the Other would himself become an object when I, in turn, look at him.
It seems that the structure Other precedes the look; the latter, rather,
marks the moment at which *someone* happens to fill the structure. The
look brings about only the effectuation or the actualization of a structure
which must nonetheless be independently defined.

13. Pp. 94–96.

14. P. 204.

15. P. 85.

16. P. 205.

17. P. 203.

18. Pp. 115–116.

19. Pp. 40–41.

20. P. 105.

21. See Henri Michaux's description of a table made by a schizophrenic in *Les*

Grandes épreuves de l'esprit (Paris: Gallimard, 1966), pp. 156ff. Robinson's construction of a boat which cannot be transported is not without analogy.

22. P. 67.
23. P. 172.
24. P. 180.
25. Pp. 211–212.
26. P. 113.
27. See the collection *Le Désir et la perversion* (Paris: Seuil, 1967). Guy Rosolato's article, "Étude des perversions sexuelles à partir du fétichisme," contains some very interesting, though too brief, remarks on "sexual difference" and "the double" (pp. 25–26). Jean Clavreul's article, "Le Couple pervers," shows that neither the victim nor the accomplice takes the place of an Other; (on "desubjectivization," see p. 110; and on the distinction between the cause and the object of desire, see the same author's "Remarques sur la question de la réalité dans les perversions," *La Psychanalyse,* no. 8, pp. 290ff.). It seems that these studies, founded on Lacan's structuralism and on his analysis of the *Verleugnung,* are in the course of development.
28. In Sade there is the ever-present theme of molecular combination.

5. ZOLA AND THE CRACK-UP

1. Émile Zola, *La Bête humaine,* trans. L. Tancock (Markham: Penguin, 1977), p. 66.
2. In an article on "Freud et la science," Jacques Nassif briefly analyzes this conception of dissimilar heredity, as we find it, for example, in Charcot. It opens the way to a recognition of the action of external events. "It is clear that the term 'family' is taken here in both of its senses: that of the classificatory model and that of the parental relationship. On one hand, maladies of the nervous system constitute a single family; on the other, this family is indissolubly united by the laws of heredity. These laws allow the explanation that it may not be the same malady that is electively transmitted, but only a diffuse neuro-pathological disposition which, on the basis of nonhereditary factors, would become specific in a distinct illness," *Cahiers pour l'analyse* (1968), no. 9. Clearly, the Rougon-Macquart "family" operates in both of these senses.
3. "Céline I," *L'Herne,* no. 3, p. 171.
4. *La Bête humaine,* p. 227.
5. *La Bête humaine,* p. 267.

6. *La Bête humaine*, pp. 331, 332.
7. *La Bête humaine*, pp. 335, 361.
8. *La Bête humaine*, p. 58.
9. *La Bête humaine*, p. 155.
10. *La Bête humaine*, pp. 55, 56.

Index

Abstract thinker, 156-57

Absurd, the, 15, 69, 135; distinct from nonsense, 35; paradox of, 35; philosophy of, 71

Abyss, 106, 164, 182, 306; groundless, 139-40; in Nietzche, 108; return to, 315; *Sans-fond,* 106-8; undifferentiated, 103, 106-7

Accident, 151, 152, 155, 244, 322; event and, 53-54

Action(s), 91, 94, 95, 192, 207; corporeal signs, 343n10; and events, 182; everyday and pure event, 238; of external events, 377n2; in language, 184; opposition between intended and accomplished, 207-8; phantasm, result of, 210

Actualization, 114; first level of, 11-12, 113, 115, 116; time of, 168

Actualization of the event, 146, 147, 148, 149, 152, 186, 210, 212; by the action, 150; in distinct worlds, individuals, 172; doubling of, 161; individuals and, 177, 178; moment of, 151; movement of, 167-68; phantasm and, 221; temporal, 100-9; willing, 159

Adsorption, 206, 211, 213

Aeneid, 286

Aesthetics, duality of, 260-61

Affirmation, 123; of disjunction, 172; of divergence, 172, 174, 175; power of, 260-61, 296, 297; in naturalism, 79; scene suspended in, 31, 32, 33, 35; synthesis, 241

Aggression(s), 220-21; thought as, 298

Aggressiveness, 192, 193, 201

Ailly, Pierre d', 20

Aion, 101, 121, 136, 141, 144, 215, 241; actor belongs to, 150; and Chronos, 77, 132; effect on, 5; in events, 53; infinitely subdivisible time, 60, 61, 63-64; past, present, and future, 164-68; pure infinitive as, 185; pure line of, in speculative form, 209; sense in, 81, 166; series of, 67, 162-68; strategic line of, 64, 176; surface organization determined by, 166-68; of surfaces, 175-76; two simultaneous directions of, 79; univocal Being as pure form of, 180

Alcohol, 156, 161

Alcoholism, 154, 157, 158-60, 193, 219,

Alcoholism (*continued*)

349*n*5; and crack-up, 321; depressive aspect of, 159; as instinct, 322, 323, 325

Aleatory point, 56, 94, 103, 113, 116, 166; Aion, straight line traveled by, 64; of desexualized energy, 241; in development of language, 81; displaced, 65, 137, 141; ideal form, 19, 59; instantaneous, 167; in problems, 114; of singular points, 114; in Stoic philosophy, 146; and subsistence of God, 176

Alice in Wonderland (Carroll), 1, 9, 10, 43, 56, 234-36; alimentary obsessions of, 23-24; caucus-race in, 58; direction, 77, 78-79; doubles (in), 79-80; double adventure of, 75; paradox, 32; paradox of repression, 30-31; parts of, 234-36; schizophrenic elements in, 92; series in, 234-38; series in serialization, 41; singularities of, 80; as story of oral regress, 37; surface in adventures of, 124

Alice's adventures, 142-43; reversals in, 3; series of, 234-38

Alimentary drives, 216, 225, 242

Alimentary obsessions of Alice, 23-24

Alimentary system, 198

Alimentary words, 342*n*10

Aliquid, 19, 26, 44, 49, 180; liberation of, 221; sense as, 22, 31

Althusser, Louis, 341*n*4

Ambiguous sign, 114, 116, 346*n*4

Amor fati, 149, 151

Amplitude: moment of, 261; series of, 242, 244

Anality, 187, 219, 246-47, 248

Analogy, 179, 180, 194, 268, 275

Anal stage, 196, 245

Anal theme, 189

Analytic predicates, 112-13, 115, 116

Anal zone, 196, 245

Ancient philosophy, simulacrum and, 253-79

Anecdotes, 142, 148; in philosophy, 128, 129-30

Animus/anima, 273, 276

Anonymity, will of, 100-1

Answers, 56

Antichrist, 281, 292, 296; order of, 294, 297, 301; system of, 298

Antinomy: paradox in form of, 48-50

Antisthenes, 132, 133

Anti-theology, 282

Anxiety, 201, 202-3, 204, 205, 352*n*2

Aphorisms, 128, 142

Appearance(s), 20-24, 253

Apperception, 105, 344*n*6

Appetites, 332; and death instinct, 326-37

Aristotle, 6-7, 18, 254, 259

Aristotelianism, 105

Arnault, 345*n*1

Art, ideal game and, 60; psychoanalysis and, 237-38; theory, 260

Artaud, Antonin, 87, 88, 89, 91, 157, 193, 343*n*11; antinomic series in, 86; confrontation with Carroll, 83-86, 91-93; "Jabberwocky," of, 89-90, 339*n*2

Ascent, 247; philosopher being of, 127-28, 135; Socratic irony as, 132-38

Assents, role and return of, 144-45

Assertion, 14

Associations (in language), 85, 90

Astrology, 171

Atom(s), 268-71, 274, 276, 277; collision of, 269-70; declension of, 183; infinite, 269, 272

Attitude (concept), 355*n*3

Attributes, 94, 276-77; in Aion, 165; as predicate concept, 97

Auto-eroticism, 197, 199, 203, 225; phantasm and, 216

Autonomy of the effect, 95

Breath-words, 88
Bréhier, Emile, 5
Brentano, Franz, 20
Brisset, Jean-Pierre, 140
Brunnius, Jacques B., 83, 338n2
Butor, Michael, 47

Cannibalism, 130, 131, 143, 202, 206,
    239; orality and, 187
Carroll, Lewis, 20, 74, 80, 83, 129; Ar-
    taud's confrontation with, 83-86, 91-
    93; desexualization in, 238; doubles,
    39, 79-80; *Dynamics of a Particle, the,*
    55; entity of the height, theme in,
    358n1; esoteric words in, 43-44, 234;
    events/things/state of affairs, differ-
    ence between, 9-11, 34; grammar in,
    91; *Hunting of the Snark, the,* 46; ideal
    game in, 58; invention in, 343n11;
    "Jabberwocky," 45-46; language,
    means of, 22; method of problems
    and solutions in work of, 56; paradox
    of, 17, 18; paradox of logic in, 16;
    paradox of neutrality in, 33, 34; par-
    adox of regress in, 29-31; paradox of
    sterile divisions in, 32; perversion in,
    244; psychoanalytic diagnosis of the
    work of, 237; recreational mathemat-
    ics of, 55-56; schizophrenia in, 92-93;
    sense/nonsense in, 111, 117; serial
    method in, 36, 42-43; series in, 64,
    65, 86-87; *Sylvie and Bruno,* 10, 11,
    23, 26-27, 42-43, 44, 55; "Three
    Voices, the," 359n1; *Through the Look-
    ing-Glass,* 1, 9-10, 43, 236; to eat/to
    be eaten, specific alternatives in, 23,
    26-27, 37; "Two Brothers, the,"
    358n1; *see also Alice in Wonderland*
Carroll effect, 70
Carroll's paradox, 340n2
Castration, 202, 203, 206, 207, 208,
    209, 211, 219, 222, 243; complex,
    203, 206, 229, 230, 231; contraries

of, 175-76; convergence of depth
into partial surfaces, 227; critique of,
11; dismissal of, in humor, 136;
depth, disturbance of, 315; drives in,
198-99; effect, 210; ego in, 203; exploration of, 108; fear, 353n4; good
object extracts, Voice from, 193-94;
history of, 187-95; hollow/full, 188-
89; humor and, 141; internal tension
of, 189-90; loss of everything in, 239;
in Nietzsche, 347n1; Oedipus complex
and, 205; in origin of, of phantasm,
218, 219; Others and, 307; penis in,
200, 202; phallus as agent of, 237; in
philosophy, 128-29, 130, 133; physics
of mixtures in, 132; reaction of
height to, 198; repressed by height,
243-44; risk, 236; in Stoicism, 143;
Subversion of, 243; thinker of, 219
Castration trace: becomes line of
    thought, 219-20; development of,
    and phantasm, 218-19; phallic line
    merging with, 228, 232
Categorical syllogism, self as universal
    principle of, 295
Categories, 139, 295; distribution of,
    311, 318; in perpetual hold, 308, 309
Causality, 59, 144, 270, 272, 295; cleav-
    age of, 6-7; Naturalism in principles
    of, 268
Cause/effect, 7, 8, 59, 94; in bodies, 4-
    5; inference in, 13; series in, 95
Causes, bodies as, 4-5; events and, 210-
    22; irreducible plurality of, 270; of
    phantasm-event, 211; present and,
    162-63; unity of, 132, 143, 144, 163,
    169, 270
Céline, 326
Center, 104; decentered, 176, 264; dis-
    placed, 183
Chance, 180, 270; affirmation of, 60;
    Aion as, 64; division and apportion-
    ment in games, 58, 59; ritual in
    games, 60-61

Chaos, 139-40, 260-61, 263, 266; eternal return, 264
Chaos-cosmos (Chaosmos) in Carroll, 111, 176
Cheshire Cat, 235, 236
Child(ren), 82-83; 210; in Artaud and Carroll, 93; good intentions of, 204-5; development in, 229, 230, 231, 232; schizoid position of, 92
Chronos, 60, 61, 64, 144, 176; and Aion, 77, 132, 162, 163, 165; God as, 150; past, present, and future in, 162-64; presents of, 168
Chrysippus, 8-9, 80, 129, 130, 131, 134, 136, 170; effect, 70
Cicero, 144
Circle(s): decenterring of, 261; and eternal return, 300-1; monocentric, 260; of proposition, 22; of time, 150
Clinamen, 269-70, 275, 276, 277
Cogito, 14, 15, 102, 123, 139
Common sense, 75, 77-80, 102, 119, 248; complementarity with good sense, 78; destroyed by paradox, 3; in Husserl, 97-98; produced by passive genesis, 116-17; representation in, 145
Communication: through incompossibility, 174
Compatibility, 170, 171; alogical, 172, 177
Compossibility, 111, 171-72, 259-60
Conatus, 269
Concept(s), 6, 19, 34, 115, 170, 171, 245; attributes as, 97; loss of identity and, 174, 296; primacy of the "I" in relation to, 15, 18; reason and, 294-95; signification in, 241
Confatalia, 8
Conjunction, 47, 174, 175; relations of, 170, 171; of series, 225, 226
Conjunctive series, 174; in Carroll, 234
Conjunctive synthesis, 175, 229, 231; in sexual series, 232

Connection, 47; of series, 225
Connective synthesis, 174, 175, 229, 232; in Carroll, 234
Consciousness, 102-3; 122, 123; effect of presence of Others on, 310-11, 312; phantasm and, 217; positions of, 101; sexuality in, 244; the transcendental and, 104
Consumptions/expressions duality, 85
Contingent futures (paradox), 33
Contradiction, 69, 111, 173, 178; development of, 175; of events, 170-71; as primitive words, 213; schizophrenic manner of living, 87, 88, 89, 91-91; principle, 33-34, 35, 74-75
Contraries: affirmation of distance of, 172-73; compatibility of, 177
Convergence, 259, 260; circle of, 183; of divergent series, 183; ideational center of, 174-75; phallus as agent of, 227; of points of view, 174; of series, 171, 172, 176, 225, 226, 227, 228, 229, 234; world constituted on the basis of series, 109-10, 11, 113, 114, 116
Coordination, 268; of ego, 203; of erogenous zones, 200; phallus as agent of, 227, 231-32; of series, 225
Copy, 2, 7, 263, 265, 266; Platonic, 259; simulacrum and, 253, 256-58; world of, 261, 266; and icon, 256-57
Cosmos, 48
Counter-actualization, 150, 151, 152, 157, 161, 175-76, 178-79, 221; present of, 168; in psychoanalysis, 212; ultimate sense of, 178
Counter-sense, 72, 341n2
Court de Gebelin, 140
Crack (the), actualized as depths of body, 222; cerebral, 241; in development phantasm, 218-19; in history of instincts, 332; heredity of, 324-25, 326; of the self, 176; silence, 155-58, 160-61; in surface, 165; trace of cas-

Crack (*continued*)
tration as, 208-9; in Zola, 321-23, 324, 333
Crack Up, the (Fitzgerald), 154-55
Crane, Stephen, *Red Badge of Courage, the,* 101
Cratylus, 2, 25
Cruelty, 190-91, 192-93; theater of, 90
Culpability, 202-3, 204, 205, 206
Cynics, 9, 129, 130, 132, 133

Death, 145, 149, 151-52, 153, 176, 208, 217, 221, 222, 261, 277, 292, 326; aspects of, 156; by castration, 206, 207; in event, 156; figures of, 209; incorporeal/personal, 156; problem of, 84
Death instinct, 198, 208, 209, 239, 240, 318, 326-27; in silence, 241; in Zola, 327-29, 330, 331
Defoe, Daniel, 302-3, 314
Denegation, 208
Denotation(s) (indications), 12-13, 14, 15, 16-17, 18, 19-20, 35, 37, 52, 86, 96, 101, 104, 135-36, 184, 241, 245; affected by quality, quantity, relation, modality, 32-34; duality in proposition, 25-26, 28; and expressions, 182-83; equivocity of, 247; of everyday language, 248; humor and, 141; and language, 182, 232; of names, 36-37, 67, 68; nonsense of, 136; of propositions, 167, relation of, 118-19, 120; and sense-object relation, 97, 98; sensible representations and, 145; series of, 37, 43; significations, 242, 244; signifier in, 38; sound, 166, 187; speech, 181; verb as, 184; of voice, 194; of word, 87; world as principle of, 176
Depressive past, present, 192
Depressive position, 187-88, 193, 194-

95, 197, 202, 208; in good object, 190; move from schizoid to, 229, 232; penis and, 200; phantasm-events, 211; and phantasmatic life, 216; reaction to schizoid position, 198
Depressive split, 192
Depth(s), 186, 188, 189, 201, 224, 245; adventures of, 315; in Alice's adventures, 234-35, 237; becoming of, 213; bottomless, 246; in Carroll, 9, 10
Depth of bodies, 5-6, 23, 87, 88, 94, 142; Artaud's language in, 84, 93; emissions from, 273-75, 276; mixture in, 130-31; and production of sense, 124-26; silent crack incarnated in, 155, 156-57
Depth-surface distinction, 187
Descartes, Réné, 14, 15, 344n1
Desert island, 302, 303, 304-5; paradox of, 309-30
Desexualization, 208, 220, 238, 242-43, 244; forced movement represents, 239
Desire(s), 13, 16, 220-21; 311-12, 313, 319; false impressions of, 277; image corresponding to, 276; in perversion, 219; and Robinson, 317-18; sense of, 17-18; unlimited, 273, 277, 278
Destiny, 169, 170, 270, 278-79; affirmation of, 169; and necessity, 6
Destructive drives, 188, 201, 202, 203, 209, 222, 225, 242, 243, 352n2; libidinal liberation from, 203, 204; sexual drives disengaged from, 244, 353n3
Dialectic, 255; Platonic, 254
Dialectics, 8, 21, 128; of humor, 9; single center of, 260
Dickens, Charles, 349n4
Difference(s), 173, 261-62, 289; authentification of, 287-88, suppression of, 172; of intensities, 297; intensity of, 289; internalized, 262; in Nature, 268; as object of affirmation, 296,

197; origin of, 116; Others and, 17, simulacrum and, 298

Differentiation, 281

Digestive-destructive stage, 245

Dilemma, 285, 286, 287, 290-94, 296

Diogenes Laertius, 8, 128, 129-30, 142

Diogenes the Cynic, 129, 130, 135

Dionysus, 107, 129, 139, 281, 301

Disjunction(s), 47, 174, 176, 268, 285, 292; affirmative power of, 183, 241; in Alice's adventures, 235; and exclusions in reality, 296; good object as source of, 227; multiple, 66; negative/exclusive, 296-97, 301; as object of affirmation, 300; in phantasm, 215; creations of, 170, 171; singularities distributed in, 214

Disjunctive syllogism, 364n2; God as principle of, 294-97; in Klossowski, 280, 281, 282, 285, 290-94, 300-1

Disjunctive synthesis, 67, 68-69, 174, 214, 226; affirmation of, 176, 177, 178, 179; in Carroll, 234; of heterogeneous series, 229; portmanteau word, grounded in, 46-47; in sexual series, 231-32; univocity of Being, 179-80

Disparity, 261-62

Displacement, 50, 51, 53, 217, 224, 228-39

Dissymmetry, 261

Distance, 173, 176, 179, 185, 215, 274, 307; affirmation of, 178; infinitive, 175

Distribution, fixity of, 59, 76, 263; in good sense, 75-76; of singularities, 59-60, 70, 345n4

Divergence, 113, 114, 260; affirmation of, 174, 175, 177, 265, 296, 297, 300; of disjunction, 172; loss of, 43; of points of view, 174; of series, 111, 171-72, 226, 229, 260, 261

Divergent series, 174, 175, 176, 299, 301; in Carroll, 234, 236; conver-

gence of, 183; in simulacrum, 262, 264

Diverse (the), 279; diversity of, 266, 268; heterogeneity and resemblance of, with itself, 271, 272; power of, 271-72

Division, method of, 253-54, 259; Plato texts on, 256; purpose of, 254-55, 256; second irony of, 254-55

Docteur Pascal, Le (Zola), 333

Dostoyevsky, Feodor, 247

Double(s), 122-23, 124, 284, 289, 315; in Carroll, 79-80; erect, 312-13; and humour, 141; language as ultimate, 284; Others and, 319; personal, 316, 317; perversion and, 319; in Sade, 320

Double causality, 102, 108; paradox of, 144; of phantasm-event, 211; series of, 94-99

Dry reiteration, *see* Paradox of sterile division (or dry reiteration)

Dualism, 6-7, 233, 308-9; heredity/acquired, 325; Platonic, 2

Duality(ies), 23-27, 37, 66; of aesthetics, 260-61; Idea/image, 257; of orality, 84-85, 86

Duns Scotus, 344n1, 351n3

Dynamics of Parti-cle, the (Carroll), 55, 56

Dynamic genesis, 186, 193-95, 215, 229-30, 241, 246

Eating, 186, 187, 240, 242

Effect(s), 4-5, 61, 62, 270; in alcoholism, 159-60; autonomy of, 95; events are (as), 210; the identical incorporeal, 7-8; phantasm in, 210-11; relations of, 169; sense as, 70-71, 86

Ego, 208; and death, 222; division of, 192; formation, 188; good subject, 190-91; id and, 188-89; Idea and, 192; as knowing subject, 113; narcissistic, 197; phantasm in, 212-14; pre-

Ego (*continued*)
  reflective syntheses of, 308; of secondary narcissism, 212, 216; surface
  in development of, 203-4; transcendental in, 116; universal, 115
Elements, 248, 302, 303, 304, 306, 317-
  18; free, 315, 316; impersonal, 312;
  liberated, 313, 319
Empedocles, 128, 129; and Etna, story
  of, 128
Empty square, 47, 56, 65, 72-73; circulation of, in structured series, 71; essential to structure, 51; in nonsense,
  81; paradoxical element as, 66; phallus as, 228; in signifying series, 50,
  51
Energy, 107, 245; cosmic, 302, 303; desexualized, 208, 218, 222, 241, 243,
  245; finite, 110; neutral, 213; potential, 103, 104, 110, 344n3; sexual,
  248; superficial, 104, 199, 203; surface, 124, 315
Envelopment, constitution of individual
  as center of, 111
Epictetus, 144
Epicureans, 6, 94, 183-84, 269-270,
  273-79
Epicurus, 266-67, 273
Equivocity, 185, 194, 241, 246-47, 248,
  282
Erogenous zones, 197, 199, 222-23,
  229, 243; in Alice's adventures, 236;
  coordination of, 200; and languages,
  230-31; series of, 225; and sexual series, 232
Eros, 239, 241
Erotic phantasm, 275, 276, 277, 278
Esoteric language, 140, 141
Esoteric words, 42-47, 50, 51, 183;
  blank word designated by, 67; in
  Carroll, 43-44, 234, 238; construc-
  tion of, 231-32; denoted by portmanteau word, 47; paradoxical element

in, 66; secret of, 175; tied to problem and question, 56; the time, 62
Essence(s), 71, 135, 257, 258; abolition
  of the world of, 253; and appearance,
  253, 266; of event, 214; replaced by
  sense, 105; as sense, 34-35; states of,
  34-35
Eternal return, 61, 62, 64, 149, 165,
  176, 240, 263-65; individual and,
  178; sense and, 299-301; phantasm as
  site of, 220; univocity of Being as,
  180
Ethics, 31, 149, 169; physics and, 272;
  Stoic, 142-44
Event(s), 64, 65, 132, 171, 176; and
  accident, 53-54; communication of,
  174, 185, 214; communicating the
  univocity of being to language, 248;
  compatibility of, 177-78; conjugation
  of, 183; death as, 156; difference
  from things and states of affairs in
  Carroll, 9-11; distributed in two series constituting metaphysical surface,
  241; double structure of, 151-52; effects in, 5, 210; castration of, 351n3;
  Epicurean notion of, 344n4; eternal
  truth of, 161; as the expressed of
  proposition, 184, 186; and experience, 170-71; Freudian theory of,
  226; heterogeneous series of, 70;
  ideational/incorporeal, 8; infinitely
  divisible, 8, 113, 114; lack of present
  in, 63-64; and language, 3, 181-85;
  logic of, 111; and metaphysical surface, 221-22; modality of, 33-34;
  movement and, 276-77; nature of,
  94, 95; Oedipus and, 212; phantasm,
  213-14; in proposition, 12, 34; problematic as mode of, 54, 56; realization of, 87, 104; relation of, 33, 171;
  representations of, 245; sense as, 22,
  107, 167, 176, 180, 211; series of,
  37, 38, 148-53, 226; signifier as, 37-

38; singularities as, 53, 56; singularity of, 152-53; in Stoic ethics, 143, 144, 146; surface-, 167; symbolic relation with state of affairs, 240; and thought, 220-21; unique, 178; *see also* Actualization of event; Communication of event; Pure event

Events-effects, 12, 23, 145, 169-70; time of, 62-63, 64

Excess, paradoxical element as, 66; in phallus, 227-281; in signifying series, 48, 49-50, 51

Exchange and repetition, 287-90, 296

Exhaustion, method of, 269, 275

Exiles (Joyce), 283

Expressed (the), 132-33

Expression(s), 20, 32, 110-12, 122, 166; denotation and, 182-83; and duality in proposition, 25-26, 28; "expressible" of, 86; founded in event, 182; relation of, 170; representations and, 145-46, 168; series of, 37, 38, 43; signifier as sole dimension of, 38

Extra-being, 7, 22, 31, 81, 123, 180, 221; impossible objects in, 35; Void in, 347n1

Fairbairn, W. R. D., 351n2

False, 13, 68, 120-21, 263; in proposition, 14-15, 17, 19; infinitive, 272, 277, 278, 279

Familial romance, 204, 237, 238, 326, 359n2

Father, 205-6, 207

Father image, 204, 205

Fink, Eugen, 97

Finnegan's Wake, 40, 260

Fitzgerald, F. Scott, 157, 159-60, 219, 321; *Crack Up, The,* 154-55

Flaubert, 324

Floated signified: paradoxical theme in, 49, 66; phallus as, 228

Floating signifier, 49-50; paradoxical element in, 66; phallus as, 228

Forced movement, 239-40, 261, 262, 265

"Forclusion" of Others, 309-10

"Fourth person singular," 141

Frege's paradox, 29

Freud, Sigmund, 72, 189, 193, 203, 208, 213, 214, 237, 244, 261, 284, 303, 304, 341n4, 352n2; *Beyond the Pleasure Principle,* 356n3; dualism in, 233; "familial romance" in, 204; phantasms in, 210; Rat Man, 357n3; schizophrenia in, 87, theory of the event, 226; use of word "series," 356n2; *Wolf Man,* 40, 230, 357n2

Future (the), 80, 150, 151; in Aion, 164-65; in alcoholism, 159-60; in Chronos, 162-63, 164; death in, 156; imminent, 63; language, 167; in the order of time, 63; language, 61-62; the untimely in relation to, 265

Future perfect, 159-60, 349n5

Game(s): implicit models in, 59; theory of, 58-61

"Gardener's song" (Carroll), 44, 46

Gattegno, Jean, 22

Genital sexuality, 208; series of, 225; zone, 200, 201, 203, 206, 207, 222-23

Geoffroy Saint-Hilaire E., 356n3

God, 78, 110, 138, 139, 245, 247, 292, 344n1; belief in, 281; calculating, choosing, 172; as Chronos, 150; experience of present, 162; and disjunction, 176; and grammar, 281; as guarantor of identity of self, 294; immutability of, 107; made man in his image, 257-58; order of, 292-94, 301; as principle of the disjunctive syllogism, 294-97; sense in, 72-73; as Traitor, 292; work of, 194

Goldschmidt, Victor, 144, 147, 340n3
Gombrowicz, Witold, 39; *Pornographia,*
281, 289-90
Good intentions, 216, 236; punishment
of, 202-9
Good object, 187-88, 189, 190-91, 203,
245; in Alice's adventures, 236; disjunction, subsumed under, 204; extracts Voice from the depth, 193; father of, 201; lost, 193, 227; penis
and, 201; positions, 189-91, 192
Good objects of the heights, 203, 204;
in Alice's adventures, 235; series converge toward, 227
Good penis, 203, 205, 227
Good sense, 3, 74-76, 78, 97, 102, 248;
characteristics of, 76; and common
sense, 78; direction of, 2-3, 75, 76-
77, 78; individuation, 119, paradox
of, 80; produced by passive genesis,
116-17
Greek philosophy, paradox of, 17
Gregory of Rimini, 19
Ground, 105; undifferentiated, 106, 120,
139-40
Gurvitch, George, 344n1

Hammer-blow philosophy, 128-29
Hegel, 19, 173, 213, 253; *Phenomenology,*
346n1; representation, 259-60
Height(s), 201, 347n1; in Alice's adventures, 236; castration of, 206; good
subject belongs to, 189-90, 191; humor and, 136, 141; and language,
246-47; Oedipus complex and, 205;
penis and, 200, 202; in philosophy,
127, 128, 130, 132, 133; pre-sense
of, 194; reaction to depth, 198; represses depth, 243-44; unlimited,
246; voice from, 233
Heimann, Paula, 243, 353n3
Heraclitean world, 131-32, 133, 165,
205

Heredity, 321; dissimilar, 367n2; great/
small, 324-36, 329, 331
Heterogeneous series, 225, 226, 232;
communicating, 261; conjunctive synthesis of, 231; coordination of, 47,
67; disjunctive synthesis of, 229; esoteric words subsumption, 45, 46; in
nonsense, 70; paradoxical element,
66; power to affirm, 260-61; singularities-events compound to, 103-4
Heterogeneity, 262, 263
Homogeneity, in series, 36, 37, 38, 225
Hugo, Victor, 100, 101
Hume, David, 13, 275
Husserl, Edmund, 20-21, 32, 99, 101-2,
113, 122, 298, 308; *Cartesian Meditations,* 344n6; *Ideas,* 96-98; *Logical Investigations,* 341n2; noematic core, 212;
theory of constitution, 116
Hunting of the Snark, the (Carroll), 46,
234

"I" (the), 13, 14, 78, 99, 102, 105;
coextensive with representation, 138;
cracked, 141; primacy of, 15, 17-18;
singularities, and, 103
Icon, 259, 261, 263, 265
Id, 190; and ego, 188-89, 191-92
Idea, 7, 128, 132, 263; action of, 2, 7;
authentification, in division, 256; deprived, 295; and images, 256, 257;
knowledge of, 258; problem subsists
in, 54; pure, 137, 138; universality
of, 139
Ideal event(s), 50, 52; spatio-temporal
realization of, 53, 54
Ideal game, 72, 116, 180; series of, 58-
65
Ideas: combination of, 131; foundation
of language in, 134; motive of theory
of, 253-54; perception of Others and,
305-6; and syllogism, 294-95
Ideas (Husserl), 96-98

Introjection, 155, 187, 188, 192

Irigaray, Luce, 215

Irony, 9, 141, 246-47, 248; classical figures of, 137-40; in Kant's theology, 294, 295-96; in Plato, 254-55, 256; Socratic, 135, 137-38; and tragic ground, 140

Isaacs, Susan, 215-16

Jabberwock, 67, 91, 234

Jabberwocky, 234, 236

"Jabberwocky" (Carroll), 62, 236; Artaud's rendering of, 83-84, 89-90, 339n2; portmanteau words, 45-46

Jakobson, Roman, 71

James, William, 318

Joyce, James, 39, 56, 260-61, 264, 343n11; *Exiles*, 283

Kant, Immanuel, 54, 97, 98, 105, 138, 139, 176, 253, 294, 345n5; causality in, 6; forms of possibility in, 18; on theology, 294-97; will in, 344n1

Kierkegaard, Sören, 300, 318

Klein, Melanie, 187-89, 200, 201, 202, 204, 215, 216, 224, 349n4, 351n3, 352n2

Klossowski, Pierre, 39, 40, 176, 178, 219, 264, 280-301, 336n7; *Baphomet, le,* 291-94, 297-98, 299; opposition between exchange and true repetition theme, 287-90; *Révocation, La,* 285-86; *Souffleur, Le,* 283, 285, 286, 287-88, 299; sexual descriptions in, 281

Knowledge: apodeictic, 145; esoteric, 243; limits of, 107; object/condition of, 105; and perversion, 360n2; theories of, 311; true, 258; types of, 146

Koan, 136, 142

Koyré, 341n2

Lacan, Jacques, 38, 40, 41, 200, 228, 229-30, 232, 309-10, 319, 360nn2,5; analysis of Rat Man, 357n3; Lacan's paradox, 48, 338n6

Lack, paradoxical element as, 66; in phallus, 227-28; in significant series, 48, 49-50, 51

Language, 8-9, 111, 125, 158, 183; and the Aion, 167; and Being, 180, 280, 281, 282, 285-87, 289, 290-94, 296, 300-1; cleavage of causality and, 6; and common sense/good series complements, 78, 79; co-system of sexuality, 61, 243-45; dimensions of, 2-3; duality of, 85; ethics of, 143; events and, 22, 56; flexional character, 286; formation of, 193-94, 232; foundation of, 134-35; in Freud, 213; of the ground, 140; height and, 246-47; irony and, 137-38; loss of denoting function of, 299; made possible by that which distinguishes it, 186; made possible by world of surface effects, 11, 166-67; negation of events/effects and, 12; order of, 18, 48, 181, 241, 244, 245-46, 248-49; organization of, 157, 183, 184, 241, 242; paradoxes insist within, 74; power of, 29; primacy of signification as, 15-16; in primacy order, 120; problem of, in relation to univocity of Being, 351n3; and pure becoming, 2; as reality of the possible, 139, 307; relationship of phantasm to, 215-216; satiric values of, 246; schizophrenic, 82-83, 84-85, 88, 91, 92-93; and sense, 25, 240; shifting function of, 294; series of, 181-85; sexual origin of, 229-33; as sign empty of meaning, 90-91; singularities within, 50; table of development of, as the surface, 80-81, 246; tertiary arrangement of, 119-20, 247, 248; as ultimate double, 284;

and univocity of series, 248; without articulations, 89

Mouth (*continued*)
242, 355n3; and thought, 240; -anus, 223

Multiplicity, 279, 292, 297

Myth, 254-55, 264, 278-79, 364n2; circular, 255; founding, 256, 263; Nature and, 278

Name(s), 24; denotation of, 36, 44, 67, 68; paradox of regress, 29-31; synthesis of, 37

Narcissistic wound, 208, 213, 216, 218

Nassif, Jacques, 367n2

Naturalism, 266, 268-72, 278-79, 324; of Zola, 322; physics as, 272-77

Nature, 278, 313; and unity of causes, 270; composition and combinations of elements of, 268-72; diversity in, 266-68; infinite in, 278; mixtures in, 131; positivity of, 279

Necessity, 137, 169, 270, 300; denial of, 169, 170; destiny and, 6; hypothesis of, 33-34

Negation, 123, 206-7; sense suspends, 31, 32, 33, 35

Negative (the), 279

Neoplatonism, 255

Neufchateau, André de, 20

Neurosis, 222, 304, 313, 314, 315, 321

Neutrality, 122-23; of singularity, 52; estates, paradox of, 32-35; of sense, 95, 96, 100, 101-2, 104, 105, 123-24, 125, 339n1

Nietzsche, 72, 106-8, 157, 173, 174, 178, 203, 289, 300, 347n1; *Birth of Tragedy, The,* 107; eternal return in, 264; God/grammar link in, 281; Klossowski's analysis of, 298; madness in, 198; and orientation of thought, 128-30; task to reverse Platonism, 253; the untimely in, 265

Nihilism, 266

Noema (noematic), 20-21, 32, 96-97, 98; attribute noematic, 182, 186, 211, 214, 221, 238, 240; event related to series as, 241; perceptual, 20-21

Noesis, 98

Noise, 182, 189, 229, 232, 246, 248, 274; passage from — to voice, 194; of depths/heights, 233; move to voice, 248

Nomadic distribution, 75, 77, 102, 113, 263

Nonsense, 8-9, 91, 134, 156-57, 246, 358n7; in Carroll, xiii, co-present with sense, 116-17; of depths, 136; distinct from absurdity, 35; double, 98; eternal return as, 301; in the event, 95; figures of, 91, 95; forms of, 341n2; functions of, 83, 241; ideal game thought as, 60; and the metaphysical surface, 244; mobile, 86; organization of, 241; passive/active, 90; phallus role of, 228, 242; of pure noise, 189; and sense, 67, 69-71, 81, 91, 106, 107, 137, 141, 176, 183, 233; series of, 66-73; sexuality mimics, 243; of the surface, 136, 166; threat to surface is, 82; two sides of, 67; univocal Being as, 180

Novalis, 53

Object(s), 119, 135; alcoholism, 160; common, 115; of depth, 216; of decision, 313; of drives, 353n3; exoteric, 51, 66; of heights, 216; instinct and, 323-24; introjected, 196; introjected/projected, 216; loss of, 159; perception of Others, 305-6, 307, 315, 318; in perceptual field, 308-9; and presence/absence of Others, 305-6, 307, 308-9, 310-11, 312-13; reaction to sense, 97, 98; series of

(Carroll), 46; and subject, 310-11; substitutive, 198-99

Ockham, 2, 19

Occupant without a place, 41, 47, 66, 81

Oedipal series, 226, 227, 228, 232, 242

Oedipal situation, 24, 353n4; in Alice's adventures, 237

Oedipus, 188, 201, 202, 205, 206-7, 212, 222, 226, 237, 244; evolution of, 230, 231, 232

Oedipus complex, 200-1, 202-3, 204-5, 208, 237, 353n4, 356n2

Oneiric phantasms, 275, 276, 277, 278

Ontological genesis: logical genesis and, 119-20; element of, 118

Ontology, 179-80

Oral-anal regression, in *Alice's Adventures*, 37, 236, 237

Orality, 37, 44, 84-85, 86, 181, 187, 188, 196, 199, 219, 223, 225, 231; series of, 186-95

Origin, 302-3, 304

Osier, J. P., 341n4

Other(s), 248, 345n2; a priori, 307, 318; concrete, 318; effects of, 304-21; meaning of, 307-10; model of, 258, 262; presence of, 304-5, 307, 308-10; structure-, 313-15, 319-21; theory of, 318, 366n12; world without, 301-21

"Overman," 107

Pankow, Gisela, 342n10, 351n3

Paradox, 1, 16, 69, 80; arguments in, 145; of Carroll, 17, 18; direction of, 75-76, 78, 79; of double causality, 144; in form of antimony, 48-50; forming theory of sense, 111-12; in good sense/common sense, 117; in Greek philosophy, 17; in nonsense, 70; in relative displacement of series,

40-41; of series, 28-35; series of, 74-81; of speech, 232-33; in the Stoics, 8-9; of the voice, 194; in translation, 85; of transmission, 321

Paradox: of the absurd, 35; Actor's, 150; of contingent futures, 33; of duality, 37; of infinite identity, 2-3; of neutrality (or of essence's third estate), 32-35; of pure becoming, 1-3; of regress (or of indefinite proliferation), 28-31, 32, 36-37; of signification; of sterile division (or dry reiteration), 31-32; of surface effects, 4-11

Paradoxical element, 81, 95, 103, 119; characteristics of, 66-67; convergence of divergent series, 183; figures of, 67-68; instant as, 168; is at once word and thing, 67; phallus as, 228; void as, 137

Paradoxical element in series, 50-51, 52; as locus of the question, 56, 57

Parain, Bruce, 17

Paranoid-schizoid position, 187-88, 192

Paris, Jean, 343n11

Parisot, Henri, 83, 90, 338n2

Parmenides (Plato), 164, 165

Partial objects, 188, 190, 191, 196, 224, 353n3; and good object, 190; introjection and projection, 187, 197, 198, 199; penises and, 204

Partial zones, 226, 227

Pascal, 59, 60

Passion(s), 88-89, 90, 91, 95, 131, 187, 192, 207, 276; bodily figures, 343n10; of body, 162-63; and events, 182; everyday and pure Event, 238; phantasm and, 210; sense and, 94

Passive genesis, 116-17

Past, 80, 150; Aion, 164-65; of the alcoholic, 158, 159; in Chronos, 162-63, 164; of event, 151; language and, 167; in the order of time, 5, 75, 76,

irony in, 138, 247, 254-55, 256; motivations in, 253-54, 256-57; *Parmenides,* 164, 165; and simulacrum, 253-66; *Philebus,* 258; *Phaedrus,* 254, 255, 256; trinity of user/producer/imitator, 258-59

Platonism, 7, 19, 191, 254, 263, 265; aim of, 259; domain of representations, 259; and eternal return, 264; images of the philosopher in, 127-28; reversal of, 53, 132, 253, 256, 262-63, 265

Pleasure, 272-73, 277, 278

Plotinus, 124

Plutarch, 146

Poe, Edgar Allan, 38, 40

Pontalis, J. N., 212, 213, 216, 352n3

Pop Art, 265

Pornagraphia (Gombrowicz), 281, 289-90

Portmanteau words, 82, 140, 177-78, 231-32; in Artaud's "Jabberwocky," 84; and Carroll, 234; designating esoteric words, 67; heterogeneity, 83, 92; infinity of interpretations, 343n11; nonsense expressed in, 86; and problems, 56-57; regulating series, 44-47; in schizophrenic language, 90

Possibility(ies), 18, 115, 137, 138; God defined by total, 295-96; originary and derived, 139; of person, 138-39; personal/individual, 118, 119

Possible (the), 138, 180, 306; being of, 35; the Other is the existence of, 307-8; as structure-Other, 318, 320

Possible world: the Other as expression of, 308, 309, 310-11, 316

Predicate(s), 21; defining persons synthetically, 115, 116; exclusion of, 174; primary, 106, 187; logic of, 111

Pregenital series, 226, 228, 232, 242, 357n2, 358n3

Pre-individual (the), 140, 344n3

Pre-sense, 194: voice from heights as, 233

Present (the), 1, 4, 5, 61-62, 75, 76, 77, 166; in Aion, 164-65, 168; of the alcoholic, 158-59, 160; in becoming, 1, 2; in Chronos, 162-64, 168; divine, 150, 151; of event, 63-64, 151; God lives in, 150; hardening of, 158-59, 160; meanings of, 168; relativity of, 162, 163; untimely relation to, 265; of verb, 184

Pre-Socratic philosophy, 128-29, 131, 132, 134, 191

Pretender(s), 259, 260; distinguishing true from false, 254, 255, 256, 257; false, 256, 262-63, 265

Primary narcissism, 203

Primary order, 91; series of, 239-49

Primitive words, 213

Problem, 56, 113, 114; events bear on, 54, 56; game of, 60; minimum of being in, 56; neutrality of, 122-23; sense expressed as, 121-23; spatiotemporal self-determination of, 121, 122

Problematic, 344n3; as mode of event, 54, 56; as object of the Idea, 54; series of, 52-57; of world of sense, 104-5

Proclus, 54

Projection, 155, 187, 192, 193; mechanisms of, 353n3; as surface operation, 197; willed action image of, 207

Proper name, 3, 13, 24, 70

Properties, 68, 70, 76, 276; grounded in the order of the person, 115, 116, 118, 119

Proposition(s), 8, 12-22, 69, 91, 134, 186; attribute of, 21; circle of, 184; conditional, 14, 16, 122; connection of, 69; corresponding to problems, 121-22; dimension of, 44, 182; duality in, 23, 24, 85; event in, 181, 182,

Proposition (*continued*)
214; form of possibility of, 18-19;
frontiers, 86-87, 125, 132-33, 166,
167, 182-83; hypothetical, 170; logic
of, 105; modalities of, 102; noematic
attribute of, 182; and paradox of regress, 29, 31; and paradox of sterile
division, 31-32; regulating series of
events (in Carroll), 43; relations with
states of affairs, 242; relations of, 12-
22, 118-20; sense in, 19-22, 24, 25,
31, 32-33, 34-35, 37, 65, 80, 81, 95-
96, 241; series of, 37, 38, 43, 44;
signifier as, 38; signified as, 38; verb
in, 215
Propositional modes, neutrality of sense
as, 101-2
Proust, Marcel, 220, 301-2; *Remembrance,* 357n3
Psychanalysez (S. Leclaire), 230-31
Psychoanalysis, 92-93, 211-12, 287,
317-18, 319, 324
Psychosis, 314-15, 321; orientation of,
222
Pujol, Robert, 352n5
Punishment, 213; fear of infinite, 273,
277; of good knowledge, 202-9
Pure event(s), 63, 123, 134, 141, 152,
172, 207, 211; in Carroll, 1; constitutive elements of, 166-67; eternal
return of, 176, 178-79; imprisoned
in its actualization, 161; neutral infinitive for, 215; noema as, 21; non-
naturalizable part of, 238; opposition
to, 35; phantasm as, 210, 211, 218;
psychoanalysis as science of, 212; are
results, 221; sense as, 19; in Stoic
philosophy, 147-48; as surface, 136;
univocity as, 180; wound as, 148

Quality, 1, 7, 12, 178, 187; in
Chronos, 165; and denotation, 32-
33; sense and, 101; and signs, 261

Quantity, 7, 12; and denotation, 32-33;
sense and, 101
Quasi-causes, 6, 148, 166, 222, 238;
event and, 144; genetic form of series inherited, 124, 125n26; instant
as, 168; paradoxical element as, 183;
of phantasm-events, 211; relation of
sense to, 94, 95, 98; in Stoic philosophy, 146-47; subsistence of God,
176
Quasi-causality of events, 33; expressive,
170; ideational and noematic, 171;
relations of, 8, 169
Question(s), 136; game of, 60; locus of,
56; minimum of being as, 56, 57
Quintillian, 285

Reality, 96-97, 137, 260; irony and,
138; of the Other, 307; of phantasms, 210; whole of, 295-96
Reason, 112, 294-95; critique of (Klossowski), 296-97
Regress, serial form of, 36-37; paradox
of (indefinite proliferations), 28-31,
32, 36-37
Regression, 246, 314; mechanisms of,
244-45
Regressive synthesis, 67, 68, 69-70
Relation(s), 12, 97; as analytical predicates of mixtures, 112-13; and denotation, 32-33; of force, 297; necessary to the conditioned, 118-20, 122;
sense and, 101
Repetition, 296, 300-1, 307; false/true,
287-88; fundamental, 287-90
Representation(s), 141, 266; actor, 150,
157; domain of, 259-60; and eternal
return, 264; of events, 221; expression, 168; Kant's critique of classical,
138; logical use of, 144-46, 147; and
person, 247; reversal of, 265; verbal,
241, 245-46; world of, 241, 262,
263

Sense (*continued*)
sitions and things, 22; in Carroll,
xiii, 26; cause-effect and, 94, 95; of
contraries, 175; denotation of, in
nonsense, 67-68, 69-71; direction in,
1, 77, 78, 81; distribution of, between sexual series, 242; donation
of, 67-68, 69-71, 76, 80-81; doubly
generative, 10, 120-21, 125-26; as
effect, 70-71, 86, 341n4; elaborated
along lines on surface, 86; essence
in, 34-35; and the event, 107, 149,
167, 176, 180, 211; expressed by
nonsense, 67-68; expressed as problem to which propositions correspond, 121-23; figures in, 81, 82;
formal and transcendental logic, 96-
99; fragility of, 94-95, 120; genetic
power of, 124-26; incorporeal events
in, 145; language and, 25, 240; locus
of, at surface, 125-26, 133, 136; and
the logical proposition, 119-20, 126;
loss of, 87-88, 315; and the metaphysical surface, 244; moment of, as
the eternal return, 299-301; neutrality of, 123-24, 125, 145; and nonsense, xiii, 106, 107, 139, 183, 233,
241; operation of, 166; organization
of, 241, 344n3; in paradox of neutrality, 32-35; in paradox of regress,
28-31; in paradox of sterile division,
31-32; paradoxes of, 75, 77, 81; paradoxical element bestows in signify-
ing/signified series, 51; passive genesis of, 116-17; of perception, 20; in
philosophy, 71-72; as pre-individual
singularity, 299; in proposition, 17-
18, 19-20, 24, 25, 31, 32-33, 34-35,
65, 125, 128; psychoanalysis, 92-93;
relation with nonsense, 67, 69-71,
81; secondary organization of, 120,
125, 239-49; series of paradoxes, 28-
35; and sexuality, 233, 243; sign and,
298; in simultaneous series, 37-38;

and transcendental philosophy, 105-
6; as truth of problems, 121; univocity of, 248-49
Sense-object relation, 97, 98
Serial form, 36-37, 225, 226-27, 229
Serialization, 36-41
Serial method, in Carroll, 39, 42-47
Serial form, in surface organization, 224
Series, 246; of the Aion, 162-68; of
Alice's adventures, 234-38; Carroll's
theory of, 56; characteristic of specification of relation and distribution
of, 39-41; coexistence of, 225, 226;
of communication of events, 169-76;
correction of, 175-76; convergence
of, 260; differentiation, 38; disappearance of, in schizophrenic language, 91; divergence of, 260, 261;
of double causality, 94-99; of the
event, 148-53; first stage, 356-
57n213; in Gardener's song (*Sylvie
and Bruno*), 26-27; good intentions
are inevitably punished, 202-9; homogeneous, 98; of humor, 134-41;
of ideal game, 58-65; internal sorrow
of, 244n3; kinds of, 224-33; of language, 181-85; and moral problem in
Stoic philosophy, 142-47; of nonsense, 66-73; of orality, 186-95; of
the paradox, 94-81; of the phantasms, 210-26; porcelain and volcano, 154-61; primary order and
secondary organization, 239-49; of
the problematic, 52-57; regulated by
portmanteau words (Carroll), 44-47;
ramification of, 183; resonance of,
104, 179, 232; reversals of, 8; separation, serialization of, at surface,
183, 186; of sexuality, 196-201; of
singularities, 100-8; of static logical
genesis, 118-26; of static ontological
genesis, 108-17; of structures, 48-51,
52-53; of thought, 217-23; of three
images of philosophers, 129-33; of

univocity, 177-80; world constituted on condition of convergence of, 109, 111, 114, 116

Sextus Empiricus, 66, 114

Sexual drives, 202, 203, 216, 224, 225, 243, 352n3; detached from alimentary drives, 242; liberation of, 235, 239, 244, 247; and simulacra, 198

Sexuality, 197, 199, 217, 219, 233, 242, 245, 247, 313; co-system with language, 229-33, 243-45; energy of, 248; pregenital, 225; and presence/absence of Others, 317-18; repression of, 244; and sense, 233; series of, 196-201, 224-33; and surface zones, 199-201; and thought, 218-20, 222-23

Sexual: history, 233, 243, 247-48; language in, 229-31; organization, 242; position, 188, 197-98, 199-201; prefiguration of organization of language, 241-42; surface, 219, 232, 239; third agent of, 231-32

Sexual series: phantasms and, 239, 240; and repression, 244

Sign(s), 63, 104, 261, 264, 298; pure, 176; in schizophrenia, 342n10; in simulation, 263

Signification, 14-15, 16-18, 19-20, 25, 34, 35, 52, 96, 99, 101, 104, 167, 184, 241, 245; analogy of, 247; absurdity of, 136; in Carroll, 22; as condition of truth, 122; connection between propositions, lines in, 69; determinations of, 68-69; of everyday language, 248; general, 122; God as principle of, 176; humor and, 141; hypostatized, 134-35; in language, 232; paradoxes of, 75; rational representations are, 145; relation of, defined by the form of possibility, 119, 120, 122; with sense as predicate, 97, 98; and series, 70,

81, 126; sexuality and, 244; of sounds, 166, 187; and speech, 181; verb and, 184; of voice, 194; of word, 87

Signified series, 48, 48-51, 91

Signifier, 37-38, 40, 41, 70; phallus as, 232; primordial, 48

Silence, 194; body and, 290-91; death instinct in, 241; in Zola, 326

Similar (the), 264, 289; eternal return of, 265; Platonic copy, 259

Similitudes, 145, 261, 284-85

Simondon, Gilbert, 104, 195

Simplificatio, 297

Simulacr(a)um, 2, 7-8, 94, 216, 219, 221, 273-76, 284-85, 289, 315; and ancient philosophy, 253-79; becoming phantasms, 165; being of, 256; copy and model, 256; demonic arbiter of, 258; divergent series in, 262-63; in Epicurean theory of time, 274-76, 277; and eternal return, 264-65; Friday and, 316; in the hierarchy of participation, 255-56; invention and, 266-79; and modernity, 265-66; perception of, 277; phantasmatic power of, 261; Plato, 253-66; as reactionary, 263; sexual drives, 198; varieties of, 275-76, 277; world of, 187-88, 261-62

Simulacra-phantasms, 256-57

Simulation, 262, 263-64, 265, 285

Singularities, 52-53, 73, 99, 116; actualization of, 109, 110; auto-unification principle of, 102-3; confined in an individual or person, 139-40; continuum of, 111; distribution of, 53, 54, 55-56, 57, 59-60, 64, 104-5, 111, 114, 214, 345n4; events, 103-4, 116; in good sense, 76; impersonal and pre-individual, 107, 109, 111, 140-41, 152, 176, 177, 213, 297, 344n3; imprisoned in supreme Self, 106; inseparable from the zone of indeter-

distinction between corporeal mixtures, 89; double causality, 94; dual attitudes of confidence and mixture, 163; nonsense in, 66-67; paradox in, 8-9, 32; sense in, 19; theory of the Voice, 347n1

Structuralism, 71-72, 92, 366n12

Structure, 71, 281; minimal conditions for, 50-51; Other as, 307-10, 313-15; presence, 319-21; series of, 48-51, 52-53

Subject(s), 99, 107; analytic predicates of, 112, 115; assignation of, 1; free, nomadic singularities, 107; knowing, 344n3; manifested states of, 96; and object, 310-11, 318; and phantasm, 212-13; position of, 216; signifies by sound, 187; vis-à-vis the world, 113

Subjectivity, 139, 140; dialectical whole of, 138

Sublimation, 208, 212, 216, 219-20, 221, 222, 237; less successful, 224

Superego, 94, 188, 189, 203, 243, 245, 352n2, 353n4; acoustic origin of, 193; "good"/cruel, 352n4; good object as, 190, 191; and libidinal drives, 205; and sexual drives, 198

Supernumary object, 50, 51, 65, 66, 81; paradoxical element in, 66; phallus as, 228

Surface, xiv, 132, 133, 141; action at, 207-8; aggregate, 245-46; in Alice's adventures, 237; ascent to, 247; Carroll's language and, 9-11, 84, 87-93, 124-25; confused, in Chronos, 165; contraries at, 175-76; in the development of ego, 203-4; discovery of, 11; emissions from, 273-74, 275, 276; humor is art of, 141, 248; ideational, 211; intention is phenomenon of, 207; in language, 183; leap between, 238; is locus of sense, 104-5; nonsense of, 136; as object of secondary regression, 244; Oedipus and,

205-6; operation of bodies at, 24; organization of, 200, 233; in origin of phantasm, 218; paradoxical element running the series, 81; phallic coordinations of, 203, 226; phallus as instrument of, 201; phallic line at, 201, 206, 208, 209; phantasm is phenomenon of, 216; in philosophy, 129, 132-33; physics of, 94-95; primary formation of, 241; production of, 187; Robinson's history of, 319; Robinson's return to, 315-16; saving, 168; schizoid fragments at, 92; sense at, 19, 136; sexuality and, 199-201; simulacra at, 298; singularities at, 103-4; split, in schizophrenic language, 86-87; in Stoic philosophy, 146; thinker of, 219; as transcendental field, 125; traversal of, 206; is what "renders possible," 186; zones are facts of, 197, 198

Surface effect(s), 7-8, 211, 232; in Aion, 165, 166; appearance as, 21; dual, 242; essence of event is, 182; in language, 11, 183; and metaphysical surface, 244; paradox of, 4-11; in propositions, 12; sense in, 70, 72

Surface organization: as determined by Aion, 166-68; serial form is, 224; of transcendental field, 99

Swift, 43

Sylvie and Bruno (Carroll), 10, 11, 23, 26-27, 42-43, 44, 55, 62, 79, 358n1; "Gardener's song," 26-27, 34; paradox of neutrality with, 33, 34

Symbolization, 188, 208, 212, 216, 219-20, 221

Syntheses, 174-75, 176

"Tangled Tale," 51, 55, 56, 67

Theology, 103, 279, 281-82; in Kant, 294-97; rational, 294

Thérèse Raquin (Zola), 323, 330-31

Thing(s), 1, 9-11, 186; attribute of, 21; denotations fulfilled in, 241; frontier between, 86-87, 132-33, 166, 182-83; as points of view, 173; series of, 37, 38; sonorous qualities of, 181

Things-propositions (duality), 23, 24-25, 28

Thought, aggression in, 298-99; apprehension of, 269, 276; crack of, 160, 208-9; denegation and, 208; erosion of, 157; ideal game as reality of, 60; intensity of, 219; nonsense as zero point of, 241; object of, 279; orientation of, 127, 128-30, 132; paradoxes in, 74; possibility, 332-33; relation of atoms to, 268; series of, 217-23; sexuality and, 218-20; surface of, 208; time of, 276

"Three Voices, the," 359n1

Through the Looking-Glass (Carroll), 1, 9-10, 43, 236

Time(s), 144, 147; of actor/of God, 150; Aion as eternal result of, 165; of decomposition, 121; deformation of, in alcoholism, 158-60; Epicurean theory of, 269-70, 274-79; of events/effects, 62-63; in ideal game, 59, 60; infinite, 60-61; language in, 185; minimum of, 269-70, 274, 275, 276, 277; restful, 277-78; order of, 75, 76, 77; and presence of Others, 311; readings of, 5, 60-61, 63, 64, 162-68; relation to movement, 276-77; verb in, 184-85

To eat/to be eaten, 23-24, 26, 37, 85, 86, 91, 182, 199, 238, 240, 241

To eat/to think, 240

Tolstoy, 100, 101, 349n4

To shit/to speak (duality), 85, 86

Totem and Taboo (Freud), 211

Tournier, Michel, 301-21

Transcendental field, 105, 109, 123; characteristics of 344n3; impersonal,

98, 99, 102, 116, 244, 343n5; surface as, 125

Transcendental philosophy, 107; sense is characteristic discovery of, 105-6

Transcendental principle, 96-99

Transcendental subject, 98

True (the), 13, 68, 120-21; in propositions, 14-15, 17, 19

Truth, 18, 121, 222; condition of, 14-15, 19; eternal, 221; logic of, 111; philosophical, 346n1

"Two Brothers, the" (Carroll), 358n1

Umwelt, 113, 116

Unconditional, 122, 123-24

Unconscious (the), xiii, 72, 204, 351n3; paradox as force of, 80; phantasm and, 217; series in, 40

Unique event, 56; Being as, 180; language as, 185

Univocal Being, 175-80, 241, 300

Univocity, 194, 241; pseudo-, 180; series of, 177-80; transmitted from Being to language, 185

Untersinn, 91, 92, 136, 233

Untimely (the), 265

Urdoxa, 97, 98, 102

Valéry, Paul, 10

Variables, 115

Veracity, 14

Verb(s), 5, 24-25, 28, 37, 182, 183-84, 221, 246; as attributing Aims, 21; on metaphysical surface, 240; move from speech to, 248, 249; phantasm and, 214-15; poles of, 184-85; secondary organization of, 241; sense in proposition expressed by, 31-32; speaking and, 241; univocity of language, 185

Verleugnung, 243

Voice (the), 195, 200, 214, 215, 229, 232, 241, 246; in Alice's adventures,

236; Being on, 179; disengagement of, 240; in language, 193-94; from above, 245, 247; of the heights, 242

Void, 268; beginnings in, 218; infinite, 269, 272; sexual surface as, 222; Stoic theory of, 347n1; univocity of, 180

Voyeurism, 214, 282-83, 284, 320

Wagner, 107

Welt, 113, 116

Whole (the), 267, 268, 279, 300; eternal return as, 300, 301

Will, 149, 157, 222, 344n1; false impression of, 277; particular, 131

Will to power, 107, 300, 301

Wittgenstein, 146

Wolf Man, 40, 230, 357n2

Wolfson, Louis, 84-85

Word(s), 82-83, 87-88, 247-48; action, 90; contracting, 47; duality of, 85; esoteric, 45, 46; howl-, 88; morality of, 142-43; neutrality of, 65; obscene, 246; passion, 90; primary function of, 241; reaction to corrupt, 14, 15-16; schizophrenic, 91; separated from bodies by sense, 91

Word/image association, 12-13, 16

World(s), 245, 247; and absence of others, 319; bottomless, 199; characteristics, 103-8; commodities, 115, 116; constituted by the convergence of series, 109-10, 111, 112, 113, 114, 116, 176; destruction, 294; diversity of, 266; elements in, 271; expressed, 110-11, 114, 116; as icon, 261; incompossible, 113, 114, 115; organization of, 312, 313; other, 260; person in, 139; perverse, 320; as phantasm, 262; principle of reproduction in, 271; real, 260; of simulacra, 187-88, 261-62; unique, 262; as universal principle of hypothetical syllogism, 295; without others, 301-21

Wound(s), 147, 148, 149; eternal return of, 157; mortal, 151-52

Zarathustra, 264, 289, 299

Zen, 136, 137, 146; Buddhism, 8; Zen's paradox, 340n2

Zola, 321-33; *Assomoir, L',* 323; *Bête humaine, La,* 321, 323, 326-27, 330-32; *Docteur Pascal, Le,* 333; optimism of, 332; scientific inspiration of, 325-26; *Thérèse Raquin,* 323, 330-31

Zones, conjunction of, 229; letters in, 230-31; *see also* Bodily zones

European Perspectives:

A Series of Columbia University Press